The Decline and Fall of the Dukes of Leinster, 1872–1948

The Decline and Fall
of the
Dukes of Leinster,
1872–1948

Love, War, Debt and Madness

TERENCE DOOLEY

FOUR COURTS PRESS

Typeset in 11pt on 13pt AGaramondPro by
Carrigboy Typesetting Services for
FOUR COURTS PRESS LTD
7 Malpas Street, Dublin 8, Ireland
www.fourcourtspress.ie
and in North America for
FOUR COURTS PRESS
c/o ISBS, 920 NE 58th Avenue, Suite 300, Portland, OR 97213.

A catalogue record for this title is available
from the British Library.

ISBN 978–1–84682–533–0

Printed in England
by CPI Group (UK) Ltd, Croydon, CR0 4YY

Contents

Dukes of Leinster Family Tree (from the 1st to the 8th duke, but including only the names of those mentioned in the text, e.g., James 1st duke of Leinster and his wife, Emily, had nineteen children but other than the 2nd duke William only Lord Edward (1763–1798) is mentioned).

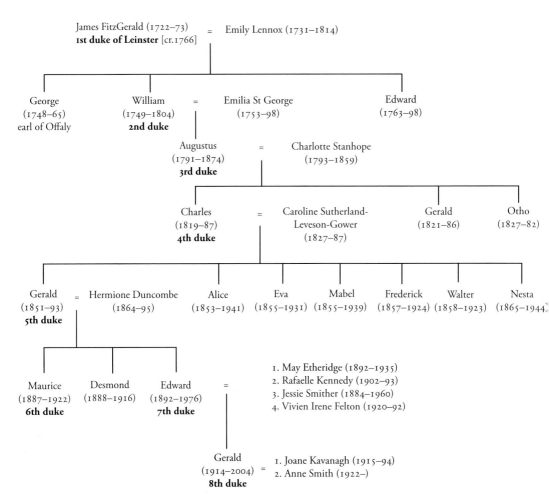

Preface and acknowledgments

O something unprov'd! something in a trance!
O madness amorous! O trembling!
O to escape utterly from others' anchors and holds!
To drive free! To love free! To dash reckless and dangerous!
To court destruction with taunts – with invitations!
To ascend – to leap to the heavens of the love indicated to me!
To rise thither with my inebriate Soul!
To be lost, if it must be so!
To feed the remainder of life with one hour of fulness and freedom!
With one brief hour of madness and joy!

'One hour to madness and joy', Walt Whitman (1819–92)

Until the last quarter of the nineteenth century, the Irish aristocracy were part of a supra-national British landowning class that controlled most aspects of economic, social and political life at estate, local and national levels.[1] They comprised a tiny minority of around 100 families in a post-Famine population of around 3.5 million people. Their power was symbolized in their grand country houses, in Ireland commonly referred to as 'Big Houses', which had mainly been constructed during the golden era of the eighteenth century. Surrounded by designed landscapes and carefully guarded by gate lodges located along their high perimeter walls, the privacy of the demesne complex represented the aristocracy's desire to remain aloof from all but their social equals.

Their ascendancy had certainly been weakened during the nineteenth century by a variety of factors, most particularly growing indebtedness and the onslaught of democratization, but, even so, by the time this work opens in 1872 few of the resident nobles in Ireland could have anticipated how quickly and dramatically their final fall would come. In just half a century their political power and socio-economic position crumbled under the weight of revolutionary developments in Ireland. Indeed, their fall might be seen as part of a much wider phenomenon experienced by the aristocracies of Britain and wider Europe who suffered similar fates; of course in other countries such as Russia this fall occurred on a much more brutal scale during the Bolshevik revolution of 1917.[2]

The impact of public events has featured prominently in the historiography of the decline of the wider Irish landed class, both north and south.[3] However, little attempt has been made to combine that history with private lives and experiences. This book attempts to provide this extra relevant dimension. It adopts a case study approach, focusing on the decline and fall of the dukes of Leinster, Ireland's premier noble and most illustrious family over an extended period of almost 800 years from their arrival with the Anglo-Normans in 1169. It sets out to provide a judicious blend of the rather sensational events peculiar to the Leinsters with the historical background common to the Irish aristocracy as a whole. Thus, the narrative of decline unfolds within the context of such public historical watersheds as the Land War of the 1880s, the concurrent rise of the Home Rule movement, the break up of Irish landed estates after 1903, the Great War of 1914–18, the revolutionary turmoil of 1916–23, and the 1920s global economic depression, and simultaneously against the backdrop of the tragic personal story of Gerald, 5th duke of Leinster, his wife, Hermione, and their children. By combining the public and private dimensions, the story of the Leinsters encapsulates the decline and fall of the Irish landed aristocracy.

While sources revealing the historical context are numerous, the dramatic private events have largely been revealed through the discovery of a significant collection of Hermione's letters to her closest friend and confidante, Evelyn de Vesci, on deposit in Somerset Record Office. They reveal Hermione as a woman sometimes kind and loving, sometimes spiteful and manipulative, often neurotic, but always intelligent and feminist, caught up in a male-dominated society. (She was once rebuked by Lady Zetland for 'unladylike behaviour' when she whistled a tune for an orchestra.)[4] Like the tragic hero of Shakespearean drama, her human flaws led her to actions that had far-reaching consequences, not only for her own peace of mind, but for the future of the family inheritance.

Lord Ernest Hamilton (1858–1939), author and the seventh son of Ireland's only other duke, Abercorn, once reminisced of Hermione that

> As a child of sixteen or so … her beauty was so dazzling as to be almost unbelievable. It was not only that she was divinely tall and absolutely flawless in shape, feature and complexion – a very rare combination – but she also had on her face that look of radiant goodness which, for some mysterious reason, is seldom seen on the face of any except those doomed to an early death.[5]

It is often the case that those who die tragically young are remembered in this way; their flaws simply soar to the heavens with them and are forgotten. This can mean that the influence of human decisions are often neglected and lost in the much wider context of change when the causality of historical events is debated. The history of the decline of the Leinsters is a case in point: while the Leinsters were affected by public events over which they had no control, they were equally affected by personal misfortune.

The story begins in 1872 when Hermione's future husband, Gerald, then earl of Offaly – his father, marquess of Kildare, and his grandfather, duke of Leinster, were both still alive – celebrated his coming-of-age with great aristocratic pomp. It moves from the estate village of Maynooth in Co. Kildare to London, to continental Europe, to an asylum in Edinburgh, to the US, before finally completing the circle and ending back in Maynooth in the late 1940s. In three-quarters of a century, the dukes of Leinster fell from being Ireland's premier aristocratic family, close friends of the British monarchy, secure within the world's most powerful empire, to relative obscurity in an Irish Republic that did not recognize titles. And while in 1872 Gerald's grandfather, the 3rd duke of Leinster, resided in aristocratic grandeur in Carton House, Edward, 7th duke, died impoverished in 1976, his body found in his home, a bedsit flat in London, where he had taken his own life.

∗ ∗ ∗

Once again the pleasure of completing a book provides the opportunity to warmly thank all those who gave so generously of their time, knowledge and friendship to make it possible. First I am grateful to the owners and custodians of collections I have consulted and/or who provided advice and guidance: Jake Duncombe of Duncombe Park; Eton School Archives; the late Anne Hamilton of Hamwood House; Paul Harris of the Helmsley Archive; Lothian Health Service Archive in Edinburgh (especially Laura Brouard); National Library of Ireland; NUI Maynooth Library (especially Cathal McCauley); Public Record Office London; Public Record Office Northern Ireland; Russell Library Maynooth (especially Penny Woods); and the Somerset Record Office.

I owe a particular thanks to those who read and commented on all or part of the manuscript and who improved it in the process: Lisa Butterly, Patrick Cosgrove, Kevin McKenna, A.P.W. Malcomson and Ciarán Reilly. I am grateful to Vincent Comerford, not only for commenting on an early draft, but more especially for his continued encouragement and friendship. I owe an immense debt to Tony McCarthy for his generosity in sharing with me his knowledge of the investment behaviour of Irish landlords under the 1903 Land Act. Chantal Stebbings very kindly allowed me to read pre-publication drafts of articles cited in this book.

I would like to thank all those who directed me to sources and answered queries, especially Joe Cleary, Geraldine Convey, Emer Crooke, Dave McCusker, Karol Mullaney-Dignam, Des Galvin, Raymond Gillespie, Jacqueline Hill and Deborah Mallaghan. Edward Tynan very kindly helped at an important stage of the project. In the early years of research, Colette Jordan provided many excellent leads and I am greatly indebted to her. I am equally indebted to Catherine Murphy for all her help with this and other projects. The friendship and kindness of the late Desmond FitzGerald, Knight of Glin, and Patricia (Paddy) Friel, and the many discussions with them on aspects of this book, are remembered with great fondness. I have also benefited immensely from long conversations with Hon. Desmond Guinness who lived for a time in Carton in the late 1950s (from where he and his wife, Mariga, launched the Irish Georgian Society), and who, of course, knew many of the people who feature in the latter part of this book. Professor Marian Lyons has been a most supportive head of history, colleague and friend at the National University of Ireland, Maynooth.

I would like to take this opportunity to warmly thank the Mallaghan family for their friendship and for providing me with unconditional access to Carton House and its collections whenever sought. Over a long number of years I have come to appreciate that Carton means a great deal to Lee and Mary, Conor and Alex.

For some time now, David Cannadine and Alvin Jackson have been constant sources of encouragement and support. This is at last a chance to thank them. I owe a similar debt to Christopher Ridgway and his wife, Rosie, not least of all for the warmth of hospitality on my visits to Yorkshire. As always, I am grateful to my siblings, their families, and the Dolan family who have helped me along the way.

Once again, I am indebted to Four Courts Press for so enthusiastically embracing this project. My thanks go to Martin Fanning, Martin Healy, Michael Potterton, Anthony Tierney and Meghan Donaldson for their professionalism, courtesy and good humour.

And finally there are those who live with me every day and whose patience, friendship and love cannot be repaid: Annette, Conor and Aine. I can only dedicate this work to them in the hope that they will know how important they are to me.

CHAPTER ONE

Gerald FitzGerald's coming-of-age, 1872

> But one, more wrathful than the rest,
> In spitefulness did swear,
> 'Your Majesty, all Ireland
> Can't rule this Lord Kildare.'
>
> 'Then by my soul', out spoke the king,
> 'By this my sceptred hand,
> Since that be so, this noble earl,
> Shall rule all Ireland.'[1]

On 16 August 1872, Gerald FitzGerald reached his majority. As his grandfather (Augustus, 3rd duke of Leinster) and his father (Charles, marquess of Kildare) were both still alive he inherited the courtesy title of earl of Offaly. In time he would become the 5th duke of Leinster and inherit one of the largest landed estates in Ireland, centred on an impressive eighteenth-century Palladian mansion on the outskirts of the village of Maynooth, about fifteen miles west of Dublin. The estate was almost 70,000 acres, taking in approximately 16 per cent of the total acreage of Co. Kildare (with around 2,000 acres in neighbouring Co. Meath). It yielded £40,000 in agricultural rents (around £3 million in 2014 terms). To put this income into some perspective, there were only 250 families in Britain and Ireland who owned in excess of 30,000 acres with rental incomes of more than £30,000 per annum.[2] At a time when Irish land was selling at around 23 years' purchase on annual rents, Gerald's grandfather, by asset definition, was a multi-millionaire. Just as significantly, from the viewpoint of status he was one of only two dukes resident in Ireland. While the duke of Abercorn's title had been created a mere four years previously, Leinster's title dated to 1766 and, moreover, the family could trace their residency in Ireland back to the building of the medieval family castle at Maynooth at the beginning of the thirteenth century. Indeed, the FitzGeralds could lay claim to having been one of Ireland's most illustrious and powerful families over significant periods of that time.

Gerald's birth in 1851 coincided with the beginning of the end of the Great Famine in Ireland. His generation grew up during a period of socio-political

stability and relative prosperity across much of the country. The widespread
celebrations to mark his coming-of-age gave the impression that the duke of
Leinster's tenants were among the most contented in the country. In estate
towns and villages such as Castledermot 'there was great rejoicing at night, the
houses were gaily decorated and lit up with Chinese lanterns'; Kildare town was
also 'brilliantly lighted up and from the famous abbey and round tower
illuminated designs were suspended'; a celebratory banquet for the more
respectable and prosperous tenants was held in Athy, the largest town in the
south of the county; and in 'the pretty little village' of Maynooth an impressive
fireworks display lighted up the night sky while the local band, recently
supplied with instruments by the duke, marched up and down Leinster Street
(now more generally referred to as Main Street).[3]

As time passed these well-rehearsed rituals to celebrate the coming-of-age,
the succession, or the marriage of a landlord's heir had become predictable
enough. In particular, the presentation of addresses on behalf of the tenantry
became an intrinsic part of proceedings.[4] These illuminated and ornate
congratulatory statements were commissioned and composed by the estate's
socio-economic elite who were then invited to attend the banquets and other
events orchestrated to present them to the celebrant. Thus, the addressees of
Castledermot and Kilkea typically reminded Gerald of his family's centuries-
old attachment to the area, physically symbolized in the medieval dower castle
at Kilkea, and 'the strenuous efforts and chivalrous sacrifices' made by his
illustrious ancestors for 'their more than fatherland'.[5] He was told that he had
'sprung from that long line of ancestry who ever sustained the interests of the
country where they loved to dwell, and who, for the good of all, perseveringly
upheld the principles of civil and religious freedom'. Kildare's Liberal MP,
W.H.F. Cogan, captured the essence of both the FitzGerald myth and the
legacy which Gerald had to live up to:

> The property of many of [the FitzGeralds] was confiscated and their titles
> attainted; we know of many of them perishing in the dungeons and
> perishing on the scaffolds … Many of that noble race suffered hardships
> for their love of Ireland (great applause). Many of them loved their
> country 'not wisely but too well'. Many of them were obnoxious to the
> powers of the day by becoming more Irish than the Irish themselves.[6]

The address of the tenantry of the core estate around Maynooth, designed by
Browne and Nolan of Dublin, and organized by local medical doctor, Edward
O'Kelly, had an image of the ruins of Maynooth Castle in the bottom corner,
symbolic of the FitzGerald family's long association with that area (see plate 9).

Reference was made to the fact that Offaly had been guided during his youth by his father and grandfather and there was the stated hope that this would stand to him in the future:

> We pray that the good and prudent guides of your youth may long be spared to you; we are proud of your name; we feel that the history of your family guarantees a continuance of its well known kindness; and we think we rightly interpret your lordship's feelings when we say that we are sure you will regard that history as the brightest and noblest guiding star of your own career.[7]

To the modern ear the speeches and the content of these addresses may sound verbose and the tone deferential and sycophantic, but they fulfilled an important function from a tenant perspective, allowing them to remind the heir that he had duties and responsibilities – social, religious, economic and political – as a landlord, and especially to those who signed their names. It was quite deliberate that the earl was reminded his ancestors had been landlords who had 'loved to dwell' in Ireland; in other words, the estate had been free of the scourge of absenteeism. By suggestion, Gerald was being advised that the future stability and prosperity of the estate was inextricably tied to his residency and any change in circumstances would be detrimental to both sides. Finally, it would have been anticipated that regaling the FitzGeralds would appeal to their sense of family pride – an emotion exceptionally important to aristocratic families throughout Ireland and the United Kingdom[8] – and that praise would be reciprocated with the maintenance of the *status quo*. Thus, instead of interpreting the rhetoric of celebratory addresses as sycophantic it is more relevant to examine the purposes that they served for the socio-economic elite on the estate, and, perhaps more importantly, the subtle nuances as time passed, reflecting imminent shifts in power.[9]

Fourteen years before, in 1858, Gerald's father, Charles (1819–87), had published his celebratory family history, *The earls of Kildare and their ancestors: from 1057 to 1773*. In a different format, this was likewise a reminder to Gerald of the legacies he would one day inherit: familial, cultural, architectural, political and so on. It is informative to now examine these legacies in order to comprehend the nature and extent of the decline in family fortunes, which arguably began the very year that Gerald came of age; for while there was evidence that the traditional deferential relationship operated on the estate in August 1872, there were cracks beneath the surface, and this relationship was to be severely tested just a few months later when his grandfather introduced the controversial so-called 'Leinster lease'.[10]

II

Those legacies stretched all the way back to 1169 when Robert FitzStephens arrived in Ireland with an Anglo-Norman army of just 30 knights, 60 men-at-arms and 300 foot archers at the invitation of Diarmait Mac Murchada, the displaced king of Leinster, who wanted them to help him restore his position. FitzStephens is said to have proclaimed: 'It is not, then, greed for monetary rewards or the "blind craving for gold" that has brought us to these parts, but a gift of lands and cities in perpetuity to us and to our children'.[11] One of the party was Maurice FitzGerald. His kinsman, Giraldus Cambrensis (1146–1223), the controversial chronicler of the invasion, later described FitzGerald as: 'a man of dignified aspect and modest bearing, of a ruddy good complexion and good features … of the middle height, neither tall nor short'.[12] It was in stark contrast with Cambrensis' much less flattering descriptions of the native Irish but in that respect it intentionally highlighted the civilized characteristics of the new settlers and thus, as Colm Lennon has argued, Cambrensis' strong polemical writings began the process of crafting the place of the FitzGeralds in Irish history from their arrival.[13]

For his role in the siege of Dublin, Maurice was rewarded with large tracts of land in Co. Kildare and other surrounding counties by Richard de Clare, earl of Pembroke (d. 1176), better known in Irish history as 'Strongbow'. Around 1203, the FitzGeralds decided to locate their great castle at the confluence of two streams at Maynooth. Over the following century, Maurice's descendants married astutely, amassing more lands and consolidating their political and martial power among the native Irish as well as the new settlers in the area of the English Pale. In 1316 the earldom of Kildare was created for John FitzGerald and in time this would be followed by the marquessate of Kildare in 1761 and duke of Leinster in 1766 (after which the heir apparent would assume the title of marquess of Kildare and the latter's son, if alive during the lifetime of the duke, earl of Offaly). But fifteen years after Maurice FitzGerald had arrived in Ireland, he articulated the ambiguity of the new settlers which would be a constant in the lives of the FitzGeralds:

> … we are now constrained in our actions by this circumstance, that just as we are English as far as the Irish are concerned, likewise to the English we are Irish, and the inhabitants of this island and of the other assail us with an equal degree of hatred.[14]

Over time, the FitzGeralds were more successful than most at bridging cultural divides. They successfully represented themselves as Irish to the Gaelic people – as patrons of Gaelic culture and language they created one of the greatest library collections of its time at Maynooth Castle, housing a significant Irish language section – while simultaneously asserting their Englishness to the Anglo-Normans of the Pale.[15] Outsiders could only hope to buy into a share of their power, usually at a price that enhanced the FitzGerald standing. During the fourteenth and early fifteenth centuries, as the English monarchy was preoccupied with the Hundred Years War with France (1338–1453) and then the struggle between the rival houses of York and Lancaster (1455–85), the ruling of Ireland increasingly fell to the FitzGeralds. Between 1495 and 1534 they were so dominant under Garret More FitzGerald (1456–1513, 'the great earl') and his son, Garret Oge (1487–1534), that historians have labelled the period the 'Kildare Ascendancy'.[16]

While the FitzGeralds successfully managed for generations to judicially balance their relations with the Old English, the Gaelic Irish and the English Court, they eventually found themselves increasingly alienated as Tudor policy created a 'new aggressive English colonial elite'.[17] The Tudor revolution in government and specifically Thomas Cromwell's programme for the centralization of administration in Ireland threatened their ascendancy. When the great earl's grandson, Silken Thomas, 10th earl of Kildare (1513–37), rose up in revolt it provided the government with the pretext to destroy their power. Thus, in 1537 Henry VIII attempted to wipe out the whole of the family line, executing the 10th earl and his five uncles at Tyburn. The castle at Maynooth was confiscated, their lands (and those of leading members of the collateral branches of the family) were attainted and their period of dominance came to an end. Steven Ellis has contended that 'there is little doubt that this heavy loss of life left real bitterness in the popular memory' and that 'nationally minded historians have good cause to see in the events of 1534–5 the origins of the modern Irish nation'.[18] This may very well be true. It certainly mattered little to those who later wanted to embrace the FitzGeralds' defiance of English authority in Ireland that Silken Thomas rose in revolt for a complexity of reasons when these could all be simplified as a rebuttal to English attempts at colonization. Later FitzGerald family members would refute or embrace the myth depending on whether they thought it would be detrimental to their cause or stand them in good stead.[19]

While Silken Thomas' ill-fated rebellion resulted in the smashing of FitzGerald power, the family's demise was neither total nor permanent. They had spent generations building relationships with notables both sides of the Irish Sea, and had kept important contacts at Court, as well as on the continent of Europe. At the height of their ascendancy, Garret More, himself a significant patron of the arts, had been keen to nurture cultural relations with his Italian ancestors, the Gherardini of Florence, as he looked to the cultural centre of the Renaissance to legitimize the FitzGeralds' position within a wider European aristocracy.[20] In 1507, he wrote to his Gherardini relatives to inform them 'of the state of your relations in these parts' who 'by their swords obtained great possessions and achieved great feats of arms'. He explained that 'we are most desirous to know the deeds of our ancestors, so that if you have in your possession any history, we request you to communicate it to us' and, in return, 'if there is anything that we can procure for you through our labour and industry, or anything you have not got, such as hawks, falcons, horses, or dogs for the chase, I beg you will inform us of it as I shall, in every possible way, endeavour to obey your wishes', signing off as 'Chief in Ireland of the family of the Geraldines'. The letter was written around the time that Leonardo Da Vinci was completing the *Mona Lisa* in Florence. The probable subject of the painting was Lisa Gherardini (1479–1542, or *c.*1551), wife of one of Florence's wealthiest merchants, Francesco del Giocondo, and possibly a distant relative of Garret More.[21] When Garret More died as a result of wounds received in battle, the Italian poet, Lodovico Ariosto (1474–1533), commemorated him in the romantic epic, *Orlando Furioso*.[22] Ariosto's consideration of Garret More's position in Ireland – even if flawed – remained for generations a source of pride to the FitzGerald family; thus when the contents from Carton's great library were sold in the 1920s they included several editions of *Orlando Furioso*.[23]

After the rebellion of 1537, such continental contacts were crucial in the survival of Silken Thomas' half-brother, Gerald, who made his escape to mainland Europe. He subsequently spent sixteen years in France and predominantly Italy supported by Cosimo de Medici (1519–74), duke of Florence from 1537 to 1574 and first grand duke of Tuscany (1569–74), who made him master of horse with an allowance of 300 ducates per annum; Cardinal Farnese (1520–89), and his father, the duke of Parma; and by Monsignor Piero Carnesecchi at Padua and Venice.[24] This continental assistance, allied to their long-established links with prominent English families at Court, allowed the FitzGeralds to gradually claw their way back to political favour and, eventually, after a good deal of international intrigue, they re-emerged to prominence in the early eighteenth century.[25] When they did, the FitzGeralds renewed their interest in a variety of aspects of Italian culture, particularly related to the artistic and architectural developments of the Renaissance period, which most clearly manifested itself in the building and embellishment of their grand Palladian mansion at Carton.

The return to national prominence was a slow, gradual process sometimes hindered by bad luck, such as the death of successive young heirs in the early seventeenth century who did not have time to establish themselves, or the more complex exigencies of national politics during the Confederate and Williamite wars of the same century. But there were also times when luck smiled upon the FitzGeralds. In 1620, the 15th earl died at the young age of eight years and was succeeded by his seventeen-year-old cousin, George, the last surviving male FitzGerald of the Kildare line. It was at this juncture that Richard Boyle, the earl of Cork, saw an opportunity of an alliance with the FitzGeralds that would further his own plans for familial aggrandisement and link him into the older network of the Old English aristocracy.[26] Boyle had made a fortune from the plantation of Munster and was now intent on 'constructing for himself and his family dynastic respectability and honour'.[27] So in 1629 he bought the wardship of George FitzGerald for the impressive sum of £6,600. Later that same year, he arranged the marriage of George to his daughter, Joan, and he could thereafter 'bask in the reflected glory of the distinguished Kildare line'.[28]

By now the medieval castle at Maynooth was in an advanced stage of decay – 'totally ruined and ready to fall'[29] – but Boyle was determined to restore it to its former glory in order that it would not only stand as a physical legacy to his ambitions but suggest a more ancient ancestry in Ireland. By 1635 the work was completed at a cost of around £2,000, embodying 'the spirit of the late Renaissance'.[30] However, because of the Confederate Wars of the 1640s, it was to be a false dawn. By descent young George FitzGerald belonged to the Old English but as a Protestant brought up in the English Court he was more sympathetically disposed towards the New English, so he found himself in a political limbo. In January 1642, the castle was seized by a group of local rebels, the contents were plundered and a great deal of structural damage was done, including the destruction of the great library. Over the next few years what remained of the structure was variously occupied by Royalists, Confederates and Parliamentarians and eventually in 1647 it was taken by Owen Roe O'Neill (?1582–1649), the most successful Confederate Catholic general, who had it dismantled.[31] Thereafter, it was uninhabited and the great thirteenth-century symbol of FitzGerald power fell once again into dereliction so that by 1682 it was simply described as 'the remains of an ancient pile, venerable in its ruins, and which did partake of the hottest, and felt the fiercest malice of a revengeful enemy in the last rebellion'.[32]

III

The injection of new wealth from Boyle stabilized the FitzGerald financial position but it was not until 1714, with the appointment of Robert FitzGerald, 19th earl of Kildare (1675–1744), as lord justice for the government of Ireland that their political re-emergence was solidified. Originally, Robert considered restoring the castle at Maynooth as his main residence 'but on examination it was found to be too much dilapidated'.[33] Instead, on 21 January 1739, he purchased the reversionary lease on an existing seventeenth-century house at Carton from the representatives of Major-General Richard Ingoldsby for £8,000.[34] Robert and his wife, Mary O'Brien, eldest daughter of the 3rd earl of Inchiquin, then began the process of remodelling the house.

The existing Baroque mansion at Carton was of an architectural form that had become a symbol of foreign absolutism. For this reason, it may not have appealed to the patriot politics of Kildare and may in part have contributed to his desire to remodel it as a Palladian mansion. However, the overriding reason was undoubtedly contemporary tastes and fashions in which Palladianism was supreme and had evolved as the popular exposition of the architectural grandeur to which the Irish grandees aspired.[35] A short distance away was the grandest house in Ireland, the Italian style palazzo at Castletown, which had been constructed between 1722 and 1729 for William Conolly, speaker of the Irish House of Commons and Ireland's wealthiest commoner.[36] The FitzGeralds could not match the Conollys in terms of wealth, so Carton would not be as grand in scale, but aspirations were to make it impressive enough to sound 'a fanfare for Kildare's re-entry into politics and high society'.[37] (In 1759, Lady Louisa Conolly became chatelaine at Castletown at a time when her sister, Emily, lived at Carton, married to James, earl of Kildare and later 1st duke of Leinster.)

Kildare employed the pre-eminent Palladian architect of his generation working in Ireland, Richard Castle (c.1690–1751), to design the new build. In time, Castle came to occupy a place of importance in Irish architectural history, at least as influential as Robert Adam in the domestic architecture of England. He was responsible for such mansions as Summerhill (1731), Carton (1739), Powerscourt (1741), Russborough (1742), and the FitzGerald town house in Dublin in 1745, now Leinster House, seat of the Irish parliament.[38] His influence was so pervasive that following his death at Carton in 1751, one contemporary wrote: 'had he lived a few years longer, the edifices of our nobility and gentry might vie with those of every other country whatever; in short his death is a great loss to the public, but his buildings will be monuments of his worth to latest posterity'.[39]

1 Leinster House, Dublin, 1792, the town house of the Kildares/Leinsters, designed by Richard Castle and built in the 1740s and sold by the family in 1815.

When Robert died in 1744, it fell to his successor James (1722–73) and his wife, Lady Emily (1731–1814), daughter of Charles Lennox, 2nd duke of Richmond and Lennox, to complete the work on Carton and its surroundings. It was not until 1759 that Emily could finally boast to her husband: 'I really think Carton when 'tis spruced up will be vastly pretty, and full as fine and I wou'd ever wish a country house to be'.[40] And so it was, with specially commissioned collections of silver and important works of art located in grand interiors, notably the Gold Saloon, the most glorious example of Italian Renaissance influence at Carton and one of the finest rooms in all of Ireland. Its design was the work of the Lafranchini brothers, highly skilled stuccadores who had travelled with architect employers throughout Europe wherever the building boom took them, reaching England around 1731.[41] As Joseph MacDonnell has contended, the commission gave the brothers 'an opportunity for the most sumptuous display of their skills in figurative stuccowork'[42] Originally used as the dining room, the ceiling design was reminiscent of many representations of the gods dining popular in Renaissance art and this may have been intentional to give guests the impression that they were dining among the deity (see plate 12).[43]

James and Emily and to a lesser extent their son, William, also reshaped an aristocratic landscape. After years of planting hundreds of trees, diverting the Rye River, constructing lakes and bridges, creating islands and cascades, moving thousands of tons of earth to form undulating hills, they created an ornate 1,200-acre demesne, enclosed behind five miles of a demesne wall, to reflect and enhance the tranquillity, stability and increased prosperity that had come with the 'Age of Improvement'.[44] They also invested heavily in the construction of a magnificent town house in Dublin and the development of the town of Maynooth on the fringe of the demesne.

All of this building and embellishment was necessary to publicly announce James' rise through the aristocratic ranks. Two years after returning from his grand tour, his political career began on 17 October 1741 when (as Lord Offaly) he entered the Irish House of Commons as member for Athy. In 1744, the year he succeeded his father, he moved to the House of Lords as the premier earl in the country. The following year, he established a popular reputation for himself when he offered to raise a regiment at his own expense to protect protestant Ireland against the Jacobite threat. In 1746 he was appointed to the privy council and thereafter his political rise continued via his elevation to the British peerage as Viscount Leinster of Taplow, Bucks, in 1747; his appointment as lord justice in 1756; master general of the ordnance (1758– 66); major-general (1761) and lieutenant-general (1770). Some of Kildare's appointments offered handsome sinecures, which augmented his vast rental income of around £40,000 per annum. In 1761 he became marquess of Kildare and then in 1766 duke of Leinster. It was an impressive rise, and one that has yet to be fully examined by historians, but his connections at Court were probably influential: as noted above, his wife, Emily (1731–1814), was the daughter of Charles Lennox, 2nd duke of Richmond and Lennox (1701–50), the illegitimate grandson of Charles II, and she was also a god-daughter of George II (see plates 1, 4 & 5).

Leinster became one of the most powerful borough patrons in Ireland, controlling between twelve and fifteen MPs, some of whom were his brothers or distant relatives and others who were openly criticized by opponents of the duke as being his sycophants and lickspittles. In 1773, for example, it was said of William Burgh of Athy that he was 'a very distant relation of the duke of Leinster by whom he was brought in …' and of Walter Hussey that he was 'brought in by the duke of Leinster as he married a distant relation of his', while Simon Digby was also 'brought in by the duke of Leinster and will do whatever he is bid by his Grace'.[45] Within the city of Dublin, Leinster enjoyed the deferential treatment of the freemen mainly because he was a considerable employer of craftsmen (particularly during the building and embellishment of his town house in the 1740s).[46] His involvement in the regulation of trade – sitting as a trustee of the Linen Board, mixing with the wealthiest merchants and professionals in the Dublin Society or Masonic lodge (of which he was grand master) and honorary member of guilds – also added to his political prestige.[47]

It was through such powerful patronage and connections that Leinster maintained his influence on a variety of different levels and so he enjoyed significant popularity as the leading patriot politician of his generation. In 1753, he presented a memorial to the king setting out the grievances of Ireland and protesting against the ambitiousness of Archbishop Stone whom he stigmatized as 'a greedy churchman, investing himself with temporal power, and affecting to be a second Wolsey in the State'.[48] Jacqueline Hill has argued that in the money bill crisis of 1753–6, Kildare was one of the individuals who emerged with their reputations enhanced and that his attempts to acquaint the king with Irish grievances 'earned him great popular acclaim, and did something to restore confidence in the aristocracy as champions of Ireland's interest'.[49] Some contemporaries believed that Kildare wanted to be lord lieutenant for more personal reasons, 'to restore the historic position of the FitzGeralds'. He never achieved that position; Eoin Magennis contends that his ambition was thwarted by his inflexibility and by 'acts of principle or pique, which were to dog his relationship with successive viceroys'.[50] His memorial also offended the king and the British ministers. For good or ill, his desire to connect with the legacy of his ancestors remained a constant with him and, indeed, with the next five generations of dukes.

IV

Until at least the end of the Napoleonic Wars in 1815, outward display was much more important than affordability. In 1813, for example, it was reported that Augustus, 3rd duke of Leinster, had sent out 600–700 invitations to the 'nobility and gentry of Dublin and its environs for a magnificent breakfast … at his beautiful seat at Carton'.[51] Several regimental bands were 'disposed at proper distances throughout the demesne' and the beautiful shell cottage 'which had all the characteristic graces of rural scenery formed the *point d'appui*' for the crowds. Thirty tents were erected to cater for dining, containing 'everything that the season could supply, that wealth could procure and that taste and art could select and arrange'.[52]

The fulfilment of social ambition and the necessity of keeping it on display in this manner were extremely costly. When the 1st duke died in 1773 he left debts of almost £150,000. However, aristocratic families such as the FitzGeralds could hope to alleviate some of these debts through astute marriages to wealthy heiresses.[53] In 1775, James' successor, William, 2nd duke (1749–1804), married Emilia Olivia Ussher St George, daughter and heiress of 1st Baron St George. She brought with her an estate of around 10,000 acres and an additional income of £4,000 per annum.[54] Over time, parts of her estate were disposed of to meet her husband's debts.[55] However, the remainder went to improving Leinster House so that they could display the impressive painting collection inherited by Emilia, improving the town of Maynooth and more-or-less completing the embellishment of the grounds at Carton. By October 1777, William could boast to his mother:

> I have now finished [diverting] the Rye Water and you cannot conceive how beautiful it is as I have carried it near two hundred yards below the park which has a great effect … Instead of carrying on the wall I have made a sunk fence and the trees being so grown that the wall is hid by them so you see no termination. I now look on the park to be nearly finished; as during the intervals that we could not work at the head and water we worked at the hill before the house which begins to make a great alteration for the better as the house stands so bold.[56]

William and Emilia had eight daughters before a son, Augustus, arrived in 1791. William used a traditional aristocratic expedient to retain close contacts at Court by inviting the Prince of Wales, later George IV, to be his heir's godfather (the Prince's father, George III, had been in love with and almost married Leinster's aunt, Lady Sarah Lennox).

There has been no full biography of William (nor, surprisingly, of any of the dukes of Leinster). He may have had a very chequered political career,[57] but what is important in the context of this work is that he built a reputation as a paternal landlord which was carried on by his successors. When he died in 1804, the *Gentleman's Magazine* described him as 'a fond father, an indulgent landlord, and a kind master' – suggestions of paternalist and feudal overlord – while his funeral in Kildare Abbey is said to have been so well attended that the mourners stretched right across the plains of the Curragh.[58] He also recognized the importance in 1795 of leasing lands at Maynooth for the establishment of St Patrick's College, the national Catholic seminary. He had been broadly supportive of Catholic relief and religious toleration but in 1792 he had withdrawn his support for outright Catholic Emancipation. However, he was pragmatic enough to realize that the granting of the lands would ultimately serve his better interests (see plate 6). As we shall see below, it won him the gratitude of Catholic Ireland and this was to serve his descendants well long into the future. And as Cormac Begadon argues: 'For the duke, the establishment of a national Catholic college in the burgeoning town of Maynooth must have been a very attractive proposition. He was a major investor in the recently constructed Royal Canal, and the location of the new college, was undoubtedly favourable, in economic terms and in adding further prestige to "his" town.'[59]

After the passing of the Act of Union in 1800, the focus of Irish politics shifted to Westminster. With parliament removed from the Irish capital, a stately home in the city to entertain and provide a power arena to plot political manoeuvring was no longer necessary. Moreover, the relative cost of living in Dublin increased rapidly and so the aristocracy began to abandon the city for the countryside. Of 300 MPs with town houses before 1800, only five retained them in 1821.[60] In 1815, William's successor, Augustus, 3rd duke of Leinster (1791–1874), sold Leinster House to the Royal Dublin Society for £10,000 and an annual rent of £600 per annum. (He continued to retain a townhouse on Lower Dominick Street.) This probably helped to finance the second remodelling of Carton under Sir Richard Morrison who before this had received commissions from 'the richest, most powerful and apparently most ostentatious families in the country'.[61] The remodelling may have been the result of an accident reported in *The Times* in August 1817, which described how the duke had a narrow escape 'when ruins of an arch which formed part of Carton fell in'.[62]

Before Morrison began his work, the main block as it stands today had been joined to pavilions by curved colonnades. Morrison extended the main block at either end and straightened the colonnades. A suite of rooms including a large dining room were added.[63] In 1822, the earl of Donoughmore visited Carton and estimated that the remodelling was 'at an expense of a great many thousand pounds – as much I think as £40,000'.[64] He described how the entrance from the south had been reversed to the north so that the best rooms and their windows were now pointed south; he was particularly taken by Morrison's new suite of rooms: 'very magnificent apartments of great height – with coved ceilings' and the elaborate plasterwork of Christopher Moore which cost £1,300.[65] He was also impressed by the 'excellent hot and cold vaporous baths… there is no private house with so magnificent a cold bath', and by 'a magnificent organ which cost his grace 2,000 guineas'.[66] Morrison's was to be the last major work carried out on Carton until the early twenty-first century. Its completion coincided with the beginning of an extended economic crisis from the 1820s, through the years of the Great Famine and which ended around the time that Gerald FitzGerald, earl of Offaly, was born in 1851.

V

In the late eighteenth century, family politics took an unexpected twist when James and Emily's fifth son, Lord Edward (1763–98), an admirer of the French Revolution, himself turned revolutionary and became a prominent leader in the United Irish rebellion of 1798. It was a major embarrassment to members of his family and, in particular, to his brother, the 2nd duke. On 20 June 1798, John Fitzgibbon, earl of Clare and lord chancellor of Ireland, wrote of Leinster's 'knavery and folly', indirectly implicating him in the actions of Edward and stating that 'whenever his grace shall return to make his appearance amongst us, he will be treated very roughly'.[67]

A generation later, the family had successfully overcome the embarrassment, mainly through the efforts of the 3rd duke, Augustus. He is important to this study because of the undoubted influence he exerted on Gerald as he grew to adulthood and because of the changes he made on the estate, which created the social circumstances in which Gerald later had to operate. Augustus' life was book-ended by his popularity in the Emancipation era (Daniel O'Connell once called him 'the finest fellow that ever bore the name of FitzGerald')[68] and his unpopularity which began with his anti-Repeal stance (in a vitriolic attack on what he called the pusillanimous Irish whigs O'Connell said: 'Oh! Plague take that shabby set! The duke of Leinster, his name operates like a vomit')[69] and ended with his opposition to Gladstone's 1870 Land Act shortly before his death.[70] Like his father, the full complexities of his character and role in local and national politics have yet to be revealed but suffice to say here he brought patronage on the estate to a different level by creating a community of strong farmers and merchants, particularly in the towns of Maynooth and Athy and their hinterlands, who considered his paternalism to be essential to their own economic and social prosperity.

Among many other things, Augustus was grand master of the Freemasons of Ireland, a popular reformist, chairman of the Board of Commissioners for National Education and founder of the Kildare county infirmary. He funded

2 Lord Edward FitzGerald (1763–98), United Irish leader, who died from wounds received during his capture in 1798 (courtesy of Mallaghan family).

the building of a school in Kildare town because he felt the Kildare Place Society indulged proselytism. His funding of both Catholic and Protestant churches on his estate led the *Freeman's Journal* to claim in 1839 that 'few men have done more to reconcile the differences and smooth down the asperities that, unfortunately for the well-being of society, exist in this country, than his Grace'.[71] He kept a finger on the populist pulse. For example, he befriended Fr Theobald Mathew (1790–1856), founder of the mass temperance movement, and at least twice in the 1850s Leinster sent £20 and £10 to the priest when he was in need of 'pecuniary aid'.[72] Leinster seems to have been abstemious himself and saw the wider social benefits of sobriety, so he supported such initiatives as the formation of a Maynooth Temperance Band, which would entertain his guests on occasions such as his heir's wedding.[73] He reared his sons in typical aristocratic fashion to serve country and empire: among other things, Charles, his heir, was MP for Kildare, 1847–52, a commissioner of national education and chancellor of Queen's University; Otho was MP for Kildare (1865–74), an officer in the Royal Horse Guards, and a privy counsellor; and Gerald was a captain in the Scots Guards.

In 1848, in the run up to the fiftieth anniversary of the 1798 rebellion, Augustus tried to divert social memory from the republican ideals of his uncle, Lord Edward, by dismantling the house formerly occupied by him in Kildare town. Notably, this was at a time when Leinster was planning for Queen Victoria's visit to Ireland but also, of course, it coincided with the 'year of revolutions' throughout Europe and at home the re-emergence of republican ideology as espoused by the Young Ireland movement, which culminated in an abortive rebellion in July of that year.[74] (It is not certain whether the dismantling of Lord Edward's house came before or after July.) Simultaneously, he tidied up the ruins of Maynooth Castle, removing the more modern buildings in its courtyard and railing it off. He wanted it to stand as a monument to a much earlier FitzGerald legacy. Augustus also employed the eminent Irish scholar, Eugene O'Curry (1794–1862), to research the FitzGerald family history. By 1846 O'Curry had 'transcribed and translated 492 pages' of family records at a cost of 2s. per page, charging the duke £49 4s.[75] In 1849, Augustus' social ambitions were achieved when Queen Victoria came to visit Carton; one historian has recently concluded that the royal visit 'was public proof that the quiet and diligent loyalty' of Augustus Frederick and of his father before him 'had dissipated any lingering doubts about the allegiance of the FitzGeralds in the wake of the very public rebellion of the 1st duke's son, Lord Edward, in 1798'.[76] In 1858, when his son and heir, Charles William FitzGerald (1819–87), published *The earls of Kildare and their ancestors: from 1057 to 1773* (based on O'Curry's researches), he notably ended it before any discussion of Lord Edward was necessary.

VI

Augustus maintained social control on his estate through a patronage system that bestowed social respectability on those provided with access to land and property. It was part of what he had inherited from his father. When the 2nd duke died in 1804, one of his political opponents, Thomas Rawson, admitted:

The late much to be regretted duke of Leinster was a lover of his country; he almost constantly resided at his magnificent seat of Carton, where he set an example of honesty and benevolence and by every humane attention to the wants of the industrious people, to whom he gave constant employment and charitable assistance, he called aloud on the nobility and gentry of Ireland to imitate so great and good an example.[77]

In turn, the patronage system gave rise to a deferential relationship in which tenants expressed their gratefulness to their aristocratic overlord in their congratulatory addresses and their willingness to adhere to estate management policies. Deference is no easier to define than it is to quantify but it is more than just the enforced actions of tenants who felt they had to please their landlords.[78] It was much more subtle and much more complex. Deference and subservience should not be confused: an Irish tenant could be deferential to suit his own needs. On the Leinster estate, the type of deferential address composed for Gerald's coming-of-age was clearly intended to articulate the mutual benefits of robust landlord–tenant relations on an aristocratic estate. It was not necessarily the same all over Ireland; indeed, there was an uniqueness about the stability of the relationship between Leinster and his tenants over an extended period and this was predicated on the economic advantages accruing to both the agricultural and urban tenants from having Ireland's premier peer in residence.

At a rudimentary level it stemmed historically from the fact that building and landscaping had provided employment for hundreds of men and women for years at Carton and in the town of Maynooth. Inside the house, Lady Caroline Dawson (1750–1813) famously remarked 'there are servants without end'.[79] There were at least 60 indoor servants in the eighteenth century, and 40 by the time Gerald came of age. Very few of these may have been recruited from the local community but there were spin offs: these people had regular wages to spend and they had to buy their own goods and commodities in the local town and perhaps some even had to take lodgings there, and so the town expanded and businesses prospered. Similarly, the demesne became a hive of industry catering for millers, tanners, brewers, granary workers, farriers, wheelwrights, chandlers, smiths, gentlemen of the horse, grooms, shepherds, cowherds, lamplighters, stable hands, lodgekeepers, gardeners and an army of estate labourers, providing much local employment. Local farmers benefited from supplying the grain for the demesne's brewery and distillery; merchants provided the flour, candles, soap, and a multitude of other goods and services to Carton. In the second half of the eighteenth century, the Carton house steward was instructed that 'when anything is to be bought, first enquire for it at Maynooth, and among Lord Kildare's tenants which, if not to be got there or among them as reasonable and as good as elsewhere, to get it where it is best and cheapest giving the preference to Lord Kildare's tenants'.[80] Nothing maintained good local landlord–tenant relations as effectively as a sound employment-based local economy and a 'shop local' policy. This was carried on through the succeeding generations right up to Gerald's time so that when he died in 1893, the Church of Ireland rector, Revd J.W. Tristram, at a general meeting called in Maynooth, proclaimed that 'the income which he derived from this country was spent in the country, and among his people'.[81] There were no dissenting voices from the prominent Catholic nationalist businessmen and strong farmers in attendance. The voice of the lower classes was not heard.

As the first two dukes developed the town of Maynooth they encouraged their wealthier employees to speculate in property development. In the 1750s, the butler, John Stoyte, and his son built grand houses: one of these, Stoyte House, later became the foundation house of St Patrick's College in 1795, while another, Riverstown Lodge, today houses the offices of the president of the National University of Ireland, Maynooth (see plate 3). Peter Bere, the house steward, who was paid around £100 per annum in the 1750s, took a number of long-term leases on properties, which he let for profit, thus giving rise to Bere Street. Other streets are named after developers such as Fagan, Kelly and Nelson (who previously occupied Waterstone Cottage before it was developed as the demesne Shell Cottage). Twelve of the duke's immediate lessees, most of whom lived in the town itself, each controlled between five and thirty properties. Of the fifty-one occupiers of property on Leinster (Main) Street, over half had an interest in at least one other house.[82] In the post-Famine period, many of these town families (and merchants) such as the Caulfields, Mooneys, Kavanaghs and Coonans were also large farmers, their impressive town houses reflecting their socio-economic standing in both urban and rural communities.

Estate employees were comfortably housed in estate cottages at the east end of the town and provided with allotments for the grazing of a cow. The 3rd duke ensured that both the Royal Canal and later the railway passed through Maynooth; urban and rural tenants would have been acutely aware that except for his presence the town might very well have been bypassed by both. Moreover, providing the land for the establishment of St Patrick's College in turn provided massive employment through the service industry or building projects, and so the availability of jobs was indirectly linked to the patronage of the Leinsters. In the 1830s, a report to the poor law commission concluded:

The labouring classes ... derive great advantages from the members of the Roman Catholic college ... From them tailors, shoemakers, seamstresses, and washerwomen obtain constant employment. To these may be added the different tradesmen concerned in building etc.; together with upholsterers, cooks, victuallers etc.[83]

Tenant farmers comprised the most important sector on any landed estate. When Caesar Otway, the Protestant clergyman, travel writer and antiquary, came upon Carton in the late 1830s, he enthused:

Now that we are in view of Carton, and the fine estate all round it, brought into its admirable state of improvement by the present nobleman's grandfather, the first duke of Leinster, I wish I could plant you, reader, for a few minutes, on the top of the [Tyrconnell] tower that crowns a summit in this fine park. Looking east, west and south, you would observe one of the best managed estates in Ireland, comfortable slated farmhouses, two stories high, with all their accompanying homesteads; the fences hedge-rowed; the lands well drained and divided, and in the centre of the property a town laid out in the English style and all this done by one man. Would that all the great proprietors of Ireland had followed the first duke of Leinster's example, whose desire was to have around him not an idle, sporting, presuming, carousing, set of squireens, but a comfortable, industrious, humble, but at the same time self-respecting yeomanry a class of men so much wanting, and, alas, still so scarce in Ireland.[84]

The evidence would suggest that Otway's observations were accurate and that Augustus and his predecessors adopted a policy of letting the Leinster estate in large farm units to progressive farmers. But the creation of large farm units was not without controversy.[85] Augustus, like many of his fellow landlords, began the process of farm consolidation after the passing of the 1838 Poor Law Act in an attempt to avoid the burden of having to pay the rates on holdings below £4 valuation (which, coinciding with Otway's visit, may perhaps suggest the latter's observations had an agenda). There were, in other words, evictions in the pre-Famine period but unfortunately no hard evidence of the exact number survives. There is evidence of further evictions during the Famine, and the duke's investment in so-called voluntary emigration schemes. In April 1849, for example, it was reported that Leinster's tenants were among those who departed for Quebec on board the *Hannah*. The following month, there were further reports that the *Princess Alicia* had brought 'large numbers' of tenants from Wicklow and Kildare and that among the latter 'were many of the duke of Leinster's tenantry'.[86] In 1868, N.W. Senior claimed that Leinster had 'cleared the land by an extensive emigration policy' (involving up to 2,000 acres) and that he had then advertised 'substantial farms with new dwelling houses in south Kildare', offering preference to Scottish tenants.[87] In the early 1850s, seventeen Presbyterian families arrived in Athy from Perthshire in Scotland.[88]

Griffith's valuation from the early 1850s clearly shows that Carton was ringed by large farms; the agent, Charles Hamilton, pointed out that 'as a rule they are large tenants paying on an average about £400 a year'.[89] It would seem that Leinster deliberately let each townland in the hinterland of Maynooth to one or at most two large tenants: Old Carton was let in one block of 287 acres to Lawrence Brangan; 130 acres in Rowanstown to Richard Suban; John Sullivan and John Chandeler held over 270 acres between them in Rail Park; Matthew Fagan leased all 196 acres in Treadstown; Edward Murray all 130 acres in Timard; Peter Fowler, 163 acres in Sion; John Fitzpatrick, 470 acres in Griffinrath; Edward Alday, 166 acres in Dowdstown and so on. The largest grazier would seem to have been Bartholomew Ellis who held all 242 acres in Donaghstown, similarly all 119 acres of Laraghbryan, 119 acres in Maravilla, 189 acres in Maws and 11 in Crickstown, a total of 679 acres. Most held on leases of twenty or thirty-one years, long enough to give them confidence to invest in their holdings and stability during the prosperous years of the post-Famine period; the aforementioned Senior had ended his report stating that after the Famine: 'the estate was re-let, the rental, which had been £35,000 a year, was, by improved management, and by the falling in of very old leases, raised to £45,000; and the tenants (especially the Scotch) are doing well'.[90]

The contentment evidenced at Gerald's coming-of-age celebrations was predicated on this prosperity for a generation after the Famine but it was a prosperity that in all probability had been created on the back of estate evictions after 1838 and during the Great Famine. Famine studies have yet to fully consider culpability at local level or to determine how neighbours benefited at the expense of the less well off during Ireland's greatest modern social catastrophe. Around Maynooth, no more than most places, the social and popular memory of the Famine did not dwell on the creation of large grazier farms at the expense of those cleared from the land; instead the bulk of blame was placed on Irish landlords and British governments. The middle classes, which emerged on the Leinster estate, simply buried any suggestions of culpability (or perhaps more accurately insensitivity to the needs of the

3 'Maynooth College, 1850', coming towards the end of the Great Famine
and shortly after Queen Victoria's visit to Maynooth.

destitute) in their own stories of success: thus the myth was created that
through their own initiatives and hard work they had emerged as the
cornerstone of a stable local society on an exceptionally well and liberally
managed estate where rents were affordable (not necessarily moderate) and
raised only at the expiration of long leases; where families remained for
generations; where abatements were granted in times of economic crisis; and
where evictions were rare.[91]

In the same social memory, it was, therefore, legitimate to represent
Augustus as a benevolent landlord and to ignore the history of evictions; in that
way both the reputation of the 3rd duke and those who benefited remained
intact.[92] Coinciding with Gerald's coming-of-age, a strong tenant calling
himself 'F.S.' wrote to the *Irish Times* claiming that by 1872 evictions on the
estate had become unknown except for the non-payment of rent.[93] On 19
August 1872, the establishment *Morning Post* claimed that 'Maynooth has good
reason to regard Ireland's only duke with feelings of esteem'.[94] At the
celebrations in Maynooth local grocer and spirit dealer, Joseph Caulfield,
praised the duke for spending an estimated £22,000 a year 'at Carton alone …
in giving employment to those around him'.[95] It is not known from where he
got these figures and they sound inflated but they might more accurately
indicate what the duke's residency meant to the local economy per annum.
Caulfield also referred to the duke as 'the father of his people', emphasizing the

patriarchal relationship on the estate (and using terminology which might have suggested a comparison with misplaced contemporaneous peasant perceptions of the Russian Tsar). Historians subsequently bought into this myth. For D.H. Akenson, Augustus was one of 'that rare phenomenon in Ireland, a conscientious landlord' who 'spent a great deal of his time performing his civic duties'.[96] Similarly, William Nolan points out that the contemporary evidence to the pre-Famine Devon Commission and retrospective opinions expressed at the Bessborough Commission of the early 1880s are 'favourable to the duke'.[97] In terms of Famine relief he has been cited as one of the more benevolent landlords: for example, one of the few commended by Cecil Woodham-Smith.[98]

But it is when Augustus' representation in social memory as a benevolent landlord is juxtaposed with the harsh realities of evictions and, indeed, ulterior motives for private relief schemes on the estate at the height of the Great Famine, that issues are raised suggesting the need for a more nuanced interpretation of the relationship between landlord and tenant. This is particularly true in terms of the participation of the middle classes in celebratory events. In October 1847, Augustus' eldest son and heir, Charles, married Lady Caroline Sutherland-Leveson-Gower, granddaughter of George Granville Leveson-Gower, 1st duke of Sutherland (1758–1833), who, when he died, was described by Charles Greville as 'a leviathan of wealth. I do believe he was the richest man who ever died'.[99] Standards of presentation for the arrival of the new bride were presumably important, which may explain much of the work on the estate, including the completion of the Midland and Western Railway in 1847 which terminated at Maynooth adjacent to the Duke's Harbour on the Royal Canal.

Even more difficult to reconcile is the hardship in the area during the worst year of the Famine, 'Black 47', and the large-scale expenditure on the wedding celebrations. On 2 November 1847, the *Freeman's Journal* reported that the previous Saturday 'was observed as a gala day at Carton. Preparations on a large scale for the festivities had been in progress for some days for the arrival of the happy couple ... and the Duke of Leinster personally superintended all the proceedings'.[1] That morning Kildare and his new bride arrived from their Dublin townhouse on Lower Dominick Street in 'a splendid new chariot and four'. A 'hospitable entertainment' was provided for up to 200 tenants and all sat down to 'an excellent dinner', which was followed by 'plumb pudding and other delicacies' laid out in one of the barns adjoining the mansion. The Maynooth Temperance Band entertained the guests and an evening of sports – 'running in sacks, rolling in barrels, climbing of poles and a variety of other

4 'Dance of the peasants on the lawn at Carton', to celebrate the visit of Queen
Victoria in 1849 (*Illustrated London News*, 1849).

rustic amusements' – was held on the lawn. This was then followed by a ball in
one of the large lofts over the stables where the guests were again treated to tea,
coffee and other refreshments (while a private dinner for around forty family
guests was held in the house).[2] There was no word in the report of the Famine.
One can only presume that those entertained in the barns and lofts comprised
the strong farming and merchant classes of the estate who were pleased to
accept the duke's invitation, perhaps not oblivious to the hardships of their less-
well-off neighbours – the population of Maynooth declined by about 20 per
cent over the period 1841 to 1851[3] – but more concerned about their own
future prospects.

The same applied to Queen Victoria's visit two years later. It came at a time
when there were 141 cases of cholera and typhoid in Maynooth, 47 of which
resulted in death. Cholera was also rampant on the duke's Athy estate,
reportedly 'adding fear to the distress and hunger of the local people'.[4] But
from Augustus' perspective, the queen's visit was of major significance to his

standing within the supra-national aristocracy of Great Britain and Ireland (as had been the marriage of his heir to Sutherland's daughter) and once again no expense was spared. The contemporary descriptions of the visit from Victoria herself show how far removed from the reality of the prevailing social circumstances were the upper echelons of society and, indeed, how well Augustus hid these realities. 'Peasants' were reported to have danced on the lawns of Carton but in reality this was a well-orchestrated entertainment planned for Victoria and Albert's amusement while the guests comprised the social elite. The only spectators allowed near the vicinity of the demesne walls were the seminarian students and the queen herself later recalled that these 'did not make a very attractive impression' on her.[5] She concluded her reminiscences: 'We walked around the garden twice, the duke leading me and Albert the duchess. The duke is one of the kindest and best of men'. The deferential manner in which the respectable tenantry behaved to the duke was, she felt, due to his patriarchal benevolence: 'the duke is so kind to them that a word from him will make them do anything'.[6]

In a sense, Victoria was right. In the post-Famine period, the strong farmers and the shopocracy built their economic strength on the relationship they cultivated with the duke and, in turn, they paid their rents on time and usually in full. They had no difficulty with using a deferential rhetoric when looking to the duke(s) for favours.[7] They consolidated their positions through their close knit social circles, which they kept exclusive primarily through marriage but also through the conduits of associational culture – for example, they invariably placed themselves at the head of any club or organization formed in the towns and country whether political or social. The middle classes also practised their own forms of patronage: they provided employment on farms and in shops; the shopkeepers and publicans and other merchants offered credit facilities; as the leaders of local societies and organizations they allowed access to recreation halls and so on. In time this would provide them with the political power commensurate with their social and economic gains.

VII

The relationship between St Patrick's College and successive dukes was a complex one. With the advent of the devotional revolution in the post-Famine period, both the 3rd duke and the Church representatives vied for authority over the people; both locked horns at times to show who was in the ascendancy. Yet, there was a mutual dependence when it came to maintaining social control.

When Augustus supported Prime Minster Peel's controversial decision to increase the parliamentary grant to Maynooth College under the terms of an act of 1845 – raised from just under £9,000 to over £26,600 with a further £30,000 once off payment for infrastructural repairs – he was appointed a Visitor there, giving him access of sorts to the hierarchy.[8] Previously, he had been influential in the development of the new Presentation convent in the 1830s (on the site of the old charter school) at the east end of the town, adjoining Carton Avenue, and directly across from a row of estate (Leinster) cottages. The Order brought charity workers, nurses and in time teachers. Everything helped in the greater scheme of things to present an image of an improving estate where examples of destitution and impoverishment were rare. Notably, the records of the Presentation Order for the Famine years claimed: 'there was not much distress in the district, so there were not extensive claims on the Sisters'.[9] If they had reported otherwise it would have reflected negatively on themselves, St Patrick's College, the Catholic middle classes who were the financial mainstay of the church, and even on the duke of Leinster, none of whom would have welcomed any charge of culpability being laid at their door for the suffering of the lower orders.

This loose post-Famine alliance of strong farmers, townsmen and Catholic clergy – and it should be noted the trustees of St Patrick' College were one of the duke's largest tenants, leasing around 400 acres of farmland – in defence of the duke was evident during Gerald's coming-of-age celebrations in 1872. The college president, Dr Charles W. Russell, told his Maynooth audience:

> It is foreign to our college habits to take part in public assemblies under ordinary circumstances but I look upon the present occasion as very far from an ordinary one (applause). I look upon it as an occasion of public importance and at the same time in the light of a domestic festival (applause).[10]

At another function, Fr Myles McManus, parish priest of Celbridge, remarked of the prosperous farmers in their midst who provided much local employment: 'It might not be so fashionable for these gentlemen to reside among them if his Grace the duke of Leinster had not set them the example'. Fr John O'Rourke, who was parish priest of Maynooth from 1869 to 1887, thought it 'a most pleasing duty' and 'a great honour' to propose the duke's health for: 'his name alone is sufficient to elicit from you feelings of bliss and gratitude [and] of affection (applause)'.[11] Three years later, O'Rourke wrote a history of the Great Famine and managed not to mention Maynooth despite the fact that he had lived through the calamity while a student there.[12]

However, like the records of the Presentation Sisters, this may say something of the censorship of both Church and the duke. For Fr O'Rourke, it was more judicious and politic to focus his Famine attentions on far away west Cork.

O'Rourke finished off his speech in 1872 by quoting Thomas Davis' eulogy to the Geraldines and while Davis may have had the Desmond branch more in mind, O'Rourke felt lines such as 'Ye never ceased to battle brave against the English sway/Though axe and brand and treachery your proudest cut away', were appropriate to celebrate the Kildare branch. Davis (1814–45) is, of course, best remembered as a radical nationalist, a founder of the Young Ireland movement that rebelled in 1848 (three years after his death), founder of the *Nation* newspaper, and writer of rousing ballads including 'A nation once again' and 'The west's awake'. He had once proposed that hereditary rank 'should be unhesitatingly swept away'.[13] But he never called for the abolition of the monarchy. The middle-class spokesmen who led the various celebrations for Gerald FitzGerald's coming-of-age did not call for the abolition of hereditary rank and they had no problem juxtaposing their nationalism alongside their loyalty to the British monarchy. At one event a toast was drunk to Queen Victoria that the proposer was confident would be received 'with that loyalty and cordiality due to the toast' and he was right for it was reported to have been 'drank amid enthusiastic applause'. This was followed by James Edward Medlicott JP, a substantial farmer on the Leinster estate, proposing a toast to the Prince and Princess of Wales, reminding all those present of 'the time his Royal Highness was at the Curragh, when he went about the houses of the gentry and about the country making friends of all he met'.[14] Medlicott went on to describe how the royal couple had arrived at Maynooth train station and were greeted by the duke and marquess, taken by carriage to St Patrick's College, passing through the town of Maynooth where they were 'enthusiastically cheered by a large number of persons, who, notwithstanding the inclement state of the weather, had assembled to greet them'. In the college they were met by the president, Dr Charles W. Russell, who addressed them as follows:

> We, the president, masters, professors, and students of the Royal College of St Patrick, Maynooth, most respectfully acknowledge the honour which your Royal Highness has done us, in affording us by this gracious visit, an opportunity of joining with our countrymen in the enthusiastic welcome which has hailed the presence of your Royal Highness and your illustrious princess in Ireland.[15]

In 1872, as he was being regaled, the evidence of his grandfather's influence at all levels of local society, among all classes and religions, was, therefore, clearly evident to Gerald. When Augustus died in 1874 stories abounded in newspapers about his paternalism. One anecdote told of an old man making his way to Carton where he met the duke, told him he had worked for him for twenty years, and asked for 10s. for a bandage that would cure a sore on his leg. The duke replied: 'That's a long time ago but here are the ten shillings'. As the man made his way down the avenue the duke called after him: 'Who will put this bandage on when you get it?' When the old man replied he would do it himself, the duke gave him 5s. more to go to Dublin to get it done properly.[16] Whether true or not, and most likely the latter, it was important for the family to ensure that such stories got reported in the local newspapers as a reminder to the tenantry of how grateful they should be. (It would be foolish to think that the Leinsters did not use the media for public relations purposes and this, as we shall see in later chapters, became much more prevalent and blatant from the late nineteenth century.) What is perhaps most striking is that the vast majority of Leinster's post-Famine tenants were content at this stage to show their deferential gratefulness that orthodox nationalist history did not subsequently recognize or acknowledge.

VIII

However, Gerald's coming-of-age in August 1872 represented the twilight of paternalism and deference on the Leinster estate. Ultimately, paternalism and patronage proved to be a double-edged sword for Leinster; as the Catholic middle classes grew in economic and social stature and confidence they began to assert their independence and look for political power commensurate with their other gains. In this respect, 1872 proved something of a watershed, not just in the history of the estate but the country as a whole. In the very month that Gerald came of age, the Secret Ballot Act was passed, which greatly diluted landlord power at elections. Two years previously, in 1870, W.E. Gladstone had introduced his first significant land act for Ireland as part of his mission to pacify the country. Gerald's grandfather, Augustus, became one of its chief critics and within three months of Gerald's birthday he introduced a lease that would strain landlord–tenant relations on the estate and give rise that November to one of the first tenant defence associations to be established in Ireland.[17] His timing would suggest that he deliberately held off until after the coming-of-age celebrations. Moreover, his absence at the celebrations was noted; his son, the marquess of Kildare, apologized that his eighty-one-year-old father had been unable to travel from England.[18] Augustus would have been keenly aware of the discord that the introduction of the lease would have created before the coming-of-age celebration and as the latter was a traditional public demonstration of the harmonious relations that existed between landlord and tenant, he was undoubtedly reluctant to interfere with that tradition.[19]

Augustus had already been galled by Gladstone's disestablishment of the Irish Church in 1869 because of the blow it dealt to the Protestant interest in Ireland and then by the founding of the Home Government Association, which over the next decade would morph into the Irish Parliamentary Party. Its demand of Home Rule for Ireland ran contrary to Augustus' unionist beliefs. In time, as the land and Home Rule questions gathered momentum, his grandson, Gerald, would have to face the choice of whether to remain loyal to the Leinster tradition of support for the Whig party or loyal to his landlordism. Like the majority of Whigs he would opt for the second alternative. The perceived democratic extremism of Home Rule was not for him, or, indeed, his father, Charles. They were as opposed to the sundering of the Act of Union as Augustus had been in the 1840s. His father would hand down to Gerald an estate much changed by circumstances and in a country, as in Britain and Europe as a whole, where the democratization of politics was pushing governments in the direction of social reform – ranging from education to land reform – as well as wider action to defend the economic interests of an expanding electorate.[20]

CHAPTER TWO

Land war and politics in a changing society, 1872–85

I look upon it as a means of drawing closer those ties which should ever
bind the good landlord with his tenantry … We are all unfortunately too
well aware that in this country circumstances … have been, nay, still
continue to be the means of creating dissension and division, of cutting
asunder the ties of social discourse … But in a meeting like the present
we establish, as it were, a sort of neutral ground, where all may meet in
peace and harmony together, and become convinced … that political
differences and private friendships are not necessarily incompatible.

Dr Edward O'Kelly, Maynooth, at Gerald's coming-of-age celebration[1]

By 1870, Irish land was a long-established political issue, along with the Irish
church, Irish education and Irish disaffection. The unsuccessful Fenian uprising
three years previously had convinced the British Liberal prime minister, W.E.
Gladstone, that positive measures had to be taken to pacify Ireland.[2] The
introduction of his land act in 1870 can be seen as his first attempt to address
the Irish land question in furtherance of his wider aim to find a solution to the
'Irish problem'. The act was an extremely long and complex piece of legislation
and ultimately was largely ineffectual. From the tenants' perspective, it suffered
from the fundamental weakness that it did not give them the basic security of
tenure they demanded.[3] It recognized the so-called 'Ulster Custom' –
recognition of the outgoing tenant's investment in his holding – but only in
areas where it previously existed. Tenants were to be compensated for
improvements they had made if they were evicted; however, as improving
tenants were probably rarely evicted, the clause did little for those impoverished
tenants whose inability to pay rents led to them losing their farms. There were
provisions for land purchase by occupying tenants but the terms were so
unfavourable to both landlords and tenants that ultimately only a handful of
the latter purchased their holdings.

Probably the most significant outcome of the act was the consternation it
caused among the propertied classes, especially the clause that obliged landlords
to compensate vacating tenants for any improvements they had carried out on
their farms. As R.F. Foster has put it, 'Gladstone had interfered with property

rights; his theoretical principles of compensation implicitly admitted the Irish tenant's *moral* property in his holding'.[4] This was anathema to traditionalists such as the 3rd duke of Leinster; he and many other landlords responded to the act by attempting to force more of their tenants to accept restrictive leases. The so-called 'Leinster lease', which Augustus introduced in 1872, was a deliberate attempt to allow him to legally circumvent the terms of the act; it contained all of the standard covenants in terms of duration, farm husbandry and so on but it required tenants to forego claims to compensation for disturbance or for improvements, except where the latter had been carried out with the written permission of the duke. Very quickly, the lease was denounced as 'an artifice to evade the law and deprive the tenants of the benefits which the legislature intended to confer' and it was proclaimed 'an obnoxious document which had the effect of depriving the tenants of the meagre benefit conferred on them by the legislature, and of reducing them to the position of the merest serfs, removable at the whim of the landlord'.[5]

The duke's agent, Charles Robert Hamilton, predictably defended its introduction on the grounds that Leinster and his predecessors had 'always treated the estate very much as an English one. They have planted, drained, built houses, erected farm offices, labourers' cottages and everything'.[6] The landlord carried out all permanent improvements (though some of the expense was usually passed on to the tenants in increased rents). Hamilton would later show that from 1874 to 1880 the 4th duke spent £75,000 on improvements, £40,000 out of his own pocket and £35,000 borrowed from the Board of Works for arterial improvements.[7] This type of expenditure went further than benefiting the large farmers; it crucially also provided work for the labouring population during the winter months when it might otherwise be scarce. Thus, it was being suggested to the large farmers that the duke's paternalism was to their benefit in terms of maintaining social order and control: if the lower classes felt grateful they would express it in docility.

While the so-called Ulster Custom – essentially a departing tenant's right to sell his interest in his holding to the highest bidder – had become increasingly widespread outside that province after the Famine, it had not been allowed on the Leinster estate. When Hamilton gave evidence to the Bessborough Commission in the early 1880s, he claimed that one of the main purposes of the Leinster lease was 'to prevent the introduction of the Ulster tenant-right upon the estate', as he and Leinster were of the opinion that even one tenant receiving money on quitting his holding would establish it as a right.[8] As is usually the case when a major controversy breaks out, a number of other issues came to prominence that had been simmering beneath the surface for some

5 Augustus Frederick FitzGerald (1791–1874), 3rd duke of Leinster,
shortly before his death in 1874 (*The Graphic*, 24 Oct. 1874).

time: for example, it seems that some of Leinster's urban tenants wanted to use
townparks for tillage and gardening purposes and the duke was completely
opposed to this, asserting that such use would 'run them out of heart entirely'
and thereby insisted townparks be used only for the grazing of cows.

In December 1872, it was reported that this was the first time in living
memory that 'a feeling of bitter hostility to his Grace and his agent' had been
aroused.[9] A few weeks before this, the Leinster Tenants' Defence Association
was established. In a letter to *The Times*, a correspondent calling himself 'J.S'
declared his surprise that a new tenant right movement should spring up on an
estate where 'under all circumstances the sympathies of the Geraldines have
been with the Irish people'. He noted it was especially surprising given that it
was so soon after a strong sense of patriarchal dependency had been articulated
in Gerald's recent coming-of-age celebrations. In some circles, democratization,

as exemplified in the establishment of the Leinster Tenants' Defence Association, following very quickly upon the passing of the Secret Ballot Act (and possibly linked to the same), was perceived to be a contagion: *The Times* pointed out that Athy was becoming the 'rallying point of a new democratic movement which threatens to be mischievous'.[10] This was significant because this was the southern outpost of the Leinster estate, not only away from the watchful eye of the duke, but also perhaps out of range in terms of the paternalistic advantages that accrued more readily to the Maynooth estate.

Trouble in Athy centred upon the eviction of a substantial tenant named Low, who reputedly had expended £2,000 on improving the land and £1,000 on buildings since taking up his tenancy, but who had refused to sign the lease. Low had the sympathy of the tenant association who collectively denounced the serving of the eviction order in 'an insulting and uncalled for manner'. They deplored the 'deep sense of the injustice and wrong done to the duke's tenants', laying the blame upon his agent, and couching their language to suggest that either the duke had been misguided or that his instructions were issued in 'a moment of hasty temper'. Charles Hamilton had a different version of events to report. In a public letter to *The Times* he told of how he had written to Low reminding him that his lease was due to expire and that the duke would be happy to renew it and provide him with a Board of Works loan for £1,600 towards improvements. He had informed Low that he would have to add 5 per cent of the repayment instalments to his rent. In order to carry through the transaction, Low's lease would have to be terminated legally and that could be best done by eviction before reinstatement.[11]

The eviction controversy led to much public and political debate. In February 1873, in the House of Commons, Prime Minister Gladstone was asked if the Leinster lease was legal under the terms of the act. Gladstone was reticent to discuss the conduct of 'one of the most respected landlords in Ireland' but he was happy to quote a telegram he had received from the duke's son, Lord Kildare, which he read with 'only one or two verbal changes' and which had reassured him that

> No tenant has been requested to sign a new agreement, except when the old one had expired or a new valuation was necessary. No tenant has been debarred from compensation where the holding was under £50 valuation; nor, in the case of large farms, has any tenant been excluded from compensation.

Gladstone made the point that it was to be expected that tenants with a rental valuation of over £50 per annum were of 'sufficient independence' to enable them 'to contract fairly with the landlord'.[12]

This very much encapsulated traditional management policy on the estate where Augustus had encouraged the creation of large viable farms let on medium- to long-term leases. These large farmers had been his security against agitation and this had worked very well during the good years of the post-Famine period. Once legislation promised to improve their situation the tenants acted predictably enough.

These large tenants had further benefited from recent social reforms which had given rise to the emergence of an educated class – 'many men of property and great intelligence' as one estate correspondent put it – now willing and able to articulate its grievances in the press.[13] Thus, on 16 December 1872, a member of the Leinster Tenants' Defence Association wrote a lengthy letter to *The Times* setting out why the tenant farmers took exception to the lease and the reasons ranged from their objections to Augustus preventing the operation of the Ulster Custom, to his wanting to reserve all shooting, hunting and fishing rights. It is clear from the letter that new ideas were spreading on the estate; the educated farmers were reading the *Mark Lane Express* and other agricultural magazines coming from Britain and they saw the plight of the Leinster tenantry not just in an Irish, but in a much wider British context. And on agrarian issues there was inter-denominational agreement: Thomas Robertson from Athy was anxious to emphasize that the Leinster Tenants' Defence Association included Episcopalians and Presbyterians, the Scottish and Welsh 'planters' as well as 'the native Irish' and he concluded: 'the movement has nothing whatever of a sectarian character about it'.[14]

The controversy over the lease signalled the first major stage in the struggle for power between Leinster and his prosperous, better educated and increasingly more confident middle-class tenants, both rural and urban. In essence, the duke was *told* that he was acting in contravention of the spirit of government legislation. Low's eviction does not seem to have been followed by others, so moral victory went to the tenants. It may be that it was quickly realized by Hamilton and Leinster that further evictions would be detrimental to social stability on the estate and that would have been too much to risk. Perhaps revealingly, while the Liberal candidate, William Cogan, retained his seat in the general election of 1874 (the last Liberal to represent Co. Kildare), the 3rd duke's son, Lord Otho FitzGerald, lost his seat to Charles Henry Meldon of the Home Rule League.

The events of 1872 took their toll on Augustus. Late that year he was reported to be exhausted but he still managed to write to his agent on 22 December that he was 'thankful for my good health & all the enjoyments I have'. He sympathized with Hamilton on 'all the bother' he had to contend with and expressed a wish that future Christmases would be less stressful.[15] But Augustus' health began to fail shortly afterwards and he died on 10 October 1874. Revealingly, he issued very specific instructions before his death that 'his obsequies should be as private as possible'.[16] On 14 October, his remains – in a suite of coffins, 'the inner being of cedar, lined with white silk, and cased in a leaden coffin, outside of which was one of Irish oak, covered with black silver velvet, with rich gilt mountings'[17] – were taken from Carton to be laid to rest in the family vault in the church in the town of Maynooth. It was reported that

> … the funeral would have been of much greater extent locally had it not been for the almost extreme measures taken to carry out the wishes of the late noble duke. Even those who were most desirous of paying their last sad tribute of respect to the memory of the late duke found it difficult to obtain admittance to the grounds or the churchyard at Maynooth, only the most select, and these in some cases with difficulty, being admitted to either.[18]

It would seem that those of the respectable classes who had stood against him, and only two years earlier had regaled him at his grandson's coming-of-age, were now being reproved. Even the Royal Irish Constabulary were deployed at the gates of the church in Maynooth 'refusing admittance to all but the more respectable of the mourners'.[19] In death, Augustus was described as 'a most kind and improving landlord, an extensive and steady employer and a constant resident on his estates in this country'.[20] But the controversy over the Leinster lease had illustrated that tenants (and this was equally true of non-nationalist Protestants as their Catholic nationalist counterparts) were not prepared to merely acquiesce to the *status quo*; even the longest established landed families such as the Leinsters found their position under threat in a new world where privilege and paternalism continued to exist but their powers were on the wane.

II

It was up to Augustus' successor, Charles (1819–87), to calm the waters. This he did by reverting to the *status quo ante* and for the first five years or so of his succession stability returned to the wider estate as prosperity once again diluted the potential for agitation. In a further attempt to diffuse the negative impact that the lease had on the perception of the FitzGeralds as paternalistic aristocrats, Charles even opened Carton demesne for tours, at least to paying respectable groups. Thus, in May 1877 the *Freeman's Journal* advertised an excursion from the Coffee Palace on Townsend Street in Dublin to Carton with a special train leaving Broadstone Station at 10.30 a.m. to stop outside the Dublin Road gates of the demesne. Tickets were 2s. each, with children half price, and visitors were set to enjoy 'athletic sports, bands of music, innocent amusement' and 'healthful recreation'.[21]

The year 1877 also witnessed the beginning of a prolonged economic depression, which expedited the transformation of the Irish political landscape. In late 1879, the Irish National Land League was established in response to the crisis, very much taking its lead from previous tenant defence associations such as had been established on the Leinster estate a few years before. Shortly afterwards, the land and Home Rule movements merged under the leadership of Charles Stewart Parnell, himself a Protestant landlord from neighbouring Co. Wicklow. This was the first time in over a generation that the strong farmers and the town traders on the Leinster estate found their prosperity (as opposed to their tenurial rights) under threat and at a time when their democratic powers had increased. They were never likely to suffer the same levels of destitution as the smallholders of the west of Ireland where the Land League first took root, so the Leinster tenants' campaign was not so much about economic survival as about maintaining new-found social status and laying claim to political power.[22]

During the winter and spring of 1880–1, relations between the 4th duke and his tenants were reportedly tense, particularly in the Athy and Castledermot areas, again notably removed from the core estate and ducal residence at Carton. The agitation was orchestrated by John Heffernan, who, as Virginia Crossman has pointed out, typified men who were 'frustrated by the severely restricted range of positions open to them in local government' and who were 'quick to take advantage of the opportunities provided by the formation of the Land League to establish themselves as figures of influence within their localities, and thus to mount an effective challenge to landlord power'.[23] Heffernan's father (died 1872) had held fifty-six acres on the Leinster and Drogheda estates but he was also a prosperous grocer and hardware merchant and property owner (with thirty cottages in Kildare town) who had mingled in the company of the local professional and gentry classes at the Kildare annual hunt balls. But his commercial success and wealth had not translated into commensurate political power and thus his frustration was undoubtedly passed on to his son, John. The latter inherited another grievance. John was set up as a small farmer of fifteen acres by his father. (His elder brother, Charles, inherited the urban properties and his mother the tenancy of the larger farm.) This meant that he was relegated to the status of a smallholder, below the social class into which he had been born (and there were undoubtedly many more like him who came to prominence in the Land League). In the early 1870s he considered emigrating to America, probably inspired by the letters from his cousin, Stephen Clery, one of which told him in February 1874: 'the man who sweeps the street is as good and as independent as any of the swells who are worth millions, there's no two classes here, and if you respect yourself everyone will respect you … . It's just the country for to live in.'[24] However, he stayed and over the next two years he prospered, advancing himself as a shopkeeper in Kildare town. At the same time he joined the Amnesty Association that campaigned for the release of the Fenian prisoners arrested in 1867, then one of the few organizations that allowed ambitious young men to be politically active.

When the economic downturn of the late 1870s began to impact on Kildare, Heffernan met with a peripatetic Land League organizer, Michael Boyton, which led to the establishment of the first Land League branch on the Leinster estate in Kildare town in March 1880 with Heffernan as secretary. One of the most iconic events of the Land War was Boyton's public burning of the Leinster lease attached to a 1798 pike in the square of Kildare town. The symbolism was difficult to ignore: the lease represented all the perceived grievances of the tenants in 1880, the pike was a reminder of Lord Edward's participation in the 1798 rebellion.

In the end, the relatively prosperous county of Kildare remained largely dormant during the Land League campaign.[25] The high of thirty agrarian crimes reported for 1880 was less than 10 per cent of the number reported for Mayo where the League had been initiated back in 1879.[26] Without estate rentals it is difficult to ascertain with any certainty what financial impact the Land League had on the duke's income. There are newspaper reports for the summer of 1880 that state that in the run up to the May gale day the tenants demanded reductions of 25–30 per cent, but Charles, the 4th duke, offered only 20 per cent. He warned that in the economic climate he would find it difficult to continue to provide employment for labourers if he was forced to grant more substantial reductions.[27] It may have been a ploy to break the Land League alliance, comprising all classes from strong farmers and townsmen to agricultural labourers. It seems, however, that Charles eventually gave in and granted 25 per cent reductions to yearly tenants under £50 annual rent and 15 per cent to those with holdings of 50–100 acres. Leaseholders received some help in accordance with the circumstances of each case.[28]

On a national level, the Land Act of 1881 was very effective in diffusing the Land League's momentum (notably Gladstone had communicated his ideas to

6 The burning of the Leinster lease became an iconic event in the history of the later Land War in Kildare. Picture shows Michael Boyton burning the lease attached to a 1798 pike in Athy in late 1880 (*Illustrated London News*, 8 Jan. 1881).

the duke on the proposed 1881 Land Bill.)[29] On the one hand, it was only marginally more successful than its predecessor in stimulating tenant purchase; in total only 731 tenants in the country as a whole purchased under the act. While the newly-established Land Commission was empowered to make advances to tenants for the purchase of their holdings, it restricted the amount advanced to 75 per cent of the purchase price, putting the onus on tenant purchasers to raise a 25 per cent deposit, a major disincentive in a depressed agricultural economy. Moreover, it was only in rare cases that landlords and tenants could reach common ground in terms of an agreed purchase price. For example, one of Leinster's nearest aristocratic neighbours, Lord Cloncurry at Lyons, who had suffered years of agrarian agitation on his Limerick estates, wrote in 1881: 'The conduct of the people in the south of Ireland during the last year has been so disgraceful and all feelings of honesty have been so openly repudiated that I shall be glad to sever my connections with the county of Limerick'. But he would not sell for less than twenty-five years' purchase on the value of his annual rents at a time when tenants were not prepared to pay more than fourteen or fifteen years' purchase.[30]

On the other hand, the act once again infringed on previously sacrosanct landlord rights by giving legal standing to the Ulster Custom or the '3 Fs' – it provided fixity of tenure for all tenants who paid their rents; it allowed for free sale of a departing tenant's interest in his holding, compelling a landlord to compensate a tenant for disturbance and for improvements carried out; and perhaps most significantly, it provided for the establishment of independent tribunals under the auspices of the Land Commission for the adjudication of fair rents on individual holdings.[31] It was this legal mechanism for the fixing of fair rents, which in the political climate of the day ultimately meant lower rents, that broke the loose alliance between large farmers, smallholders and the labouring class; the large holders had secured the rent reductions they had desired. Revealingly, in October 1881, the police made it known that the strong farmers of Kildare had never been fully committed to the Land League; the county inspector surmised that if Heffernan was arrested, the vital arm of the League would be cut off and concluded rather revealingly that: 'there is no one to take his place. In fact all the respectable farmers would be pleased at the arrest as, though they sympathize with the movement, they do not approve of the advanced steps to which Heffernan is prepared to go.'[32] The Land League did not take a grip on the core estate around Maynooth. Perhaps what Richard Cobden (1804–65), the Liberal reformer, said of the situation in Britain in 1849 when famine was ravaging Ireland, was just as true of Maynooth during the Land War: 'We have the labour of Hercules in hand to abate the power of the aristocracy and their allies, the snobs of the town'.[33]

Charles should be given some credit for astutely keeping the Land League at bay with his willingness to compromise on tenant demands; the landlord-sympathetic Finlay Dun claimed 'the duke is always accessible and ready personally to see them and hear and remedy any grievances'.[34] Moreover, he made it clear that he did not agree with the government's coercive approach to the escalating land agitation, which he expressed in a subtle rather than public way. In her Irish journals, Florence Arnold-Forster, the adopted daughter of W.E. 'Buckshot' Forster, chief secretary of Ireland 1880–2, recalled that on 10 December 1880 her parents were planning on a visit to Carton when a letter arrived from Caroline, duchess of Leinster: 'Sorry not to have the pleasure of seeing Mr and Mrs Forster, but owing to the disturbed state of the country, and

7 Charles FitzGerald, 4th duke of Leinster (1819–87)
(courtesy of Mallaghan family).

the doubtfulness of getting rents, they were giving up their party and felt obliged to reduce everything'.[35] Florence was discerning enough to note: 'there can … be little doubt that their Graces were glad to take this impressive if somewhat undignified manner of marking their displeasure with the government'.[36]

From the spring of 1882, Leinster and his agent began to negotiate with the tenantry, the duke arguing that it would be best for him to appoint a valuator to determine a 'fair rent' rather than allow the tenants to go into the Land Commission courts. By the end of May, nearly all of Leinster's tenants around Kildare town had signed agreements and Charles Hamilton was happy that everything was now in order for a more peaceful future. Writing to the duke on 31 May 1882, he claimed: 'There is the best feeling here and I do believe that the rents will be paid punctually and pleasantly in future'.[37] Around Maynooth some of the tenants decided to contest their valuations (it seems as many as 25 per cent) but Hamilton was not perturbed: 'I am just as well pleased that a few cases shall be tried as it will show what relation the valuations made by the sub commissioners bear to those made by your valuers'.[38]

Hamilton was more concerned by the fact that a sub-commissioner, Archibald (who had earlier surveyed the duke of Abercorn's estate in the north of Ireland), had made significant reductions on the large farms in Kilkea Manor, something that he was not anticipating. Yet, he was prepared to yield to Archibald's better judgment: 'I am sure Archibald from his great experience in the management of that class of land is a good judge of what rent can be paid for it'.[39] Reductions were much smaller on the Athy and Castledermot estates, on average around 13 per cent (which was about 8 per cent less than the national average).[40] Writing to the duke in July 1882 Hamilton pointed out that not only had he 'saved a considerable sum in law expenses' by staying out of the courts but in the future 'you cannot ... be called upon to make any improvements for the tenants, and [given] the large sum per annum which has been usually devoted to these improvements, I do not think you will be dissatisfied'.[41] Around Marshallstown, Knockroe and Castleroe where Archibald reduced rents by 15 per cent, Hamilton had told the tenants they should be 'very grateful' and he 'fully explained to them all that at the rents now fixed, they are to do everything for themselves and not to expect anything from you'.[42] It might be said to have been akin to swings and roundabouts. However, as we shall see below, Charles did not stop investing in improvements. And he even got over his personal animosity towards W.E. Forster; on 6 April 1882, he and the duchess paid the chief secretary and his wife a visit and Mrs Forster was surprised to find them 'benignant' and friendly.[43] (It was only weeks before Forster would resign over Gladstone's decision to release Parnell from Kilmainham and his successor, Lord Frederick Cavendish, was murdered in the Phoenix Park.)

III

Before leaving this discussion of the Land League campaign, one other issue of some importance requires mention, the relationship between the duke of Leinster and the Catholic Church during the Land War.

Back in the 1840s, A.W.N. Pugin had been commissioned to build his great Gothic suite of buildings at St Patrick's College, creating a structure that surpassed in size the aristocratic mansion at Carton; its Gothicism was a symbolic departure from Protestant ascendancy architecture. In the decades that followed, the Catholic Church built imposing structures throughout

8 Pugin buildings, Maynooth, constructed in 1840s at the height of the
Great Famine (courtesy of Lisa Butterly).

Ireland, usually on prominent sites, in effect emulating what landlords had
done in the Georgian period to symbolize their power. At the same time, the
Church began to wrest the allegiance of the people away from landlords. A
popular story in local lore has it that when a duke of Leinster – probably
Charles – travelled to service each Sunday morning in the little Protestant
church at the gates of St Patrick's College (connected to the tower where
Augustus had been entombed), the local people, on their way to mass in nearby
St Mary's Catholic church, stopped in deference to allow his carriage pass. The
local parish priest, fed up with members of his congregation arriving late, is
said to have stopped one Sunday and proclaimed: 'There is only one Lord in
this parish and it is not the duke of Leinster'. Fact or fiction it was revealing of
the power struggle that played itself out during the Land War at local level
between the duke of Leinster and the Catholic Church.

The college trustees had held a 140-acre farm from the duke at Laraghbryan since 1849. The rent had been revised in 1867 and set at £300 per annum, but no lease was signed. In 1877, just as the economy was about to turn, Charles Hamilton suggested that the rent should be raised to £400. The college agreed but then Leinster insisted the trustees should sign a lease. This they were not prepared to do.[44] When the college president, Monsignor William Walsh, an ardent supporter of the land movement (as a means of maintaining the loyalty of the rural population), became disconcerted by the lack of support on the north Kildare estate, he observed that 'the people of Athy have always spoken out manfully and boldly. The Maynooth people feel their grievance no less intensely but they are much more reticent about expressing them openly.'[45] The point has earlier been made that Athy was at the southern extremity of the estate where traditionally the paternalistic influence of the dukes of Leinster was much less felt. Walsh was well versed in land law, valuation and all other related issues.[46] (Interestingly, Walsh had no personal background in the land question; his father was a Dublin watchmaker.)[47] He urged the college trustees not to sign the lease on principle.[48] Later in his evidence to the Bessborough Commission he stated:

> the great reason why our trustees were so unwilling to sign the lease was that being all Roman Catholic bishops they felt that they would place themselves in a false position before the country, if they gave sanction by their signatures to such a lease as this. Of course the fact of their signing it would be quoted all over the country as an argument for calling on other people to do so.[49]

The trustees were holding themselves up as the champions of the people. It was a propaganda war they could not lose if they held out, even if it meant eviction from the farm at Laraghbryan. For two years there was a stand off and then in 1879 the trustees passed a resolution:

> That considering the great depreciation of agricultural produce of every kind the trustees feel constrained to withdraw the offer made some time ago to the duke of Leinster, of an increased rent for the farm of Laraghbryan, but they will, with his Grace's kind approval, continue to hold the farm as yearly tenants at the rent hitherto paid.[50]

The resolution contained some of the language of deference traditional to such requests – 'with his Grace's kind approval'. The offer was somewhat dis-ingenuous; the trustees could well afford at this stage to pay the extra rent, but

9 Archbishop William Walsh (1841–1921) walking alongside King George V
and Queen Mary during their visit to Maynooth in 1911 (NAI, KE 180).

they were now using the economic downturn as a pretext not to do so. Again, Walsh's comments were revealing: 'the people [of Maynooth] feel they are completely at the mercy of the duke and they are unwilling to speak out'.[51] This was akin to psychological warfare: Walsh was attempting to change the mindsets of the Maynooth tenants who do not seem to have been nearly as aggrieved as he would have liked to believe. Throughout the country there were much better examples of exploited tenants than on the Leinster estate and even Walsh admitted: 'Up to this, so far as I know, nothing has occurred, at least in the Maynooth district, from which his Grace could form the faintest suspicion, that his Maynooth tenants, as a body, was not fairly content with the management of the estate'. There was a certain air of caution in his pronouncements; he suggested that the duke must have been blinded to the plight of his subjects by the duplicity of those around him: 'I have as yet seen no evidence that if the duke was made aware, by those concerned, of the state of feeling that really exists, he would not make some substantial concessions, in deference to it'.[52]

Eventually, the college was evicted from Laraghbryan farm. But Walsh saw this as a victory: 'we were successful to this extent that they did not succeed in obtaining the sanction of our bishops for the lease'.[53] When Walsh addressed the Bessborough Commission he concluded his evidence by pointing out that the British government had no problems in the past in spending £20–30 million to cover the expense of the Crimean War or voting £20 million for the emancipation of slaves in the West Indies:

> So that I think the money difficulty is not likely to stand in the way of an efficient measure for the emancipation of the poor tenants in Ireland from the misery of their present condition … I have experienced a good deal of kindness from His Grace, and from members of his family; but I feel it is due to the college, and to our trustees, that the history of this transaction should be laid before the public, and before parliament, and that the circumstance should be made known, in which the trustees, as the O'Conor Don says, 'successfully' resisted the pressure that was put upon them to obtain the sanction of their signature for the Leinster lease.[54]

The controversy mirrored a much wider power dispute that went beyond aristocratic landlord and tenants at local level to the heart of the struggle between the landlords and the Catholic Church for control of the people. It was not until 1902 that the great spire of the College Chapel was completed, by which time the Catholic Church had assumed ascendancy over a declining landlord class. Shortly before its completion, the *Kildare Observer* noted: 'when the edifice is completed 116 feet of it will be composed of white stone, which will make the memorial strikingly conspicuous at a distance of many miles and effectually locate the famous college to travellers passing within its view'.[55] Until then the most imposing architectural structures on the Maynooth skyline were Carton itself, the Conolly folly bisecting the horizon between Carton and Castletown, and the Tyrconnell tower on the Carton demesne. The spire superseded all of these; indeed, there were (and are) very few places on the Carton demesne from which it was (is) not clearly visible, a message to the duke – perhaps not as deliberate or intentional as is being suggested here – of who held authority and power over the people in the area.

But the damage in the relationship between the estate and Church was certainly not irreparable; the college eventually took back the farm and the relationship between the trustees and the FitzGeralds remained at least amicable for decades to come. For example, to celebrate the centenary of the foundation of the college, the trustees of the Leinster estate donated a magnificent Villavicenzio in 1895 and in 1904 Cardinal Vanutelli, the papal legate, who was on an official visit to St Patrick's College, was warmly welcomed to Carton.[56] For some years to come the middle-class farmers and merchants in and around Maynooth would continue to support the Church but retain a loyalty to the FitzGeralds.

IV

The expenditure involved in the eighteenth century in the grand development of Carton and its demesne and the town of Maynooth; the building of a mansion in Dublin and the upkeep of a London house; providing for exceptionally large families in three out of the four generations of dukes (Emily and James had nineteen children, William and Emilia had nine, and Charles and Caroline had fifteen); and living a ducal lifestyle beyond what their modest rental income should have allowed meant financial problems were never far away for any of the first four dukes of Leinster.[57] In successive generations, there was always the great contradiction of impending poverty juxtaposed with grand plans to embellish house, interiors and landscape and to continue to live the lifestyle associated with a ducal title.[58]

By the mid-1880s, Charles, the 4th duke of Leinster, was in a very precarious financial position: the passing of legislation in 1870 and 1881 had statutorily recognized dual ownership in his estate, lowered his rents, and had decimated confidence in Irish land as a source of investment. For generations, the FitzGeralds, like most great Irish landed families, had survived by borrowing on the collateral strength of their vast estates. Now all of that was changed and the value of Irish land in real terms and as collateral both plummeted. Lending institutions and other creditors not only closed avenues of borrowing, they began to call in their mortgages at an unprecedented rate. For many Irish landlords, the writing was clearly on the wall. As early as 1880, the duke of Argyll had been warned by a prominent Irish land agent that: 'Already the insurance offices, the greatest mortgagees in Ireland, have declined to lend any more money, and all negotiations for loans have been broken off … I have bought £3,000 worth of land, and no one will loan £5,000 on it'.[59] And soon after the Land Commission began the process of fixing fair rents, the same agent, Samuel Hussey, wrote to *The Times*: 'No capitalist will now lend on Irish estates as they naturally argue if the government forcibly reduces rents 25 per cent in an exceptionally good year, what in a bad year?'[60] In 1881, Argyll was also informed by Lord Dufferin that the form of British politics was rapidly changing in the face of increased democratization: 'The tendency of the extreme section of the Liberal Party is to buy the support of the masses by distributing among them the property of their own political opponents, and it is towards a social rather than a political revolution we are tending'.[61]

By the mid-1880s, as the second phase of the Land War gained momentum, another financial crisis threatened as the 4th duke's inherited financial obligations and accumulated debts caught up with him. He had no room to manoeuvre except by selling land. But just as he readied to do so, Gerald, marquess of Kildare, was preparing to marry and once again talk of diminishing incomes and the need for retrenchment would be juxtaposed with the extravagance of an elaborate London wedding. While the last two chapters have taken the rather traditional approach of describing the major events that were impacting on the future of Ireland's premier aristocratic family in the last quarter of the nineteenth century, the narrative now changes focus to take into consideration the private stories of those most intimately affected by change and, indeed, who effected change themselves through personal decisions, which were as catastrophic as any external event beyond their control.

CHAPTER THREE

The marriage of Gerald and Lady Hermione Duncombe, 1884

The place [Duncombe Park] in this country is by far the most worth the attention of the curious traveller … The ornamented grounds, some of the most beautiful in England, cannot be viewed without a most exquisite enjoyment.

Arthur Young, 1771[1]

> Home I must leave thee, the sweet days here are numbered,
> I turn and look upon you with regretful eyes.
> Fate beckons to me with her unrelenting fingers,
> Hope and lost love have no answer for my sighs.[2]

Lady Hermione Duncombe, daughter of William, 1st earl of Feversham (1829–1915), was nineteen years old when she wrote the above lines and just one month away from her marriage to Gerald FitzGerald, marquess of Kildare. If 'December 1883' is taken literally, its depressed tone, doleful imagery, and the personification of Fate as a thief with her 'unrelenting fingers' stealing her away from 'hope and lost love' suggests that it was with great trepidation Hermione faced the future. Her reluctance to leave home and to abandon all her ambitions was echoed in the second stanza. Here she used the River Rye, which ran close to her home, as a metaphor for her carefree youth: once she dreamt beside it, 'With pulses beating high with proudest hope and youth', but only despondency lay ahead:

> Ah never, never more my illusions thus delight,
> For these bright things have vanished and I must face the truth.

Home for Lady Hermione was Duncombe Park, near Helmsley in north Yorkshire, an imposing early eighteenth-century Baroque mansion (with some elements of Palladianism) built for her ancestor, Thomas Duncombe, heir to a great banking fortune.[3] Like so many of the early eighteenth-century *nouveaux*

10 Duncombe Park, Helmsley, Yorkshire, Hermione's childhood home.

riches, the Duncombes, in the words of one descendant, quickly devoted their money and energies towards establishing themselves 'as great landed magnates: building houses, laying out parks and gardens, improving their estates, representing their interests in parliament as MPs and improving the bloodline by marrying the daughters of earls'.[4] The house was located on a virgin plateau overlooking the valley of the River Rye which rises just south of the Cleveland Hills and flows through a series of Yorkshire towns and villages before joining the River Derwent near Malton.[5] Hermione later reminisced that she grew up loving Duncombe Park's surrounding parkland with:

> its great thick woods that are never thinned, where one can wander all day [without] the chance of meeting a single human being, the wild moors waving and billowing, covered with tufts of heather & bracken, the dark pine woods breaking the sky line and standing black & mysterious against the sun when it sets. The very noise of the screech owls at night is delicious.[6]

If the thoughts of moving to Ireland to settle in a foreign country held little appeal for Hermione she was not alone in that respect; Sir Shane Leslie (1885–1971) of Glaslough could recall in his childhood that

> We moved over to London frequently – as soon as the foreign wives tired of Ireland … It was no wonder that my grandmother and mother sat down all morning and wrote endless letters to their happy friends on the banks of the Thames deploring the state of Ireland, weather or politics, and making rainbow plans to return to London as soon as possible.[7]

Less than two years previously, in March 1881, as a seventeen-year-old London debutante, Hermione was: 'universally acknowledged as the belle'. The *Penny Illustrated* reported: 'So lovely in face is rarely seen. When she appeared … at Lady Marlborough's ball, there was an absolute sensation among the guests.'[8] During the months that followed, her every sighting was reported, as she attended race meetings throughout the country and various society events in London.[9] The high society hostess and poet, Clara Grant Duff (1870–1944), later recalled: 'I have seen men in top hats running like hares down Rotten Row to see the duchess ride past on her big black horse'.[10] One of her closest Irish friends, Elizabeth Fingall, told of one of her male friends who had walked 'the length of Dawson Street behind Hermione Leinster, for the delight of seeing her move'.[11] Elizabeth described her as 'divinely tall' with a 'wonderful long neck, and a skin so delicate and transparent that … you could almost see the passage of the wine through her throat'. When she met her for the first time at Lord Cloncurry's home at Lyons in Co. Kildare, she thought her 'the most beautiful creature that I had ever seen' with long brown hair that hung loose around her shoulders, soft brown eyes, a 'slightly retrousse nose, and brilliant pouting lips'.[12] And Winston Churchill remembered Hermione as the most beautiful woman he had ever met.[13]

If, as Anita Leslie (1914–85) claimed, Hermione 'dazzled every London drawing-room',[14] it was inevitable she would attract the attention of some of the most powerful eligible aristocrats in the United Kingdom of Great Britain and Ireland. Indeed, that would most likely have suited her father's ambitions. The 1st earl of Feversham had been Tory MP for East Retford 1852–7 and the North Riding of Yorkshire 1859–67. He moved to the House of Lords when he was created earl in 1868. Feversham was prosperous enough to keep a house in fashionable Belgrave Square in London. With four beautiful cosmopolitan daughters, the London townhouse was an essential springboard to introduce them into society.[15] Lady Helen married Sir Edgar Vincent, later Viscount

11 A young Lady Hermione Duncombe, c.1884
(private possession).

D'Abernon, one-time governor of the Imperial Ottoman Bank in Constantinople and later MP for Exeter, and she became 'the most celebrated hostess of her age' and 'by reason of her outstanding beauty, intelligence and charm, one of the most resplendent figures'.[16] (The architect Edwin Lutyens was somewhat less complimentary, once describing her as 'sponge cake or a lovely Easter egg with nothing inside, terribly dilettante and altogether superficial'.)[17] When the writer Thomas Hardy met Lady Cynthia, who married her maternal cousin, Sir Richard Graham of Netherby Hall in Cumberland, he wrote: 'In appearance she is something like my idea of Tess [of the d'Urbervilles], though I did not know her when the novel was written'.[18]

It is not known how or when Hermione met Gerald FitzGerald but their engagement was first announced in October 1883.[19] The fact that his son-in-law was to become one of only twenty or so dukes in Britain at the time and that his daughter would, therefore, become duchess of Leinster probably appealed to him. Such 'suitable' marriages brought social prestige. Hermione's foreboding in 'December 1883' suggests she had little say in the matter but that

12 Gerald FitzGerald, 5th duke of Leinster (1851–93),
(courtesy of Mallaghan family).

was not entirely unusual: young aristocratic women were lucky if their fathers permitted them to marry solely for love and romance. Shortly before the wedding, *The World* reported rather revealingly: 'It is indeed a great day for the Dunscomes [*sic*] ... in which they see a daughter of their house united to the heir of the illustrious Geraldines'.[20] Thus, while there is no substantive evidence, it seems likely that this was an arranged marriage, possibly based on long-standing family connections.

If Hermione was 'a daughter of the gods, divinely fair' and 'divinely tall', beautiful and vivacious,[21] Kildare was quite the opposite: physically he was a rather squat, square-shaped thirty-two-year-old man. Contemporaries variously described him as measured, ponderous, serious and quiet in a way bordering on dour. The nuances in one of his obituaries failed to mask what was perceived (possibly unfairly) to be a rather boring personality.

> He weighed every word that was said with a view to arriving at a right conclusion; in this, as in county, political and estate matters, laboriously striving to know what was right to do; and when once satisfied as to his

duty, he followed it out with an almost painful conscientiousness. The duke seldom spoke, but when he did, his quiet thoughtful utterances always commanded the attention of the House.[22]

Other than the bare facts that Gerald was one of fifteen children born to the marquess of Kildare and his wife, Lady Caroline Sutherland-Leveson-Gower, and was educated at Eton College and groomed to become Ireland's premier peer, we know very little about his early life. In his adulthood, he remained studious: he devoted much of his time to cultural pursuits, much preferring to be locked away in his library pursuing antiquarian interests; he was an avid stamp collector (he later bequeathed his collection of around 10,000 stamps to the Dublin Museum of Science and Art); he was a Visitor of the Science and Art Museum of Dublin; and director of the Irish National Gallery (to which he presented Francis Wheatley's 1779 painting of the Dublin Volunteer on College Green). Obviously not accepting these as alluring characteristics, the *Belfast Newsletter* could only conclude: 'It is the old story – beauty draws us by a single hair – and Lady Hermione Duncombe must have conquered without an effort'.[23]

The engagement was accompanied by a long and complex pre-marriage agreement (in contemporary terms a 'disentailing deed'). Hermione was to receive £5,000 from her father's estate, a very modest dowry to bring into a ducal family. This money was to be placed in trust to pay an income to Lady Hermione during her life. During the lifetime of his father, Kildare was to receive a subsistence allowance of £4,000 per annum payable quarterly; Hermione was to be paid £600 per annum in pin money during the joint lives of herself and the marquess; she was to receive £2,500 per annum during the joint lives of herself and the duke if the marquess was to die during the lifetime of the duke. Hermione was to be entitled to a jointure of £3,800 per annum if she should survive her husband and trusts were to be raised to finance portions for their children: £20,000 if there was only one son, £30,000 for two and £40,000 for three or more. She was given the right to reside at Carton in the event of the death of the duke and the minority of his successor; thereafter she would move to Kilkea. Any necessary repairs and maintenance costs would be paid out of rents and not her annual income.[24]

II

In January 1884, the *Belfast Newsletter* anticipated that whatever other weddings were to take place that year none would exceed 'in brilliancy' that of the marquess of Kildare and Lady Hermione Duncombe.[25] It was the first great society wedding of the year, with *The World* reporting that 'all Ireland takes an interest in the Kildare–Duncombe nuptials', at least all of Ireland of a certain social standing.[26]

Friday, 18 January 1884, was a cloudy and dull day in London with temperatures slightly above normal for the time of the year at around seven degrees Celsius.[27] Early that morning, Hermione arrived at St Paul's Church in Knightsbridge wearing 'a very handsome dress of cream *velours épinglé*, made with a very long train, and the petticoat of cream satin, was elegantly trimmed with exquisite old point lace'. Accompanied by eleven bridesmaids, she was met at the door by the choir boys who led the procession up the church singing 'How welcome was the call'. The bride was met at the chancel steps by Gerald (who the newspapers noted was shorter in stature than his bride) and the archbishop of York who officiated along with Revd Charles Norris Gray, rector of Helmsley. The groom had entered the church a short time earlier with his mother on his arm, she dressed in a silk dress of dark purple, trimmed with old point lace, a large white Indian shawl, and a white straw bonnet with cream lace. After he had led her to her seat, Gerald made his way to greet the principal guest at the wedding, Her Royal Highness Princess Louise, which was described by the *Belfast Newsletter* as 'quite a pretty little incident of the occasion'.[28] Princess Louise (1848–1939), fourth daughter of Queen Victoria, and a close friend of Hermione's, shared many of the bride's interests: she was an ardent feminist and an able sculptor and artist who in the 1870s and 1880s exhibited at the Royal Academy, the Society of Painters in Watercolour, and the Grosvenor Gallery.[29] She was also married to John Campbell, marquess of Lorne and future duke of Argyll, a FitzGerald family friend.

The fashion columnists described the ladies' costumes: Lady Feversham, Hermione's mother, wore a bonnet trimmed with shaded feathers to match her mouse-coloured velvet dress; the duchess of Westminster wore a dress of striped red velvet with a red bonnet and black velvet mantle bordered with fur; the duchess of Sutherland stood out in her 'superb costume of blue velvet, richly trimmed with magnificent sable'; while the younger Lady Alexandra Leveson-Gower wore 'a very pretty and graceful toilette composed of brown velvet and cashmere which suited the youthful wearer to perfection'. Velvet and cashmere, fur trimmed mantles, and bonnets *en suite* were the popular choice of the ladies

13 'Lady Hermione Duncombe in her wedding dress',
taken from *Lady's Pictorial*, 26 Jan. 1884.

for this winter wedding.[30] After the blessing, and as the couple carried out their
registration duties in the vestry, bouquets of orange flowers and shamrocks tied
together with loops of white satin were distributed among the wedding party;
it would be difficult not to presume some degree of symbolism.[31]

Newspaper columns throughout Britain and along the east coast of America
carried lists of the many wedding gifts. It was customary for the bride to receive
jewellery so Hermione was given a diamond necklace and matching bracelets
from the duke and duchess of Leinster; three diamond stars, a diamond
bracelet and 'a handsomely fitted dressing case' from her own parents; a large
pearl star, three pearl rings and a pearl bracelet from her husband; a gold locket
set with cameo from the earl of Granville; a diamond and sapphire crescent
from Baron Ferdinand de Rothschild (at least six members of this famous
banking family gave her gifts of precious stones); a pearl and diamond ring
from her brother, James. *The Court Journal* listed dozens of the other presents
received, such as a marqueterie bureau from Princess Louise; a pair of silver
candelabra from the duke of Westminster; a pair of ponies from Lord and Lady

Maurice FitzGerald (the groom's uncle and his wife); a jewel case from Lord Walter FitzGerald (the groom's brother); a bronze Indian peacock from Viscountess Clifden; Dresden china dishes from Lady Isabel Stewart; a (Boulle) clock from Lady Jane Repton;[32] and a white ostrich feather fan from her sisters, Helen and Cynthia. There were more modest presents: an umbrella from the Wombell sisters; twelve menu holders from Lord and Lady Legard; a silver pencil case from Tom Musgrave; a book from Miss Campbell; a calendar from Mrs Stewart Gladstone; and opera glasses from Mr Spofforth.[33]

As for her husband, his list of gifts were equally impressive: Princess Louise gave him an Argyllshire marble inlaid table and a gold pen and pencil case; he received a grand pianoforte from his parents; a Chippendale bureau and pair of matching side tables from the countess of Harrington; three pearl shamrock pins from Lord and Lady Castletown; a silver and leather writing set from the Cloncurrys; an Italian embroidered quilt from his sister, Mabel; a cuckoo clock from his other sister, Nesta; a mahogany cabinet from his brother, Lord Frederick, while other family presents included a Russian leather jewel case, and a chest of Assam tea.[34] Gifts on both sides added another generation of material culture to the FitzGerald homes.

On leaving the church the couple and guests went to the Feversham's residence at Belgrave Square for breakfast.[35] They left early that afternoon – the bride now dressed in brown velvet trimmed with fur and a bonnet to match – and took the train from the London and North-Western Railway terminus to Eaton Hall in Cheshire where they stayed for a few days honeymoon with Hugh Grosvenor, 1st duke of Westminster (1825–99). He had married Lady Constance Sutherland-Leveson-Gower (1834–80), fourth daughter of the 2nd duke of Sutherland and his wife, Harriet Howard, daughter of the 6th earl of Carlisle, mistress of the robes to Queen Victoria and, therefore, at the head of the queen's household.[36] Lady Constance was also Gerald's aunt. Westminster's son, Victor, was married to Sybill Lumley who in 1887, after Victor's untimely death, would marry George Wyndham, future chief secretary for Ireland and a kinsman of the FitzGeralds. In time, all these relationships would be important, as influential aristocratic and Court connections had been in the past to the Leinsters. Westminster, for example, was a hugely influential politician and one of the most prominent commercial and residential developers in London; as one biographer put it: 'he was a one-man planning and enforcement officer, sometimes arbitrary or capricious in his rulings, but generally liked by the wealthy and fashionable for whose comfort and convenience Mayfair and Belgravia were regulated'.[37] Westminster's connections consolidated the Leinsters' position within Court circles for another generation.

As detailed already, Gerald's grandfather, Augustus Frederick, 3rd duke of Leinster, had hosted Queen Victoria at Carton during her Irish visit of 1849; Gerald and Hermione would also host royalty at Carton, including Prince Edward (later King Edward VII) and Princess Alexandra in 1885. Their eldest son, Maurice, would later be a pageboy at Edward's coronation in 1902, while their second son, Desmond, would become Edward, Prince of Wales' (later Edward VIII's) 'greatest friend'. And their younger brother, Edward, would have an affair with Wallis Simpson during Edward VIII's abdication crisis![38]

Meanwhile, in Maynooth on the wedding day 400 schoolchildren were treated to 'an elegant dejeuner' on the grounds at Carton by a Dublin caterer; the racket court in the yard complex was set out for a banquet for 100 employees who were treated to a 'substantial dinner'; the town of Maynooth was illuminated with tar barrels and a large bonfire lighted in front of the courthouse; there was an impressive fireworks display outside the Leinster Arms Hotel, and a large banner proclaiming 'Cead Mile Failthe [one hundred thousand welcomes] to the bride of Kildare' hung across the street, while two bands paraded amidst 'joyous scenes'.[39]

III

After their short honeymoon, Hermione and Kildare returned to Ireland, to Kilkea Castle, on the southern part of their county Kildare estates. It was a medieval FitzGerald house dating to around 1180. In 1849, at the height of the Great Famine, Gerald's grandfather, Augustus, 3rd duke, had reclaimed the lease of the castle from a middleman, Peter Caulfield, who presumably had fallen upon hard times.[40] Caulfield had allowed the castle to fall into a ruinous state. In the course of a major restoration project, Augustus added a new storey, windows were enlarged and 'its interior, while preserving the picturesque character of the days of chivalry, [had] all the graces of a modern domestic dwelling'.[41] Kildare's father and mother continued to reside in the main residence at Carton until the 4th duke died there after a short illness on 10 February 1887. His wife died just three months later.

The early years of Hermione's marriage were, it seems, relatively happy. At first she basked in the reflected glory of being the wife of a duke. She was regularly seen at all the best social events in Dublin and London. She attended the race meetings at Punchestown and Ascot; was a constant visitor to the picture galleries in Dublin and London; and became a benefactor of several charities and schools, including Alexandra College in Dublin. But she did not hunt, which the *Kildare Observer* commented was surprising given that she resided in 'the premier sporting county'.[42]

In Carton, Hermione was surrounded by all the material symbols of the duke's position in society on display in the spacious halls and saloons of the house: collections of portraits by Wissing, Ramsay (including his very impressive representation of Emily, 1st duchess), Reynolds, Kauffman, and Hamilton; landscapes by Ashford, Dalens, Lorraine, Cuyp and many others; the magnificent library with its 'many rare and choice volumes of the great writers of old'; the collections of objects of *virtue* especially of old china. The ornately designed Gold Saloon was a room with a stucco flamboyancy which few mansions in Ireland (or even England) could boast.[43] The entire north-east wall of the saloon was taken up by a magnificent organ case, typically mid-eighteenth-century Baroque in keeping with the room, but designed much later in 1857 by Kildare's uncle, also Lord Gerald FitzGerald (1821–86). It was in this room that Hermione, herself an accomplished keyboard player who had been tutored by Robert Prescott Stewart (1825–94), liked to entertain her guests.[44] Long after Hermione's death, Elizabeth Fingall recalled the 'wonderful musical evenings in that white and gold music-room'.[45]

Despite diminishing income, lavish expenditure and the employment of a veritable army of staff at Carton, and on the demesne, remained part of aristocratic living. The household bill for the month in which Hermione and Gerald got married came to £1,234, the equivalent of 120 years' wages for the average labourer employed on the demesne. The highest single payment made was £337 to Kinahan & Sons, Grocers and Wine merchants. Smaller payments included £70 to Jameson, Pim & Co., distillers; £50 to Samuel Roe, flour merchants; £60 to W. Fleming for cheese and bacon; £33 to Greene & Co. for fish; and a fairly substantial £34 to S. Boyd, druggist. The remainder went to a variety of fruit merchants, lamp oil merchants, ironmongers, china and glass merchants, brushmakers, doctors, silver smiths, cutlers, upholsterers and so on.[46] There were at least 100 servants and estate employees, of whom 44 were indoor servants, at Carton, including a house steward (James Bradley on a salary of £100 per annum); a valet (Bernard Flynn, £60); a housekeeper (Mrs Baker, £60); a cook (Mrs Harris, £60); an under-butler (Charles Jordan, £35); six housemaids, three kitchen maids, four laundry maids, a dairymaid, a still room maid, two footmen, a hall boy, a coal boy, a coachman and grooms, a pot boy, a clock winder, a chimney cleaner and a house porter.[47]

In a contemporary description of the demesne Revd Charles Ganly described how family and guests could 'wander beneath the shade of ancestral trees that spread their luxuriance over the green sward, or take a boat and float dreamily over the placid lake, or stroll through the gardens, loitering a while to admire some rare exotic'.[48] The description may have been overly romanticized but it was a fact that Carton ranked as one of the most impressive eighteenth-century landscapes created in Ireland.[49] Hermione enthusiastically threw herself into putting her own mark on it, although her designs were much less ambitious than her predecessor, Emily.

Sometime around 1887, Hermione visited Granston in Queen's County where she was 'immensely impressed' by Clare Castletown's 'genius for arrangement and the vision of the long border in the open garden door and under the hanging chestnut branches is one I shall never forget. And then the wild garden with the unexpected flashes of scarlet poppies – 2 beds of shimmering blue irises is too ideal'.[50] On another visit to the Botanical Gardens she fell in love with the rows of daffodils 'beautifully arranged under trees in long grass' and found the whole scheme 'really very near perfection and full of hints & ideas'.[51] She was less impressed by the designs of William Robinson (1838–1935), the champion of the so-called 'wild garden', who is credited with vanquishing the Victorian pattern gardens and having them replaced with the more natural and informal plantings of hardy perennials, climbers and shrubs. Referring to him as the 'garden man', she wrote: 'it seems to me his ideas that I like the best are generally stolen from other people. For instance his ideas about herbaceous borders and their artistic plating are not his at all but [Gertrude] Jeckyll's whose garden about an hour from London is beautiful – really a sight to see'. Jeckyll (1843–1932) had a huge influence on gardening over much the same time period as Robinson and was a collaborator with the architect Sir Edwin Lutyens (who, it might be worth noting, was employed by Hermione's brother-in-law, Viscount D'Abernon, to create the great amphitheatre at Esher Place).[52] However, there were aspects of Robinson's designs that appealed, particularly 'the garden for all sorts of primroses and cowslips in amongst some Scorch firs & with a background of brown winter heather which I have dreamt of at intervals ever since'.[53]

In 1888, Hermione wrote to one of her closest friends, Evelyn de Vesci, describing her delight at her Carton creations: 'I am quite pleased with my new garden. It really is rather pretty and picturesque & with a few alterations will be very pretty indeed. Some of the tall white lilies are two feet high and against the green background & with tall hollyhocks and tritomas'.[54] She planted snowdrops everywhere: 'giant snowdrops that make the grounds of Carton white and beautiful each year, as though someone had strewn snow under the trees for pleasure'.[55] She created an extraordinary pergola that Elizabeth Fingall claimed was the first ever constructed in Ireland: 'when the sun shone on its red brick and the roses growing over it, it seemed to bring Italy to that Irish garden'.[56] Her children would later delight in the legacy she created; her eldest son, Maurice, wrote to Evelyn de Vesci: '[I hope] I will be able to bring you here [Carton] and show you how mother's gardens have grown and how nice they look. Her pergola is lovely and so is the bog garden'.[57]

In those early years of marriage, Hermione enjoyed the freedom of Carton in the spring and summer, when she could escape to the woods and open parkland with her young children.[58] It seemed for a while as if she had found a substitute for Duncombe Park:

> Such a beautiful evening – I walked with the children thro' the woods – Rhodendrons, Syringa in full flower, ferns uncurled and purple and white Columbinus in the long grass. The grass very green and all the birds singing … The children are very loving and affectionate & tonight dancing thru the green grass with their hands full of wild flowers and their rosy laughing faces they seemed an embodiment of all that is young & happy & beautiful & spring-like.[59]

IV

In those same early years of marriage, the 4th duke and Gerald were pre-occupied with estate and wider political matters. After a temporary recovery in 1882–4, the economy went into freefall once again. A new movement, the National League, emerged in response and adopted similar no rent tactics and boycotting to those that had been practised by its predecessor, the Land League, and extended these into a concerted Plan of Campaign, which was adopted predominantly on financially embarrassed estates to force landlords to reduce their rents.[60] On the May gale day in 1886, Charles Hamilton informed the 4th duke that while he was doing all he could to get the rents in, it was more of a struggle than he had anticipated.[61] He blamed the impending introduction of the Home Rule bill for having a negative impact on the value of land, citing the example of George Patterson, a large tenant farmer from Athy, who had tried to sell his interest in his holding in April but not a single bid was received. Patterson confided in Hamilton: 'a few years ago had that place been put up for sale I have no doubt that it would have sold at £1,500 at least. The prospects of Home Rule are telling on the value of land.'[62] Hamilton warned of the difficulties that depreciated rental income would have; it was difficult 'to find money just at present'.[63]

With diminished income, cutbacks became necessary. When in March 1885 the duke proposed cutting Hamilton's salary the latter complained that he had already taken a salary cut of £200 to take up the Leinster position (down to £1,500) and he 'had no other agency but yours and am entirely dependant upon it'.[64] The duke, mindful of Hamilton's worth, came to an amicable agreement with him but this meant getting rid of another employee named Duffy (role unspecified).[65] Hamilton informed the duke of his relief; now despite 'the disturbed times' he could focus his full attention on his work.[66]

Once again, the absence of estate rentals and accounts makes it difficult to determine the true extent of indebtedness but lack of money would seem to have been the reason for compiling the *Catalogue of pictures, plate and antiquities at Carton, Kilkea Castle and 13 Dominick St Dublin and 6 Carlton Terrace, London*, which was privately published in 1885, and another slightly earlier inventory of diamonds and jewellery. Works of art, curios, silver and valuable furniture were now more likely to be sold than collected in light of the passing of the 1882 Settled Land (Ireland) Act, legislation that facilitated sales by allowing trustees to set aside a will in order to sell the contents of a house.[67] The time had come to be more discerning regarding what needed to be kept as family heirlooms. Moreover, there was a vibrant market for works of art, silver and antiquities which, unlike Irish land, were appreciating in value, particularly among the increasing number of American plutocratic families emerging in the late nineteenth century from the banking, steel, publishing and oil industries. Art dealers such as Joseph Duveen, who worked on behalf of American collectors, manufactured an extravagant market for paintings in the late nineteenth century, again possibly explaining the sale of around 140 paintings from Carton at the turn of the century, including works by Brueghel, Gainsborough and Van der Hargen.[68]

A few paintings here and there or some other valuables were not as noticeable as the sale of broad acres and much less detrimental to one's social position but the seriousness of Leinster's financial position became apparent when the 4th duke was forced to sell almost one quarter of his estate – a sale facilitated by the 1885 Ashbourne Land Act (which provided £5 million to finance land purchase). Ashbourne's act was a major improvement on the land purchase terms of the earlier 1881 act, enabling tenants to borrow the full purchase price of their holdings and to repay it in annuities fixed at 4 per cent over forty-nine years. For heavily indebted landlords such as the duke, the act offered a window of opportunity and so he was advised by Hamilton in April 1886 that because the estate was struggling he 'might take advantage of the present Land Purchase Act'.[69] A short time previously, a small (presumably

Dublin) property was sold to the Science and Art Department; at the time money had been so scarce that Hamilton had to impress upon the duke the need to sign the conveyancy deed 'urgently' so that the money could be used to pay his annual interest on Board of Works loans.

By the end of March 1890, lands on the Kildare and Rathangan estates, comprising 337 holdings on 19,200 acres, were sold for £246,400. Virtually all of this money went to paying off encumbrances.[70] There are only a few scraps of evidence that inform on the levels of rental income from 1893 to 1898 and they suggest that it declined to an average of £31,000 per annum, or around 25 per cent from just over a decade before.[71] The sale of one quarter of the Leinster estate had wider implications than loss of revenue: it was reported in 1886 that sales also 'deprived the duke of a large share of his patrimony'. In other words, he had to face labourers on the parts of the estates sold and inform them that 'under the new conditions … his power of giving immense employment was crippled and curtailed and that his labour bills must be contracted accordingly'.[72] It signalled yet another diminishing aspect of paternalism.

Charles died on 10 February 1887, and was followed a few months later by his wife, who died in May. Gerald and Hermione moved to Carton and the 5th duke was immediately faced with the prospect of completing the sales negotiations begun by his father. The fact that his parents had fourteen children, ten of whom survived to adulthood, meant he faced the same burden of family charges that had compromised the financial position of his predecessors. When Gerald died his obituary in the *Freeman's Journal* rightly pointed to the fact that 'the duke's income was not as large as one might be inclined to think from the extent of his estates and the great position he held. Family charges and the lessened value of land as letting farms cut off much of the ducal resources'.[73] Gerald was immediately forced to retrench: the servants' wage accounts for December 1887 list only 19 (with 4 occasional) employees as opposed to 44 three years previously. Elizabeth Alexander doubled as both housekeeper and cook at a salary of around £50 per annum and gone were such symbols of aristocratic extravagance as the pot boy and clock winder.[74]

V

Gerald's burdens were not just financial. The point has already been made that the 1880s represented a major turning point for the Irish landed class and, indeed, for the European aristocracy as a whole. The global agricultural recession did not just give rise to a land war in Ireland; it spawned similar agrarian revolts and nationalist movements in Germany, Russia and Austro-Hungary. In parts of Europe land banks were established to prop up the nobility and in Prussia new state legislation allowed for the take over of bankrupt estates. Emerging middle classes all over Europe were no longer content to leave the government of their countries in the control of traditional landed elites; as David Cannadine has put it: 'The age of the masses had superseded the age of the classes. At the same time that the economy became global, politics became democratized.'[75] The FitzGeralds were simply the most powerful Irish family among thousands of landed nobles throughout Europe caught up in a maelstrom that would irreversibly change their fortunes.

In the Irish case the passing of the Franchise and Re-distribution Acts in 1884–5 made the possession of vast estates, money and titles irrelevant to popular political power. At the same time in Britain, the landlord class were being assailed from all directions – by the press, pamphlet literature on the land question, land reformers and politicians in parliament, including David Lloyd George who would spend much of his political life attacking landlords; as B.B. Gilbert said of his obsession: 'The landlord – there was the enemy. Idle land in the hands of idle men.'[76] By the mid-1880s Irish landlords had lost control of national politics and the Irish Parliamentary Party's strong presence at Westminster put Irish Home Rule to the forefront of British politics.

Conscious of his position as duke of Leinster, Gerald now involved himself in a variety of civic, religious and political positions – as a member of the General Synod of the Church of Ireland, committees of the Royal Dublin Society, a trustee of the National Library of Ireland, president of the Royal Horticultural Society, a privy councillor, lord lieutenant of Kildare, and chairman of various local government bodies. He took a more prominent part in public affairs than current Irish historiography allows for. In 1891, Gerald became president of the Irish Unionist Alliance upon its establishment to combat the threat of the introduction of the second Home Rule bill.[77] He shared the concern of all unionists that Home Rule would dismember the empire, undermine their loyalty to the monarchy, result in economic disaster and threaten the future of landlord and tenant alike. In June 1892, he addressed a unionist convention in Dublin in his position as president of the IUA. He admitted that in the past he had 'personally [taken] little part or pleasure in politics' but now proposed the first resolution at the convention calling for 'the preservation to the people of Ireland of equality of rights and privileges with the people of England and Scotland, as fellow citizens of the United Kingdom'.[78]

In retrospect it is easy to comment on the irony of the wording of the resolution; the 'equality of rights and privileges' was primarily what nationalist opponents demanded. Gerald would have had no difficulty in reconciling his love of Ireland with his wish to be British but, in a departure from the toasts at his coming-of-age in 1872, nationalist definitions of Irishness had become unequivocally associated with being Gaelic and Catholic as well, and that marginalized the vast majority of Irish aristocrats.[79] In 1893, after Gladstone's second Home Rule bill was passed by the House of Commons, Leinster was one of the 419 peers who voted against it in the Lords.[80] The Irish aristocracy (and patricians elsewhere in Britain) knew, however, they could not stem the tide of democracy; all they could hope for was to secure concessions – economic and political – that would ease their fall. In particular, by the last decade of the nineteenth century the heavily encumbered Irish landlords were looking towards the British government to introduce a land act which would extricate them from their indebtedness. It would be ten years after the defeat of the second Home Rule bill before that would become a reality.

In the meantime, Gerald's pre-occupations with matters political and financial may have contributed to the marital problems that he and Hermione began to experience.

CHAPTER FOUR

'In this black dog haunted place': Hermione's melancholia

Much Madness is divinest Sense -
To a discerning Eye -
Much Sense - the starkest Madness -
'Tis the Majority
In this, as All, prevail -
Assent - and you are sane -
Demur - you're straightway dangerous -
And handled with a Chain -

Emily Dickinson (1830–6)

Within a year of their marriage Hermione and Gerald's first child was born, a daughter, but she died shortly after birth. Two sons followed: Maurice (born March 1887) and Desmond (born September 1888). Sometime around 1890, Hermione wrote: 'the little boys have been so happy here [Carton] – little Desmond laughs and jumps and tumbles & shouts all day'. Notably in the same letter, she described her eldest son, Maurice, as 'quiet and undemonstrative', perhaps an early indication of her concern for his future well-being.[1]

Victorian aristocratic parents were not known for their close personal attention to their children who generally remained in the care of a nanny or governess. Anita Leslie, who admittedly had a particularly lonely childhood, generalized that 'the parents of Victorian times seem to have been un-amused by their offspring. Mothers might see their little ones once a day, the fathers about once a year. It is curious, really, that they did not want small children tumbling around when there were so many servants to clear the debris away'.[2] As a father, Gerald was not atypical in this respect but Hermione, even though she spent considerable periods away from her children, seems to have been a dutiful and concerned mother. She fretted about typically maternal things – illnesses, fevers, her children's future education – once declaring: 'Sometimes my heart faints when I think of the never ending struggle their education and bringing up will be'. When they were around two and three years old she

14 Hermione with her two eldest sons, Desmond, on the left, and Maurice (Kildare) by her side.

confided in a friend that Maurice and Desmond 'are very dear now & I am also going through agonies asking myself how it would be best to educate them and rejecting each and every plan as odious ... I am too ignorant to teach them myself tho' I am learning Latin to keep pace with their studies'.[3]

Choosing the right governess was difficult. The first Hermione employed – because her testimonials delighted her – was Ms Morton, a twenty-three-year-old Newenham College girl, a classical scholar, 'full of life and spirit', head of a hockey club and a 'first rate cricketer'. Hermione was happy to promise Ms Morton generous holidays, a day a week with her family when they were in London and 'many evenings too' if she liked. She emphasized to the young governess the importance of educating her young sons. Preaching of the 'infinite patience' often required in such a task, Hermione told the young woman that 'teaching boys has this advantage over teaching most little girls – one feels that it lies with one to ground them thoroughly and thus lay the cornerstone of their future career'.[4] However, the boys proved a handful and Ms Morton proved a 'great disappointment'. When Desmond cut three fingers after 'she gave him the open knife to <u>play with</u>', Hermione was incensed: 'I was an idiot to engage a young inexperienced girl. It has all been my fault really. I am very, very sorry.' Thus, she decided she would have to go to London to find another governess: 'some one young and strong who would not mind rather spirited children … the boys like her but will not obey her'. She stoutly defended her boys: 'they do not mean to be naughty and want very little to make them good'.[5] And she was delighted when they played as children did – running through the demesne shooting sparrows with their pop guns.[6] Her affection for her children was regularly articulated in her correspondence; once after a sojourn away from them she wrote to Evelyn de Vesci: 'I do pray that the children may be my life – they are very dear and loving & I feel even closer to them already than I have ever done before'.[7]

However, while Hermione's letters suggest a young woman with strong maternal instincts, they also reveal a very highly strung personality which, as time passed, became increasingly more susceptible to long bouts of depression, or melancholia as it was termed in the late nineteenth century.

II

The death of her daughter at birth had a profound emotional affect on Hermione, as might be expected. In one of her darkest moods, she later wrote to Evelyn de Vesci:

> After my first little baby was born – the one that died – I don't know if I fancied it or if it is true but a great large fly kept on flying around the ceiling and all that night its wings kept on beating 'the baby won't live, the baby won't live' and now it is the legions of black dogs keep on saying it's all of no use & perhaps it isn't.[8]

Indeed, Hermione's letters suggest a coincidence between her darkest periods and the birth of her children; she may, therefore, have been susceptible to what in the modern day might be diagnosed as post-natal depression. To compound her emotional vulnerabilities, the children also came along as Gerald's responsibilities increased: Maurice, the eldest son, was born a month after the 4th duke died and by the time of Desmond's birth in 1888, his responsibilities had evolved into burdens.

Hermione's susceptibility to dark moods is clearly evident in the tone of 'December 1883' or as a corollary the poem may very well suggest what triggered her melancholia: having to leave behind her family, friends, home and personal ambitions to embark on a loveless arranged marriage to a man who, as we shall see, was determined to control every aspect of her life. After Desmond's birth, the couple became increasingly estranged and according to her friend, Elizabeth Fingall, Hermione would regularly retreat to her boudoir with its Chippendale furniture, cabinets of china and rows of books, and which looked over the Dublin and Wicklow mountains, and write long letters to her sister, Helen, in which she articulated her frustrations.[9] These letters clearly show that she was a young woman, full of energy and creativity, who felt stifled at every turn by her husband. She longed, for example, to indulge in her passion for painting but Gerald saw it as a mere waste of time. She was aggrieved that she had no power in her own household, no room to make her own choices, no independence of mind was allowed to her, and so she felt humiliated on a number of levels. Thus, in one letter to her sister, she complained:

> If I had less vitality and less energy, I should not mind things so much, I should not be so rebellious, nor restless, nor so irritable. I have nothing on which to expend my energy, no object or aim in life, no great interest. If I was more domestic, I might have given all my mind to managing the house, but even here the field is not my own. It is not a housekeeper K[ildare][10] wants, it is an under-housekeeper. I may not choose my occupations – I thought this winter I would work hard at my modelling – but here is a fresh apple of discord. It is not an occupation K. approves of. Therefore I may not go upstairs to my painting room till (under his direction) I have performed my household duties, written my letters and *practiced for one hour on the organ*, within his hearing. I may not have a fire there because the time I spend there is a wilful waste. I am humiliated before the servants; every order I give is countermanded unless I have consulted K. about it first. And fault is found with me for anything and everything I do and say.[11]

Soon Hermione came to resent Gerald's lack of support in anything she suggested. When, for example, she wanted to have her children taught German or French before they went to school 'K[ildare] set his face against it as he does against everything'.[12] Life became a bitter struggle and so she wrote to Evelyn de Vesci:

> I have fought so hard and so desperately about these things [unspecified] and so little seems gained in the end and if ever anything will be really

gained in the end seems more than problematical. Only the bite of cold blooded creatures is dangerous and there is a cold senseless unmovable hardship which one can beat one's heart and life out in vain.[13]

She became ground down by fighting and arguing with Leinster; she was fed up, she confided in Evelyn, 'struggling against it all. Things just drift on. It is hopeless'. She began to look to death as a final solution: 'anything to stop fighting, cease caring and be at rest'.[14] The 'black dogs' became the favourite symbol of her depression; finishing a very despondent letter to Evelyn, she requested her not to reply for 'very likely the black dogs will have gone by tomorrow'. She had no hesitation in informing her family and friends of her unhappiness. Thus, in October 1890, she again wrote to Helen:

> It is true things have been very blue … no danger is imminent. I shall not go away, I am not dreaming of eloping. I shall not press Gerry to allow a judicial separation, and I am not doing all I can to goad him into wishing it himself. On the contrary I have been trying to come within less immeasurable distance of his standards of excellence, so that if I cannot please him there may yet be less reasonable cause for complaint. But … it is very difficult. We cannot understand each other and it is hopeless to expect we ever shall. If K[ildare] would only accept this fact (as I would willingly do), if we could agree to pull together, to keep up appearances before the world and live separate in our own lives and households – not trouble and weary each other by constant friction, there would yet be some possibility of things coming straight. But to this Gerry will not agree. While admitting there is no love nor sympathy between us, he still insists upon trying to force me to become something different to what I am, or to what it lies in my nature to become. For this reason he uses petty tyranny on every imaginable sort of occasion.[15]

The same letter even suggested how uncomfortable she was with sharing Gerald's bed:

> What I resent is that K. has no more wish than I have that we should live *maritalement*, he still insists on sleeping in my room for fear of what the servants may think! Even though he knows what a bad sleeper I am and that except alone! I cannot sleep. And that the servants have only to listen at the door to be aware that recrimination continues late into the night and begins early in the morning.[16]

All of Hermione's letters are very personal; they are essentially about her, yet we get no indication of who was influencing her thinking or what she was reading or what new ideas or philosophies appealed to her. This was a time when women were demanding equality within marriage and greater freedom of activity. Sixteen years before Hermione had married, the highly influential English philosopher and political and moral theorist, John Stuart Mill (1806–73), had argued that 'Men hold women in subjection by representing to them meekness, submissiveness, and resignation of all individual will into the hands of a man, as an essential part of sexual attractiveness'.[17] His essay on 'The Subjection of Women' (1869) would have resonated with Hermione and it is not beyond the realms of possibility that she read Mill and been engaged with his argument that

> the principle which regulates the existing social relations between the two sexes – the legal subordination of one sex to the other – is wrong itself, and now one of the chief hindrances to human improvement … it ought to be replaced by a principle of perfect equality, admitting no power or privilege on the one side, nor disability on the other.[18]

Hermione felt a prisoner of the rigid social conventions preferred by her husband.[19] When she met George Frederick Watts (1817–1904), the eminent artist and sculptor who would later become her tutor, she was drawn to the Symbolist movement he espoused – perhaps hardly surprising as the Symbolists were concerned with the darker Gothic side of Romanticism and for them art became a contemplative refuge from the world of strife – and rather revealingly she contrasted him to Gerald as a man who 'is different from most great men. He does give one his mind.'[20]

When she first married, the young Hermione was a socialite who revelled in what today might be termed 'celebrity status'. In the short period between her coming out as a beautiful young debutante and her wedding, she had experienced the gaiety of society. Gerald, on the other hand, had little interest in social events and shared little of Hermione's passion for the social whirl of aristocratic society, a fact which was captured in his obituary in the *Kildare Observer*: 'the late duke was of a singularly quiet and unobtrusive disposition; he loved the quiet, homely, simple country life, and had no yearnings whatever, for the gay whirl of society gaieties'.[21] He was 'a man of simple tastes, preferring the quiet routine of a country gentleman's life to the more exciting pursuits of fashion and pleasure'.[22] Thus, he much preferred to remain at Carton than socialize in other houses, which often disappointed Hermione. Following an invitation to Abbey Leix for a shooting party, she was forced to reply to Evelyn de Vesci: 'I think I had better decline for both of us for I know Kildare will not be persuaded to go to shooting parties – even if he is not called upon to shoot.'[23]

Gradually, Hermione transformed from the perfect hostess full of 'attractive personality and charm of manner',[24] to one who could in private be acerbic when commenting on her husband's friends. In 1891, in a letter to her cousin, Lord Houghton (later lord lieutenant of Ireland), she was less than kind to George Wyndham (maternal great-grandson of Lord Edward FitzGerald, and at that time private secretary to Arthur Balfour, chief secretary for Ireland) and his wife, Lady Sibell Grosvenor, after one of their visits to Carton:

> … she so aged and he almost looking like her son! To him I took a frantic dislike (I don't know if you have discovered that I am a person of strong prejudices!) indeed I refuse even to acknowledge his good looks … Moreover he has a superciliousness of manner, which, had he remained much longer – would most certainly have irritated me into slapping or scratching him, so perhaps it is fortunate he went away![25]

Depressed and unfulfilled, there were claims that she had 'many lovers' but only one lover has come to light in this research.[26]

III

Hermione's letters exhibit a shift in young aristocratic women's attitudes towards their role in married life that occurred in the late Victorian period. Her assertion in the letter quoted above – 'I may not choose my occupations' – is strongly suggestive of the fact that she was increasingly frustrated by the docile life assigned to her by Gerald. Whatever about outside influences such as the writings of J.S. Mill, crucial in Hermione's search for independence was her relationship – sometimes very ambiguous – with Evelyn de Vesci (1851–1939), daughter of Francis Richard Charteris, 10th earl of Wemyss, who in June 1872 had married John, 4th Viscount de Vesci, and become chatelaine at Abbey Leix in Queen's County. Described as 'saintly but one of life's martyrs',[27] Evelyn was an enigmatic beauty. Elizabeth Fingall recalled: 'She was and is simply unlike any one else. She had something much more rare than beauty. I think now that she was like a Rosetti picture with her deep-set eyes and her priestess look'.[28]

Hermione met her shortly after coming to Ireland. Their friendship grew quickly and soon Evelyn became Hermione's closest confidante. As her very intense affection for Evelyn deepened, she would often proclaim: 'I love you with <u>my whole heart</u>' or 'Only I know I love you & worship you – I never knew what goodness & kindness really meant till I knew you and I know now that to keep a little of y[ou]r affection … I would make any sacrifice in the world'.

In the beginning, she turned to Evelyn continuously for support, which was generously given. For example, after a day in London interviewing servants, Hermione wrote effusively: 'I don't know why you are so good to me. It is very undeserved but it has changed everything for me and has turned it to peace. Sadness but still peace.' She had just seen Leinster the previous night but their relationship remained fraught: 'he said he thought it was time I returned to my household duties', and off he went to visit the Bartons at Straffan. Every so often there is a frustrating cryptic insight offered to her husband's personality: 'he <u>is</u> what I thought him. He has proved it to me before and I never would have doubted it for more than a minute.'[29] As her trust in Evelyn grew, Hermione time and again poured out her emotions to her:

> If Kildare [Gerald] could understand, I would tell him everything, and ask him to help me. But if he knew all he would only think me hopelessly wicked and vicious and I am not, I am not that! My better self has perhaps left me for a little, but it will come back to me, I know it will. I am horrified and disgusted at the shallowness of my present ways and feelings, but there used to be deep pools somewhere and I will find them again. You don't know what I have been through lately, the humiliation, the despondency, and despair and the loneliness – who will, who could understand such a hopeless and complex frame of mind.[30]

As her unhappiness at Carton became intolerable she revealed to Evelyn that she could no longer remain in a marriage which was going to ruin her:

> I cannot live like this any longer. I am too wretched. K cannot realize what I feel. I <u>know</u> he does not. I worship him, you must remember that. And I feel as if I <u>cannot</u> hurt him. And yet I feel as if to go on like this would kill everything in me. You know him and you must love him too. Tell me he is capable of sacrifice, that he would know how I have loved him, that he would be good and noble. He <u>cannot</u> realize what I feel. I <u>know</u> he does not. He does not see how wretched it makes me. He

refuses to believe it – he thinks he <u>can</u> give me happiness. I made so <u>sure</u> that when I told him I was not happy that he would let me go but everything I said was wrong – he could not realize it.[31]

Unfortunately, Evelyn's letters to Hermione, if they survive, have not been traced but she seems to have advised Hermione to become more independent. During periods of great vulnerability, Hermione's letters are particularly unrestrained but equally they are frustratingly ambiguous. For example, is the following letter simply more revealing of the increased freedom of expression and the movement away from stricter conventions or is it suggestive of a deeper relationship with Evelyn?

I beg your pardon a thousand times – first for having allowed myself to love you and then for having troubled you by revealing what I had no right to reveal. My only excuse for that is I could not bear the thought of the false estimate you had formed of my character and as far as I am concerned I am glad that you know. Don't write. There is nothing more that either of us can say & once more for the last time goodbye Evelyn dearest. Don't write – I should burn the letter without opening it.[32]

Probably sometime in 1889, Hermione confided in Evelyn that her relationship with Leinster had completely broken down. Her attempts to 'grasp a mirage of peace and happiness' with Gerald had failed but Hermione could only blame herself: 'I <u>failed utterly</u> for reasons I had been too blind to foresee. But they are for me insurmountable reasons', reasons she could not even discuss with Evelyn.[33] By then Carton had become for Hermione, 'this black dog haunted place'.[34] And to complicate matters further, she was about to embark on an affair with Evelyn's brother, Hugo.

IV

Evelyn's social circle opened up a whole new vista in Hermione's life. She was at the Irish centre of a social clique that had become known as 'the Souls'. Various interpretations of the Souls have survived but most generally agree that this was a group of pseudo-intellectuals, predominantly aristocrats, who revelled in each other's company.[35] The name derived from Lord Charles Beresford's remark in 1888: 'You all sit and talk about each other's souls, I shall call you the Souls'.[36] For almost thirty years the members were 'monotonously well-born', the majority coming from aristocratic landed backgrounds of significant wealth, invariably with important national and imperial service, most of whom had made each other's acquaintance at public school (exclusively Eton or Harrow) or later at university (in the majority of cases Balliol or Trinity, Oxford). Around the time Hermione would have been introduced to the set, Wilfrid Scawen Blunt (1840–1922), poet, polemicist, opponent of British imperialism, supporter of Irish causes, and notorious womanizer, recorded in his diary in June 1891:

> I turned with redoubled zest to my social pleasures of the year before, and … [to] that interesting group of clever men and pretty women known as the 'Souls' … It was a group of men and women bent on pleasure, but pleasure of a superior kind, eschewing the vulgarities of racing and card-playing indulged in by the majority of the rich and noble, and looking for their excitement in romance and sentiment.[37]

The Souls were dominated by the five families of Charteris, Wyndham, Tennant, Balfour and Lyttleton. Over time, they created a coterie united by political and social ambitions and helped progress the careers of each other and their respective families. There were at least seven marriages between the children of Souls' families in the years leading up to the Great War. Five of the Souls were to be members of Balfour's cabinet of 1902–5 (and Lord Curzon was viceroy of India).[38] Even when Gladstone's flirtation with the Irish national and land questions came to the fore in the 1880s, dividing London society, the Souls transcended political divides and offered a forum to families, who might otherwise have split, to continue to perpetuate their social positions. As Ellenberger found: 'The group … contained two nephews of Salisbury and two of Gladstone, classic Whigs like Cowper, Ribblesdale, and Frances Balfour, a daughter of the duke of Argyll, representatives of old-world Toryism such as the Wyndhams and Betty Balfour, and elements of the newer commercial Liberalism in the Tennants and Willie Grenfell'.[39] In her autobiography, Margot Asquith could remember Gladstone, Asquith, Morley, Joseph Chamberlain, Rosebery, Salisbury, Hartington and Harcourt all come to Souls' parties at the height of the Home Rule crises.[40]

When Arthur Balfour (1848–1930), one of the most prominent Souls, arrived in Ireland as chief secretary in 1887, he brought with him as his private secretary the aforementioned George Wyndham. Shortly after their arrival, Wyndham wrote to his new wife, Sibell Grosvenor (1855–1929): 'Arthur is very kind and pleasant to me. We have been talking about poetry, politics etc. and playing an extraordinary game of politics – all conversation and misses'. Wyndham enthused that in the fashion of the Souls they talked about 'Shakespeare, Shelley, the story of Hero and Leander, the difference of accent, quantity and numbering of syllables in English, Latin and French territory, politics, principles, warfare etc etc.'[41] Balfour had been in love for many years with Wyndham's sister, Mary (1862–1937), who was married to Hugo Charteris (1857–1937), styled Lord Elcho and later earl of Wemyss. And it seems Mary remained in love with Balfour all her life; she once wrote to him: 'Mama wanted you to marry me… you got some silly notion in your head because circumstances threw Hugo and me together and accidentally kept us apart – you were the only man I wanted for my husband and it's a great compliment to you!'[42] In Ireland, Balfour became a regular visitor to Evelyn de Vesci's home, Abbey Leix, which, as noted, was the centre of the Souls in Ireland. Evelyn was Hugo Charteris' sister.

At first, it was the excitement of the intellectual freedom offered by the Souls that captured Hermione's attention; as Lady Frances Balfour later recalled: 'We were, in this period, on the brink of society, enlarging its borders, and entertaining new personalities and new ideas'.[43] Viscount D'Abernon, Hermione's brother-in-law, wrote in high praise of the Souls' contribution to *fin de siècle* society, how they effected change 'in the manners, customs, and prejudices of London in the nineties',[44] while Cynthia Asquith recalled in her memoirs:

> …we tried to define the distinction between genius and talent, happiness and pleasure, intellect and intelligence, beauty and prettiness; we asked one another where good manners left off, and insincerity began; whether we would choose to be widely popular or caviare to the general, whether we believed in love at first sight, affinities, and table-turning; whether, if we could, we would abolish pain. And of course, over and over again, we tried to decide which six friends, six books and six pictures we would take to a desert island.[45]

Thus, Evelyn de Vesci's circle of friends was so much different in type to Leinster's, for whom calm superiority was a social convention, that Hermione found their company irresistible. The Souls were also credited by contemporaries with having loosened the strict social morals of Victorian Britain and thereby created a *jeunesse dorée*.[46] Despite the huge degree of etiquette that previously was supposed to have controlled sexual relationships between

15 Abbey Leix, the home of Evelyn de Vesci, and the meeting point of the Irish Souls.

gentlemen and ladies, extra-marital affairs proliferated and it was widely known that members of the Souls had outrageous love affairs with each other.[47]

It was around the time that Hermione confided in Evelyn that her relationship with Gerald had broken down that she was first introduced to Hugo Charteris. It may have been at a social gathering to celebrate the birth of the de Vescis' only child, Mary, in April 1889 (after seventeen years of marriage when Evelyn was thirty-eight years old). In a letter written after this first meeting, Hermione enquired after Evelyn's 'poor brother' and hinted at her fondness for him: 'His own patience and courage touch me more than I can say'. Hermione clearly wanted to make contact: 'I don't know his address but will you give him this little note from me [not found]. I am only an outsider but I think of him <u>often</u> & and my wishes about him are almost prayers.'[48]

At the time Hugo was thirty-four years old and had been married for six years to Mary Wyndham. By his own account, he had a remarkably dull upbringing. He resented the boredom of life in his parents' home at Stanway, the lack of intellectual stimulation and the restraints imposed by social mores. He wrote:

> Their circle was limited and, more probably by chance than design, included no elements of disrepute. There was a sense of formality and observance at their dinners – people arrived with punctuality, and left about eleven – having conversed in contiguous groups after dinner with apparent decorum and liveliness; there were no cards or diversions; tea was spread out in the drawing room at about ten-thirty on a table at which my mother presided, and after that the guests drifted away … I think there was less laughter and certainly less freedom, whether of speech or suggestion – taboos were in the air – and restraint guided conversation into safe channels.[49]

While for Hermione, the Souls offered an alternative outlook from the insipidness of her marriage, for Hugo they provided an alternative from the strict machinations which had restricted the youthful exuberance of his parents and their generation.

Hugo had been educated at Harrow and Balliol and went into a life of politics, becoming MP for Ipswich in the 1880s. He was what his contemporaries might describe as 'a cad'. He could be amusing but unscrupulous; he could be charming but sulky; later in life he could play kindly with his grandchildren but cheat in order to win; and he was possibly best remembered in the House of Commons for his regular suggestion that all business should be adjourned on Derby Day.[50] He was a gambler extraordinaire, treating life 'as a huge roulette table'. By the 1880s he had run up massive debts including losses on the stock exchange, which caused his family severe financial embarrassment. So much so, that he was disinherited by his father who then set up a trust fund of £100,000 for him to be managed by others acting as trustees.[51]

Hugo's mood swings were as severe as Hermione's: 'He was moody and unpredictable; he could be very witty. Some days, he set the table in a roar, talking very fast … Next day he would be sitting aloof or glum, imposing his own silence on everyone else'.[52] On a visit to his family home at Stanway, Laura Tennant found him 'very amusing' but 'completely unscrupulous'.[53] In one of their intellectual amusements in which members of the Souls described another member in rather candid terms, Arthur Balfour described Hugo as 'too indulgent to succeed and too clever to be content with failure'.[54] Of course, as noted already, Arthur had long been in love with his wife, Mary, who was Hugo's polar opposite – charming, unselfconscious and kind to a fault.

16 Hugo Charteris (1857–1937), styled Lord Elcho from 1883 to 1914.

More particularly in the context of this study, Hugo was noted for being 'flagrantly unfaithful'.[55] Hermione's beauty would have been a magnet for him. While he was experienced in extra-marital affairs and, given his knavish personality, hardly likely to have had any moral qualms, the same was not true of Hermione. Her initial excitement with the affair gave way to endless paranoia as she became obsessed by her descent into sexual immorality. Feelings of self-loathing took hold of her and she wrote to Evelyn that her punishment on earth was to have found happiness at last but to have it taken away by her feelings of morose despair:

> My soul has consented to earthly darkness and my punishment is to see and love the light and to know that I have failed … I told you – I repeat – earthly love brings no peace, no happiness, only wild unrest and if delight, then delight which is nearer torture. But I chose it. I loved with all my heart and strength and blindly and selfishly I gave everything up to it.

17 Full-length portrait of Hermione, 5th duchess of Leinster, which hangs at Carton
(courtesy of Mallaghan family).

At first, she fretted that she had compromised her friendship with Evelyn:
'... all along I have marvelled you should have seen anything in me to love or
care about and now you know the extent of my moral blindness. What could
you feel but scorn or even perhaps loathing?'[56] And it does seem that Evelyn

was initially furious about the liaison, but this we can only surmise from the content of Hermione's letters when she wrote, for example:

> You have not realized the one wide essential difference between us – that what to you seems 'revolting', 'miserable', 'hideous' and 'squalid' – to me in my love seems <u>none</u> of these things. It is the natural irresistible impulse to express it in every way I can in the language which comes of itself to me and which I could not stop to criticize.[57]

In another, Hermione denied being a conjurer who had snared Hugo and prayed that Evelyn might not grow to hate her. In a typical passage she prays that 'If my stupid ugly shadow has fallen for a moment on anyone's life I [?live] & hope – as I do believe – that it will quickly fade out of all recollection'.[58] And she had to face the very real prospect that her love for Hugo would mean the loss of her children:

> Will it matter to the children? Will it make any difference? I love them & any way they <u>must</u> love me back again … I would <u>cut myself in pieces</u> to save them trouble and suffering … and only just lately it has occurred to me I wish my children might feel some sort of feeling for me as yours will feel for you.[59]

Then in August 1891, Hermione became pregnant to Hugo (based on the fact that their son, Edward, was born in May of the following year). She took the decision to leave Carton and move to London, informing Evelyn: 'I love Hugo and as long as it is his happiness to keep me I cannot go back'. Their relationship became common knowledge.[60] Hugo admitted that the child Hermione was expecting was his.[61] Hermione was twenty-seven years old but, as her letters suggest, she was still emotionally immature. She had literally been swept away by the type of romantic love she felt she had been denied by her arranged marriage to Gerald. The worldly-wise Evelyn was more realistic about a future with her brother. The following letter, probably written shortly after Hermione left Gerald and Carton, suggests Evelyn advised Hermione to guard against her brother's insincerity but she did not listen:

> I <u>will not</u> change – the worst is over now – it <u>is done</u>. And he is already beginning to prove I did not put my faith in him in vain. I know I did not. I did not make this sufficiently clear the other day but I have proof that there are great possibilities in him. And there will be a return to ours in his life. I feel it and know it. And do not be afraid. <u>I will not see him</u>

until I know it has come to pass. I know I must not see him. I shall say this to you over and over again – for the temptation will be terrible & I am not always brave. And believe me if I love him with all that is best of me for always it is the least return I can make for his infinite kindness & unselfishness to me. I am not writing wildly when I say this – my knowledge of this fact proves that it is true. Some day I would like to tell you all about it. You will think more of Hugo and less of me. Some day – when all is right – & you see for yourself what he is I will tell you.[62]

This was the era of the Parnell divorce scandal. In November 1890, probably a few months after Hermione had first met Hugo, the divorce trial revealed to the public what was already widely known in Victorian political circles that Charles Stewart Parnell, leader of the Irish Parliamentary Party, had for many years been living with Katherine O'Shea, wife of Captain William O'Shea, and had fathered three of her children. The public scandal that ensued was enough to bring down the leader and bitterly split the party. It was the type of scandal which Ireland's premier peer, the duke of Leinster, would have wanted to avoid and he was obviously extremely successful in keeping Hermione's extra-marital affair out of the public arena.

A son, Edward, was born to Hermione in London on 6 May 1892. But as Evelyn had anticipated, Hugo was not readily going to leave his own wife or settle down in a scandalous relationship with the duchess of Leinster. Soon, Hugo abandoned Hermione and their son. The latter was despondent when she wrote to Evelyn:

I am not eloquent enough or clever enough to make him see things as I see them. I failed utterly in making him understand. I only succeeded in further convincing myself of my own utter selfishness & cruelty in having made him care for me. I only felt the strength of my overwhelming love for him & misery that he should doubt me.[63]

She ended the letter blaming herself, as she was wont to do: 'he has a right to feel bitter – for I made him love me'.

Hugo's wife, Mary, would later retaliate by having her own affair with her cousin, the aforementioned Wilfrid Scawen Blunt, who seduced her in a tent in Egypt; she returned home to England pregnant.[64] Many years later, Cynthia Asquith, the legitimate daughter of Hugo and Mary, contemplated the illegitimacy of her half sister fathered by Blunt, and in the process revealed much about the moral milieu in which the Souls operated:

Although she must have long suspected it she had not given the possibility much thought. After all, given the moral climate in which she had been brought up most of her contemporaries were potentially illegitimate. When Charles Lister was killed [in the First World War] she would not have thought he might have been my half brother, nor would she when the newspapers reported the bankruptcy of the [7th] duke of Leinster [Edward]; neither would she have wondered whether the rising politician Anthony Eden was her first cousin (his mother had had a long affair with George Wyndham and there was a clear resemblance). She would have been interested in that typically Edwardian conundrum of things not being what they seem and no-one ever really knowing the truth …[65]

V

From London, Hermione moved for a time to Nubia House, home of the Baring family on the Isle of Wight, to escape from the 'tangled condition' of her life, but not before she had talks with her husband in London. She confided in Evelyn: 'I met Kildare in London on Saturday & before returning to Ireland he must accede to five conditions I make and which I think necessary for the probability of the continuance of our life together and for the happiness of the children and the peace of their home'.[66] She claimed to be 'asking very little & nothing but what I am sure Kildare when he thinks it all over & considers it calmly and dispassionately will see it is for the best'.[67] Unfortunately, she did not reveal what her pre-conditions for return were. But Gerald's willingness to reconcile with Hermione would not have been unusual. As Anita Leslie reminisced of the time:

> Once married, a young woman could be eyed thoughtfully, but it would not be *de rigueur* not to attempt to waylay her before she produced a few sons to carry on her husband's name and inherit his estates… it did not matter terribly if one or two rather different-looking children arrived at the tail-end of the family.[68]

Similarly, Angela Lambert makes the claim that no Souls' marriage ended in divorce and 'the erring wife or husband was always welcomed back, and any children of these outside liaisons were always accepted and reared as the husband's child'.[69] Gerald had two sons, Maurice and Desmond, to succeed him; as far as he was concerned the FitzGerald bloodline was safe.

After Gerald and Hermione's London meeting nothing immediately happened. It may have been because Gerald's attentions were firmly focused on fighting the introduction of the second Home Rule bill. In August 1893, Hermione went home to Duncombe Park with her young son. (It is not known if she had access to her other sons after she left Carton.) While at Duncombe, her sister, Helen D'Abernon, became increasingly concerned for Hermione's emotional state. Again, it is perhaps illuminating that such concern was expressed after Hermione had given birth to another child. However, she had been through a great deal more besides, not least of all the break up of her marriage and her abandonment by the man with whom she thought she had found love.

Hermione's depression deepened. In her letters she frequently referred to her soul when contemplating her moral dilemmas and her self-loathing at having descended into sexual immorality. In one she wrote: 'My soul has consented to earthly darkness and my punishment is to see and love the light and to know that I have failed' and in another 'But then again when he is here I <u>hate</u> myself for thinking of my "Soul" – it seems it ought to be nothing in comparison to my love.'[70] (Of course, 'my "Soul"' in the second letter may have been a clever play on words to camouflage Hugo's name.) Interestingly, in the eighteenth century the German physician, Johann Christian Heinroth, had put forward the theory that melancholia was a condition of the soul related to moral conflict within the person. Throughout his work, Heinroth regarded sin to be the predominant cause of mental illness.[71] At any rate, Helen took it upon herself to write to Gerald, reprimanding him on how he was treating Hermione:

> … more freedom should be secured to her and in which it should be agreed that seven or eight months per annum is the limit of time she should be expected to pass at Carton. No one can regret more than I do that such a compact should have become necessary, but the circumstances of your married life have been peculiar to the highest degree and I think that after consideration you will not fail to recognize that in common fairness and equity she has a right to some of the liberty on her side that you exercise so freely on your own…. I only write in order to express a hope that you may see your way to some agreement independently of all publicity and without other arbitration than that of justice and commonsense.[72]

The liberty that the duke exercised so freely is not clear – was she charging him with having affairs? – but Helen's letter took Leinster by surprise and he replied rather tamely by telegram: 'Thank you for your letter and advice. Hope to act on it.'[73] Shortly afterwards, Hermione returned to Carton; perhaps as Anita Leslie contended: 'The break up of a home was the price never to be paid for romance'.[74] Hermione, it seems, was not welcomed with open arms by the duke's spinster sisters. When much later in the 1930s, Edward's wife, Rafaelle Davidson-Kennedy, met his aunt, Lady Nesta, she got the distinct impression that Nesta 'thoroughly disapproved' of Hermione and 'had rejected her from the day she had married a Geraldine'. Nesta informed Rafaelle that 'she never trusted pretty women'.[75]

There are a number of letters to Evelyn which date to around the time of the reconciliation but they throw up as many questions as they provide answers. In one written from Carton, Hermione refers to a gift of the *Saint Esprit* which she has received from Evelyn but which she felt she had to return with the morose note: 'I send you back the *Saint Esprit* … I cannot bear to keep it any longer. I always thought I should be able to wear it some day. I do not kill myself because wretched as it all is I can be of no use to the children [if dead]. They do want me'. In the 'long dark hours' of the previous night she came to realize 'how impossible it was you should be kind to me any longer' and concluded 'Goodbye dear beautiful Evelyn & try to realize that in spite of everything your love and tenderness have not been quite thrown away'.[76] Another refers to a note received by Hermione in the 'middle of a nightmare dinner' at 46 Cadogan Square:

> I <u>know</u> it is only goodbye for a time – some day you will feel I may come back to you. And I love you darling with my whole heart. I will not [?] yet. I could not bear it. But I know you love me a little – for myself – and that thought brings me <u>infinite peace</u>. And some time I shall see you again and your Baby [the pet name which Hermione used for Mary de Vesci] and go to Abbey Leix. I know it.[77]

As the letters quoted below will further indicate, it does not seem to have been the case that the duke forbade any further contact between Hermione and Evelyn, even if he thought her an unsuitable influence on his wife. Instead, Hermione, for whatever reasons, made the conscious decision to try to sunder the emotional bonds.

VI

By November 1893, Hermione and her son, Edward, had returned to Carton. In the eyes of the law Edward was a FitzGerald; it mattered little who knew what about his actual paternity. Later that month Gerald took Hermione to stay with George Campbell (1823–1900), 8th duke of Argyll, at Inveraray. The duke was related through marriage to Leinster: Argyll's first wife was Lady Elizabeth Sutherland-Leveson-Gower (d. 1844), daughter of the 2nd duke of Sutherland and, therefore, sister of Leinster's mother. His heir was married to Princess Louise, the principal guest at the Leinsters' wedding. The visit may have been purely social – a second honeymoon, so to speak – but it may just as easily have had a political agenda. Argyll had been a vehement opponent of the Irish Land League (and the Scottish crofters),[78] and broke with Gladstone over the terms of the 1881 Land Act which he felt were a sell-out in response to the intimidatory tactics of the Land League. He was also a staunch unionist, and just a few weeks before the Leinsters' visit, the second Home Rule bill had been thrown out by the Lords.

While in Inveraray, Hermione wrote to Evelyn (who must have been staying in one of the Wemyss' Scottish homes):

> Some ridiculous small feeling made me resolve not to write to you while I was in Scotland & so near you. But I am ashamed of feeling anything so silly & so small & last night as I lay awake listening to the wind and watching the fitful gleams over the water & looking in the direction where I imagine you to be my whole heart went out to you and I felt I must write to tell you how I love you & how the thought of your sadness weighs upon my heart. I think you are an angel, Evelyn, darling. Knowing you has made a lot of vague thoughts and ideas real and tangible to me. Everything beautiful makes me think of you and everything good and alas too everything sad! … I can imagine no grief, however terrible, from which your dear presence would not take some of the despair away … I do not want you to write to me darling – unless you feel inclined. I think letters can be such a terrible trial. Only write because my whole heart goes out to you because I love you with a humble and adoring love, because I have been thinking of you day and night and because I am ashamed of the feeling that prevented me writing to tell you so and because my heart aches at the thought of all the hideous misery.[79]

The rest of the surviving letters indicate that Hermione was no more contented after the reconciliation than she had been before, but it hardly mattered because the visit to Inveraray had grave consequences for the duke. When he returned home, Gerald was taken violently ill and subsequently diagnosed with typhoid fever. At first it was suspected that he had contracted it in Dublin (possibly after a visit to the estate offices in Dominick Street)

where fever was 'rampant' but it was then deemed more likely he had contracted it in Scotland.[80] He was confined to bed at Carton and two of the most
eminent medical practitioners of the time, Dr Wallace Beatty and Dr James
Little (former president of the Royal College of Physicians of Ireland), were
brought from the Adelaide Hospital in Dublin to attend to him. Two nurses
from the same hospital, Miss Sayers and Miss Pringle, bathed him in iced
cloths as he spent days in bed suffering severe shivering fits, his temperature
rising to a high of 105 degrees, and then falling dramatically.[81] Despite their
efforts his heart was unable to withstand the fever and he died on 1 December
1893.[82] He was only forty-two years old. Had he died just a few months later,
after death duties had been introduced by the government, his passing would
have had an enormous impact on the financial position of the estate.

Gerald was buried in the private graveyard at Carton, a little space about
100 yards from the house enclosed by wire railings and red-berried holly trees.
It was a strictly private affair with only immediate relatives and friends in
attendance. His remains were placed 'in a massive lead coffin, enclosed in an
oaken case'. The coffin was carried from the house by some of the estate
labourers and household servants as the bells of the Protestant and Catholic
churches in Maynooth tolled their last respects. The blinds were drawn in the
village houses and business was suspended for the day. The archbishop of
Dublin presided at the graveside where the chief mourners included Hermione,
the duke's brothers – Frederick, Walter and Henry – and Monsignor Browne,
president of Maynooth College. When the service ended, Hermione walked
over to the grave and dropped in a bunch of violets and white hyancinths and
'though she bore up bravely during the comforting service of the Church, she
now completely broke down, and was led away'.[83] If true, and one must bear
in mind this was written by the duke's private chaplain, it is difficult not to
surmise some degree of melodrama in her actions. She chose lines from a
Shelley sonnet for the inscription on his cross: 'Death is the veil which those
who live call life/ They sleep and it is lifted.'[84]

The news of the duke's premature death was met with widespread sympathy.
Queen Victoria telegrammed Lord Kildare that she was 'Deeply grieved to see
in the paper the death of your excellent father … and am most anxious to
know how your dear mother is.'[85] The tenantry were led in their condolences
by the large Catholic and Protestant farmers. Celbridge guardians lamented
that 'his loss will be deeply felt by all classes in this district where he was equally
liked and respected by rich and poor'.[86] Athy town commissioners passed a
similar resolution led by nationalist chairman, Thomas Whelan. M.J. Minch
MP said he spoke on behalf of the tenant farmers and merchants and noted

their collective sorrow; in his eulogy he claimed that the duke had been known to grant up to 50 per cent reductions to tenants in time of recession and 100 per cent to widows and orphans. It was more fiction than fact but the type of post death tribute that creates myths. The Revd W.J. Tristram, rector of Maynooth, described him as a patriarchal landlord who spent his income in the country as an example to all others. He told an ecumenical meeting at Maynooth:

> I can confidently say that there is scarcely a family in the town of Maynooth that has not directly or indirectly experienced the advantages of having a residential duke at Carton … The duke and duchess of Leinster were seldom absent from Carton. They lived in the midst of their people. They were anxious about their welfare. They knew their wants and relieved them.[87]

The Catholic parish priest, Fr J.J. Hunt, similarly described the late duke as a friend to the people:

> In the death of the duke the poor have lost a sincere friend and the working people of Maynooth a good employer. I can confidently say that there is scarcely a family in the town of Maynooth that has not directly or indirectly experienced the advantages of having a residential duke at Carton.[88]

The significance of Fr Hunt's tribute should not be missed: even in the midst of a nationalist upsurge that demonized landlords and their Big Houses there remained on the Leinster estate around Maynooth a contemporary appreciation of the economic value of a leading aristocrat residing in a locality.

The *Freeman's Journal* portrayed Gerald as having the common touch – possibly another symptom of democratization – describing him as a man with 'genial, sociable, unaffected ways'. It described how 'in the summer months he might be often met tramping along the roads in a plain homespun suit and soft hat, or engaged in friendly converse with some farmer of the district'.[89] In death, any faults he had were swept away and Gerald was represented in a variety of ways to epitomize all that was good in a patriarchal landlord.

An untitled and undated, but evidently early twentieth-century newspaper clipping survives in the Leinster archive that reads:

The writer remembers hearing a story told on many occasions with
reference to the Leinster estate, in the hottest part of the Land League
times when the people in a just and indignant uprising were clamouring
against and even shedding the blood of rackrenting landlords, a late duke
of Leinster was reported to have said he could walk round his Kildare
estate with an umbrella in his hand. This was the time when the firing at
landlords and landlords' agents was as common almost as firing at crows.
Such a state of things in Kildare reflected credit both on the landlord and
tenant – the former gave no cause of complaint and the latter recognizing
that they had one of the best landlords in Ireland appreciated accordingly
and consequently unpleasantness between them was of rare occurrence.[90]

It may have been a pro-establishment newspaper and it did edit out the
Leinster lease controversy but it adequately serves to make the point that the
family's legacy stood to them in the darkest hours of anti-landlord feeling in
Ireland and, indeed, was important enough for them to keep a record of the
same. While the Leinster estate had seen its fair share of controversy during the
Land War era, it still emerged as one of the type identified by K.T. Hoppen
where 'distinct feelings of social and political esprit de corps' were built up
'which cut across most other barriers and distinctions'.[91] When Gerald's heir,
Maurice, came of age in 1908, there was, as we shall see, an interesting change
in the rhetoric of the addresses presented to him, reflecting the great socio-
political changes since 1872, but still no one around Maynooth was calling for
the removal of the duke of Leinster from their midst.

VII

There were no contemporary newspapers that reported on the scandal of the
duchess's affair or her return to Carton with Edward. Shortly after Gerald's
burial the estate press office began its job of responding to the messages of
condolence. A statement was issued from Hermione that she was

> … deeply touched by the expression of sympathy felt by the people of
> Maynooth with her in her heavy trial. She would desire to convey to
> them her heartfelt thanks, together with the assurance that the affection
> they express for her late husband will be kindly remembered and
> reciprocated to them by her and her children as long as they live.[92]

It is unlikely that Hermione had any say in the management of estate business after the death of Gerald, as it passed into the hands of trustees. It is equally unlikely she had any interest. None of her surviving letters make any reference to estate matters, her attitude to the trustees or even to the FitzGerald family or any commentary on their perceived attitudes towards her.

After Gerald's death, Hermione's relationship with Evelyn de Vesci was restored. Very shortly after the funeral, Hermione wrote to her of her plans:

> I think of leaving Carton for 4 months and not returning till the spring. I take all my children with me and shall go first to Duncombe & then to Netherby & then take a house somewhere at the sea. I want to go on living here & for this to be the children's home. I am very impractical and stupid about all things but I feel sure I ought to manage it easily. I am so grateful for being left practically sole guardian of the children – only life has suddenly become a very solemn thing and I am oppressed by the sense of my own terrible deficiencies. Do pray that I may become a little less ignoble and selfish and above all less impulsive and wildly injudicious. I should like never to think of myself again and I should like more strength and patience and self command. In fact I feel I have nothing but <u>love</u>. Do pray God for my little children Evelyn that I may love them right.[93]

However poignant the tone of the letter, it is still Hermione's personality and her state of mind that is most evident. Fourteen times in this short passage she uses 'I'. It is perhaps revealing that modern psychology studies suggest that the frequent use of 'I', and by extension too much attention to the Self, 'is associated with highly negative emotional states such as depression'.[94] Certainly, after Gerald's death, Hermione's emotional state worsened. In another letter to Evelyn, she wrote: 'I was very unhappy when I wrote to you. I had had those nervous breakdowns before but had never so fully realized how near one can be to that strange wild land of grotesque [?]'. On a later occasion, after a lengthy period of confinement, she wrote of having 'what the doctor kindly calls a "nervous collapse" but which was really a sort of brain break-down. I feel shaky and frightened as if I should always be haunted by the terror of <u>going mad</u>.' She continued: 'the doctor talks of me as a discharged convict & says I must remain "under observation" for a fortnight. But I think one will be surprised at how quickly I recover. I have had these wretched fits of nerve-slavery before. I know I shan't get well till they let me get home and I <u>long</u> to go.' She did not specify where home was, if it was Carton or Duncombe Park. Perhaps her real problem was that she had never really known where home was, at least not since she left Duncombe as a young twenty year old, emotionally unprepared for the journey ahead.[95]

Her last surviving letters to Evelyn reveal all her vulnerabilities: often a lack of self-confidence, sometimes self-loathing, a craving for love, a need to be the centre of the attention of those she loved. She could be desperately possessive and often petulant when ignored or when she felt attention was not adequately bestowed upon her. Thus in one letter she was forced to apologize to Evelyn for recent behaviour:

> I was overtired that evening I got to Abbeyleix and you don't know how silly I am on those occasions & how easily I imagine all sorts of nonsense. Please realize if you have not done so already that I am idiotic & forgive me for having been so ridiculous … I do love you, Evelyn dear, who could help it.[96]

Her penchant for feeling sorry for herself was even reflected in her envy of her children's innocence: 'they at least have no misgivings about life or their own enjoyment of it'.[97]

As planned, she made her way to her sister Cynthia's home at Netherby Hall in Cumbria. After a period of contemplation, she wrote from there to Evelyn expressing her regret about things unsaid and undone before Gerald died:

> I am haunted by the recollections of kind words left unsaid and little kind acts that might have given pleasure left undone. Our lives all went wrong – I don't think anything could have ever made them right. But he was often very kind to me – I can remember nothing at all but being odious & judging harshly.[98]

Hermione's personality makes it difficult to judge the sincerity of her feelings. Her letters may suggest her own road to Damascus experience but a degree of scepticism would question whether her portrayal of her sense of loss was merely another guise to attract sympathy for her own situation:

> Those last weeks we spent together in Scotland he was very kind and dear to me – kinder and dearer perhaps than he had ever been – and my last recollections of him are of tenderness and love… and now he is dead, I remember only his merits, his dearness to me in many ways, the strong foundation of love and affection that underlay his apparent coldness. He did everything, managed everything – took the whole burden of life from

my shoulders – and now I am conscious of a great blank. A feeling that the arms of a silent encircling love have been withdrawn. No words can express his goodness and patience all through his illness … these last few days have been a terrible strain and the misery of each hopeless detail haunts me day and night.[99]

Ultimately, her marriage had not been a happy or fulfilled one. Elizabeth Fingall recognized that while the duke was 'good and kind', he was, however, 'not the man for her [Hermione]'. According to Elizabeth Fingall, Hermione had 'wanted a man whom she could look up to and fear a little, as well as love', but the duke merely 'used to sit in the library at Carton, cataloguing his books and tidying them' and if Hermione went to him with a plan for domestic arrangements and he did not approve, 'he would argue and tell her "I have settled it" before walking out of the room to leave her looking after him'.[1] Perhaps Elizabeth Fingall was right when she suggested that she had been unable to carry the burden of the FitzGerald history, too much of which 'looked down at Hermione from the walls of Carton'.[2]

CHAPTER FIVE

Hermione's death

Some say 'God wills it'
And some say – ''Tis fate',
My heart – and none stills it –
Says, you loved him too late.

Hermione, on the death of her husband, Gerald

Yes, I always think of her [Hermione] now as a radiant vision gone before age has touched her beauty and before time and disappointment had broken her spirit.[1]

In December 1893, Hermione returned briefly to her home at Duncombe Park, exactly ten years after she had composed 'December 1883'. Its restoration after a disastrous fire in 1879 had just been completed to the design of William Young. It was the first time Hermione had seen the remodelled house and even though the rebuild was based on original designs there were a number of changes to the interiors, notably reductions dictated by financial exigencies, which did not appeal to Hermione. She wrote despairingly to Evelyn of her great disappointment:

> I went all over the new house yesterday & the result was frantic tears. Everything reduced, everything ruined. The hall which was the feature of the house reduced by 30 ft. Staircases mean and wretched … I came to the melancholic conclusion that the improvements in <u>no way</u> counterbalance what they have sacrificed. I trust I may never meet Mr. Young for I cannot congratulate him on what he has done … [I am] fully convinced he can have no real feelings for art or he <u>could not</u> have wantonly sacrificed much that was so beautiful.[2]

However, the visit did inspire her to begin writing verse once again. In lines presumably composed during her visit, she reflected on the ten years since she had left Duncombe Park:

Could I feel sure that failure trod
Would bring me so much nearer God
That I should find again the theme
And mystic music of my dream
That blessed death would take my hand
And bid me know and understand
That dreams, once seen, are never lost
But all we feel and long for most
Will meet us at Death's golden door
Then I could wait and weep no more.[3]

There is no evidence that Hermione ever read Emily Dickinson but there are strong suggestions of Dickinson's funereal themes in Hermione's composition and Dickinson's first volume of poetry had been published just three years before in 1890. There are also by coincidence strong parallels between Hermione's correspondence with Evelyn and Emily Dickinson's with Susan Grant, her cherished friend who would become her sister-in-law. Their correspondence over a period of decades might be interpreted as nineteenth-century romantic friendship, or like Hermione's letters to Evelyn de Vesci they might be read as more than mere effusive expressions of love.[4]

After Gerald's death, Hermione certainly devoted more of her time to artistic pursuits. She moved to a cottage in Surrey to pursue her interest in painting and sculpting and presumably to be close to her tutor, George Frederick Watts, whose home was in Compton. Her love of art was not some whim; she seems to have been genuinely talented. When back in July 1891, Arthur Balfour was invited to the Leinster residence in London to view one of her works in progress, he reported back to Mary Elcho:

> … certainly I think she has talent. The subject is a little nude nymph – about two feet high – with her hands above her head looking down with a glance half of malice half of triumph on a discomforted Cupid; the latter not yet modelled. It seemed to me very clever and spirited: and if she has had as little training as I gather she has the work is really remarkable.[5]

Balfour may have been more perceptive than he realized: the sculpture might have been an allegory for her life at that point with Gerald (and Hugo). It was in London that she had the freedom to sculpt, away from Carton and from the duke's disapproving gaze and Balfour's visit was at the height of her affair with

Hugo. The following month she would become pregnant with Edward. Moreover, it was Watts' lifetime ambition to create a universal symbolic language through allegorical works.

Hermione also began to spend more time in the company of Emily Lawless (1845–1913), writer and sister of Lord Cloncurry of Lyons, Co. Kildare. They first met shortly after Hermione arrived at Carton but it was not until after Gerald's death that they became close friends. Hermione's cottage in Surrey was close to where Lawless frequently stayed with her companion (and possibly lover) Lady Sarah Spencer, sister of the former viceroy, Earl Spencer.[6] Emily's own life had been blighted by the deaths by suicide of her father (1869) and her sisters (Mary in 1885 and Rose in 1891), her own deteriorating health, depression and drug addiction.[7] They would have had quite a lot in common, not least of all the fact that both, through their artistic endeavours, were trying to contemplate what it meant to be female and aristocratic at a time when class and gender definitions were radically changing in Britain. Unfortunately, no sooner had Hermione begun to find refuge in her art, than more personal misfortune befell her.

II

In August 1894, less than a year after her husband's death, rumours began to circulate that Hermione was seriously ill. Arthur Balfour had met Elizabeth Fingall early that month and he wrote to Mary Elcho: 'she gave me – second hand from L[ad]y Helen [Vincent] – a very gloomy account of the duchess'.[8] In her memoirs, Elizabeth Fingall (described in 1902 by George Wyndham as 'a dear but indiscreet')[9] recounted how Hermione rushed into her bedroom one morning and announced wildly, almost with a childish excitement: 'I must tell you … You won't believe it! The doctors have just told me that I have only a year to live; and even to live that year I must go abroad at once.'[10]

Hermione was much more sombre when she wrote to break the news to Evelyn de Vesci: 'I have had a cough for some months and they now say it is tuberculosis of the lungs. It can quite well be arrested in the early stage – they tell me I am taking it in time'. There was something tragically inevitable in the fact that she fell victim to consumption, a disease that was not simply the great killer of the nineteenth-century western world, but one which transcended morbidity to assume a certain romanticism as real life and literary heroines succumbed to it. At first she did not agonize: 'I am quite happy about myself. I know I shall get well'.[11] But her mood quickly changed and she became fretful and agitated when she realized that her illness might be terminal. Now, she wrote angrily and in denial to Evelyn: 'Don't waste any time talking about my stupid health … I am not really ill & I don't feel ill. In my heart of hearts I believe there is nothing the matter and I shall go on believing it till it becomes a reality.'[12] She reverted to type, reproaching herself and viewing her illness as a punishment visited upon her for past neglects and indiscretions: 'my own thoughts disquiet me. Remorse for the past ingratitude … for all the loving kindness which was not in me'.[13]

The dreaded cough grew worse. Her throat swelled so much she could not talk and doctors even feared throat cancer.[14] She attended a number of medical experts and consultation committees composed of specialists of international standing who were authorities in the field of TB and throat disease: Dr Bezly Thorne (an expert on pulmonary disease who, Hermione noted: 'wrote enthusiastically about the cure to his friends for the reason it evidently is doing his son good'); and Dr J.L. Gimbert, author of the pioneering *Mémoire sur la structure et la texture des artères* (1865) who proclaimed creosote as a cure for throat illnesses and coughs. But Hermione was not convinced: 'Personally I have a horror of his creosote treatment. I know it has succeeded in some few cases but I know also from other sources in how very many more cases it has failed utterly and only caused pain and discomfort'.[15] The thought of taking creosote orally was bad enough, she proclaimed, but having it injected into the blood stream was out of the question. However, Evelyn, desperate for her to find a cure, seems to have advised her to try anything, for Hermione later wrote to her: 'I am also ashamed of having made such a fuss about Gimbert. Believe me, if necessary, I will try his treatment. I have spraying (daily) & inhalations for my throat. I have great hope these may work wonders.'[16] In the end she was advised by her private consulting team of doctors not to go ahead with the treatment. They had learned that Gimbert's treatment had been tried at the Brompton Consumptive Hospital and at Ventnor on the Isle of Wight, the leading hospitals for consumptive diseases in Britain, and the results were 'so unsatisfactory that it has now been definitely abandoned'. They were not inclined to make her endure months of 'hideous suffering of dreadful abscesses' and Hermione was happy to abandon the treatment: 'I am so thankful I heard of some of his victims when I was seriously thinking of putting myself under him 2 months ago. I can quite understand somebody trying it as a "last chance" but I think they would have to be stronger than I am.'

In the winter of 1894, probably December, Hermione set out with her mother, Mabel, countess of Feversham, and her sister, Lady Cynthia Graham, in search of a climate that would bring relief from her symptoms. First, they tried Malaga but it did not work. They travelled on to Tarasp in the picturesque Swiss canton of Graubunden within the lower Engadin valley. From there on to the spa town of Meran(o) in what is now part of northern Italy, located within a basin surrounded by mountains and where the radon water was said to cure circulatory problems. At times their journey resembled a pilgrimage: Cynthia would often sing 'the hymn to the virgin'. Her mother had hoped that Hermione would try various traditional cures but she was not at all in favour of these and often got quite angry at their mention.[17] Gradually, Hermione grew weaker; Mabel wrote to Evelyn that she was 'too ill to write herself and her clear voice is only a whisper now'. They were forced to stay over in various places including Genoa and Dondighera, unable to travel further. At Monte Carlo, Mabel wrote that Hermione 'hardly ever gets up now'. She was so debilitated that her mother thought they would have to get a second nurse. All this time, Hermione longed to see the children and lamented how she had 'achieved nothing but one's own banishment'.[18]

As her condition deteriorated in the spring of 1895, she gave 'up all hopes of going back to Ireland'. The party moved on to Mentone, a small town on the French-Italian border about sixteen miles east of Nice. It was a most picturesque area, described as follows by one contemporary traveller who had gone there in search of a cure for his own consumption:

> As the road descends, winding along the mountainside, a brown sunburnt village appears – Roccabruna [Roquebrune], clinging to the rocks. Then a corner is turned, and behold a magnificent mountain amphitheatre appears, that of Mentone. The higher mountains, receding round a beautiful bay opening to the south east, form this amphitheatre, the centre of which is about two miles from the seashore. The entire bay and the town of Mentone, with its background of swelling olive-clad hills closed in by the amphitheatre of mountains, are thus thoroughly protected from the north-west, north and north-east winds.[19]

For some time Mentone had become a haven for sufferers of consumption. In 1859, J. Henry Bennet, a member of the Royal College of Physicians in London, and himself a consumptive, had discovered its climactic qualities and a decade later wrote a book that influenced many others to go there to arrest the progress of their disease: 'During the ten winters that I have passed at Mentone … I have never seen a fog, either at sea or land, day or night, morning or evening. Generally speaking the sky is clear and the sun shines in the heavens like a globe of fire'.[20] While Bennet could claim in his book that 'after ten winters passed at Mentone, I am surrounded by a phalanx of cured or arrested consumption cases', he added a cautionary note that 'Those who are in the last stage of the disease ... appear to derive but little benefit from the change'.[21] Unfortunately, Hermione was among the latter.

Hermione and her entourage booked into the Hotel des Isles Britanniques. A traveller remarked in the 1880s: 'Everything at the hotel was comfortable and satisfactory, cleanliness and courtesy were predominant, and I should think altogether it was one of the best conducted hotels on the Riviera'.[22] It was beautifully located surrounded by a rich diversity of vegetation, where mesembryanthemums blended with aloe, oleander, verbascum and antirrhinum and where terraces of lemon and orange trees stretched into the distance, but where one traveller also noted 'the gnarled and twisted olive has a strangely sad and sombre effect',[23] a poignant symbol pointing to the fact that in the midst of all this scenic beauty consumptives were succumbing to their disease.

At Mentone, Hermione received three letters of support from W.E. Gladstone who had resigned as prime minister of Great Britain the previous year; she was blessed with Lourdes water in the hope of a miracle cure; and visited by the Prince of Wales.[24] She was also visited by Hugo Charteris. Whether she had seen him in the intervening years since the birth of their son is not known and seems unlikely. Likewise, it is not known if she requested him to come or somebody did so on her behalf. He does seem to have come with the blessing of Mabel who almost immediately reported an improvement in her daughter's condition, at least psychological, and wrote to Evelyn: 'She could not bear two days here ... after he is gone! I can't tell you how I dread the pain of parting for her. She said to me the other day I <u>know</u> I am very ill – but I am very happy – happier than I have ever been in my life for Hugo is an <u>angel</u>.' Mabel praised Hugo's 'infinite tenderness, thoughtfulness & <u>unselfish</u> devotion. Night and day he has nursed her ... He has inspired her with the deepest affection & I think it must be a privilege to belong to him ... She so adores him.' But then he left and Hermione went into relapse.[25] On 18 February 1895, Mabel wrote: 'I thought her so aged and altered. It was immediately after dear Hugo left and I know she has been crying so this explained a great deal ... Hugo's return will be the signal of improvement ... I am a poor substitute.'[26]

Mabel quite obviously had a liberal view of her daughter's relationship with Hugo and considered that both of them deserved some happiness in their lives: 'the few pleasures they have been able to match in the course of their existence need cause them no remorse'.[27] Hugo was, of course, still married to Mary but he believed she would approve of his actions. He wrote to his sister, Evelyn: 'I think Mary will approve of my staying here'.[28] In one sentence he could write that Hermione 'found as she told me so often the one happiness of her unhappy life in my love', but in the next profess that 'Mary is so good and I am so fond of her'.[29] The scandal of his being at Hermione's bedside was hidden from the public; at least one newspaper reported that it was actually Mary who was nursing Hermione.[30]

Mary was not, however, as understanding as Hugo might have wished. Shortly after he returned to the bedside of his former lover she went off to Egypt on an expedition with her cousin, Wilfrid Scawen Blunt, who was over twenty years older than her. As has been noted earlier Blunt was among other things a diplomat, poet (he was married to Lord Byron's granddaughter), traveller, philanderer – described as a 'connoiseur of women and Arab horses'[31] – an anti-imperialist, and supporter of Irish Home Rule having unsuccessfully contested the 1885 election on that ticket. When he toured Ireland in late 1887 he was imprisoned during Arthur Balfour's term as chief secretary for inciting Irish tenants to revolt against the system of landlordism.[32] He did not enjoy the experience and it was sometimes surmised that he exacted a particularly cynical revenge on Balfour when he had an affair with Mary Elcho.

When Hugo began to contemplate that his wife might be having an affair, he became increasingly more anxious about Blunt and her than the dying Hermione. He complained to Evelyn that he was 'in an abnormally depressed state of mind. I am wretched. I suppose stupidly anxious about Mary. She went for a long expedition into the desert on camels with Blunt. I had a sort of foreboding dislike of it – I did all I could to stop her'. Ten days had passed and he had not heard from her and so he admitted: 'I can't help feeling nervous'.[33] Now it was his turn to revert to type; according to Angela Lambert, he simply 'got tired of waiting for his mistress to die',[34] and so he made up his mind to leave. He informed Evelyn:

> I am going tomorrow. I have thought and thought about it and I feel now I should go … *The World* said Mary was nursing Mione. I think I ought to go – to let it be known I have been in Egypt. Mary is [?] happy – enjoying herself – feeling better than she has for years & not really wanting me. But that does not make any difference really, also she is leading an odd sort of life camping out in the desert [with Blunt] and I fear people may be talking about them.[35]

Hugo made his way to Egypt to seek reconciliation with his wife. Blunt had led his Arab servants to believe that Mary was his Bedouin wife and so Hugo was banned from sharing her tent. Blunt later wrote: 'I would not allow Mary

18 Hugo Charteris, his wife, Mary, sister of George Wyndham, and their children, *c.*1890: from the left, Guy, Mary, Hugo, Bibs (on her mother's knee), Yvo, Ego, Cynthia (taken from Ridley and Percy (eds), *Letters of Arthur Balfour and Lady Elcho*, before p. 203).

to share her tent with Hugo, as that would not have been proper. Surleyman and all the Arabs know that she is my Bedouin wife and I would not hear of it. So ... I slept under a bush a little apart, where Mary could come to me as in the night of the honeymoon.'[36]

In the meantime, Hermione was growing weaker and now longed to return to Carton.[37] There had been long stretches when she did not mention the children; Mabel wrote: 'the children are well I am thankful to say. She hears of them daily but she seldom mentions them and I avoid the subject, I am so afraid of upsetting her.'[38] Hermione knew she could not have them with her;

not talking about her sons may simply have been, as Mabel surmised, her way of dealing with her separation from them.

By the middle of March 1895, Hermione's condition deteriorated rapidly. Hugo was sent for and he returned to her bedside. When she died on the afternoon of 20 March she was just thirty years old. Hugo told his sister: 'She died this afternoon – it lasted a long time, 24 hours and was terrible to watch … She was hardly conscious at all.'[39] A violent gale blew the night that the ship carrying Hermione's remains crossed the channel. She would have appreciated the symbolism of it. On 25 March, her body arrived in Dublin and was conveyed by road to Carton, accompanied by a cortege led by Lord Frederick. The earl of Feversham and Lady Cynthia Graham arrived at the ancestral FitzGerald home that evening. Maurice and his younger brother, Desmond, were reported to have been taken to Kilkea Castle by Lady Eva 'for a change of air' after an attack of Scarlatina. Perhaps significantly there was no mention of Edward.[40] Similarly, when *The Graphic* reported on her death it stated 'she leaves two sons'.[41] The children did not attend the funeral.

On the days that followed, Hermione's remains were laid out in the duke's study at Carton and at 1 p.m. on the very wet afternoon of 28 March 1895 they were enclosed in a suite of coffins and taken from the house in traditional style on a double shaft cart covered with ferns and drawn by a number of the estate employees. The cart made the short journey from the house through an avenue of cedar trees to the secluded cemetery where she was laid to rest beside her husband. The grave, under a beech tree, had been dug 'very deep and wide' and adorned by the head gardener, Mr Black, with violets mixed with ferns and lilies mingled with papyrus.[42] The bottom of the grave was lined with large palm leaves. The largest wreath was five feet in diameter from the Prince of Wales, composed of orchids, white roses and lily of the valley. Just as the service began a 'drenching downpour of rain' fell incessantly.[43] It was a 'solemn ceremony of internment … conducted with great simplicity and in a semi-private manner' by Revd F.W. Gason, rector of Maynooth, and 'the attendance … was not accordingly very large'.[44] Inside the cemetery railings were family and close friends and a number of dignitaries including the lord lieutenant (Hermione's cousin, Lord Houghton), Viscount Charlemont representing the queen, and Sir Arthur Vicars, Ulster king at arms (who later became embroiled in the scandal surrounding the theft of the Irish crown jewels and was murdered by the Irish Republican Army during the War of Independence in 1921). Hermione had requested that on the stone cross which marked her grave there should be written: 'My God, I know that all Thou ordainest is for the best, and I am content'.[45]

Posthumous tributes abounded. The *Freeman's Journal* said Hermione was 'a lady whose name was synonymous for goodness and beauty'; she had endeared herself to all classes, but particularly the poor of Maynooth to whom she was 'always a very kind and generous helper', regularly contributing £5 a month to Canon Hunt, the parish priest, for distribution.[46] Edmund Burke's description of Marie Antoinette ('Surely, never lighted on this orb, which she hardly seemed to touch, a more delightful vision') influenced eulogists to make the comparison and so A.W. Quill published a poem in the *Irish Times* in memoriam:

> Hermione! Spirit of beauty!
> Hermione! Spirit of grace,
> Nor crown or of diamond or ruby
> Could add to the light of that face!
> No colours of Orient empurpled,
> No hues of the weavers of Tyre
> Could rival those blushes that mantled,
> Or vie with those glances of fire.[47]

The local *Kildare Observer* reported the

> feelings of the most profound sorrow [felt] by the servants of the family and the many persons engaged about the house and demesne … On the faces of the workmen and servants appearances of sorrow and regret are plainly stamped, and in and around the place the sombre gloom following in the wake of death is all too plainly visible. At every turn it is manifest that a great loss has been sustained and that a central figure, one dear to the people, has disappeared.[48]

One of the most generous tributes paid to Hermione – 'our duchess' – was written by Katharine Carmarthen on behalf of Alexandra College in Dublin, a private school for girls to which Hermione had acted as patron for a number of years (and where there remains a bust of her donated by Lord Frederick FitzGerald in October 1908).[49] The tribute referred to her 'loveliness, magic and grace', the inspiring power of her personality, her generous efforts to promote the welfare of the college, her own 'great gifts, artistic and intellectual', 'her insatiable longing to <u>know</u>, to understand all that is best knowing' and the power 'to recognize the essential truth and meaning of things'.[50] The duke's chaplain, Revd Ganly, remembered her 'grace of manner, charm of person, and innate goodness of heart' that he believed not only 'graced Irish society, but contributed in no small degree to the successful and happy state in which all connected with the estate at present obtains'.[51]

Thus, the social memory of Hermione's death was imbued with the great sense of loss felt by public bodies, educational institutions, the impoverished of Maynooth, family and servants. Hermione's private persona was, however, much different to her public persona. This hardly made her unique then or historically; she was neither the first nor the last tragic and flawed character to achieve iconic status in light of her premature death. Perhaps revealingly, in none of her letters which have survived did she make mention of her concerns for public matters or public duties.

III

When Mary Elcho arrived with Wilfrid Blunt at Sheyk Obeyd, a stud farm that he had established near Cairo to raise Arabian horses for export to his Crabbet Arabian Stud in England, there was a telegram awaiting her from Hugo: 'I am unhappy. Shall wait for you at Rome'.[52] Mary knew that Hermione must have died. Shortly afterwards she and Hugo met and were reconciled. On 30 March 1895, a week after Hermione's death, Hugo wrote a rebuking letter to Blunt:

> You have wrecked the life and destroyed the happiness of a woman whom a spark of chivalry would have made you protect. She was thirty years [recte twenty-two] younger than yourself. You had known her from childhood. She was your cousin and your guest. She was a happy woman when she went to Egypt, and her misery now would touch a heart of stone.[53]

A few weeks later in a secret meeting with Blunt, Mary confessed that Hugo had allegedly said to her: 'If it had been Arthur [Balfour] I could have understood it, but I cannot understand it now. I forgive you but I shall be nasty to you.'[54]

IV

Hermione's three children were now orphans. There is no evidence that Edward had any contact with his biological father thereafter. He never mentioned his extramarital paternity in any of his writings and it never seems to have come up during his lifetime. Did he know? Maurice was eight years old and

Desmond seven when their mother died. They had not seen her for seven months before her death and so their uncle, Lord Frederick, wrote to Evelyn: 'I do not think from what I hear that they thoroughly realize their loss. They had got accustomed to her absence, as they have not seen her since August.'[55] His note said more about the unmarried Frederick's lack of understanding of the children's emotions.[56] As we shall see, the physical and emotional loss of both parents undoubtedly contributed to the fashioning of at least two of the personalities of Hermione's sons, those of the eldest, Maurice, and the youngest, Edward.

The children lived away from Carton for most of their youth, in particular with their aunt, Lady Cynthia Graham, at Netherby. She had been particularly close to Hermione and her constant companion, along with her mother, in her last few months. The children became extremely fond of her. As Desmond, for example, grew into friendship with Edward, Prince of Wales, later King Edward VIII, he would tell him of his affection for Cynthia, while Edward's mother, Queen Mary, would write to her some years later: 'he was almost like a son to you and so devoted … Desmond always spoke so affectionately of you'.[57] If not with Cynthia, the children spent their time with their grandparents in Duncombe Park or their London residence on Belgrave Square and occasionally newspapers reported their return to London 'having spent a delightful holiday at Carton'.[58]

Years before, when Maurice and Desmond ran carefree around the demesne, Hermione had dreamed of future summers at Carton and 'the life that I may live there with my boys', sharing 'their fresh young lives, angelic natures, glad life spirits', and hoping that 'their lives may be in harmony with their dear beautiful natures'.[59] Much changed for her in the years that followed and much more would change for her children in the years after their parents' deaths. For now, though, the narrative must shift away from the children's lives in order to focus on a decade that was a watershed period for Carton and the Leinster estate, when all-important decisions were in the hands of trustees.

CHAPTER SIX

The sale of the Leinster estate, 1903

This [1903 Land Act] is a very far reaching measure; and the Irish government are sanguine that it will settle for all time the Irish land difficulty. The objections to it – and there are objections to all things – arise from the fact that it makes a heavy call on British credit, already handicapped by the past war loans and the Transvaal borrowings; and that it will be represented as a great gift to the Irish tenants and landlords at the cost of the British taxpayer. The cabinet did not underrate the force either of the financial or the political argument, but they were clearly of the opinion that in the interests of a great policy, minor difficulties must be ignored.

Arthur Balfour to King Edward VII, 1903[1]

Gerald was the first duke of Leinster to die before an heir had reached his majority. Maurice, his eldest son, was only six years old; Desmond was just gone five; and Edward was around eighteen months. There was no perceived threat to the family dynasty, but it did mean that trustees had to be appointed to take control of estate administration until Maurice would reach his majority in 1908.

The chief trustee nominated in Gerald's will was his brother, Lord Frederick (1857–1924). He had been educated at Eton and afterwards, following the long family tradition for younger sons, his family purchased a commission for him in the army; he became a captain in the King's Royal Rifle Corps. He saw at least fifteen years of active service: in the Afghan War of 1878–80 he fought at Ahmed Khel and Urzoo and in August 1880 he took part in the famous march from Kabul to Kandahar under Lord Roberts to relieve the besieged British garrison.[2] He went on further expeditions to South Africa and Egypt and saw action at Kassassin and Tel-el-Kebir. During the Sudan expedition of 1884 he was mentioned in dispatches and promoted to brevet-major, eventually rising to lieutenant-colonel.[3]

In between, on 16 January 1882, 'Lord Fred', as he was known locally, returned home for his sister Lady Alice's wedding to 'general rejoicings in Maynooth'. This was a time when land agitation and the continued

TORD F FITZGERALD
MAYNOOTH

19 Lord Frederick
FitzGerald (1857–1924)
in military dress.

imprisonment of the Irish nationalist leader, Charles Stewart Parnell (reported
in the same paper as the celebrations), might have curtailed any show of local
enthusiasm for the returning son of the duke of Leinster. But this was not the
case; instead the town of Maynooth was 'brilliantly illuminated' and tar barrels
were lighted in the ruins of the ancestral castle and on the Tyrconnell tower on
the demesne. There was a larger bonfire in the market square and an impressive
display of fireworks. When Lords Frederick and Walter, his brother, appeared
on the streets it was 'the general signal for a splendid ovation … The local band
played during the night and merrymaking was kept up till about ten o'clock'.[4]
One report claimed that the locals peered closely at Frederick 'to see what
changes an Indian sun had wrought upon his face'.[5] After that, it seems he
came just once more to Ireland, for his father's funeral in 1887, before taking
charge of the estate in 1893. From then until his death in 1924, the surviving
sources suggest that Lord Frederick became duke of Leinster in all but name.
Unfortunately, he has left no personal papers that might shed light on his
personality, life, ambitions and so on, but that may well have been a deliberate
act on his behalf.

20 Carton House, *c.*1920

The second trustee nominated in Gerald's will was Arthur FitzGerald (1847–1923), 11th Lord Kinnaird of Inchture and 3rd Lord Kinnaird of Rossie, a distant cousin but close family friend. Kinnaird was an extremely interesting character. His grandfather had married Olivia, the youngest daughter of William, 2nd duke of Leinster. Born in London, he attended Eton in the 1860s, at the same time as Frederick, where he excelled at sport before moving on to Trinity College, Cambridge. After leaving university, he went into banking and quickly became a partner in the West End firm of Ranson, Bouverie & Co. – a firm with which his family had been associated with since the eighteenth century. Following a series of amalgamations the firm became Barclay's Bank Ltd in 1896 and Kinnaird was appointed a director (the local head office in Pall Mall was subsequently named after him). From an early stage of his career Kinnaird immersed himself in charity work, following the example of his mother who was a founder of the Foreign Evangelization

Society, and he became co-founder of Homes for Working Boys. His work for Christian youth organizations (such as the YWCA and YMCA) continued throughout his life. However, it is for his role in the development of association football that he is chiefly remembered. Acknowledged as one of the greatest footballers of his generation, he played in eleven FA cup finals (including two replays, a record unlikely ever to be beaten), winning five times, and he was capped at international level for Scotland. As an administrator he oversaw the transition of soccer from an amateur to professional sport and he became president of the FA in 1890. One biographer has noted:

> Although real power on the FA council had shifted towards more bourgeois types, Kinnaird's position as a nobleman, his presence, and his personality helped to develop the game's ties both with the leaders of the political parties and with the monarchy. Lord Rosebery, A.J. Balfour, and the king himself were all guests of honour with Kinnaird at cup finals before the First World War.[6]

As well as his family connections and his experience in the world of financial affairs, his political connections made him an attractive choice as trustee.

II

Frederick took up residence at Carton enjoying all the trappings of life there, albeit with a diminished retinue of servants (only eight were returned in the 1901 census although more may, of course, have been living outside the house). As main trustee he managed all estate affairs and retained the services of Charles Hamilton as estate agent. He never married, though there are many anecdotes passed down in local lore – unsubstantiated it should be noted – of his penchant for young women. Thomas Nelson has pointed out that 'Local folk memory describes Lord Frederick as being amorously predatory on the female servants and the rate of turnover of staff may give some credence to the local gossip'.[7] Nelson shows that none of the servants returned for the house in 1901 were returned in the 1911 census but, of course, there may have been many other reasons for this turnover.[8]

At the highest level, he maintained close relationships with the royal family. In January 1895, he dined with Queen Victoria at Osborne.[9] In April 1899, the duchess of York visited Carton and in July of the same year, the duke and duchess of Connaught.[10] It has already been noted that in June 1902, his nephew, Maurice, by then 6th duke of Leinster, was a pageboy at the coronation of King Edward VII, while Maurice's younger brother, Desmond, would become Edward, Prince of Wales' closest friend. And, as was noted in chapter two, Frederick kept the Catholic Church on side.

But within Frederick's social and political orbits revolutionary change was underway. Over the previous two decades Irish politics had been transformed by the growth of the nationalist Home Rule movement (closely associated with the Land League) and the Franchise and Redistribution Acts of 1884–5, which greatly expanded the electorate. Farmers, shopkeepers and publicans, the very sectors who led the Land League, were clamouring for political representation that would reflect their new-found prosperity. It was a trend that was not, of course, unique to Ireland. Equally in Britain, the idea that the landed class had some traditional right to parliamentary representation and political leadership at local and national levels was becoming anachronistic as the rapidly expanding electorate and a rising urban middle class clamoured for a share of power. In 1880, Benjamin Disraeli, former Conservative prime minister, had forewarned that the politics of Great Britain would 'probably for the next few years mainly consist of an assault upon the constitutional position of the landed class'.[11] In Ireland the assault was completed over a relative short period of time. Of the 105 MPs returned for Ireland in 1859, 87 had been landlords; of the 103 MPs elected in the 1885 election, only 5 were landlords with more than £1,000 valuation and 75 were Catholics.[12]

Their decimation at the polls in the 1885 election heightened landlord and wider Protestant apprehensions about their prospects under a Catholic nationalist-dominated Home Rule parliament in Dublin and encouraged all Protestant classes and denominations, former Liberals and Conservatives, to unite as unionists 'in an attempt to maintain minority ascendancy interests and influence'.[13] It has already been noted that Frederick's brother, the 5th duke, had been prominent in the unionist movement which had defeated the first two Home Rule bills in 1886 and 1893. Frederick took up the unionist mantle. Thus, he was opposed to the popular political will of nationalist Ireland: outside of the Leinster estate he was noted for 'his hostile feeling towards Home Rule', and charged with 'not understand[ing] the feelings of the people' and being 'a bitter unionist'.[14] However, Frederick played local politics very well. His election to the first Kildare County Council in 1899 was testament to this, but also to the deep-rooted local loyalty to the FitzGeralds of Carton.

The general case stated was that nationalists wanted to use the local government elections of 1899 to prove that Ireland demanded Home Rule and that the people (meaning the Catholic nationalist majority) were capable of governing themselves. At a meeting in Ballitore in Co. Kildare, about eight miles from the Leinster residence at Kilkea castle, to select nationalist candidates for the elections, it was contended: 'The first great measure everybody has before him is Home Rule (applause). This local government board is an intermediate system of education for Home Rule'.[15] John Redmond would later argue that the act brought about a social revolution that 'disestablished the old ascendancy class from its position of power and made the mass of the Irish people masters of all the finance and all the local affairs of Ireland'.[16] The statistics agree: by 1907, only eighteen of the 694 councillors in the twenty-six county area of the present Irish Republic could be considered unionists and just a third of these were landlords.[17]

In the run up to the elections, an editorial in the nationalist *Freeman's Journal* had urged the electorate to reject unionist candidates, specifically naming Lord Frederick, whose family, it claimed, had oppressed the people of Kildare in much the same way as a Russian oligarch.[18] It was orthodox nationalist rhetoric that would have appealed to tenants on many estates in Ireland but not to the electorate of Maynooth.[19] As surrogate duke of Leinster, Lord Frederick had the support of the local Maynooth power brokers. In February 1899, two months before the elections, a meeting took place in the town to nominate candidates. On the motion of Dr Edward O'Kelly, seconded by John Haughton, a butcher on Main Street, the chair was taken by Robert Mooney, a substantial farmer who also resided on Main Street. Mill owners, James Kavanagh and Joseph McArdle, were appointed secretaries. O'Kelly proposed Lord Frederick and 'in the course of an eloquent speech pointed out the many claims Lord Frederick had upon their support', alluding to the legacy of the FitzGerald residency for over 700 years, meaning the social and economic benefits accruing to professionals such as himself and the businessmen of the town and large farmers of the surrounding hinterland. The motion was 'carried unanimously amidst great enthusiasm'. The middle-class cliques in Maynooth had few problems, even at this late stage of the nineteenth century, with supporting the candidature of the local landlord in the face of wider nationalist opposition. They did, however, make their point that political agendas were now dictated by nationalist agendas and so they passed motions that would have simultaneously resonated with the expanded local government electorate, expressing support for Home Rule; a Catholic university bill; the release of political prisoners (those convicted of the Fenian dynamiting campaign in Britain in the 1880s towards whom it seems Lord Frederick was particularly opposed and was accused of having 'a callous attitude');[20] the restoration of evicted tenants; a compulsory land act and an amendment to the

21 A group of young thistle cutters about to begin work on Carton demesne *c*.1910
(courtesy of Bridie O'Brien).

Labourers Act to enable them to purchase their homes along with small plots
of land.[21]

In the neighbouring town of Leixlip, which was not part of the Leinster
estate, Frederick's star was not quite so bright; from there it was reported that
the feeling was that 'if Lord Edward were living today in Maynooth there is
little doubt how he would vote. It would not be for a Geraldine who had
deserted to the Union.'[22] Frederick was politically astute enough to turn the
tables and he used the iconic status of Lord Edward to his advantage with his
election posters proclaiming: 'Remember the spirit of Lord Edward and
1798'.[23] He might also be described as a late nineteenth-century spin doctor
who manipulated the press, especially the local press, for his own purposes (and
this will also be evident in later chapters). In the run up to the elections, stories

of his sympathy for the tenantry began to appear in the local newspapers. One anecdote placed him at the centre of an eviction in the north of Ireland. He was there in his capacity as an army officer to oversee proceedings but notably the eviction was located in the remote north, well removed from his native county. He was asked by an old man if he was a relative of Lord Edward (who had estates in Co. Down that were attainted after the 1798 rebellion). When Frederick replied that he was a direct descendant, the old man enquired further why he was in the eviction party given that Lord Edward was 'such a friend of Mr Parnell'. Frederick told the old man that Lord Edward had been dead a hundred years, but the former retorted: 'Divil may care. If he was alive wouldn't he be on Mr Parnell's side', to which Lord Frederick replied: 'I believe he would be'.[24] Thus he managed to portray the United Irishman as a would-be supporter of Charles Stewart Parnell, thereby linking the FitzGerald legacy with the late champion of Home Rule and former president of the Irish National Land League.

Moreover, when the passing of the Local Government Bill for Ireland became inevitable Frederick opened up Carton to visitors in what might be considered another astute political move, just as his father had done after the Leinster lease controversy. As well as tours of the demesne and house, people could visit the 'estate museum [which exhibited] varied collections of curios and antiquities including Irish bog wood ornaments'.[25] The local press coverage of this development presented Frederick as an enlightened supporter of the people. Shortly after the first elections were held in 1899, and he had been safely elected, he closed the demesne once again on the pretext of 'the conduct of some excursionists who, being privileged to meander through the extensive and lovely grounds, did a considerable amount of damage'.[26]

In the meantime, Frederick defeated his opponent, William Rutherford, a strong farmer from Tipperkevin, by 235 votes to 163 under the first past the post system.[27] News of Frederick's election gave rise to celebrations in the Maynooth area and when he arrived on the outskirts of the town, locals unhitched the horses from his carriage and pulled it up to Carton.[28] For over twenty years he remained a member of the nationalist dominated council (and for much of that same period sat on the executive committee of the Irish Unionist Alliance).[29] The council remained conservative and cautious right up to independence and Frederick played a conspicuous role in its deliberations, his attendance being exemplary even at the height of the War of Independence in 1920–1, when travel was dangerous. But Tom Nelson makes the relevant point: 'It is understandable, given that he was a trustee of the largest estate in the county and a substantial rate payer himself … that he should wish to keep an eye on proceedings that led each year to the striking of the rates for the county'.[30] And in the early years, some of the estate's most influential tenants sat with him on the same council.

Frederick was the last of the Kildare FitzGeralds to become a public representative in that county or anywhere else. In the broader context, the political landscape once dominated by his ancestors had vanished after 1880 and especially with the Franchise and Redistribution Acts of 1884–5. While he might sit comfortably on the council he was still reminded at the initial meeting that its majority supported 'the right of the Irish nation to a full measure of self government' and resolved to: 'accept the Local Government Act as the first instalment of the same and call on the imperial parliament to proceed with the full restitution of our rights'.[31] Democratization had overtaken the aristocracy in Ireland and even the senior representative of the most powerful noble family had to recognize the impact of the growth of nationalism. And while the Maynooth estate may have continued to acknowledge the traditional deferential dialectic in the election of Frederick, it was within the context that the new political elite, ironically created in the post-Famine decades by the Leinsters' desire to create a progressive class of tenant farmer, no longer had to compete with the landlord for political control at local government or national level. Moreover, four years after his election, Frederick was faced with an even greater challenge than a county council resolution in support of Home Rule: the negotiation of the sale of the Leinster estate.

III

In late nineteenth-century Ireland, national and global economic developments meant that the future sustainability of great estates was becoming increasingly problematic. The worsening state of agriculture in the face of massive international competition, the decline in rents due to government intervention and increasing interest rates on borrowing meant that landlords' diminishing incomes were, at best, just enough to cover their expensive lifestyles. Estate ownership had become a burden few could any longer afford. The land acts from 1881 to 1896 had been only moderately successful in terms of the transfer of landownership and so in March 1902 the chief secretary for Ireland, George Wyndham, announced in the House of Commons that they had reached 'the end of the landlords who are prepared to sell for a capital sum which can be advanced under the existing law'. The most important landlord organization, the Irish Landowners' Convention, suggested in October of the same year that landlords would be prepared to sell their estates 'at a price which if invested at three per cent [would] yield an income approximately equal to their present net income'.[32] A conference followed in December of that year which brought together landlord and tenant representatives in an attempt to bridge the gulf between what landlords would settle for and what tenants were prepared to offer. The result was a report published in January 1903 which became the basis for the land act introduced that year by George Wyndham.[33]

Wyndham's act was the first serious attempt to provide the inducements for landlords to sell (while simultaneously making purchase a realistic goal for Irish tenants). Payment of the entire purchase money was to be advanced to landlords by a newly established branch of the Irish Land Commission, the Estates Commissioners. As an extra inducement landlords were paid an additional 12 per cent cash bonus on the sale of estates, which made them more confident that the capital they would receive would allow them to move smoothly and profitably from a rental income to an income derived from investments.[34]

Unfortunately, no Leinster estate rentals or accounts seem to have survived for this crucial period but it is to be presumed that the estate's financial situation was no different to most and, therefore, the trustees could ill afford to ignore the generous terms on offer. Nor is anything known about the actual decision-making process regarding the sale of the estate except that Maurice, the heir, was still a minor and would not come of age until 1908 and so the trustees were empowered to act on his behalf both under the terms of the existing settlement, and within the terms of the 1903 legislation. It may simply be the case that Frederick, like most Irish landlords at the time, saw an opportunity that was too good to overlook – the Wyndham act represented the first recorded bailout (to adopt a modern phrase) of a previous elite. His fellow trustee, Lord Kinnaird, was an experienced financier who probably recognized that the sale of the estate followed by astute investment would benefit the family much more than any continued rental income in a prolonged period of agricultural depression. In the absence of contemporary evidence, there is little point in speculating as to how Frederick and Kinnaird perceived the sale would benefit them personally.[35]

While landownership in Ireland no longer went hand-in-hand with political power, there were still those who did not believe that a ducal title should be separated from the traditional symbol of its status and that a ducal title without land would simply be an aberration. Thus, in the House of Lords, Lord Muskerry was scathing of the trustees' decision to sell: 'One great estate, which used to support the highest dignity in the Irish peerage, has been sacrificed for ready money by the guardians of a minor, with little respect for the future of a title divorced from property and residence'.[36]

One of the more interesting questions is whether Wyndham's personal attachment to the FitzGeralds was important enough to ensure that the Leinster estate was the first great aristocratic estate to be sold under the terms of his act in November 1903. As noted above, Wyndham was a direct descendant of Lord Edward FitzGerald. In the period 1887–91, Wyndham had been private secretary to Arthur Balfour when he was chief secretary for Ireland and by 1903 Balfour was prime minister of Great Britain. Both men were familiar with Carton during the years of agrarian agitation. In their official capacities they had paid numerous courtesy visits to the 5th duke, and had met with him formally and socially in Carton and his Dublin town house. In April 1893, when in opposition during the second Home Rule crisis, Balfour travelled to Belfast and Dublin to deliver keynote addresses at two massive unionist demonstrations and stayed in between at Carton. (Balfour and Wyndham also knew Hermione through the Souls.) It is hard to imagine they would not have discussed land matters with the duke: after all, he was both Ireland's premier peer and one of the largest vendors under the 1885 Land Act, so his advice would have been valuable. There may have been an element of truth in the claim that Wyndham's 'great [personal] ambition … to do something for Ireland', was linked to his FitzGerald lineage.[37] Elizabeth Fingall was in no doubt of this when she recalled that the 'most romantic and beautiful' Wyndham was 'as conscious of that [FitzGerald] heritage as was the country that welcomed him' and she noted that his 'first pilgrimage' on his arrival in Ireland was to the tomb of Lord Edward in Thomas Street.[38] Elizabeth presumed to know enough about Wyndham to claim that he could never pass Leinster House in Dublin without 'a feeling of deep emotion'.[39] Unfortunately, access to Wyndham's private papers at Eaton Hall was denied to this author, but it is notable that six weeks after the act received the royal assent, Wyndham happily reported to Balfour that the purchase agreement for the Leinster estate represented 'a good deal' for the trustees.[40]

IV

The sale of the most high profile estate in Ireland aroused enormous media attention and, of course, caused great excitement among the tenantry in Kildare. On 25 September 1903, an irony-laden report in the *Irish Times* thought it 'a remarkable coincidence that the oldest estate in Ireland is the first to be sold under the new act' and concluded that this enormous sum, of which a substantial amount consists of a bonus given by the State which the Geraldine family tried so often to wreck, should come into the possession of the chief of the famous family after all its 'treasons, stratagems and spoils', is a most extraordinary proof of the tremendous power and influence wielded by it in the past.[41]

It made no direct reference to contemporary family connections from Wyndham to the Royal Court.

But it was not just the power of the FitzGeralds or their connections: much also depended on coming quickly to an agreed price with the tenantry and this is where the estate policy in the past of populating the land with large prosperous farmers became significant. Ten days before the *Irish Times* article the trustees first informed the tenants of their intention to sell. An emergency meeting of the larger tenants was convened at very short notice in the town of Athy on the southern Kildare estate. The elected chairman was Matthew J. Minch. He was a very large farmer who resided at Rockfield House – symbolic of his aspirations towards squirearchy – and a very prosperous corn and malt merchant, owner of Minch Nortons Maltings. Rather typically of his class, he had propelled himself to political prominence via the Land League in Kildare and became Irish Parliamentary Party MP for the southern constituency from 1882 to 1903. He educated his sons at Blackrock College in Dublin; one of them, John Benchman Minch, would become (to date) the only Athy man to win full international caps for Ireland at rugby. John qualified as a doctor, joined the Royal Army Medical Corps and spent his army career in India, dying in 1942. Two of his brothers joined the British army during the Great War, both reaching the rank of captain.[42] Thus, Matthew J. Minch was one of those late nineteenth-century emerging Catholic middle-class men who could simultaneously benefit from the patronage of his aristocratic landlord, use the empire for the benefit of his sons, and still credibly become a nationalist MP and place himself at the forefront of mass land movements (in 1903 he still claimed to be a member of the United Irish League).

Minch's speech to the large tenants at Athy was equally illuminating: 'Of course our meeting here today does not comprise all the Leinster tenants, inasmuch as the time was short and circulars were only sent out to those whose names we could secure at very short notice'.[43] It is probably safe to conclude that few attempts were made to contact the smaller, socio-politically insignificant tenants. When, during the following month, the agrarian agitator, Denis Kilbride (1848–1924), who had recently replaced Minch as MP for South Kildare, addressed another meeting in Athy, he clearly suggested that there was an element of subterfuge in the negotiations to date: 'he had heard that a circular was sent out to the Leinster tenants calling a meeting in Athy. That circular was received in most cases on Monday, and the meeting was called for Tuesday, while several tenants never got a circular at all. How could a tenant imagine that he is bound by an agreement made behind his back?'[44] He did not say he had heard of the meeting too late to attend, but perhaps the subterfuge went as far as keeping an experienced agitator such as himself away until the grazier element had made their bid.

Minch's membership of the UIL was a political smoke screen: the organization that was founded in 1898 with the motto 'The land for the people' (not by any means an original one) and with the objective of removing the very graziers that the likes of Minch represented in order to alleviate the plight of small uneconomic holders was largely moribund in Co. Kildare. Notably, the county executive remained aloof from negotiations on the Leinster estate.[45] Instead, various committees, appointed at local level, negotiated with the estate's representatives. The Athy committee, for example, was comprised of men of significant property, just like Minch, and Protestant as well as Catholic. Of ten men named in the newspaper, only one, Anthony Reeves (80 acres), farmed less than 150 acres. As well as Minch who was an MP until 1903, the others included Edward Hayden who was a county councillor and Thomas Anderson, Richard Wright and John Gannon who were all socially respectable enough to have been nominated as justices of the peace.[46] After the deputation had met the Leinster agent, Charles Hamilton, in Dublin on 17 September, two days after the Athy meeting, the *Freeman's Journal* sniped that the large farmers who were dictating the terms were men 'with heaps of money, made in business, and others who have splendid situations'. Nearer home, the *Nationalist and Leinster Times* was more cutting; these were 'the big men and Scotchmen who have got the fat of the land'.[47] Social memory had, it seems, reserved a special mention for the Scotch planters brought into the Athy area after the Famine by the 3rd duke of Leinster but fell short of recognizing that they were still in a minority when compared with their Catholic grazier and merchant counterparts.

The situation was similar in Maynooth where a meeting was held on 21 September chaired jointly by Laurence Ball and Thomas Shaw. Ball described himself in his 1901 census return as 'Grazier J.P.' Shaw was also a grazier but he was a Presbyterian who had been born in Co. Down. Thus, there was an ecumenical aspect to the various estate deputations. As the *National and Leinster Times* rightly pointed out the Maynooth estate 'was mostly made up of grazing lands, held by some of the leading graziers of Kildare and Meath', so it was small wonder that 'the grazier element predominated and took charge of the meeting'. The deputation chosen to negotiate included (as well as Shaw and Ball) John Langan, Mark Travers, James Patterson and Richard McKenna, all of whom farmed in excess of 100 acres. They were to be accompanied by local solicitor, Stephen Browne, who was also chairman of the Kildare County Council.

In the estate meetings that followed, platforms were crowded with the professionals, the shopocracy and the large farmers of the county, members of the county council, urban district councils, rural district councils, boards of poor law guardians and not least of all the local Catholic clergy. These meetings were an opportunity for political and social capital that no existing or aspiring politician or Catholic clergyman could afford to miss. Effectively, the day of the big farmer and the prosperous townsmen who had won the Land War had come. The purchase of their farms under the terms which they were happy to negotiate would represent what might be regarded as their final victory.

One can sense from what was reported to have been said and by whom that there was a desperation on the part of the large graziers to get things settled as quickly as possible, while the smaller tenants and those in the agriculturally poorer parts of the estate, especially around Castledermot, wanted more time to assess their position.[48] One smallholder represented the case of his class: 'it's all very well for the big bugs around Athy to give twenty-five years' purchase, but it's different with us'.[49] When the smaller tenants around Castledermot eventually met on 27 September the meeting highlighted once again traditional perceptions of paternalism on the estate: '[the duke] always gave the tenants better terms than other landlords (hear, hear). A voice – he was a good man. Another voice – better than the government will be.'[50] The latter was an interesting comment: it suggested that the smaller tenants were apprehensive of purchasing and becoming liable to the state, which during economic recession might not be as sympathetic as a patriarchal landlord had been in the past. Was the Irish Land Commission likely to grant a 20 per cent annuity reduction if agricultural prices collapsed as they did in the late 1870s?

At another meeting, Denis Kilbride also highlighted the question of the labourers:

> From his twenty five years' experience of Irish politics he believed that the most unselfish class in the community – the men who sacrificed most for the advancement of the National cause – were the labourers (hear, hear). They all could remember what took place in the early Land League days

of '79, '80, and '81. When the labourer in those days was going to meetings a distance of 7 and 10 miles, where was the farmer? (A voice: at home). He was hiding behind the ditch to see who was going (laughter and applause), afraid of his life that the bailiff and the rent warner would see him going to Land League meetings, and report it to the office and probably bring him into disrepute.[51]

There was certainly an element of truth in what he said. All over Ireland, leaders of the Land League had made promises during the Land War that proved empty when the large farmers secured the fixing of fair rents under the 1881 Land Act. Politicians like Kilbride might now want to appease labourers once again but their plight was not high on the agenda of the larger Leinster tenants who had waited to become purchasers. Proprietorship would be the fruition of all the gains they had made in the post-Famine decades. From their perspective, the advantages of having annuities lower than annual rents were clearly articulated by a 'Leinster tenant' to the *Irish Times*. 'Leinster tenant' pointed out that under the 1881 Land Act rents had been reduced by 20 per cent in the first term, which were to last until 1897, but because of continued agricultural depression they were further reduced before then by 12.5 per cent in what became known as 'the second term'. 'Now', he argued, 'we have a further reduction of 18.75 per cent, making a total of nearly 50 per cent on the original rents'.[52] While landlords and tenants were still allowed freedom on agreeing upon the purchase price, sales were no longer limited to individual tenants or holdings but applied *en bloc* to a whole estate, in which case the larger and more socially prestigious tenants held the upper hand. The further reduction that 'Leinster tenant' referred to arose from the fact that the purchase price could only be fixed between certain maxima and minima laid down by the act which were termed 'zones'. This guaranteed the tenant that the annuity payable by him represented a 10–30 per cent reduction on his formal rent in the case of second-term judicial rents and 20–40 per cent in the case of first-term rents.[53] Thus, D.J. Cogan, MP for neighbouring Wicklow, could draw only one conclusion from the negotiations on the Leinster estate: 'the wealthier and stronger tenants rushed the sale to the disadvantage of their poorer neighbours'.[54] And he was right.

Under the final terms of agreement, the tenants gave twenty-five years' purchase, arrears up to March 1903 were added to the purchase money, and all sporting rights were reserved to the young duke. There were some exaggerated estimates of what this would mean financially to the duke, putting the figure (including the 12 per cent bonus) at almost £1.4 million.[55] In fact, the trustees received £500,278 from the sale of the unsettled estates and £254,347 from settled estates (including bonuses in both cases), a total of £754,265.[56] But this was still huge by any standards – around £73 million in today's terms. To put this into some perspective: the highest paid employee in Carton, the butler, would have had to work 6,650 years to earn that much; an estate labourer would have had to work 66,500 years; at a time when there were 240 pence in the pound, milk cost 8 pence per gallon, oats 2 pence per bushel, wheat 3 pence per bushel, potatoes 6.5 pence per hundredweight, a craft worker was paid 80 pence a day and a building labourer 58 pence.[57] The *Irish Times* concluded that for a family that had received its lands from the crown and who then provided generations of rebels, the settlement was a transaction without 'romantic parallel' anywhere else in Europe.[58]

If the British government had been intent on bailing out the Irish landlords and doing them a financial favour, there were two very different schools of thought on the Leinster sale. On the one hand, there were those landlords who supported the negotiated prices, hoping that they would set the precedent for others to follow: the right mix of strong prosperous tenants and good agricultural land was a cocktail for high prices. On the other hand, such high prices were never going to be universal; they would simply have made the act unworkable. Given that the British Treasury had agreed to allocate only £5 million per annum, one estate out of thousands in the country as a whole had already gobbled up 15 per cent of the allocation for year one. The simple fact is that the trustees acted quickly enough to have got away with it. On 31 January 1905, a Charles P. Johnson wrote privately to Lord Frederick explaining his disappointment that the Dunsany estate in neighbouring Meath had not been sold on the same favourable terms as the Leinster estate. Johnson claimed that Lord Dunsany's uncle, Sir Horace Plunkett (1854–1932), a pioneer of agricultural co-operation in Ireland, had told him: 'if negotiations between the duke and his tenants were to be initiated now I have good reason to believe that his Grace would not fare nearly so well, even if, which is doubtful, all the tenants were accepted as purchasers'. Johnson concluded: 'I think that it will be satisfactory to <u>you</u> to have this opinion of an expert to place with your papers as confirmatory of the propriety and wisdom of the action which you took on your nephew's behalf'.[59]

The more prosperous tenants had no difficulties with the prices agreed or, indeed, having to make up the cash difference where the maximum advance from the Land Commission was not enough to meet the full price of a holding. Kildare county councillor, Edward Hayden, defended the 25 years' purchase and was warm in his praise of Leinster: 'he always gave the tenants better terms than other landlords,' he told a gathering and reminded his audience that 'You all know that the duke acted very liberally and allowed the tenants half the county cess'.[60] But Hayden was one of the largest purchasers on the estate, having paid £152 in excess of the maximum of £7,000 that could be advanced by the estates commissioners under the terms of the act for an individual purchase.[61] Others who paid in excess of the £7,000 limit included 'gentleman farmer' and deputy lieutenant of Kildare, T.W. Greene of Kilkea (paid £1,604 in excess); the widowed Eliza M. Walsh of Newtown (£650); and Thomas Anderson JP of Nurney (who paid £83 in excess and could afford to employ a governess, a cook and two housemaids).[62] In total, almost seventy-seven tenants on the Leinster estate received advances in excess of £3,000.[63] Even when there was disgruntlement expressed at a meeting in Castledermot against the duke being allowed to retain the sporting rights, John Rice, a prominent shopkeeper, responded: 'It is better to have these men in the country than have no one. We want the landlords to stop in the country and spend their money in it.'[64] It summed up how those who lived and prospered on the Leinster estate felt about paternalism.

However, the large Leinster tenants were widely assailed from within the county and further abroad. 'W.H.', writing from Maynooth to the *Freeman's Journal*, concluded that 'a more grievous wrong could hardly be inflicted … on the small tillage tenants than by their inclusion in Mr Minch's cast-iron mould of uniformity, and this is just the body of tenants least capable of understanding the injustice'.[65] Another correspondent to the same paper, identifying himself only as 'Nemo' (which may be instructive if he was influenced by Jules Verne's anti-hero driven by anti-imperialism and hatred of oppression) wrote:

> In the negotiations which have been carried on with the Leinster trustees, I have seen the names of these shopkeepers and businessmen in a very prominent position, together with the names of a few descendants of those Scotchmen, who in the old days were fondled by Hamilton and his master, the then duke of Leinster, and who got their farms at a figure never dreamt of by Irish men. These men certainly have cogent reasons for the eulogies which they have passed upon the dukes of Leinster.[66]

The Leinster estate set too high a precedent for sales elsewhere in the country, particularly in areas of the west where the farmers could not possibly justify paying such a high rate for their land and then hope to make it viable. William O'Brien (1852–1928), founder of the United Irish League and an

56   RETURN OF ADVANCES MADE UNDER THE IRISH LAND ACT, 1903.

Estate of THE TRUSTEES OF THE DUKE OF LEINSTER.

Record No. E.C. 84.   (Manor of Maynooth).

Counties KILDARE and MEATH.

Nature of Proceedings:—Direct Sales—Estates Commissioners.

No.	Date of making the Advance.	Purchaser.	Townland.	Area.	Tenement Valuation (where known).	Rent.	Tenure of Tenant—Judicial or not Judicial.	Purchase Money.			Observations.
								Price.	Amount of the Advance.	Amount of payment in Cash.	
1	2	3	4	5	6	7	8	9	10	11	12
	1904			A. R. P.	£ s. d.	£ s. d.		£	£	£	
		County Kildare.									
1	April 29	Meleady, John	Blakestown	4 1 3	5 10 0	3 16 0	Judicial	84	84	.	
2	,,	Reilly, Peter	,,	73 2 5	91 0 0	87 6 4	..	2183	2183	.	
3	,,	Meleady, John	,,	95 1 36	103 0 0	96 7 0	Not Judl	2150	2150	.	
4	,,	Frayne, Patrick	Barreen	117 1 37	96 10 0	82 14 0	Judicial	2068	2068	.	
5	,,	Moloney, Eleanor (The assignees in Bankruptcy of)	Ballycurraghan / Maws	72 0 29 / 13 2 0	66 10 0 / 12 0 0	72 12 0	..	1644	1644	.	
6	,,	Graham, John J.	,,	122 3 27	142 0 0	137 2 8	,,	3428	3428	.	
7	,,	Bailey, Ellen	,,	287 0 4	356 15 0 (Part of)	300 0 0	,,	6672	6672	.	
8	,,	Cox, Mary	Crinstown	72 3 0	63 15 0	67 16 6	,,	1565	1565	.	
9	,,	Robinson, Mary	,,	145 2 0	131 15 0	140 0 0	,,	3370	3370	.	
10	,,	Dunne, Julia	Dowdstown	32 3 21	27 0 0	31 0 0	..	688	688	.	
11	,,	Lawless, Edward	Donaghstown	27 0 5	20 0 0	23 3 2	.,	579	579	.	
12	,,	Butler, Patrick Geo.	,, / Cormickstown	164 2 8 / 162 0 27	124 10 0 / 120 0 0	274 1 0	,,	6988	6988	.	
13	,,	Murphy, Anne	Graignesallagh	86 0 0	51 10 0	59 3 0	,,	1288	1288	.	
14	,,	Travers, Mark	,, / Cowanstown	119 1 22 / 0 0 32	102 15 0	96 17 0	Not Judl	2109	2109	.	
15	,,	Haulon, James	Graignesallagh / ,,	128 3 38 / 1 0 32	106 10 0 / 139 10 0	138 19 6	Judicial	3028	3028	.	
16	,,	Mooney, Joseph	Cowanstown / Kealstown	142 1 4 / 25 0 0	20 10 0	164 4 4	..	4105	4105	.	
17	,,	Dunne, Hugh	Johninstown	25 2 28	19 15 0	18 7 6	,,	400	400	.	
18	,,	Mooney, Robert	,,	58 2 23	36 15 0	43 0 0	..	1075	1075	.	
19	,,	Dunne, Michael	,,	42 0 4	26 15 0	27 3 0	,,	591	591	.	
20	,,	Burke, Tobias	,,	25 3 19	18 15 0	13 9 6	,,	337	337	.	
21	,,	Travers, Ellen	,,	36 1 14	20 5 0	26 10 6	,,	579	579	.	
22	,,	Travers, James	,,	35 2 0	20 15 0	17 8 6	,,	387	387	.	
23	,,	Connolly, Christopher	Laraghbryan, East / Maynooth, South	23 1 15 / 12 3 3	22 10 0 / 10 15 0	46 18 6	,,	1044	1044	.	
24	,,	Meabe, Alicia	Laraghbryan, East	48 2 28	58 5 0	53 6 6	Not Judl	1208	1208	.	
25	,,	McKeever, Mary Anne	Maynooth	4 2 38	.	8 14 2	,,	218	218	.	
26	,,	Kavanagh, Margt.	,,	16 0 0	55 0 0	62 0 0	,,	1550	1550	.	
27	,,	Keely, James	,,	68 2 10	81 10 0	93 6 6	Judicial	2033	2033	.	
28	,,	Hunt, Rev. Jas. Canon	,,	10 0 20	13 10 0	13 12 0	,,	296	296	.	
29	,,	Kelly, Martin F.	,,	34 1 20	49 5 0	36 19 0	..	924	924	.	

22 Parliamentary Return of Advances showing details of purchase agreements on part of the Leinster estate under the 1903 Land Act (http://eppi.dippam.ac.uk/documents/21078/eppi_pages/585074).

early proponent of the Wyndham Act, argued that the selfishness of the Leinster tenantry was to be deplored.[67] The *Irish Times* feared that the act would not be the final solution to the Irish land question if the price set a precedent for the smaller landlords who were closer to bankruptcy than the duke of Leinster. After all, it contended, his estate was the complete opposite to struggling estates along the western seaboard: it was more typical of an aristocratic English estate with large and improving tenants, very good and productive agricultural land, a number of relatively prosperous towns, well served by the railway system, and most of the estate was in close proximity to Dublin.[68] The circumstances of the Leinster estate were, in other words, in stark contrast to estates in the congested and impoverished areas of the west of Ireland. Thus, the report could only conclude that it was wrong 'to give advantages to those Irish tenants who are as well off as the agricultural tenants of England' rather than giving 'state aid to poor landlords and impoverished tenants, so that the State would be relieved of an agrarian agitation which has been a drain on the resources and patience of both countries'.[69]

Augustine Birell (1850–1933), the Liberal chief secretary for Ireland (1907–16), censured the amount received by the duke of Leinster when introducing his 1909 amending land act to parliament:

> … though it is eminently desirable that the imperial exchequer should assist in the agrarian revolution in Ireland, and in bringing about a satisfactory solution, yet nobody will say that for a well-managed estate like that of the duke of Leinster's the duke should get £80,000 [his estimate of the bonus received] into his breeches pocket for selling at market value an excellent estate upon which there has never been any particular amount of trouble.[70]

In the midst of all the controversy, there was no doubt but that the Leinster estate fared exceptionally well under the 1903 Land Act and that Augustus' policy of populating his estate with strong, progressive farmers and merchants had paid off. The question was how could the capital sum be invested so as to sustain a ducal lifestyle for the generations to come?

V

After expenses of sale (£22,815), including a commission of almost £5,600 to estate agent, Charles Hamilton, redemption of charges (£78,831) and duty (£294), roughly £665,000 was available for investment.[71] Now free from a myriad of familial and other financial obligations that traditionally had come with estate paternalism – upkeep of tenant properties, schools, charitable donations and so on – net income had the potential to be more substantial than at any time in recent generations. But most landlords who sold under the act were now in virgin territory and dependent upon outside advice from bankers and investors as to how best to invest the capital sum so as to ensure long term financial stability. The trustees of the Leinster estate relied on Lord Kinnaird, now director of Barclay's, the sixth largest bank in Britain. About twenty years before, one contemporary described a typical 'great merchant banker' in terms which would have applied to Kinnaird:

> The great merchant banker of today is an English gentleman of the finished type. He is possibly a peer, and an active partner in a great City firm: if he is not a peer the chances are he is a member of the House of Commons. He is a man of wide culture … There is in fact but one standard of 'social position' in England and that is that which is formed by the blending of the plutocratic and the aristocratic element.[72]

Merged aristocrats and merchant bankers such as Kinnaird were the financiers of British and overseas governments, the contact points for diplomats and men of power, by extension mainly aristocrats themselves, so that his position put him at the centre of elite society. Moreover, the prominent presence of members of the Rothschild family – probably the wealthiest banking family in the world at the time – at the 5th duke of Leinster's wedding to Hermione in 1884 further suggests that the FitzGeralds had long been blending the aristocratic with the plutocratic.

For the vast majority of Irish landlords the safeguarding of the capital received from the sale of their estates for succeeding generations was a daunting challenge. This was, after all, a massive cultural shift for them when one considers that in the past they had relied on their ownership of vast estates to maintain their economic, social and political status. Land had been the major constant in their lives; if mistakes were made in the lottery of share and mortgage dealings there would be nothing to fall back on. While they could control land in a variety of ways – who they gave access to as tenants, how much they charged in rents and so on – they were now dependent upon financial instruments they knew little about and worse over which they had no ultimate control.[73] Lord Frederick was more fortunate than most, confident in his cousin's ability to plan for a long-term return. However, an examination of the share portfolio raises more questions than it provides answers about the wisdom of its composition.

The vast bulk of the capital (£603,000) was initially invested in five mortgages – to Lord Tankerville (£298,000 at 3.5 per cent); Duncombe Shafto (£82,500 at 3.75 per cent); Col. H. Dennison (£59,000 at 3.75 per cent); Lord Fitzwilliam (£41,000 at 3.75 per cent) and Lord Hastings (£122,500 at 3.5 per cent). The most obvious question is why did the trustees invest 90 per cent in mortgages that had as their underlying security the very asset type they had just sold, namely land? Moreover, the point has already been made that for some years past banks and life assurance companies were cutting back on their investments in mortgages.[74] David Cannadine makes the point in relation to British aristocrats in the late nineteenth century with money to spare that they 'preferred to put it in equities rather than in land. As an investment it was probably more secure; it was certainly more liquid; and, if it was overseas, it avoided British income tax or death duties.'[75]

Other questions might be asked such as why did the Leinster trustees not invest in commercial property in London or even Dublin where residential properties were generating rental yields of around 9 per cent? Was it because of the ingrained aristocratic mindset that still convinced them that land, even if not their own, was the safest option? Or why did they not buy foreign land as Earl Fitzwilliam did in Canada; the duke of Westminster in Rhodesia, Canada and Australia; the duke of Sutherland in Canada and Florida; and others to the extent that Lord Esher explained to King George V (reigned from 1910 to 1936) that

> of late years, some of the greatest landowners among Your Majesty's subjects have been acquiring large estates in the dominions overseas. No one who has watched the course of recent legislation in this country, both fiscal and social, can fail to understand and to see the wisdom of those who have capital to invest, taking advantage of the fields still open in western Canada and certain parts of Africa.[76]

The decision to invest so heavily in mortgages defies rationality if, and this has its difficulties, one looks at the portfolio in terms of good investment practice in the modern era when a diversified portfolio might be created along the lines of 5 per cent retained in cash to meet immediate cash requirements; 25 per cent in government bonds to provide security and income; 40 per cent in property to provide income and capital appreciation and 30 per cent in equity to provide capital appreciation and some income. As one investment expert put it to this author:

Within each of the asset categories, with the possible exception of property, it would be considered ill advisable to have any single investment
accounting for more than 5 per cent of the particular asset class. Thus, in
the case of the bond and equity portfolios there would be a minimum of
20 individual securities and probably significantly more.[77]

Yet the trustees opted for an extraordinarily undiversified portfolio, investing
over 90 per cent in mortgages to just five parties, 6 per cent in bonds and 3.3
per cent in equities. Granted, the mortgages returned on average 3.6 per cent
per annum and the Irish Landowners' Convention, as noted above, had
suggested that Irish landlords would be prepared to sell their estates 'at a price
which if invested at three per cent [would] yield an income approximately
equal to their present net income'.[78] So the estate was getting the required
return. But mortgages did not have the liquidity of say colonial government
bonds, which according to contemporary quoted prices for dominions such as
Canada, Victoria, New South Wales and the Cape Provinces likewise yielded
3.5 per cent per annum. Back in September 1903, when the trustees were
meeting the Leinster tenants, the *Irish Times* was pointing out that it was
'equally important that landlords should sell quickly, and get as much of the
bonus as possible while "gild edged" investments are at their present price'.[79] It
had government stock in mind rather than mortgages; indeed almost twenty
years earlier the *Economist* had pointed out that 'No security was ever relied
upon with more implicit faith, and few have lately been found more wanting
than English land'.[80] And yet this is where the trustees looked to invest over
£600,000.

Only ten per cent of the capital received, just over £61,700, was invested in
stocks, including around £10,100 in Belfast Corporation stock; £9,200 in
Dublin Corporation 3.25 per cent stock; £8,600 in Belfast Corporation 3.25
stock; £6,213 in Bank of Ireland 11.5 per cent stock; and £9,700 in Irish
railways. There was investment in Caledonian Railway stock (around £5,900),
Bristol Corporation 3.25 stock (over £3,000), Lagos 3.25 inscribed stock
(under £3,000) and £2,000 (Cape 3.25 stock).[81] The obvious avoidance of
large-scale investment in equities is at odds with other Irish aristocratic
landlords such as the Dufferins, Ormondes and the Clonbrocks who in their
portfolios seem to have been much more confident with this asset class, while
Alvin Jackson has found that in relation to the sale of the 10,000-acre
Saunderson estate in Cavan, the owner converted the proceeds 'into an
extensive colonial share portfolio' and that 'only in Ireland did Somerset resist
investment'.[82] Like Saunderson, the Leinster trustees did not invest in Ireland.

This was contrary to what advocates of the Wyndham Land Act had hoped for. Galway landlord, John Shawe-Taylor, for example, had urged that 'it is of the greatest importance that income derived from the sale of property in Ireland should be expended in Ireland'.[83] Similarly, the 4th earl of Dunraven had hoped that by providing landlords with a large capital sum they would remain solvent and resident, and continue 'farming their own land, retaining the amenities of their position and finding … a larger scope for usefulness than they have hitherto enjoyed'.[84]

The general reluctance of landlords to invest in Ireland said much about their confidence in the future prosperity of the country and may have been influenced by the fallout from the so-called Devolution Crisis of 1904–5, which led Wyndham to resign. Then again, there were also the traditional cultural considerations of the aristocracy: they had not tended to use Ireland to educate their children or to look for career outlets for them; their political and spiritual home was very much England; and since the 1880s Irish nationalism had clearly marginalized them as the descendants of interloping colonizers with no place in the emerging Catholic, nationalist, Gaelic patrimony. But Patrick Cosgrove has identified another very important reason for this reluctance among Irish landlords – their fear of investing in an Ireland facing, once again, not only political uncertainty but another phase of agrarian agitation in the guise of a ranch war that erupted around 1907.[85] That year, Lord Ashtown from Galway claimed agitation was frightening landlords and their capital out of Ireland and told the Royal Commission on Congestion: 'As matters are going on now, the money they invest will leave the country. It will not be invested here'.[86] Cosgrove also quotes Hugh de F. Montgomery from Tyrone who declared that same year: 'in the present state of Ireland no conscientious trustees for any limited owner would think of investing one halfpenny in the trust funds of this country'.[87] And the earl of Donoughmore from Tipperary was quoted in the *Irish Times* as having asked: '… was it advisable to invest money in Irish undertakings when they did not know whether it would assist in the development of these undertakings? Was it advisable to do so with the prospect of Home Rule.'[88]

In the medium term the asset allocation had another major defect, namely a failure to protect its 'real' value from the ravages of inflation. It probably was not a consideration in 1904 because in the previous twenty years inflation had averaged only 0.1 per cent per annum, whereas in the twenty years following, largely as a result of the war years, it averaged over 4 per cent per annum, rising to 15.5 per cent in 1914–18. For a portfolio with little if any ability to generate capital appreciation and earning a yield of 3.6 per cent, this meant that in real terms its value would decline by roughly 0.5 per cent per annum.

There are not even any obvious clues as to why the trustees put faith in the integrity of the mortgagees in whom they invested. If there were connections between the five (and the FitzGeralds) they were in the main tenuous. George Bennet (1852–1931), seventh earl of Tankerville, who was granted the largest mortgage of £298,000 (a staggering £26.6 million in today's terms, representing an extreme over concentration of risk) had been in Ireland in the late 1870s as aide-de-camp to the then lord lieutenant, the duke of Marlborough. He was an officer in the Royal Rifles. George Astley, 20th Baron Hastings, received £122,500 (almost £11 million in today's terms) but died in September 1904. He belonged to a middle-ranking patrician family; he was a successful horse owner who won the Derby and the St Leger, and, interestingly, one of his most successful horses was named 'Lord Kildare'. In the 1922 portfolio the mortgage stood at £118,000, so only a marginal repayment of £4,000 of the principal had taken place in the intervening period. Col. H. Dennison was probably a member of the Dennison family of Ossington in Nottinghamshire who had large estates in Lincolnshire, Durham and Yorkshire and business interests in Leeds, and whose Victorian ancestors included a speaker of the House of Commons (John Evelyn Dennison, created Viscount Ossington). He may not have been a good investment. On 14 May 1916, a solicitor wrote to the duke of Portland who was trying to recover debts: 'I expect that we shall find that Col. Dennison is much more involved than he had led you to understand and that the whole of the estates are mortgaged very fully'.[89] His mortgage does not appear in the 1922 portfolio, so was it written off? Duncombe Shafto's first name is not given but it was likely Robert (d. 1909) whose father had been MP for North Durham in the mid-nineteenth century. Back in the late eighteenth century his ancestor had married Anne Duncombe, daughter and sole heir of Thomas Duncombe of Duncombe Park, and therefore he would have been a distant relation of the young duke. Perhaps of most interest is William Charles de Meuron (1872–1943), seventh earl Fitzwilliam, who himself sold considerable Irish estates under the 1903 act. He had become earl following his grandfather's death but he inherited a run-down estate and Wentworth Woodhouse in Yorkshire. He shared his second name 'de Meouron' with his place of birth, Pointe de Meouron in Canada. The circumstances of his birth were controversial; he was born in an extremely remote part of the Canadian frontier and there was later speculation that, in fact, he was a changeling, introduced into the Fitzwilliam line to rid it of inherited epilepsy.[90] It was, as we shall see in the next chapter, an ironic connection given Maurice FitzGerald's medical condition.

In summation, the 1904 Leinster share portfolio did not meet even rudimentary modern rules of portfolio management, devoid as it was of diversification, liquidity, counter-cyclicality, risk equivalency or inflation protection. It is difficult to understand the aversion to purchasing commercial property, overseas estates or equities and why Kinnaird, in particular, was so reluctant, for as a director of Barclays he would have been aware of the attractions of these asset classes in terms of providing some form of inflation proofing to the portfolio. And there is a major question over the concentration in private mortgages which were risky, illiquid and indivisible, thus reducing the opportunities to take advantage of new investments or indeed to meet a substantial cash demand when required. To adopt such a strategy for the relatively low level of return secured did not represent good investment practice.

But that is to view much of this through modern eyes and does not take into consideration the aristocracy's aversion to the City and possibly the dilemmas of an aristocrat such as Lord Frederick struggling to come to terms with the dawn of a whole new era. And there may have been other considerations which have not come to light. For example, did Frederick and Kinnaird believe that investments in mortgages were a safer option than the stock exchange given that the heir apparent to the estate, who was to reach his majority in four years time, had been diagnosed with epilepsy, a disease which, at the time, was closely associated with lunacy?[91] Would he be capable of managing financial affairs?

VI

In the 1950s C. Wright Mills wrote an influential study of the power elite in America in which he made the point that 'their failure to act, their failure to make decisions, is itself an act that is often of greater consequence than the decisions they do make'.[92] And in the context of the Irish aristocracy this may be just as relevant. For centuries, the decision-making process at all levels of estate and state was in their hands. Gradually, this power was eroded by the rise in democracy from the 1880s and the aristocracy response was too weak to counter this erosion. Their inactivity was shaped by their perception that it was pointless to act; there would be no room for them in a Home Rule Ireland dominated by Catholic nationalists. With few exceptions – the obvious being Charles Stewart Parnell and John Redmond – Irish landlords did not contemplate that a New Ireland might have been willing to take them on board. The Land League was hugely influential in this respect; the rhetoric practised by those who wanted to justify the long land war from the 1880s suggested to landlords that they would be run out of the country without ample compensation for their lands if a Home Rule parliament was to be established in Dublin. For Ireland this proved a double-edged sword. It meant that when the British government eventually bailed landlords out, they invested their capital throughout the empire but hardly any in Ireland, perhaps fearing that it also might be confiscated. If they had invested in developing Irish industry, infrastructure and agriculture, might it have changed the course of Irish history and prevented their marginalization?

CHAPTER SEVEN

Maurice: epilepsy and madness

Kildare, too, is a happy [?] sensitive child & likely to suffer <u>torture</u> with anyone incapable of understanding him – this gives me a great sense of responsibility about the child & a great wish to spare him all the suffering I can.[1]

Unfortunately, no evidence has been found as to how Maurice felt about the sale of his estates. The only hint we get of his attitude towards the 1903 Land Act is a letter written three years later, in April 1906, to Evelyn de Vesci lamenting that she had decided to move to England and adding: 'one feels so sorry for Ireland in the loss of some of her noblest inhabitants by the 1903 Land Purchase Act'.[2] Much work has yet to be done to ascertain the correlation between the act and the migration of Irish landlords, but in Maurice's case his was now a peculiar situation – a ducal title without a vast estate. On the other hand, although landless, he was potentially wealthier than many peers either side of the Irish Sea. The sale of the estates did not affect either Carton or Kilkea Castle and their demesnes, which remained in family hands; thus, the residential trappings of grandeur in Ireland were left untouched and the sale of family heirlooms was no longer a necessity, so Maurice proudly, though somewhat naively, proclaimed to Lady Evelyn: '[I] intend to remain in Ireland & behave like my father, grandfather and ancestors towards this country'.[3] He, too, had bought into the myth and legacy of the FitzGeralds.

II

The sale of the estates did not bring about any dramatic change in attitudes to the FitzGerald family; relationships with the wider community remained as they had been, with some qualification to take into consideration the seismic political shift. Ducal residency continued to give Maynooth a status that no other town in southern Ireland could claim. As far as the people around Maynooth were concerned Carton remained the economic cornerstone of their community because of the employment it continued to provide directly on the

139

demesne and indirectly through the support of local businesses and agricultural initiatives. A few examples will illuminate. After 1904, Lord Frederick's campaign to promote good agricultural practice in Kildare was widely reported. The campaign resulted in a number of initiatives including the establishment of the North Kildare Farming Society Ltd in November 1904. He farmed the demesne intensively, thereby retaining a good number of labourers, and became a renowned breeder of Kerry Blues, winning numerous prizes at the Royal Dublin Society Show, the Ulster Show and various county shows. In 1908, he introduced the Leinster Cup as a perpetual trophy to stimulate competition among local farmers by rewarding them for excellence in livestock breeding and market gardening. Indeed, there was a great deal of rivalry between Frederick and a number of his former tenants, especially the chairman of the Kildare County Council, Stephen Browne, who had acted as solicitor for the tenants under the 1903 act, with both more-or-less monopolizing the top prizes at the county shows in alternate years.[4] Frederick was also vice-president of the North Kildare Horticultural Society and served as chairman on the County Kildare Committee of Agriculture and the County Kildare Technical Committee. In 1904, his gesture to local industry – the purchase of shares in the recently founded Naas Rug and Carpet Company – was reported in the local newspapers as a significant patriarchal act.[5] Strangely, there seems to have been no public curiosity in Kildare about where the bulk of the vast capital sum received in 1903 had been invested or any criticism that much more of it had not been invested in the country to create further industry and employment.

In 1908, when Maurice came of age, the event was celebrated in the same way that such events had been for generations on the Leinster estate. In Maynooth, bonfires blazed and barrels of beer 'flowed freely' and a torchlight procession led by two marching bands processed through the streets to Carton. In the planning stages for the presentation of an address the local socio-political elite were represented by large farmers such as Robert Mooney; town merchants such as James Kavanagh, the miller (he and Mooney had organized the Maynooth estate tenants during the 1903 negotiations); professionals such as Dr Stanley Moore (who noted on his 1911 household schedule return that his ten-year-old daughter, Veronica, could speak both Irish and English, in what was probably a gesture of his support for the Gaelic revival movement); and the Catholic clergy by the elderly parish priest, Canon James Hunt (elected committee chairman), and his curate, Fr Patrick McDonnell. But perhaps the most interesting of the committee was the forty-two-year-old shopkeeper and merchant, Domhnall Ua Buachalla (1866–1963). Ua Buachalla was a Gaelic League enthusiast whose father was a native Irish speaker from Kerry. In 1905

23 Maurice FitzGerald (1887–1922),
marquess of Kildare, as a child, c.1890.

he had been prosecuted and fined for using the Irish version of his name on his business cart (Patrick Pearse had acted as his barrister) and in 1911 he returned his census household schedule entirely in Irish. Ua Buachalla would later become involved in the 1916 Rising and subsequent revolutionary period.[6] And yet in 1908 he had no difficulty in involving himself on a committee to organize the celebration of the coming-of-age of the 6th duke of Leinster; even for an aspiring republican it probably made good business (and political) sense to remain publicly involved.

The committee decided on an address to be presented in album form bearing the FitzGerald family coat of arms, beautifully bound in the finest morocco leather, and engraved in gold. It was decorated throughout with Celtic ornamentations based on the Book of Kells and the Book of Durrow. The ornamentation was the work of P.P. O'Malley who had won first prize in his craft at the Royal Dublin Society's Annual Art and Industrial Exhibition from 1903 to 1907 inclusive. The creation of the album came just a year before the formation of the Guild of Irish Art Workers in Dublin who 'would play a key role in visualizing the better-known literary and linguistic Celtic Revival over the next two decades as Ireland sought her own cultural identity' and that

Nicola Gordon Bowe claims had its genesis 'among businessmen, connoisseurs, and amateurs on the hunting fields of Co. Kildare'.[7]

The wording of the address was traditional and had been drafted by the organizing committee. At the final meeting Canon Hunt 'referred in eloquent terms to the good qualities that distinguished the Leinster family, of the close ties that bound them to the town, and of his own personal knowledge of their great charity to the poor of the district'.[8] Like his father before him in 1872, Maurice was told that while 'the people of Maynooth rejoice and heartily congratulate you on this propitious occasion of your coming of age' he had to be mindful of 'the close and felicitous association which has at all times existed between your noble family and our town'.[9] He was also subtly reminded that much had changed since 1872: now 'it was legitimate for the nationalists of Ireland to honour the Geraldine name', which by extension meant he was expected to recognize the new force that had superseded the old order. Finally, the address emphasized such imperatives as 'the magnanimous interest' that former dukes and duchesses took in local affairs, the 'whole-hearted co-operation in all that tended to our material progress' and 'their great munificence to our poor'. The landed estate may have gone but some evidence of the traditional deferential relationship still remained. The final paragraph made it clear what the 200 or so signatories expected to gain: 'We trust your Grace's advent to the duties appertaining to your exalted position at a time of intellectual and industrial awakening will presage a future of much happiness and prosperity for our motherland'. The *belle époque* had not entirely passed Ireland by and there was an expectation that the duke's patronage would continue to be important whether this was within the empire or in a Home Rule country that the more prominent aspired to govern.

There were no reports of dissension at any of the local government boards now dominated by nationalists. At a meeting of Athy Urban Council, Thomas Plewman, a Church of Ireland farmer and public representative for almost forty years, praised the FitzGeralds for improving the town of Athy and providing the people with a magnificent park: 'he had never known them to refuse to do anything which was for the good of the town'.[10] On 1 March 1908 a torchlight procession took place through the town's main streets. As part of the traditional paternalistic rituals, Lord Frederick, on behalf of the duke, reciprocated the gift of an address by announcing a donation of £25 to the board of guardians for the relief of destitution in the area, while Canon Joseph O'Keefe, the local parish priest, was given a cheque for £160, the Church Auxiliary Fund received £100 and the Sisters of Mercy £30.[11]

There was, however, one crucial difference between this and previous coming-of-age celebrations: the intended recipient of the addresses, Maurice, did not receive the deputations at Athy or those who processed up the avenue to Carton. Nor was he seen in public at any of the celebratory events. When the Maynooth committee arrived at Carton they were simply told he was unavailable. As Kevin McKenna's work shows, the whole ritual surrounding the presentation of the address required the heir to receive the same personally and then to reply, whereafter the traditional paternalistic social contract continued to play itself out.[12] Maurice's absence was, therefore, highly unusual and caused some degree of controversy and speculation. The following week the *Carlow Sentinel* reported that the illuminated address would have to be presented 'as soon as his Grace favours them with a visit'.[13] Rumours went out that he was ill; Athy Urban Council, for example, passed a motion stating that 'It was with feelings of very great regret that the people of the district heard of his protracted illness'.[14] The same week, a report in the *Kildare Observer* gave Maurice's address as 140 Earls Court Road in London but it did not make the connection that this was the address of Dr (later Sir) Donald Pollock (1868–1962) who was at the beginning of what would be a most distinguished career in medicine.[15] Nor would they have known that the previous year Pollock had been appointed personal physician to Maurice.[16]

III

From childhood, there had been fears about Maurice's health. In an early letter to Evelyn De Vesci, quoted at the opening to this chapter, Hermione expressed concern that her eldest son would require special care.[17] On another occasion she replied to a letter from Evelyn who, at the time, was caring for the children: 'Your account of the children this morning delighted me and I am so glad my little Kildare is looking stronger and rosier. I thought him looking rather bloodless when I left London and am rejoiced to hear he has picked up so quickly.'[18]

As a child, Maurice was of slight build and always affectionately referred to by his mother as her 'little Kildare' and after his father's death as 'the little duke'.[19] Hermione always depicted him as 'exceedingly delicate', 'quiet and undemonstrative' and prone to ailments. On one occasion she wrote to Evelyn that 'the doctor says he never saw a wilder attack of whooping cough'.[20] In the early 1890s Hermione proposed to take him to Switzerland: 'They say it is very healthy and it may do little Kildare good'.[21] On another occasion she wrote of her fear that Maurice might be hunchbacked: 'his little back', she wrote to Evelyn, 'is rounder than ever and it is not work for I won't let him write and he does do his lessons lying on the floor'.[22] Given that he had a twisted spine and breathing difficulties, he may have suffered from scoliosis. However, Hermione's worries later came to focus more on Maurice's timorous personality. In one of her very few dated letters of 16 March 1893, she told Evelyn: 'he does not look very strong or else it is the contrast with Desmond who as usual looks bursting with health'. Maurice had 'his own quiet shy way' while his brother was 'the more boisterous Des'.[23] Desmond had 'an uproarious courage' while Maurice's personality encapsulated 'triumph tempered by timidity'.[24] In February 1894, while the children were staying with their grandparents at Duncombe Park another disastrous fire broke out, which destroyed much of the house. The children were lucky to escape.[25] They were brought to London where Hermione was staying at the Cadogan Hotel. She wrote to Evelyn that 'Des and the baby [Edward] had been more excited than frightened' but 'little Kildare with his deeper understanding and hyper-sensitive nature was in a very nervous condition. I took him to sleep with me in my room'.[26] Perhaps Hermione's own emotional instability had transferred to her eldest son.

In 1897, two years after his mother's death, Maurice was diagnosed with epilepsy.[27] This was an illness about which very little was known in the nineteenth century and was erroneously associated with the cause of lunacy; thus for the aristocracy it became an illness to be hidden more than treated. In 1851, Anthony Ashley-Cooper, 7th earl of Shaftesbury (1801–85), who introduced the 1845 Lunacy Act, and whose own son suffered from epilepsy, was critical of the fact that: 'Fits are treated as madness and madness constitutes a right as it were to treat people as vermin'.[28] But even he shuddered when his son, by coincidence also Maurice, had a fit in public: 'Maurice fell yesterday in the Park. I trembled lest a vast crowd should be gathered. Sent away the children and sat by his side as though we were lying on the grass, and by degrees he recovered and walked home.'[29] Catherine Bailey notes that the 6th Earl Fitzwilliam's relationship with his eldest son and heir, who also suffered from epilepsy, was severely strained because of the father's less-than-sympathetic attitude towards the illness:

> The stigma of lunacy threatened the Fitzwilliam's fortune and position – their potential for alliances through marriage with other great noble houses. It also threatened their social omnipotence. Endemic to epilepsy was the risk of public humiliation – an eventuality of which members of the aristocracy were particularly fearful.[30]

His father's solution was fairly typical of his class at the time – the boy would have to be kept out of sight: 'Like other wealthy "lunatics", he was exiled from his family from an early age, funnelled into the shadowy network of "madhouses" that offered a cloak of secrecy: the private asylums and single-lodging establishments, both at home and abroad, that had proliferated in the first half of the nineteenth century.'[31] The representation of the illness in fiction only propagated the mythical links between epilepsy and madness. In William M. Thackeray's novel *Catherine* (1869), one of the protagonists suddenly 'fell down grovelling among the stones, gibbering and writhing in a fit of epilepsy' and:

> Some hours afterwards, when, alarmed by the Count's continued absence, his confidential servant came back to seek for him in the churchyard, he was found sitting on the flags, staring full at the [human] head, and laughing and talking to it wildly, and nodding at it. He was taken up a hopeless idiot, and so lived for years and years, clanking the chain, and moaning under the lash, and howling through long nights when the moon peered through the bars of his solitary cell and he buried his face in the straw.[32]

Modern medical studies have shown that there are strains of epilepsy which can be genetically inherited and there is some evidence that there was epilepsy in the FitzGerald family background. Back in 1755, Emily, 1st duchess of Leinster, described a frightening experience she had of seeing her nephew, Stephen Fox, taking an epileptic seizure (note how it is confused with a disorder of the nerves and perceived to be a stigmatized disease):

> Ste is better, but he frightened us yesterday with a return of his disorder on his nerves. The poor child was quite convulsed, his head all awry and full of involuntary motion. I was terrified to see him so; today it's gone off, but he is weak and low and looks sadly. It seems he is subject to these returns when he over fatigues or heats himself – don't talk of it, for tho' they don't mind it, I think one shou'd not like to have it mentioned if he was one's own child.[33]

Modern medical studies also point to the correlation between the onset of epilepsy and emotional strain in a child's earlier life. Maurice certainly had a troubled childhood. There were first the physical ailments that he suffered, and about which Hermione continuously fretted (which in itself would not have helped his emotional development). By the time he was eight years old he was an orphan. The death of his mother had a particularly devastating effect upon him – he lost his emotional crutch – and he carried this with him throughout his adult life. When Maurice visited Carton during his vacations he began to obsess about memorabilia there relating to Hermione and to seek out artefacts and photographs to enhance his childhood memories (as we shall see later, his brother, Edward, did exactly the same).[34] He yearned to show Evelyn de Vesci 'how I approve of all that mother has done to Carton and how I try to learn how to know about gardens and forestry and all at which she was so clever'.[35] More especially he looked towards Evelyn for comfort; there was, he wrote, 'no person whom I ought to honour, love and aclaime [sic] than my dear mother's best friend'.[36] At first his exuberant letters simply expressed his 'boundless thanks' for 'innumerable kindnesses to us when small', or 'the kindness you showed Des & I and the happiness we always enjoyed whenever near you and Mary'. (Revealingly, he made no reference to their half-brother, Edward, but then it may have been deemed inappropriate to send him to Abbey Leix.)[37] And he expressed his desire to repay Evelyn for all she had done in a youthful innocent way:

> Please remember if you want any seeds for flowers or creepers for your cottage you write to me and I will get Black [the gardener] to send them to you; it will give me the greatest pleasure to do anything that will help to oblige you in any way for I am sure that you will never be repaid for your kindnesses to everybody you have met. I know I will never be able to return nor ever thank you for your kindness to my mother and to me.[38]

Then Maurice began to look to her as the direct connection between himself and his mother and his letters became increasingly more nostalgic for a lost time. He shows all the signs of a young man in a depressive time warp, constantly harking back to his visits to Abbey Leix, visits which left only rose-tinted memories: 'I can remember the village teas quite well, there used to be sports, such delicious buns, & tugs of war in which the ropes were always cut. The Abbeyleix villagers pulled against another village.'[39] But more especially his letters reveal his obsessive quest for information about Hermione. (There was, it should be added, never any reference to his father in his letters.) Eventually, in 1906, Evelyn promised him she would copy Hermione's letters to her as a gift. She sought advice from Hermione's mother, Mabel, countess of Feversham, and asked her to read a sample of what she intended to copy. Mabel advised:

I have read all these letters through, with deepest loving interest, and I am quite sure you must leave them just as they are – to let them be the mirror of her mind, which seems and feels reflected in them. My same promise to Leinster has remained unfulfilled, because when I came to re-read my letters they were less full than these and more difficult to give him. I am sure she loved and trusted you more than anyone else and these letters are quite in keeping with all Leinster knows of her. What a strong support and blessed friend she found in you dear Evelyn and how thankful one is for the love and help you gave her – which was returned a thousandfold.[40]

It is difficult to decipher from this what exactly Mabel meant by 'in keeping' with all Leinster knew of Hermione. How select was the choice of letters? Did they avoid contentious issues? Or were they warts and all, revealing her relationship with Hugo Charteris? Whichever, Evelyn delivered on her promise much to Maurice's delight:

I cannot tell you with what delight, joy and love those letters have filled me, now, for since my arrival in France I have commenced to read them. I am afraid that I shall never be able to thank you sufficiently for your great indescribable kindness in copying out and giving the copy of these letters to me. I can assure you that they will always be in my company & close to me ... I can assure you that nothing will receive more affection, love, respect, than this lovely book of letters and my darling mother's books with her little markings in pencil in them.[41]

And so he did: years later, on Christmas Day 1912, Maurice wrote to Evelyn that he had spent most of his day reading 'over and over again' the copies of his mother's letters.[42]

There were other events in Maurice's childhood, equally as traumatic. In 1897, when he was diagnosed with epilepsy, Maurice had been a pupil at Cheam Preparatory School in Berkshire for about three years, probably having started around the time that his mother's illness was diagnosed in 1894. (Desmond also attended this school but Edward was sent to Mr Wilkinson's at Eastbourne.)[43] The evidence suggests that his physical and emotional difficulties – his introvert shyness, weakly disposition and even hunched back – led to him being bullied and this compounded his emotional vulnerability.

Although Cheam's most famous headmaster of the nineteenth century, Revd R.S. Tabor (1819–1909), had been retired since 1890 his reputation lived on.

24 Maurice, marquess of Kildare, as a teenager.

Cheam was regarded as one of the leading preparatory schools in England; Major Fitzroy Gardner remembered it as 'the most luxuriously appointed private school in England'.[44] But it was also noted for its 'intensely oppressive evangelical atmosphere'.[45] General Sir Ian Hamilton (1853–1947) resented the effects of Tabor's strict, religious regime and deemed him choleric and callous with very little feeling for the sensitivities of young boys.[46] If the general atmosphere of Hamilton's time endured during Maurice's the whole intense socialization process would not have been favourable to a young boy of his sensitive nature. The evidence of Maurice's bullying at school is contained in his later medical reports drawn up by Dr Walker Chambers shortly after he was institutionalized in Craighouse Asylum in Edinburgh at the age of twenty-two (see below). In an early assessment, Chambers noted that he had a very poor sense of humour and was particularly sensitive to being chaffed. He was 'extremely self conscious and always thinks he is being laughed at'.[47] Above all Maurice 'dislike[d] very much to hear of any form of ill treatments or abuse. He was greatly bullied at school & badly treated by the other boys & dislikes to hear even of practical jokes being played, unless of the mildest description.'[48]

The evidence also suggests he was possibly sexually abused. His medical reports are not specific on this but then in Britain or Ireland in the early twentieth century it was a taboo subject and, indeed, only in more recent times has it become a subject for scholars.[49] In fact and in fiction aristocrats were more likely to have been accused of sexual deviance rather than having been the victims and, moreover, sexual abuse in Victorian England was always associated with female children.[50] Yet, in 1896, Sigmund Freud (1856–1939), the founding father of psychoanalysis, first put forward his theory that childhood sexual experience produced later psychopathology. In *The aetiology of hysteria* he wrote:

> I therefore put forward the thesis that at the bottom of every case of hysteria there are one or more occurrences of premature sexual experience, occurrences which belong to the earliest years of childhood, but which can be reproduced through the work of psycho-analysis in spite of the intervening decades. I believe that this is an important finding, the discovery of a *caput Nili* in neuropathology.[51]

The suggestion that Maurice had been a victim was first recorded in March 1912, almost three years after being admitted to Craighouse, when he called for a doctor who later wrote in the case book:

> The duke sent for me and made the following statement. When he was about ten years of age he was at school [and] had there made friends with a boy slightly older than himself … The boy practiced a habit which he had never taken part in [and] which he called 'forcing'. One day he was walking with this boy and although he does not know clearly what happened he remembers finding the front buttons of his trousers undone and of his friend say, 'that will do. There are some boys coming up.'[52]

The report connected this to an earlier interview with Maurice in which he told of another school incident when he had been asked 'if he would take the part of a man or a woman … and he immediately replied he would take the part of a woman'.[53] He lived 'under the impression that since the incident mentioned he has been taking the part of a woman, but now because of the physical exercise which he has been having he is forming into a man'.[54] This was tied in with an obsession he had with his genitals. In January 1911, he spoke of a vision revealed to him by God that showed that 'some blood had been taken from a child and transferred to him with the result that some harm was done to his genital organs'.[55] On the night of 6 September 1912, he suddenly jumped up, looked towards Heaven and exclaimed: 'I am a man! I have fully developed! Thank God, the Father, Son and Holy Ghost'. The report went on:

> He then rushed out into the corridor, partly buttoning up his trousers. He paced up and down from one end to the other, walking very fast and stamping heavily. After some time he began blowing hard and then proceeded to roar like a lion, all the time walking fast and spitting on the carpet.[56]

This went on for the best part of an hour before his trousers fell around his ankles and he tripped, falling heavily on the floor. He then became aggressive and violent and eventually had to be sedated through a cocktail of several injections of hyoscine and morphix and other medications. Thus, the doctors at Craighouse were aware that there were demons in Maurice's childhood past with which he struggled, but psychoanalysis was too new for them to comprehend their long-term consequences. It is now medically accepted that there is a compelling relationship between child sexual abuse and depression in adulthood.[57]

Maurice moved from Cheam to Eton in 1900. Here his house master was the much respected Revd Henry Thomas Bowlby (1864–1940) who was assistant master from 1897 to 1909 (after which he moved on to become headmaster at Lancing College in Sussex). Maurice did not excel at his studies. The only available school record of any note is a transcript of his maiden debate on the motion 'Whether intervention be advisable in the present war'. It is not dated but the content suggests it was around 1905 during the Russo-Japanese war. Obviously, a debating speech does not necessarily indicate a person's genuine attitudes on a subject but Maurice's speech does show evidence of an interest in warfare which he was to maintain throughout his life:

The present war has been going on for a year… yet no decisive point has been reached. It is true that in the far-east the Russian fleet has been practically annihilated, that the Russians have been beaten back in Manchuria … The Russians are a greedy land-acquiring nation and deserve to get beaten. Japan is a clever, energetic and only lately civilized nation, in fact a wonder of the world.[58]

His years at Eton were probably happier than those at Cheam but still public school may have continued to be difficult for him in light of what he had gone through and, indeed, the very nature of the emphasis which the Etonian ethos placed on character building. Sir Shane Leslie (1885–1971) of Glaslough was born two years after Maurice and both attended Eton around the same time (Leslie arrived in 1902, two years after Maurice). Leslie painted a very bleak picture of 'that house of schoolboy horrors' from 'the battered warren' in which he stayed to the 'wretched and tasteless food' and appalling teaching but he was particularly condemnatory of the excessive 'thrashings which tyrannized rather than disciplined our house' and the endemic bullying which some regarded as a requisite part of masculine formation. Moreover, 'Irish boys were ridiculed especially on St Patrick's Day'.[59]

Leslie is not entirely representative of the Irish aristocratic experience of Eton and he was later blackballed for his novel *The Oppidan* (1922). But both his novel and his own memoirs create the impression that Eton, just as Cheam, would not have provided the type of educational environment suitable to Maurice's sensitive temperament. In the preface to the novel, Leslie claimed that Edmond Warre (1837–1920), renowned athlete and headmaster of Eton from 1884 to 1905, ruled Eton as a 'Philathlete'.[60] Such an ethos had little appeal for Maurice but, as we shall see below, it did suit the more boisterous and athletic Desmond. By coincidence (presumably) *The Oppidan* is populated with characters who in some respects mirror the three young FitzGeralds who were there in Leslie's time: the orphan who 'wishes he had a father or a mother to write home the story of his Eton days' and who felt terribly 'the loneliness of his soul in the Eton crowd!'; the Oppidan (which Desmond FitzGerald became in real life) whose athletic prowess allowed him sacred status within the school; and the boy who is whipped along the corridor amid 'fearful suggestions as to his paternity'. As for those who 'showed the least sign of being unconventional in dress or taste, they were pecked by the others and worried as birds worry another wearing a ribbon attached by some human owner'.[61]

After Maurice left Eton he went on to Oxford. It was there he suffered his first recorded nervous breakdown. On 29 October 1905 he wrote to Evelyn de

25 Maurice, marquess of Kildare, third from the left after the queen, at the
coronation of Alexandra of Denmark, 9 Aug. 1902.

Vesci from The King's Mound: 'my nerves went all wrong & I was in bed for
over a fortnight in London'. (He was kept in his Aunt Cynthia's flat.)[62] There
are scraps of evidence that suggest his family were already conscious of his
emotional instability. At the end of 1909, Lady Cynthia informed Evelyn: 'My
only comfort for all that has happened this year is that strange as it seems he is
more content and near to happiness than I have ever seen him!'[63] She followed
up shortly after in another letter that Maurice was 'better now mentally than
he has been for years'.[64]

But Maurice's high social profile meant that it was impossible to keep stories
out of the newspapers at a time when the very nature of British newspapers had
fundamentally changed in response to an increased mass literate audience
wanting to read about scandal more than about high politics or the latest
foreign or financial crisis. As David Cannadine puts it: 'the old liberal, rational,
provincial press was gradually superseded by the new, cheap, vulgar,
chauvinistic, mass circulation, London-based papers, beginning with Alfred
Harmsworth's *Daily Mail* in 1896, and soon followed by the *Sketch*, the *Herald*,
and the *Express*'.[65] The aristocracy deplored the advent of these newspapers,
which infringed upon the privacy of their lives.[66] Frederick (or some form of

estate press office that does seem to have existed) counteracted any potentially damaging stories about Maurice by spinning information to the newspapers. Thus, while it was frequently reported in newspapers and society magazines that Maurice's education was disrupted 'by his delicate health', epilepsy was never mentioned. Instead it was more often surmized that he had inherited the frail constitution of his mother and that was the reason he was sent 'on several lengthy voyages' to the Antipodes, most of which were fictitious.[67] In 1905, as Maurice allegedly made his way to America, it was reported that he had 'outgrown the danger' and developed into a 'tall, healthy, handsome lad'.[68] In December 1907 the *Irish Independent* reported that the 'young duke' had lost all traces of the 'physical weakness he had inherited from his beautiful mother'.[69] At the beginning of March 1908, the *Irish Society* and *Social Review* noted how he had 'outgrown his boyish delicacy' and improved from the 'pathetic little figure' of thirteen years previously when he became heir to the estate.[70] He was now described as 'a fairly strong youth, fully six feet in height, and gifted with an engaging personality, and frank, courteous manner'.[71]

The news that Lord Frederick had circulated in 1908 was that the estate's future was safe in the hands of a young handsome duke who was about to be appointed at the Vice Regal Court and as Master of the Horse to the lord lieutenant following the resignation of Captain Walter Waring who was taking a seat in the House of Commons.[72] Indeed, Maurice's name was now being 'freely quoted' on the English and American marriage markets as one of Ireland and Britain's most eligible bachelors.[73] In reality, his mental health was deteriorating sharply.

IV

In 1907, less than a year before his coming-of-age, Dr Donald Pollock was appointed private physician to Maurice. The son of a Presbyterian minister, he was born in Galashiels in Scotland in 1868 and educated at Glasgow University. Pollock qualified as an MD in 1895 and, as noted earlier, practised out of Earls Court Road in London.[74] He was twelve years into a very promising medical career in a growing practice in a fashionable area of London, so he must have been generously compensated for taking on the new private commission. (In the early 1920s, Pollock would go into partnership with S.J.L. Hardie and R.W. McCrone to establish Metal Industries Ltd, a ship-breaking company, the success of which, along with other business interests, made him a vast fortune.)[75]

It had been ten years since Maurice had been diagnosed with epilepsy so why was Pollock called in just a few months short of Maurice's coming-of-age? It may have been medical necessity; Maurice's mental health was certainly deteriorating and perhaps this was related to the extra strain of preparing to assume the more public role of duke. Also, Frederick may not have expected Maurice to live to inherit. Contemporary medical thinking on the life span of someone suffering from epilepsy is evidenced in a report published in 1910 on inmates of Craighouse (where Maurice would be committed):

> death is imminent at a time of seizures, unless help is at hand … Each patient must be seen every few minutes, for as has been noted these deaths occur very rapidly at times … The duration of life after the onset of the disease may be several years, but as the onset is very common in the early years of life, the net result is the premature death of an epileptic compared with normal people.[76]

But now the fact that Maurice was going to inherit the estate made it incumbent upon Frederick to devise an alternative strategy. At one level, Pollock's employment might be interpreted as an attempt to prepare Maurice as best as possible for his very public role: Pollock may have been to Maurice what Lionel Logue became to King George VI. But it is likely there was a much more devious motive. If, in Lord Frederick's view, epilepsy and nervous breakdowns equated to permanent insanity, the future of the estate in the hands of a lunatic (to use the accepted terminology of the time) would have been fraught with danger. It is, therefore, the timing of Maurice's committal to a mental institution that gives rise to suspicion. Did Frederick deliberately wait until Maurice was a legal adult to commit him under the Dangerous Lunatics Act (1838), which would mean he was held indefinitely at the pleasure of the lord lieutenant and so permanently out of harm's way?

In order to have Maurice committed under the Dangerous Lunatics Act Frederick knew he had to have medical evidence – evidence that he was a danger to himself or to others – thus the employment of Pollock, somebody with a growing reputation in the area of mental health. The evidence would have to be built up over a period of time, thus the timing of Pollock's employment a few months before the coming-of-age. Moreover, from Frederick's perspective Maurice could not be declared a lunatic and institutionalized before his birthday because the estate had first to be legally resettled – without him knowing the implications – while he was still technically *compos mentis*. On 1 May 1908, a few weeks after Maurice's coming-of-age, Lord Frederick went alone to the family solicitors' offices of Johnson Raymond-Barker & Co. at Lincoln's Inn in London and drew up a draft resettlement of the estate, replacing the one of 1884 which had come into being following the marriage of Gerald and Hermione.[77] Four days later, Frederick and Pollock brought Maurice to the same offices where after 'a long conference' the epitome of the resettlement was read to the duke and according to the solicitors: 'he expressed his approval of it subject to one or two modifications'.[78] The resettlement was, therefore, presented to Maurice as a *fait accompli*. It ensured that the tenant for life, namely Maurice, could not dispose of Carton or its contents without the consent of the trustees. Maurice was entitled to the income of the estates but he was prevented from having access to the capital represented by the fee simple that remained tied up in the control of the trustees.

Two months later, on 14 July 1908, Maurice drew up his will, appointing Lord Frederick and Lord Kinnaird as his executors. He bequeathed all the contents of his mansion houses at Carton, Kilkea and 13 Lower Dominick Street to his successor and charged him with providing for the children of his uncle, Lord Charles, and 'other dependents not kept on in the service of the family after my death'. He left £5,000 to Lord Frederick and the same sum to Cynthia Graham. To Evelyn de Vesci, he left a portrait of his mother with the inscription: 'If love be dead why dost thou rise oh sun'. He left £1,000 each to his uncle, Lord Charles, his aunt, Lady Alice, and his old house master at Eton, Revd H.T. Bowlby (revoked under a codicil of 26 October 1908). Annuities of £100 were bequeathed to Lord Walter and Lady Nesta, as well as £52 to his former governess, Miss Brand, and his former nurse, Marianne Timmins of New Street in Carlow (effectively a year's salary each).[79] He expressed the wish 'to be buried in the private burying ground at Carton in the immediate neighbourhood of the graves of my father and mother' and requested his successors 'as an imperative duty to keep the said burying ground free from trees, shrubs and other growth so that it may always be available as a burying ground for the family'.[80]

No sooner had these arrangements been put in place than Maurice was sent away. In August, he failed to make an expected appearance at the Horse Show in the Royal Dublin Society – 'contrary to his custom' – and was reported instead to have gone on vacation to Connemara with his brother, Edward.[81] Another edition of the same paper later that month reported that he was due to return from Killarney where he had holidayed with Desmond.[82] But these were mere alibis for Maurice not turning up at public events. By November 1908, it was reported that he had arrived in Cairo where he was expected to spend the winter.[83] This was true: the trip had been organized by Pollock – Maurice thought him at that stage 'a v[ery] nice fellow' – who hired a sailing boat from Thomas Cook & Son to accommodate six people to sail up the Nile. The other four persons were Aunt Nesta and three servants. Nesta was the youngest of his aunts, and, like two of her sisters, would remain a spinster the rest of her life in a changed aristocratic world where even the daughters/ sisters of a duke found it difficult to find appropriate marriage partners. In January 1909, after visiting Luxor, Karnak and Thebes, Maurice wrote to Evelyn de Vesci: 'I admire the Nile and desert scenery that there is out here; I am delighted with Egypt & also with all its archaeological buildings and ruins & feel that I could spend years out here'.[84] In May 1909, it was reported that he had arrived home to Carton having 'benefited greatly from his sojourn in Egypt'.[85]

Somebody was once again spinning information to the media; Maurice did not return to Carton; instead he was brought straight to Scotland, for reasons which will become clear below. There is no evidence of what happened between the time he wrote excitedly to Evelyn de Vesci in January 1909 and the end of the trip. However, on 11 June, after five days of labouring 'under intense mental excitement', Maurice attempted 'to commit suicide by slitting his throat'.[86] Shortly before this incident, he had allegedly seriously assaulted his valet and Pollock. There was now evidence that he was a danger to himself and to others. A court order immediately placed his affairs in the hands of the trustees. Five days later, a medical report by Dr Angus Matheson stated that Maurice had been suffering from 'delusions of persecution'.[87] These delusions remained a constant for years to come and Pollock would always feature prominently. Given that there is no existing evidence of Maurice having previously been disposed to violent behaviour there remains the question as to whether he was deliberately provoked into attacking his valet and Pollock and driven to some form of dementia to inflict self-harm.

Lord Frederick sought the opinion of Dr (later Sir) Thomas Clouston (1840–1915). The thin, wiry, bearded Clouston was widely regarded as one of the most eminent practitioners in the bourgeoning field of psychiatric studies. Frederick had been well advised, probably by Pollock, as Clouston's expertise was unlikely to be refuted. In 1873, he had been appointed superintendent of the Royal Edinburgh Asylum and six years later lecturer in mental diseases at the University of Edinburgh. In 1883, his book *Clinical lectures on mental diseases* established his international reputation. He had pioneered 'the insanity of adolescence', which he defined as an inherited developmental disease arising in early adult life and often leading to mental deterioration in later years.[88] By the time he examined Maurice, Emil Kraepelin had discovered Dementia Praecox, or the Kraepelinian dichotomy, which we now know as schitzo-phrenia.[89] Clouston reported back:

> I am of the opinion that he [Maurice] is of unsound mind and under-standing, under many insane delusions viz. that Pollock, his valet and other persons present are trying to injure him. He is also dangerously suicidal and homicidal, having inflicted a serious wound on his throat and several other wounds on his chest and arm as well as having seriously assaulted Dr Pollock.[90]

Clouston's opinion was crucial because confinement to an institution was predicated upon the inability of families to control dependent and violent relatives.[91] Lord Frederick and his brother, Henry of Babergh Hall in Suffolk, a major in the Bedfordshire Regiment, then petitioned the masters in lunacy in the borough and county of Berwick-upon-Tweed to 'enquire concerning the alleged lunacy' of Maurice.[92] This was a formal process reserved for lunatics 'who were both propertied and whose physicians believed were unlikely ever to recover'.[93] On 15 July, the enquiry found that 'the said Duke of Leinster is a person of unsound mind so that he is not sufficient for the government of himself, his manors, messuages, lands, servants, goods and chattels'. He was now legally certified insane.[94] When Lord Frederick had signed the commit-ment order a short time before he had answered the question 'Length of time insane' with 'a few days'; the question 'Supposed cause' with 'epilepsy'; and 'Whether dangerous to others', he answered, 'I am afraid so'.[95] Most notably, the length of time insane was only 'a few days'. It was now about sixteen months after he had come of age and over a year since he had legally resettled the estate and made his will, enough time to make the arrangements legal and binding.

Frederick was not a man given to sentimentality and for thirteen years he had been master of Carton and, as noted earlier, duke in all but name. As trustee for a minor he had used the power to make important decisions, most notably concerning the sale of the estate and the investment of the proceeds. He had also, through Maurice, used his position to embellish Carton once again with a fine art collection and to build the family portrait collection.[96] He may have regarded the committal of Maurice as just another decision to safeguard the family's future, assured in the knowledge that his brother, Desmond, was eminently qualified to replace him.[97] The formal declaration of lunacy in cases such as that of Maurice was essentially for two reasons: 'to lawfully detain the individual or to protect his property from dissipation'.[98] Frederick was undoubtedly reluctant to see the family fortune dissipated by Maurice, but equally he may have been just as reluctant to give up his position of power and authority. None of his personal papers seem to have survived and that may be instructive. Did Frederick cleverly manipulate the law in order to secure the future of the estate and, indeed, to continue as duke in all but title for his lifetime, for as long as Maurice lived Desmond would not supersede him as chief trustee of the estate? Notably, from the time he was committed Maurice's aversion to Frederick and Pollock was abundantly evident in his behaviour whenever they came to visit him, and that was rarely.[99]

V

Maurice was institutionalized in Craighouse Asylum in Edinburgh (after 1922 the Royal Edinburgh Hospital for Mental and Nervous Disorders).[1] The neo-Gothic asylum had been opened on 24 October 1894 at a cost of around £110,000. The aforementioned Dr Thomas Clouston had planned the development to replace the pre-existing Morningside Asylum, which had become 'so surrounded by buildings and railways that it became necessary to find a new site where privacy and possibilities of extension could be had'.[2] This was as much about capacity as anything else: in less than a hundred years the number of patients had risen from four in Morningside in 1813 to 870 at Craighouse in 1894.

Why was Maurice institutionalized in Scotland? One could argue it was because of the lack of quality (and exclusive) facilities in Ireland and the family need for privacy.[3] There is, however, another reason suggested in this letter of 14 July 1909 from Pollock to the family solicitor:

> I may tell you that the medical impression is that he will sooner or later commit suicide wherever he is but that the chances of his doing this are very much less where he is than in an outside establishment. Of course there is another point. There is no coroner in Scotland and all the abominable publicity attached to his court.[4]

Was it mere coincidence that the most violent breakdown he had suffered (allegedly) to date had happened in Scotland where Pollock had trained, where Clouston was one of Britain's leading psychiatrists, where there was no coroner, no coroner's report that would lead to adverse publicity, and finally where there was a progressive asylum which catered for the 'superior classes'?

26 Craighouse Asylum, Edinburgh, where Maurice, 6th duke of Leinster, became a patient in 1909.

Craighouse had originally been a Victorian mansion purchased from John Hill Burton. It was located on 'a finely wooded slope' commanding 'many lovely views of the surrounding countryside' amid sixty acres of parkland.[5] There was a great oak-panelled hall measuring 63 feet long, 33 feet wide and 45 feet high which was 'decorated brightly and handsomely'; a drawing room; a billiard room and five dining rooms of various sizes on the north side of the great hall. In addition to the central block, there were two detached hospitals on the east and west sides and a number of detached villas for members of the 'superior' class who, instead of being confined in a monolithic asylum building, lived in a degree of comfort commensurate with their status outside the hospital. These included Maurice who took up residence at number 1 Morningside Drive. The philosophy of villa-style living in an asylum had emanated from the psychiatric schools of Germany and Austria where the therapeutic qualities of freedom and maintaining human dignity were promoted.[6] At Craighouse the visual impressions in the expansive parkland and gardens, its magnificent views of the Edinburgh countryside, superb indoor facilities, excellent lighting, and sports facilities (at least cricket and tennis) built on the philosophy that surroundings and freedom would through some form of osmosis bring insane patients back to reason.[7]

After some time it seems Maurice settled into his new surroundings, though it is unlikely that he considered them permanent. As far as he was concerned he was there to be treated for epilepsy and not permanent insanity. This is suggested in one of the earliest letters he wrote from Craighouse to Evelyn de Vesci. It was the day before Christmas Eve 1909 and his letter was intended to wish her and her daughter, Mary, a happy Christmas: 'I hope that the receipt of this letter will not trouble you or cause any worry, but I write from part of Craighouse because I dwell here as a person suffering from fits of epilepsy and am under medical care as well as having my property etc under the charge of the Lord Chancellor'.[8] He regretted that for a time he had been forbidden to read his mother's 'beloved books of letters' but having got them back he was delighted to assure Evelyn that they were 'a most lovable companion, comfort and cause of happiness. I shall never get tired of them and am quite happy and comfortable here with the above book & some of my dear mother's.'[9] A year later, thinking that he might be able to get away from Craighouse to visit Evelyn, he told her: 'I am thinking of bringing the beloved letters in their wooden case to show you how they are loved, marked and details – words and sentences – are associated'.[10] It was further affecting evidence of the sense of loss Maurice experienced after his mother died.

Maurice had been admitted as 'a handsome, pleasant, well nourished but rather pale young man', and designated an 'extraordinary patient'. His fees were set at £2,500 per annum.[11] This included use of the semi-detached villa, 'special board, the service of a doctor, the exclusive service of five attendants, one of whom was the duke's recently-assaulted valet, and the use of a carriage and pair'.[12] Early on, he played cricket and tennis (or acted as judge), went walking in the hills around Edinburgh and played the card game, picquet, at night. He was even permitted to go driving (provided he was accompanied by two doctors). That could be dangerous for those he met on the road; in March 1910, Dr Walker Chambers reported: 'in every light, the duke is a thorough aristocrat and hates everything democratic. His attitude to pedestrians etc when motoring is significant', the suggestion being that he did not consider pedestrians to have a right to the road while he was driving on it.

In accordance with the philosophy of the hospital, he was allowed to issue instructions, to dictate his pastimes and to think that he was being attended by personal servants (Fritz, Bella and Jenners). He grumbled about the standard of the lavatory paper, particularly when he found it to be superior in the rooms next door, or he would 'kick up a fearful dust' if lumps of coal were not the right size.[13] At one stage Fritz got so fed up with being blamed 'about imaginary neglect of duty' that he threatened to leave.[14] Dr Chambers' 1910 report suggested just how ingrained privilege was in Maurice's life:

1. Arthur Devis (1712–87), one of his famous conversation piece portraits showing James FitzGerald (1722–73), later 1st duke of Leinster, and his wife, Emily (1731–1814), designing the Carton landscape.

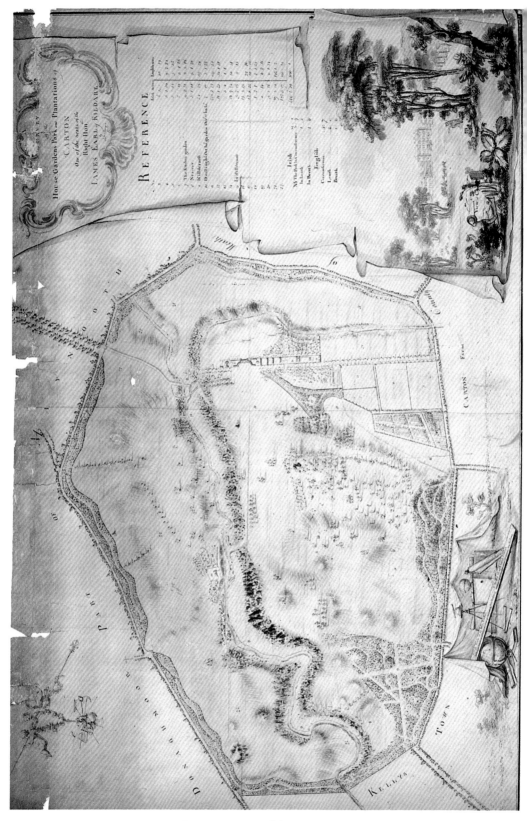

2. Carton House and demesne, *c.*1750.

3. 'Maynooth, *c.*1803', showing both the ruined castle and the recently established St Patrick's College with Stoyte House, the former home of the duke of Leinster's butler, at its core (courtesy of the president of St Patrick's College, Maynooth).

4. Emily FitzGerald (1731–1814), 1st duchess of Leinster, one of the magnificent family portraits that hung at Carton on Hermione's arrival as chatelaine (courtesy of Mallaghan family).

5. James FitzGerald (1722–73), 1st duke of Leinster (courtesy of Mallaghan family).

6. William Robert FitzGerald, 2nd duke of Leinster (1749–1804) (courtesy of Mallaghan family).

7. G. Hamilton, 'Augustus Frederick FitzGerald, 3rd duke of Leinster' (1791–1874), (courtesy of Mallaghan family).

Lord Edward Fitzgerald,
Hamilton. 1796.

8. Lord Edward FitzGerald (1763–98), son of the 1st duke of Leinster,
United Irish leader, whose portrait at Carton allegedly saved it from destruction
during the Civil War.

9. Address to the earl of Offaly on the occasion of his attaining his majority,
16 August 1872 (courtesy of Mallaghan family).

10. Hermione's portrait, which hangs in her ancestral home at Duncombe Park (courtesy of Jake Duncombe).

11. The Gold Saloon at Carton in the twenty-first century.

12. Ceiling of the Gold Saloon at Carton, photograph by Stephen Farrell.

13. The Chinese Room at Carton designed by Emily, 1st duchess of Leinster, and, according to house lore, prepared as a bedroom for Queen Victoria's visit in the 1840s, but she did not stay there.

14. Carton in 2013.

When playing games with the duke, he must be treated with impartial fairness – he is annoyed to think he is being given advantages e.g. at golf, in being allowed to pick up his ball when in a bad position. He insists on being kept rigidly to the rules ... so that if he is playing badly and it is necessary to give him a hole or two, it must be done artistically! He is extremely sharp in such matters.[15]

Chambers found that he liked 'very much to think he [was] a varsity man', imagined himself an authority on the navy, was 'extremely Conservative' on political and imperial questions ('culled from *The Times*'), which were 'fixed and unalterable and must be swallowed' for 'he scarcely ever admits that he knows nothing about a subject'.[16]

But after about eight months in Craighouse, Maurice's medical reports began to make continuous reference to his 'delusions of persecution'.[17] In March 1910, Chambers concluded that 'the keynote of the duke's character ... is suspicion', that he believed that he was 'being either tricked or cheated in some way ... certain things have been done for the purpose of getting level with him for some supposed trouble he has given rise to'.[18] Delusions of persecution were not, of course, uncommon among the patients at Craighouse: Allan Beveridge has found in a study of the letters of those admitted from 1873 to 1908 that most believed they were victims of injustice, conspiracy and persecution; some felt that their lives were threatened by those who wanted to poison them; while many others claimed that they were persecuted by their own families, and sometimes even the asylum staff.[19] About 20 per cent of the patients in Beveridge's study suffered from hallucinations, and would often complain of hearing loud noises, or words of abuse spoken or screamed.[20]

Maurice's early participation in activities in Craighouse and, indeed, his December 1909 letter to Evelyn de Vesci would not suggest he was insane. But as the months passed, and he gradually realized that he had been more-or-less abandoned by his family, a prisoner of an asylum where he had nothing but time to contemplate his position, Maurice's behaviour began to take on all of the symptoms of his fellow inmates. He became paranoid about plots to make his life miserable: cats deliberately made noise to vex him; people intentionally slammed doors; Mr Cooper, a fellow patient, wilfully played 'inharmonious strains' to create havoc to Maurice's 'perfect ear for music'.[21] In May 1911, he 'was very much annoyed ... because Mr Gallagher and Mr Smith were cutting the grass in front of the windows in a fairly backward and forward movement instead of going right on'.[22] The duke believed Smith was doing it out of spite because he had hit him by mistake with a tennis ball in the foot earlier that morning. On 1 July 1911, while sitting in the summer house watching a cricket game he became upset that 'both sides were playing badly for that special purpose' of annoying him.[23] Thus, he told the attendants, in his aristocratic manner, that 'he was not accustomed to it [noise] and would not stand it'.[24] At the end of his first year his condition was summarized in his case book as follows:

> The patient exhibits many of the mental characteristics of an insane epileptic. He is enfeebled and childish with somewhat impaired memory at times, he is cheerful, pleasant and communicative, while at other times he is morose, suspicious and delusional ... and irritable.[25]

Maurice often accused the doctors, with the exception of Dr S.J.A. Walshe, of 'plotting against him, not to let him get better but to keep him in a medium state of health, so that he should stay on here and they get his money'; he complained that 'his food had some harmful substance in it and they were giving him deleterious medicine'.[26] Walshe was the only doctor whom he trusted and his reasons may even suggest something about the duke's sense of national identity. Walshe wrote: 'He had previously told me that I was one of the very few people here whom he did not suspect of plotting against him and appealed to me as an Irishman and fellow countryman to be watchful for him'.[27]

It is unlikely ever to be revealed what was going on in the deep recesses of Maurice's mind for him to suspect that he was being poisoned or deliberately imprisoned so that 'they get his money'. He certainly came to resent family members and, in particular, Donald Pollock. His family, on both his maternal and paternal sides, to all intents abandoned him after his committal. On 22 June 1909, Lady Cynthia Graham, his aunt and former guardian who had looked after him in childhood and adolescence, instructed the doctors at Craighouse that Maurice should never be left alone, not even if he improved, for fear that if he 'escaped' and made his way to Netherby Hall in Cumbria the shock would be too much for her husband and son both of whom allegedly suffered from heart trouble. She washed her hands of the situation, instructing that all future business concerning Maurice was to be conducted solely through Frederick, and that if Maurice requested her he was to be told 'that in the changed condition of things Lord Frederick is solely responsible'.[28] She would change her mind with the passing of time.

The rest of his family rarely visited. The above mentioned genital incident occasioned Lord Frederick's first visit on 27 September 1912, over three years after Maurice had been admitted. Maurice was 'in a state of nervous tension', and ordered Pollock, who had accompanied Frederick, out of the room before he proceeded to give his uncle 'his life history since infancy'. Frederick merely 'thought it useless to speak to him'.[29] It had taken him over three years to visit and only a few minutes to decide it was not worth talking to him. Thus, it was hardly surprising that on 1 December 1912 Maurice's medical report read: 'spoke [a] little about his relatives and where they were today. The subject made him morose'.[30] The first recorded visit of one of his brothers took place just three days later when Edward came to visit with Pollock. It was to be Edward's only ever (recorded) visit and rather strangely he brought with him as a present a letter opener, a rather inappropriate present for one who had attempted suicide by cutting his throat. As it was against the rules for a patient to have a knife in his possession, the medics attempted to take it from Maurice but he became aggressive, 'very imperious and curt' and refused to hand it over.

There is no evidence whatsoever of his Duncombe grandparents ever visiting him or enquiring about him (they both died in 1915). The stigma of having a grandson in an asylum may have been too much for them. When Hermione's closest friend, Evelyn de Vesci, found out about Maurice's illness and considered visiting Craighouse, she was dissuaded by the Duncombe's daughter, Lady Cynthia, who wrote to her: 'It was dear of you to think of seeing Leinster tomorrow but sudden plans cannot be made for him. He always needs time to accustom himself to any idea & had you seen him tomorrow you would not have found him calm as I want him to be'. She proposed postponing the visit for a few days to prepare him but revealingly concluded her letter: 'I hope you will be *alone* Thursday!'[31] It was deemed imperative that Maurice's condition should be kept as secret as possible.

Most of Maurice's worst periods of 'melancholia' coincided with family visits – infrequent as they were – or news about family members. For example, he suffered a major setback, having been through a period of relative calm, when he read in the *Evening Dispatch* in May 1913 of Lord Edward's engagement; he became 'very bad' and resorted to 'roaring like a lion'.[32] For months afterwards, he remained confused, depressed, violent and suicidal and in September he tried on three occasions to cut his throat with a knife or to stick a fork into his throat.[33] This suicide attempt led to new and stricter regulations being issued in November: one clinical assistant had always to be on duty with the duke and all staff were warned that 'a very strict watch must be maintained all the time'.[34] In October, Frederick came to visit but this only sent Maurice deeper into morose silence. The following January 1914, Lord Desmond paid his one and only visit and briefly 'remained to tea'. The following September Maurice read of Desmond's wounding at the Front but he was unperturbed and 'said that one must have patience and hope for the best'.[35] Lady Cynthia visited on 25 October and Maurice 'was very high that evening'.[36] However, the following weeks he was 'completely off', aggressive and attacked at least one attendant. Lord Frederick was sent for and when he arrived Maurice 'presented himself to him with all the blankets in his bedroom wrapped round his head, neck and shoulders'.[37] This was the general trend. When Lady Cynthia and Lord Frederick visited again in April and June 1915 respectively, Maurice went through the highs of welcoming her and the lows of wanting to avoid Frederick. He went through bouts of refusing food and taking to bed almost as a form of protest.[38] In April 1913, he drew up a fourth codicil to his will, revoking the £5,000 legacy to Lord Frederick, giving it to Lady Cynthia instead. None of their visits lasted much more than an hour. In total Frederick visited only six times during Maurice's time in Craighouse from 1909 to 1922.

As noted already, Maurice displayed a particularly vehement hatred of Donald Pollock. On 5 May 1911, Dr Walshe reported that 'the duke was very much upset at 8 o'clock tonight owing to the birds singing outside the window which he feared would annoy other people, and which he said was due to Pollock and he having called them in the afternoon by whistling to them'.[39] On 23 June 1911, his medical report stated that 'he did not appear friendly towards Dr Pollock and slanged him badly while at tea'.[40] Dr Walshe was acutely aware of the lack of trust Maurice had in Pollock and on one occasion reported the 'freezing reception' given to him.[41] On 2 September 1912, during his worst episode of delusion up to then, he sent for Walshe at 4.40a.m. and asked him to tell Frederick privately of all the faults to which he had been subjected: born an idiot; cross sighted; shoulder out of joint; spine twisted; difficulty with breathing (his admission report showed he had a problem with his lungs); 'father and mother killed'; 'blood taken out of me'; two marriages; two knocks on the head leading to neuralgia, rheumatism, bad stomach; 'made to touch electricity'; and for all of these things Pollock – 'a scoundrel', 'a cur' and 'a blackguard' – was to blame.[42] In a later report, his doctors concluded that his 'dull and delusional' days usually coincided with a Pollock visit.[43]

The physical problems he listed were, in the main, real. The letters of his mother quoted earlier certainly point to some of the physical ailments he alluded to and one may have compounded the other: his twisted spine may have led to difficulties with his breathing, which prompted Hermione to take him with her to Switzerland in the early 1890s, believing the air there 'may do little Kildare good'.[44] The killing of his mother and father and his two marriages were, of course, delusional. However, blood may very well have been taken from him as in the late nineteenth century bloodletting was still used to cure hypertension.[45] Similarly, the use of electricity as a treatment for insanity had been espoused by Julius Althus in his *A treatise on medical electricity: theoretical and practical* (Philadelphia, 1870) and hailed as one of the great medical breakthroughs of the day.[46] He probably believed Pollock to have been responsible for his institutionalization, making the connection between his appointment as his personal physician in 1907 and his committal to Craighouse about eighteen months later. Perhaps, as Friedrich Nietzsche once said, there is 'always some reason in madness'.[47]

VI

Attempts continued to be made to suppress rumours and gossip and to keep Maurice's true condition and location secret from the press. In March 1910, the *Irish Independent* reported he was wintering abroad because of his 'unfavourable state of health' but it was anticipated he would return to Carton in the summer.[48] That summer, after a year in Craighouse, it was speculated that he was suffering from 'delicate health' and that he had been unfortunate in inheriting his parents' 'delicate constitutions'.[49] In October 1910, the *Kildare Observer* noted: '[his] health has been far from good for some time [and he] is at present very unwell'.[50] But it seems there was an objection to this report as the following week the paper was forced to retract the story and say that he was in fact 'very well and is enjoying his stay in Scotland'.[51] No mention was made of Craighouse. In March 1911, on his twenty-fourth birthday, the same newspaper reported that 'happily the young duke of Leinster's illness last October was not so serious as was represented'.[52]

For years after Maurice's committal, society magazines such as *Woman at Home* were publishing photographs and articles that invariably described him as one of the most eligible bachelors in Britain.[53] An untitled and undated newspaper clipping in his medical files for early 1916 stated: 'there is an interesting rumour in society that the young duke of Leinster ... is about to be married ... the matrimonial catch of the season'. It also made the point that 'the ducal resources are considerable, for the property was so well managed by trustees during his Grace's long minority that when he attained his majority in 1908 he came into a large fortune'. His long absences from Carton were passed off as being due to his foreign travels. Every so often a report would claim that he had returned briefly to Carton for a short stay. A newspaper in 1916, headlined 'Gossips on a duke', claimed that Maurice was about to embark on his travels once again and the writer could brag that 'I hear from a friend of the family that he may marry before very long. A very pretty girl is spoken of.'[54] This appeared the same week that he had three fits, two convulsive, at Craighouse. Whoever was responsible for that report annoyed and angered Sir James Crichton Browne (1840–1938), the eminent psychiatrist and the lord chancellor's visitor in lunacy, who wrote to Dr Robertson at Craighouse describing the report as 'preposterous' and demanding that Robertson assure him the 'duke is still under your care and that no matrimonial approaches of any kind have been made to him'.[55]

The rumours continued for years so that even in 1918 when his 'process of deterioration [was] steadily going on',[56] the *London Mail* asked if he would 'really marry after all, or is it only irresponsible gossip?'[57] And Maurice may very well have been reading these newspaper reports himself for his case notes in May 1919 reported that 'he is always expressing a desire to become engaged', and again in November that: 'He has of late evinced a desire to become engaged and marry several of the matrons in the house'.[58] In between, in July 1919, the *Gentlewoman* reported: 'The duke of Leinster who is now thirty-two, leads a quiet life in Ireland'.[59] Not only was it far removed from the truth but by then a series of events had taken place that threatened the very future of the FitzGeralds in Ireland.

CHAPTER EIGHT

War and debt, 1914–22

A lonely impulse of delight
Drove to this tumult in the clouds;
I balanced all, brought all to mind,
The years to come seemed waste of breath,
A waste of breath the years behind
To balance with this life, this death.

W.B. Yeats, 'An Irish airman foresees his death'

In previous chapters, we have learned something of Desmond as a child: he was invariably described by his mother, Hermione, as energetic and boisterous, more confident and physically stronger than his elder brother: 'little Desmond laughs and jumps and tumbles & shouts all day'.[1] He was always portrayed as the courageous one: for example, the fearless young child who did not cry when he cut three fingers on a penknife, or who rode a new pony without any apprehension of being thrown.[2]

In 1901, at the age of thirteen, Desmond arrived at Eton from Cheam Preparatory School, less than a year after Maurice. Destined to go the way of many younger sons of the Irish aristocracy, he was enrolled in the Sandhurst army class and stayed at Eton for six years, where his house master was also Revd Henry T. Bowlby. He came from a family with a long tradition of service to the empire – in the army, the navy and the diplomatic corps (and this excludes their military tradition in the pre-Carton generations when the FitzGeralds were overlords of Ireland). Among his eighteenth-century ancestors Lord Gerald, son of the 1st duke of Leinster, had joined the navy and was lost off Florida in 1788; his brother, Edward, before he became a rebel, fought in the American wars against the American revolutionaries and was seriously wounded at the battle of Eutaw Springs in 1781; another brother, Charles, rose to the position of rear admiral in the navy by 1799.[3] His uncle and mentor, Lord Frederick, had served in the Afghan and Zulu campaigns. Frederick likely took a great deal of satisfaction from grooming him as an army officer, with a possible eye on the fact that the discipline and training Desmond would acquire would serve him well in later managing the family affairs.

167

Desmond enjoyed a much better academic and sporting life than Maurice. The *Eton Calendar* set out that 'the work of the army class will be separated from that of the rest of the school so as to admit of more continuous instruction in the special subjects required'.[4] It was compulsory for him to take English and either French or German, mathematics, history, Latin or Greek and science, with free hand drawing as an option. He particularly excelled at mathematics for which he won an academic prize in 1904. He was treasurer of Revd Bowlby's House Debating Society. He won his maiden debate on 'Whether horse racing should be abolished'. A sense of his identity can perhaps be gleaned from the text: 'In my opinion the abolition of horse racing would be the destruction of the greatest *English* sport … It causes the breed of *English* race horses to be one of the best in the world [my italics].'[5] Bowlby later wrote that at an early stage Desmond 'formed also wise and independent views about his ill-starred country'.[6] Those views may never be known but the adjective possibly suggests aristocratic apprehensions of Home Rule that had been inculcated in Desmond before he arrived at Eton. In various other debating speeches, he made comments that were sometimes ironic in light of what was to transpire for his family and perhaps also revealing in terms of attitudes he had acquired: 'I do think that lunatics ought to be excepted [*recte* accepted] as people not in their right minds, otherwise a man might say he wishes to commit suicide'; '… spendthrifts … ought to be allowed to do what they like with their own property for they only show what fools they are'; '[men] are not so easily upset by trifles, while many little things are always troubling and annoying the women'.[7]

In 1907 he was a school sergeant and an Oppidan Wall.[8] One of the annual highlights of Eton's school year was (and is) the rather obscure Eton Wall Game in which the Collegers (King's scholars) took on the Oppidans (rest of the school) in a game which can loosely be described as a cross between football and rugby union. In the programme for that year Desmond at 11 stone 3 pounds was described as 'a strong second … very useful in loose bullies' (something akin to a rugby-style scrummage).[9] The objective of the game was/is to move a ball from one end of the playing area to the other (about 110 metres from end to end), essentially in a series of mauls and scrums. It is said that 'The Eton Wall Game is exceptionally exhausting and is far more skilful than might appear to the uninitiated. The skill consists in the remorseless application of pressure and leverage as one advances inch by painful inch through a seemingly impenetrable mass of opponents.'[10] As well as an accomplished Oppidan, Desmond helped to win the Football Cup twice and the Section Drill Cup three times, on the last occasion as sergeant in command.

27 Lord Desmond FitzGerald (1888–1916), in uniform, *c*.1914.

Some years later, Bowlby acknowledged his leadership and personable qualities: '[Desmond was] beloved from the first for a certain sunny simplicity and directness which made him free from variable moods, clear in his choice and unswerving in his loyalty to any friend or cause or institution to which he had once given his heart'.[11]

From Eton he went on to Royal Military College at Sandhurst where he displayed 'innate soldierly qualities' and soon, to Maurice's delight, became colour sergeant of his company.[12] After he left he joined the Irish Guards in 1909, rising to lieutenant in 1910, captain in 1913 and major in 1915. By the latter date he was at the Front.

II

Edward was the polar opposite of his older half brother. The love child of
Hermione and Hugo Charteris had been born on 6 May 1892 in London. As
we have already seen, his estranged mother and (non-biological) father lived
apart for the best part of a year before the duke accepted his wife's infidelity and
invited her back to Ireland. However, because of his extra-marital paternity,
Edward's position within the family was undoubtedly compromised by the
early death of his parents. When the 5th duke died, the *Irish Times* reported
that he was succeeded by his eldest son, Maurice, that his second son, Lord
Desmond, had been born in 1888, but made no mention of Edward.[13]

Unlike the other two boys, he was not sent to Cheam, but instead to Mr
Wilkinson's Preparatory School at Eastbourne. He arrived in Eton in the third
term of 1905 but stayed less than four years. His record at Eton was
unremarkable: he did not achieve excellence in any subject; he did not partake
in sports and was fined 1s. and 6d. for violation of rules of Revd Bowlby's
House Debating Society in Michaelmas term 1907.[14] According to the
sensationalized autobiographical account of his life sold to a newspaper in
1957, he and Oliver Lyttelton, later Lord Chandos (1893–1972, secretary of
state for the colonies 1951–4), once stole out at night from Eton, bought a
bottle of whisky, smuggled it back into their rooms and drank it out of mugs.[15]
Other than these few details nothing further has come to light about Edward's
childhood and youth. Even Hermione made only a couple of passing references
to him as a baby and it is very doubtful if he received very much attention from
the FitzGeralds. As time passed, his relationship with his half-brothers became
remote. Writing from Egypt in 1909, Maurice was able to tell Evelyn de Vesci
that Edward was at Eton and 'getting on all right there' but he continued 'I am
afraid I do not receive any letters from him and so cannot give much news
about him'.[16]

From an early age Edward established a reputation for being reckless and
disreputable. The vast majority of his life was to be clouded in extreme
controversy, in what Michael Estorick has described as 'an electric storm of
publicity', where he was sometimes an object of embarrassment, sometimes an
object of ridicule and derision, and at all times dissolute.[17] His behaviour could
be blamed on the fact that he had no restraining parental influence as a child,
but while this may have been a factor there have been many profligate sons
who have had parents well into adulthood.

In 1913, around the time when Desmond was promoted to captain in the
Irish Guards, Edward reached his majority and acquired a degree of financial

28 A young Edward FitzGerald (1892–1976), Hermione's third son
whose biological father was Hugo Charteris, Lord Elcho, c.1913.

independence from his inheritance of an annual allowance of £1,000.[18] In 1930
George Cornwallis-West recalled that during the Edwardian 'hey-day':

> A bachelor in London with a thousand a year was comparatively well off.
> He could get a very good flat in Mayfair, to hold himself and his servant,
> for a hundred and fifty pounds per annum. Dinner at his club cost him
> about four shillings, and any good restaurant would have been prepared
> to provide an excellent dinner, if he chose to give one to his friends, at ten
> and sixpence a head. The best tailor in Savile Row would make a suit of
> evening clothes for eleven guineas, and a morning suit for about eight
> guineas; dress shirts could be bought for ten and sixpence.[19]

As brother of the duke of Leinster, he began to attract the attention of the
newspaper media that was expanding rapidly and becoming more attentive to
the gossip and scandals of celebrity lifestyles. Barely a month after coming-of-
age, the press widely reported his first involvement in a major social scandal

29 May Etheridge (d. 11 Feb. 1935), the 'pink-pyjama-girl' of
Shaftesbury Theatre, Edward's first wife.

when on 12 June 1913 he married May Etheridge, the so-called 'pink-pyjama-girl' of Shaftesbury Theatre, in a private civil service at Wandsworth Registry Office.[20] The wedding was described as 'easily the most romantic and most exciting … of the season'.[21] But this is certainly not the impression it made on Edward's family or in aristocratic circles because May was a gaiety girl.

In the late-Victorian period, gaiety halls had become a favourite haunt for young male aristocrats. Some of these such as Hermione's brother, Hubert

(1862–1918), and Geoffrey Taylour, 4th marquess of Headford (1878–1943), became so captivated by young actresses that they married with fatal social consequences: when Headford married Rosie Boote in 1901 he was forced to resign his commission in the Irish Guards, while Hubert was disinherited and disowned for a long period by his father and eventually ended up in bankruptcy court.[22] Similarly, when George Fitzwilliam married a gaiety girl he had to resign from the Royal Horse Guards, and his cousin, Charles, wrote disparagingly: 'George hasn't one ounce of family pride or feeling in his constitution'.[23] In her 1914 memoirs, Lady Warwick quoted one *grande dame* who was disgusted to find a chorus girl fiancée of an aristocratic son in the same newspaper as her respectable niece: 'I found a portrait of my niece on one page, and opposite to her was the chorus girl whom that fool – is going to marry! Why should one rub shoulders with a creature like that, even in a weekly paper? What are we coming to?'[24] In Ireland, Hermione's close friend, Elizabeth Fingall, recalled that when she went hunting, her hair had to be irreproachable under her top hat for 'if one had appeared in curls ... one would have looked like a chorus girl, and if I had dared to do such a thing Fingall would have sent me home at once'.[25] Yet, by 1914, seventeen peers, including Edward, had married gaiety girls (and countless other peers, not to mention King Edward VII, had well documented affairs with actresses).

Thus, the young and naive May Etheridge – 'a very charming brunette' – entered an aristocratic lions' den of social snobbery. And even more fatal for her was the fact that while Edward was initially infatuated by her beauty he was completely disingenuous in his intentions. He later wrote (and his own egotism is worth noting):

> I was twenty, easily impressed and ready to enjoy the company of any pretty girl. May was more than pretty. She was tiny, dark and looked like an angel. Other people envied my being with her, and that pleased my vanity. I saw her again and again, I was fond of her, she liked me. Her interest flattered me. She was gay, too, and adorable. But I was not in love with her.[26]

The young actress understandably was in awe of her new-found position; in an interview with the *Daily Mirror*, she allegedly told the reporter: 'we became acquainted and gradually got to be very good friends, and – oh, well – then we just became engaged. I suppose it is really rather romantic'.[27] She believed that her stage career would end with her marriage and that she would be brought back to Carton by Edward.[28]

The wedding service was a bewildering occasion. May arrived at the London registry office dressed in a powder-blue coat and skirt and a close fitting hat 'with a big osprey in it'. Shortly afterwards, a car pulled up directly opposite and Edward, dressed in 'a lounge suit and a straw hat', got out. The location of the wedding was supposed to be a secret, but as the registry office was located beside a busy polling station on the day of the Wandsworth by-election, the cars and the fashionable style of the couple attracted a curious crowd.[29] Edward decided not to proceed and got a message to May to leave the registry office immediately. She got into a taxi and headed off in one direction; Edward got into another and headed in the opposite direction. The disappointed crowd dispersed. The couple returned a short time later but when they emerged from the office another crowd had 'mysteriously gathered'. The couple ran back inside, exited a back entrance, 'escaped into the scullery of an adjoining restaurant, thence into the restaurant proper, ran past the astonished diners and eventually reached the street and a taxi cab'.[30]

There was no honeymoon – Edward made the excuse that he could not afford to pay for rooms at the Cavendish Hotel so he went to a house in Belgrave Square (probably the Duncombe London house), while May went to her home at 76 Amesbury Avenue. For the next two days he did not contact her and when she tried to contact him she was fobbed off by the butler at Belgrave Square. Edward soon regretted his decision to marry a gaiety girl. Years after they separated, he confessed that his marriage to May would not have happened had his family 'not acted as they did'; in other words, he rebelled against their objections to him being associated with a gaiety girl. May had naively thought that she would be brought to Buckingham Place to be presented to the Royal family; Edward callously told her he had made 'sufficient fool' of himself by marrying her without presenting her at court.[31] But as Marcus Scriven has concluded: 'His sensitivity to social decorum was less acute when his own amusement was at stake'.[32] His behaviour towards May became increasingly more dishonourable, while at the same time he became increasingly estranged from the FitzGeralds. In 1930, his uncle Henry admitted that this was because the family had frowned upon his marriage.[33]

On 27 May 1914, May gave birth to a son, Gerald. Almost immediately after the birth, Edward deserted both mother and infant and May was forced to bring Gerald back to the impoverished surroundings of her mother's flat at Baron's Court in London. He was reputedly dressed in clothes made by May's grandmother in Brixton and his medical bills were met by her pawning some of the presents given to her by Edward. Not being able to afford a nanny, May had to take her young son with her to the club where she worked.[34]

The FitzGerald family may have wanted to keep Edward at arm's length but, as we shall see below, as circumstances changed, Lord Frederick did not want the possible future duke of Leinster being reared at the back of a gaiety hall. In 1914, he, therefore, began a long four-year legal battle that eventually resulted in Gerald being made a ward of court. In 1918, young Gerald was allegedly dragged screaming from the arms of his distraught mother and brought back to Ireland where he was reared at Johnstown Castle in Wexford by his grand-aunt.[35] The following year, May was paid off in the form of a less-than-generous allowance and forbidden to see her child except on specified occasions. Her enquiries about her son were met by curt and cold messages from the FitzGerald solicitors, typically: 'The marquess of Kildare is in good health'.[36] There is a rather poignant letter that survives written by Gerald to his mother, undated [the spelling has not been changed]:

> Dear Mummy.
>
> I hope you are very well and I wish you a very happy Xmas and a happy new year. I am sending you a card witch I painted with the lovly paint box you sent me and I have the lovly <u>Macano</u> you gave me and thank you very much for the lovly photo you sent me. I hope you are having a nice time. The hounds were down here the other day [Wexford]. How is daddy. I hope you are having nice weather. I hope you will like the card. Give my best love to daddy. From your dear son Gerald love and kisses [followed by over forty Xs].[37]

In 1926, Edward began divorce proceedings against May on the grounds of her adultery with a professional footballer, George Newall, who played with Swanage FC. By then she was living in 'a very small and humble' cottage 'in one of the poorer parts' of Bournemouth. She vowed she would 'fight to the last ditch'.[38] But Edward held all the aristocratic ace cards and he was eventually granted a divorce in 1930. A short time after, May unsuccessfully attempted suicide. However, five years later she succeeded in taking her own life: the heart-broken 'pink-pyjama-girl' had died after long years of isolation from her son, penury and depression.

III

Around the same time as the birth of his son, Edward was declared bankrupt for the first time. Since he had come of age he had indulged in a spending spree financed by loans easily acquired because of his social credentials. His extravagances included staying at the Buckingham Place Hotel, opera-going in Paris and the purchase of two yachts in a short space of time. He recalled many years later: 'The world was as rosy as the pink champagne I drank at the Cavendish Hotel'.[39]

As a bankrupt, he was technically not allowed to hold a rank in the regular army but when war broke out in the summer of 1914 he managed to covertly secure a commission as a lieutenant in the 8th Service Battalion of the West Riding Regiment.[40] On 2 July 1915, his battalion set sail on the *SS Aquitania* and on 22 July they reached Gallipoli. On 8 August, at Suvla Bay, Edward was shot in the arm causing severe damage to his muscospiral nerve; it meant he could not fire a rifle and so was taken out of the field.[41] When he arrived back in London in December the army medical personnel noted that he was also suffering from 'over-strain of the nervous system'. He was probably like so many others affected by his experiences at the Front but his file also noted: 'The present worry about his private affairs may be one of the contributory causes of his state of health'. In December he was judged 'still unfit to resume military duties' and so he was honourably discharged in March 1917.[42]

To surmise that Edward went to the Front to escape his financial difficulties would be unfair (although some heirs did).[43] His service record was an honourable one and his reason for enlisting should be seen as part of an aristocratic mindset that historically characterized any outbreak of hostilities.[44] In 1914, there was an initial expectation among many aristocrats in Ireland – even if not publicly articulated – that the war would provide them with an opportunity to re-establish their position in Irish society as they answered 'the call of the empire'.[45] Douglas Hyde's 1915 boast that 'All the gentry have suffered. *Noblesse oblige*. They have behaved magnificently' was not an idle one.[46] As time passed it became clear that aristocratic families suffered for a variety of reasons during the Great War, and the FitzGeralds were no exception. In many respects their war experiences typified the clichéd conclusions that 4 August 1914 was 'the last day of Ireland's *ancien régime*';[47] or 'the last chapter in the history of many families'.[48]

IV

Desmond's position was different; he was already a serving captain in the Irish Guards who, at the outbreak of war, was living at 44 Curzon Street in London. Desmond, his Eton generation and the children of the Souls went to the Front with little idea of what faced them. By the end of 1914 alone, the death toll from his social class would include 6 peers, 16 baronets, 95 sons of peers and 82 sons of baronets.[49] At home, the older generation, including Lord Frederick, did all they could to support the war effort through fundraising and encouraging recruitment in their localities. Upon the outbreak of war, Frederick opened up Carton demesne to the Maynooth company of the National Volunteers to allow them to drill, probably in anticipation that many of them would enlist in the British army, and therefore before John Redmond's famous Woodenbridge and House of Commons speeches declaring the support of the Volunteers for the war effort.[50] In August 1914, he pledged £1,000 to the Prince of Wales' National Relief Fund.[51] He would continue to allow the demesne to be used for fundraising purposes during the war: for example, on 2 September 1916 a garden fete at Carton raised £300 for the prisoners of war of the Royal Dublin Fusiliers.[52] That September Frederick was elected chairman of the County Kildare War Pensions Committee.[53]

Meanwhile, on 12 August 1914, Desmond left England with his battalion and a couple of weeks later took part in the retreat from Mons. On 1 September, he was wounded at Villers Cotterets.[54] It was the first signal to his family and friends that he might be in danger. When Dr Donald Pollock, Maurice's physician, heard of his wounding, he wrote revealing his apprehensions: 'I am glad that Desmond's wound is no worse. Personally I feel thankful that he is not in the middle of it and may be kept out of it for good. With Ed as successor things would be too dreadful.'[55]

Desmond did not share these concerns and so he rejoined his battalion during the first battle of Ypres in October–November 1914. Just a few days beforehand, he had dined with Edward, Prince of Wales (1894–1972), at Calais. The young prince had unsuccessfully tried to persuade his father, King George V, to allow him join the 1st Battalion of the Grenadier Guards. Permission was denied and he was compensated by being allowed regular visits to the front where he entertained officers in his temporary quarters.

A few weeks later, and six days before the battle of Ypres ended on 22 November, Desmond wrote to his Aunt Dolly (Lord Henry's wife) revealing the horrors of war: 'the casualties have been so awful that I shall not find more than two officers out of the 30 that started with me and not so many as 100 men out of the original lot'.[56] The following day, 17 November, he wrote a letter obviously intended for his family, but addressed to nobody in specific. A cloud of pessimism had descended upon him:

> This is just to say that except for the sorrow it may cause to my dear relations, I have no reason to fear death and I hope this will be a comfort to anybody who sorrows over it. I am most anxious that on no account

should there be a memorial service for me and as far as possible that nobody should mourn. I should however like a small tablet put up for me in the Guards Chapel and at Eton where I spent the happiest days of my life. Silence alone can express my love for and gratitude to my relations for all they have done for me. To a great extent I am a futurist but if I am granted to die for my country, it is the one death above all others that I should wish for and gladly accept.

As far as I know I leave no unpaid bills
Desmond FitzGerald, 17/11/14.
I should like to call attention to *Harvest gleanings and gathered fragments* by Marianne Farningham in which is a poem called 'Too Soon' with which I entirely agree.[57]

As well as the obvious poignancy, the letter is illuminating on a number of levels: firstly, the total carnage Desmond witnessed at Ypres was leaving an obvious psychological scar; the initial enthusiasm to become involved in the war had dissipated and was replaced by despair and despondency; and the foreboding of his own death was palpable, the tone and content of the letter similar to thousands more written by young officers at different stages of the war. Desmond made claim to be fighting for 'my country'. Before the war, he would have had no difficulty in reconciling his Irishness with his Britishness; it was like his soul within his body. The sense of patriotic heroism that would, he believed, come with death is suggested (and not dissimilar to that shared by fellow Irishmen of a different political persuasion in 1916 but who had a very different sense of 'country').

Finally, his choice of hymn is instructive. The latter generations of FitzGeralds had been devout evangelicals. Marianne Farningham (1834–1909, born Mary Ann Hearn) is now almost anonymous but in the early twentieth century her writings and her lectures had a strong influence on the changes within popular evangelicalism.[58] The theme of 'Too soon' not only suggests Desmond's own evangelical beliefs but it is also quite similar (on different levels) to Yeats' poem quoted at the beginning of this chapter:

> God loves them, and He spares them much,
> Not theirs to wait alone,
> And feel the ache of useless years,
> With strength and vigour gone,
> They are not stranded derelicts…
> Not theirs to lift their fading eyes
> And find no comrades left;

> Not theirs to dwell among the graves,
> Forsaken and bereft,
> They pass from work to better work.

The lines would have resonated with young aristocrats like Desmond who, as the war dragged on, found themselves becoming increasingly disillusioned. When his cousin, the earl of Feversham, was killed in 1916, his friend Lord Londonderry recorded: 'those who fall in the war are the truly happy ones'.[59] In May 1915, Desmond's battalion suffered further severe losses at the Battle of Festubert. This had a hugely demoralizing effect on the Irish Guards but the battalion doctor, W.H.L. McCarthy, was later to write about Desmond:

> I will never forget his cheery optimism during and after those days in May when the battalion had such heavy casualties at Festubert. I myself felt then that the spirit of the battalion was broken forever, our losses in officers and men were so serious. But Desmond, with wonderful confidence and capacity, devoted himself at once to the task of building up the unit afresh, and before many weeks had passed the old spirit and tradition had returned.[60]

The following October, Desmond was seriously wounded a second time during the taking of the Hohenzollern Redoubt.[61] According to Dr McCarthy: 'although wounded he endeavoured for days in extreme pain to carry out the duties of Commanding Officer'.[62] McCarthy remembered him as an officer of 'splendid character', with 'wonderful pluck … brave, steadfast, loyal and courteous, he was a great example of the chivalrous knight of history'.[63] Shortly afterwards, he was awarded the Military Cross, the third level decoration awarded to officers 'for an act or acts of exemplary gallantry', and mentioned twice in despatches.

As the war continued reports of casualties began to flood the newspapers, local and national, back home. In 1915, Douglas Hyde wrote to a friend: 'Nearly everyone I know in the army has been killed. Poor Lord de Freyne and his brother were shot the same day and buried in the same grave … MacDermott of Coolavin, my nearest neighbour, has lost his eldest son shot dead in the Dardanelles.'[64] Most of the families of the original Souls coterie were launched into mourning for their sons: Hermione's nephew, Lt.-Col. Charles Duncombe, 2nd earl of Feversham (he had succeeded his grandfather), was killed at Flers-Courcelette in 1916 when commanding the 21st Batallion of the King's Royal Rifles. (Because his grandfather had died only the year before, the family were now left with two sets of death duties and a ten-year-old heir and so the house they could no longer afford to maintain became a girls' boarding school for the next sixty years.) Lord Kinnaird's eldest son, Douglas, was killed in only the third month of fighting and another son was killed in 1917; Yvo Charteris, son of Hugo and Mary Elcho, was killed in October 1915, just six weeks after leaving Eton to join the Grenadier Guards; his older brother, Ego, was killed in Egypt in April 1916. Hugo, Hermione's former lover, now Lord Wemyss, was deeply affected; his daughter wrote: 'Poor Papa is most piteous – heartbroken and just like a child – tears pouring down his cheeks and so naively astonished. I think he really loved Evo [sic] the most of his children [possibly because he had been the result of his reconciliation with Mary] and was so proud and hopeful about him.'[65] His sister, Lady Cynthia Asquith, wrote in her wartime diary: 'Really one hardly knows who is alive and who is dead'.[66] George Wyndham's only child, Percy, was killed in the first year of fighting; Billie and Julien Grenfell were killed within six weeks of each other in 1915; Edward Wyndham Tennant, nephew of both Margot Asquith and George Wyndham, was killed at the Somme in September 1916. In total, Madeline Wyndham, George's mother, lost five grandsons. Cynthia Charteris, Mary's daughter (married to Prime Minister Asquith's second son), summed up the feelings of an aristocratic generation: 'Oh why was I born for this time? Before one is thirty to have known more dead than living people'.[67] And later in 1918:

> I am beginning to rub my eyes at the prospect of peace. I think it will require more courage than anything that has gone before … One will have to look at long vistas again, instead of short ones, and one will at last fully recognize that the dead are not only dead for the duration of the war.[68]

By March 1916, most of Desmond's senior officers had either been killed or were out of action because of injury.[69] During the first battle of Ypres, he is said to have 'carried on the command, though in extreme pain from his own wounds, refusing to go to hospital while work remained to be done'.[70] But before the second battle of Ypres (22 April–15 May 1916) broke out in earnest, Desmond was killed at Calais on 3 March. He was not killed, like many of his fellow officers, leading his men over the top, but rather as a result of an unfortunate accident. There are slightly conflicting reports but it seems that during a practice drill he was with the company chaplain, Fr Lane-Fox, when the latter picked up a live hand grenade that had a defective fuse and it exploded wounding Lane-Fox – he lost an eye and several fingers – but fatally wounding Desmond who died within an hour at the Millicent Sutherland Red Cross Hospital.[71] Regimental lore provided a more heroic end for Desmond:

the chaplain had dropped the live grenade among a group of Guardsmen standing in the trenches and Desmond 'without pausing for thought … hurled himself on top of the grenade with a second to spare and was blown to pieces'.[72]

Desmond was buried in a public cemetery at Calais, according to the instructions of his letter quoted above. There was no formal parade but the battalion lined the road to the graveyard.[73] Immediately on hearing the news of his death, Prince Edward wrote to Desmond's aunt, Lady Cynthia Graham:

> Please forgive my troubling you with a letter at such a time as this, but I must ask you to accept my very sincere sympathy on the great loss you have sustained. I got a wire this evening to say that dear Desmond had been accidentally killed in a bombing accident at Calais. It is one of the greatest blows or shocks I have ever had for in Desmond's death I have lost my greatest friend. I can't yet realize what has happened or bring myself to think I shall never seen him again … It is too terribly tragic for me to be able to express myself better … <u>Please</u> do not bother to answer this; but I can't help writing to you who I know was ever first in Desmond's thoughts! He was my <u>greatest</u> friend and that is really why I write.[74]

Queen Mary wrote two days later expressing how 'deeply distressed' she and her husband, King George, were at the news of 'the death of your dear and charming nephew' and went on: 'His loss will make a big blank in my boy's life'.[75] Lady Cynthia returned to the prince a 'little charm' that Desmond always wore and the latter promised: 'I shall ever value it more than most things I possess as a remembrance of him and I have put it on my watch chain where it will ever remain'.[76]

At home in Kildare, Desmond's death was celebrated as an act of heroism. The democratization of war meant that he had fallen with the sons of former tenants. (In the town and region of Athy alone, over 2,000 men enlisted during the war and 118 were killed.)[77] The *Journal of the Kildare Archaeological Society*, founded in 1891 by his uncle, Lord Walter, published Lord D'Abernon's tribute from the *Morning Post*.

> … he had already written his name large in the annals of a regiment which, beginning with the retreat from Mons, continued in the severest fighting, and has borne itself most bravely among the brave. By the testimony of brother officers, none of their number had served more faithfully than he, to establish the reputation of the younger regiments on a par with the glorious past of the Guards Brigade.[78]

His courage was compared to 'the ardent national enthusiasm of a celebrated member of his family in 1798' (even though Desmond's and Lord Edward's patriotic aspirations were hardly similar). The tribute was standard: the men of the Irish Guards 'felt the inspiration of his example, and loved him for it'; they felt also that he was 'distinguished by singleness of heart, purity of life and unflinching idealism of conduct' and none saw him other than 'steadfast, loyal and unselfish in a supreme degree'.[79] D'Abernon concluded that 'it will be long before either England or Ireland produces a finer example of what is best in both races, or of those qualities which each nation esteems most worthy of praise'.[80] The *Kildare Observer* reported: 'Dying at the age of twenty-seven he had already written his name large in the annals of a regiment which beginning with the retreat from Mons continued in the severest fighting'.[81] Meetings of the Distress Committee in Naas and the Kildare Committee of Agriculture, chaired by the vice chairman of the county council, both passed motions of sympathy with Lord Frederick.[82] The county council passed the following resolution:

> That we, the members of the Kildare County Council, hereby express our sympathy with our colleague, Lord Frederick FitzGerald, and the other members of the Leinster family in their sad bereavement through the death … of Lord Desmond FitzGerald, and we are confident that the sympathetic knowledge which is shared by an appreciative and grateful people, that he gave his life for his country after a brief but glorious period of service will tend to mitigate in some degree the great sorrow which they feel for the early ending of a promising and brilliant career.[83]

Notably, the nationalist members, supporters of the constitutional Home Rule movement, perceived that he 'gave his life for his country', while a few minutes later they unequivocally condemned the more radical separatist leaders of the 1916 Easter Rising:

> That we, the members of the Kildare county council, strongly deprecate the recent deplorable action of a section of our countrymen in resorting to force of arms. At the same time we strongly appeal in what we consider the best interests of this country, and the empire as a whole, to the government to extend the greatest possible clemency to the rank and file, who we believe were deceived into taking part in the Rising.[84]

In Maynooth, when the war ended, John Doran, secretary of the Maynooth branch of the British Legion, wrote to Lord Frederick enquiring if the trustees would grant a site to build a wooden hut to be called 'The Lord Desmond FitzGerald Club', assuring him that 'the people residing in the vicinity of the Square have not the least objection to the proposed building and wish it every success'.[85]

Lord Desmond was undoubtedly a gifted and talented young aristocrat. His mother's first impressions of her son were always that he would be much stronger, braver and more accomplished than his elder brother; his school record was impressive both from an academic and sporting perspective; his early military career was equally impressive as he rose through the ranks and then showed commendable leadership qualities at the Front; he had made all the right type of social connections before the war, including becoming a future king's best friend. His potential had been noted before the war and not invented in commemoration. His death had frightening implications for the estate. As Donald Pollock had pointed out, 'With Ed as successor things would be too dreadful'. Now it was a probability instead of a possibility. Perhaps Lord Frederick shared Hugo Charteris' 'naive astonishment' that such a calamity could possibly befall their class.[86] He now had to reconcile himself to the fact that there was the likelihood that a philanderer would inherit the Leinster title and fortune. But even worse was to come.

V

The Kildare County Council vote of sympathy disguised the fact that a great deal had changed outside the demesne walls of Carton, and within the country as a whole. While the 1916 Rising had initially been deplored subsequent events led to an upsurge in support for the more radical separatist movement, Sinn Féin, which had as its aim the establishment of an Irish republic. In Maynooth, one of its main organizers was the previously mentioned merchant, Domhnall Ua Buachalla, who a few years previously had been part of the coming-of-age committee that presented an address of congratulations to Maurice. Aged fifty at the time of the Easter rebellion in 1916, he was leader of the local Irish Volunteers and secured a place for himself in local lore when he organized his company to march from Maynooth to Dublin. Their participation in the fighting was minimal but it brought Ua Buachalla to the attention of the authorities and he was imprisoned after the rebellion. In the 1918 general election (after the Fourth Reform Act had given the vote to all adult men and women over the age of thirty), Ua Buachalla won the North Kildare seat as a Sinn Féin candidate, signalling another change of the political order. He later became a Fianna Fáil TD, from 1927 to 1932. After he lost his seat in the general election of 1932, the Irish government appointed him governor general of Ireland – the representative of the British Crown – a position he held until the office was abolished in 1937 as a result of the deliberate political policy of the de Valera administration, supported by Ua Buachalla, to make the governorship irrelevant.[87] Meanwhile, in 1920, Lord Frederick felt that there was no further role for him on the county council and so he retired. His seat was taken by Ua Buachalla. It encapsulated the swing in aristocratic political fortunes during Frederick's lifetime.

Away from Maynooth, political developments in Britain were equally ominous. The year 1916 also witnessed the appointment of David Lloyd George as prime minister of the United Kingdom at the head of a wartime coalition government that would last until 1922. Not only would he negotiate a peace deal resulting in the independence of the twenty-six county area of the Irish Free State (while a new state of Northern Ireland was also established), but his whole administration was viewed by the aristocracy as the culmination of 'all those distasteful aspects of British public life that had been on the increase since the 1880s'.[88] The leading southern Irish unionist, Lord Midleton, was so disgusted with Lloyd George's Irish policy that he refused the lord lieutenancy in 1918. The world that the dukes of Leinster had inhabited for so long was fast disappearing, as the old social system in Britain and wider Europe gave way to a new order, plutocratic and vulgar to the eyes of the aristocracy, but with a momentum built on the back of mass democracy and the emergence of parvenu wealth, which culminated in the separation of social life and political life. According to Lord Dunraven, who published his memoirs in 1922, 'disintegration' had well and truly set in since the late nineteenth century and the London scene now included those who 'before the war, would not have formed part of what the press is pleased to term society'.[89] Very soon after Desmond's untimely death, the FitzGerald family would have to confront head on the *nouveaux riches* intent on taking their position.

VI

In March 1916, Dr Donald Pollock informed Maurice of the death of Desmond; Lord Frederick did not visit until late March and Lady Cynthia a month later. At first Maurice was 'very indignant' that the message was not sent direct to him, and all of the following week he became 'depressed and dull' and sat in quiet melancholy.[90] His mood was not simply because of his disgruntlement; primarily, he had lost a brother of whom he was very fond and proud.[91]

In the months that followed his September 1912 breakdown, he became a good deal calmer and in March 1913 it was reported that he had been well 'for a considerable time. He is extremely good humoured with everyone and is experiencing no delusions.' However, he was still having regular epileptic fits and as time passed these became more and more frequent and severe and were increasingly accompanied by convulsions. Occasionally, during attacks of *petit mal*, he would drop his tennis racket, stand still for a minute, pick it up and resume his game.[92] By 1915 his weight had ballooned from around twelve stone to fifteen-and-a-half stone but this was 'a source of great satisfaction to him and he frequently [referred] to how well he is developed and especially his voice'. However, his doctor was less impressed and good-humouredly reported: 'those of us who have had the painful experience of hearing him singing sometimes at service will have other views, no doubt, about the vocal development'.[93]

The war reinvigorated him for a time; he began to 'study his war maps and papers relating to the military and naval situation with a zeal and assiduity that would do credit to "eye witness" at general headquarters'.[94] But 1915 became his worst year to date. In July, the half-yearly summary of his condition read: 'on the whole, however, one notices a process of deterioration going on. He has been more insane and more stupid this year.'[95] While in 1911 he had eleven very severe epileptic attacks, the number rose to forty-eight in 1915.[96] Possibly the biggest disruption came during the war years from the loss of the doctors who had come to know him so well, and who had been very sympathetic to him: Doctor Walshe moved to Australia, and Drs Cramie and Power to Mary's Hospital in Manchester. Notably, the tone of his medical reports changed after the war; he was now merely 'this patient'. Then, of course, many things changed during the war, not least of all attitudes of deference towards the aristocracy.

VII

The £1,000 per annum Edward received from the family estate fell a long way short of financing his high roller lifestyle and after he was discharged from the army he had no other regular form of income. By 1917, Edward had borrowed £15,000 at such extortionate rates that he owed over £60,000 by 1918.[97] It seems that after Desmond was killed, Edward's bargaining powers as the successor to the duke of Leinster increased exponentially and he had few qualms about exploiting this. Moneylenders swarmed around him like sharks around their prey for this was a time when there were plenty of men 'on the make', only too happy to exploit the changing circumstances of aristocrats desperately clinging on to a vanishing era of power and elitism.

Sometime in 1914, Edward met James Fraser of 7 Henrietta Street, Covent Garden, whom he later unflatteringly referred to as the son of a Scottish gillie: 'a strange individual who delighted in meeting young men in trouble … whose business was to introduce them to money-lenders and then collect a nice commission'.[98]

In Edward's own words, Fraser assisted 'in introducing me to money-lenders and that kind of thing'.[99] (Fraser would later call himself Edward's secretary but Edward insisted on the use of the term 'agent' as he paid him commission 'by results'.) In the early years, Edward paid as much as £2,700 for introductions, effectively into a sordid world of moneylenders and corruption. He paid extortionate interest rates; for example, he borrowed £1,000 from B. Lipton Ltd and had to repay £2,075 (Fraser received £350 of the £1,000); he borrowed £500 from the Regent Trust for which he had to repay £1,950 (Fraser received £150); £1,000 from Samuels and Company for which he repaid £2,000 (A.V. Cole received £250).[1] William Cooper Hobbs charged him interest rates of 400 per cent. He borrowed at similarly extravagant rates from a London financier, Frederick S. Salaman, who operated out of 1 & 2 Bucklersbury in London, and who was later to be disparagingly referred to as one of his 'Jew moneylenders'.[2] Salaman would later lead the bankruptcy suit against him.[3]

Edward signed dozens, perhaps hundreds, of promissory notes and swindled money in a variety of scams. In May 1922, he received a loan of £3,000 worth of jewellery from Fishers in Molton Street – as some Hollywood actors might in the present day before an Oscars ceremony where they would effectively act as an advertisement for the jeweller. Within a few days he had pawned it in consideration for a loan of £1,000.[4] In October 1922, he gave the afore-mentioned William Cooper Hobbs promissory notes for £2,500 in return for £50 cash and the loan of a Daimler car. He immediately sold the car for £150 and so made himself liable for £2,500 for the sake of raising £200 in cash. Out of that he paid Fraser £100 in commission for making the contact with Hobbs.[5] He gave another man named Partridge ten promissory notes for £1,000 each in return for £1,000 cash and some antique snuff boxes later sold for £760 (he later admitted he thought the boxes were worth a lot more). He paid £300 in commission to those who arranged the transaction.[6]

Edward simply did not care about the consequences as long as he had quick access to money. In fact, a wider study may suggest it was a symptom of the age of aristocratic decline. For example, on 23 July 1920, Edward's contemporary, the 5th earl of Clancarty, was tried at the Central Criminal Court for among other crimes obtaining money and goods under false pretences; using cheques to buy jewellery for a lady-friend and for meals at the Ritz, Berkeley and Oddenino's, knowing that they were going to be dishonoured, as he was a bankrupt. Like Edward, all of this credit was allowed, as one waiter put it at his trial: 'on account of his being a noble earl'. Thus, the judge, when passing a three-month custodial sentence, told Clancarty:

> You are one of those unfortunate men who have not been brought up to do anything for a living. You might have been in happier circumstances if you had been called upon to discharge the sufficiently onerous and responsible duties of a landlord. But owing to the state of the country in which you live you were deprived even of that occupation.[7]

About April 1922, Edward was introduced to Messrs Williams and Simmons, operating as stockbrokers. They invited him to act as a director of their company – his title, he was assured, would lend credibility to their enterprise. Again, characteristic of the age was the belief that the name of a peer upon the front page of a prospectus would be an attractive enticement to potential investors or a bonus to a corporation if the newly appointed director had influence in politics or Court.[8] Who duped who became the question in this transaction: Edward had little credibility and Williams and Simmons were far from legitimate. They promised him a 'consideration' of £1,500 per annum and in July told Edward 'they had a big deal on in shares'. They asked him to accept bills to the value of £10,000, assuring him that 'the bills could not be dealt with, but simply put in a drawer' to be given back to him later when they sold the shares at a profit. He gave the bills without making any enquiry about the reputations of Williams and Simmons. When it was too late he found out that Williams and Simmons was in fact a 'bucket shop'. Edward got his solicitor to write to them but received no reply. The bills for £10,000 passed on to a man named Webb who purchased ten Sentinel wagons. In turn they were sold to the Golders Green Garage for £5,000. When Edward approached Sentinel Wagon Works Ltd and told them he had been swindled they simply informed him 'that was not their problem'.[9]

Simultaneously, he ran up a long list of unpaid accommodation bills for hotels, cottages rented, and guesthouses. On occasion some of the world's leading hotels, such as the Waldorf Astoria in New York, were happy to let him stay free or at cost, as long as they could advertise that the duke of Leinster was staying with them. He later boasted how 'the Connaught and Dorchester were anxious to have us stay with them at nominal rates'.[10] Edward was even happy that there were tailors who felt he was a good advertisement for their clothes and so when Scott Thornton Ltd offered to make two coats for him: 'I told them I had no money to pay and they said it would do them good if I had them, and finally I consented to have two coats, which I have never even worn'.[11]

Edward was also a compulsive gambler; his second wife, Rafaelle Davidson Kennedy, recalled his rooms 'ankle deep in form books, bookies' slips and football pool coupons'.[12] In July 1922, Edward placed a huge bet of £3,000 that he would drive from London to Aberdeen in less than fifteen hours. He made the journey of just over 400 miles (or 650 kilometres) in thirteen hours, driving a Rolls Royce, probably a Silver Ghost. It was quite a feat without motorways. (That same month he had his license endorsed having been found guilty of speeding at 33 m.p.h. along Constitutional Hill and there had been previous convictions in 1914 at Bromley, Lambeth and Brighton.)[13]

Throughout the early months of 1923, reports of Edward's activities appeared regularly in the papers, usually relating to conspiracy to fraud charges. Between April and June 1923, he was summoned at Marlborough Street police station on at least four occasions for unlawfully obtaining credit and not declaring himself a bankrupt.[14] In November, when he was called before a public examination in the High Court of Justice to enquire into the extent of his debts, he was unsurprisingly accused of having lived way beyond his means by borrowing. Edward pleaded: 'I have signed for a lot of interest, but they will be paid, and I thought they would be paid much sooner'.[15] One of the prosecutors, Mr Waterer, pointed out to Edward: 'You have given so many promissory notes for large amounts, and, apparently, in such a reckless way, that it is not surprising you cannot remember all the details'.[16] It was a trend his life followed to the end. In a later bankruptcy proceeding in 1953 an official report read: 'The bankrupt was quite reckless in the way in which he raised money, or allowed it to be raised for him, and was unjustifiably extravagant, having regard to his available means'.[17]

VIII

Soon after his first declared bankruptcy in 1918 Edward was introduced by James Fraser to Henry (Harry) Mallaby-Deeley (1863–1937), a fascinating and enigmatic character, eminently worthy of an extensive biography in his own right. Born Henry Deeley he assumed his mother's maiden name of Mallaby by deed poll in 1922. His father, William Clark Deeley, was a prosperous merchant who lived at Curzon Park in Chester and who had extensive business interests in Liverpool. (His other son, Frank Curzon (1868–1927), who took his business name from the family home at Curzon Park, was the well-known musical comedy producer.)[18] Henry was educated at Shrewsbury and studied law at Trinity College, Cambridge. He became a highly successful businessman and property speculator/developer. With his economic status came a desire for commensurate political status and so in 1910 he successfully contested the seat for Harrow as a Conservative and then Willesden East in 1918. After the war he opened a tailor's shop in the former headquarters of the Art Union of London, a late-nineteenth century Palladian building, 'for the purpose of defeating the flagrant profiteering in men's clothes' that had become a characteristic of the wartime boom.[19] Even in far flung places of rural Ireland, the 'fifty-shillings tailor' achieved a reputation; thus, in March 1920, the provincial *Dundalk Democrat*, in a satirical piece on the theme of dancing, claimed that the fictitious Freddie Fitzjazz would overcome all obstacles to attend a dance 'even if he has to do with one of Mallaby-Deeley's suits this summer. That's the kind of man he is.'[20]

Throughout his life, Mallaby-Deeley gained a reputation for his philanthropic and charitable work. It was well known that most of his many contributions to various charities were 'made anonymously; he hated the limelight but could not always escape from it'.[21] He was also extremely astute in the way he created the social and political networks that enhanced his standing. He bought his way into the centre of British society by paying for the re-facing of the Portland stone exterior of the Carlton Club in London.[22] But it was probably his foresight to use golf clubs to create social networks which was most remarkable for its time.

In an era of expanding democracy, Mallaby-Deeley believed golf clubs had the same potential for the middle classes as gentlemen's clubs such as the Carlton, Boodles and the Kildare Street in Ireland had for the aristocracy and landed gentry in the past. The social climbers of London – bankers, doctors, merchants and lawyers who now practised and lived among their clients – witnessed in the American experience how 'Businessmen quickly found it [golf] an ideal recreational vehicle for the social lubrication so vital to the flow of commerce'.[23] On the other hand, the aristocracy saw golf clubs as the 'emblem of the stockbroker luxury that was eroding the old, virile values'.[24] One of the few aristocratic exceptions at this stage was Arthur Balfour who was an avid golfer and had introduced George Wyndham to the sport when they both arrived in Ireland in the late 1880s.[25] When Mallaby-Deeley began to design courses himself – in 1914, he was described by Josiah Newman, editor of the American magazine *Golf*, as 'the finest amateur golf architect in the world'[26] – he likely used his Party leader's influence as well as 'shamelessly' using his position as chairman of the local Conservation Committee to protect the lands necessary to build Prince's Mitcham in London, where Balfour became a regular player.[27] Mitcham became the club where the socialites of Mayfair and Belgravia gathered and where the disdain of the Lords for golf was gradually eroded so that it eventually became known as the playground of the members of parliament.

The cultural clash very much mirrored the emerging power struggle between the *nouveaux riches* and the traditional upholders of government office, the aristocracy. While the latter continued to dominate at cabinet level, a new generation of wealthy aspirants such as Mallaby-Deeley were coming to prominence within the Commons and many of these felt that the political and wider societal privileges enjoyed by the aristocracy were anachronistic in a democratic (and in Britain, largely industrialized) society. (This had played itself out in Ireland, except the north-east, some years before when the land and Home Rule movements removed virtually all political power from the landed class at both national and local levels.) Shortly before Mallaby-Deeley had been elected MP for Harrow, David Lloyd George (1863–1945), the Liberal chancellor of the exchequer, introduced his so-called People's Budget of 1909. This represented a major watershed in the history of the decline of the aristocracy. Presented as a major social reform, Lloyd George proposed to finance the old age pension and the National Insurance Act (1911) through a dramatic increase of taxation directed unequivocally at the landed classes. In his budget speech, Lloyd George, pandering to the expanded electorate, claimed: 'I am one of the children of the people. I was brought up among them and I know their trials and their troubles. I therefore determined in framing the budget to add nothing to the anxieties of their lot, but to do something towards lightening those they already bear with such patience and fortitude'.[28] As David Cannadine has put it: 'This was not just a budget designed to raise money from the rich: it was the landed rich who were its principal target and victim'.[29]

The following year, the Lords, fearful that the House would be swamped with newly titled supporters of the Liberal Party, gave into Prime Minister Asquith's resolutions to curb their powers; they could now only reject a bill in two successive sessions and if it was presented a third time, it had to pass into law. This meant that the third Home Rule bill, intended for introduction in

1912, was certain to be enacted. On 11 October 1913, at Bedford, Lloyd George continued to make it clear that he was determined to break the land monopoly of landlords: 'to free British land from landlordism and get the people back on it'. 'Oh these dukes', he proclaimed, 'how they oppress us'. To strengthen his argument about the evils of landlordism he turned to Ireland where he exaggeratedly claimed: 'millions have been driven away from the land by legal process'.[30] 'After Limehouse', Cannadine argues, 'the House of Lords was never quite the same again'.[31]

IX

What is the relevance of all of this to Mallaby-Deeley and by extension to the FitzGeralds? After 1909, Liberal policy influenced many notables, thinking they saw the writing on the wall, to dispose of both their vast agricultural estates and their London properties, and there were property speculators like Mallaby-Deeley ready to exploit the situation. The notables included Herbrand Russell (1858–1940), 11th duke of Bedford. During the 1890s he had developed much of the area around Covent Garden and between 1890 and 1912 saw the income of this investment rise dramatically from £54,000 to £104,000 per annum. In 1913, he began to sell off his London properties. His reasons were encapsulated by his agent, the author and later politician, Rowland Prothero (1851–1937), 1st Baron Ernle, in his memoirs:

> Public opinion was setting strongly against the accumulation of large landed properties in the hands of individuals. The ownership of land had lost its political importance; financial legislation had already made its tenure more unprofitable; further legislation in similar directions was threatened. The proverbial danger of carrying all the eggs in one basket was now increased by the possibility that the bottom of the basket might fall out. Experience of a quarter of a century of adversity had shown the precarious nature of an income derived entirely or mainly from an agricultural estate. Meanwhile, the gradual return of prosperity was restoring the selling value of land, and the opportunity of transfer to other investments was favourable.[32]

(The quotation may be helpful in understanding the Leinster investment portfolio, or rather not understanding it.) Two years before, in 1911, the duke had been the subject of personal attack when he was accused of retaining 'vast slums' in London 'where tenants live under conditions of misery and of squalor'. While he defended himself in a letter to *The Times*, it seems the cumulative effect persuaded him to sell.[33] In 1913, when he put Covent Gardens on the market, it was reported 'as an omen of ducal fears of the coming land legislation designed to rescue tenants from the tentacles of ground landlords'.[34] Bedford was approached with a bid of £2 million by Mallaby-Deeley, who was then a director of the Norwich Union Life Insurance Society, chairman of the General Explorers' Company (concerned with mining in the Gold Coast) and director of the China Clay Corporation. He had only recently made a reputation for himself through the purchase of the Piccadilly Hotel and St James' Court and was reported to have 'startled London' by buying the site of St George's Hospital at Hyde Park Corner 'against the opposition of American financiers'.[35] Mallaby-Deeley had not sought media publicity for his ventures; the *New York Times* reported that 'the man who by this operation has startled the imagination of London and the country is a reserved man who early in life gave no hint of the vast ambition he is realizing today'.[36]

Covent Gardens was Mallaby-Deeley's biggest speculation to date. Although it was internationally reported as a 'done deal' between him and Bedford this was never actually the case. On 24 November 1913, Bedford and his trustees agreed to the outline terms of the proposal: by 25 March 1917, one-third of the purchase price was to be paid in four instalments; the other two-thirds were to remain on mortgage to the duke for up to twelve years at 4.5 per cent interest. In May, Mallaby-Deeley, frustrated by legal wrangling, instituted legal proceedings to expedite the agreement. In the meantime he was receiving offers for the resale of the property he had not yet even purchased.[37] In June, he agreed to sell his 'option to purchase' to Sir Joseph Beecham (owner of the famous pill-making industry) for £250,000.[38] He, therefore, made a quarter of a million without actually purchasing Covent Garden. It was a mark of his financial astuteness and, indeed, an indication of the type of canniness which the aristocracy, un-experienced in the City, could expect to face in the future.

Not only was Lord Edward FitzGerald inexperienced, he was also dissolute. When he was introduced by James Fraser to Mallaby-Deeley he was more concerned with his immediate personal financial situation than the long-term future of the FitzGerald estate. Lore has always had it that the agreement was reached prior to Desmond's death – a means of exaggerating the extent of the 'gamble' – but in fact it was over a year later towards the end of 1917 when he had become heir to the dukedom of Leinster. Mallaby-Deeley was not given to risky investments; if Desmond was still alive the chances of Edward ever inheriting were slim. With Desmond dead and Maurice ill, the odds were much more favourable. While Maurice's illness had been kept out of the public arena, there is little doubt but that Mallaby-Deeley knew of his condition and if he had taken medical advice he would have been informed that, as a lunatic epileptic, Maurice probably had only a short time to live. That, of course, means Edward would have known likewise, but Edward was myopic when it came to his own personal financial needs. Edward's profligate personality and his desperation for money were a dangerous combination in the face of Mallaby-Deeley's financial astuteness: it was said of the latter that

> When the idea of acquiring any particular property had occurred to him he would follow it up with an interview with the owner, and usually, if the latter had the least intention of disposing of his interest, Mallaby-Deeley would come from the meeting place with a half sheet of notepaper recording the proposed contract.[39]

The agreement was that Mallaby-Deeley would pay off Edward's debts of over £67,000 (estimated at around £16.4 million in today's terms)[40] and pay him £1,000 per annum (tax free) as an allowance.[41] If Edward inherited, Mallaby-Deeley would become recipient of Carton and all the income from the estate entailed with the dukedom, in the region of £50,000 per annum. Mallaby-Deeley was under no obligation to spend any of his personal income (that is, his income from sources other than Carton) on the upkeep of the mansion house.

Lord Frederick and the trustees did not have to be party to the agreement for it to be legally binding. However, according to Edward himself, he approached them before he made the deal with Mallaby-Deeley and asked them to provide him with a small estate in Scotland for about £20,000 and about £3,000 per annum. They turned him down and so, in Edward's own words, 'that refusal led to the folly which followed'.[42]

From Mallaby-Deeley's point of view, an initial capital investment of £67,000, pocket money to him at that stage, had every possibility of realizing much greater long term reward. Edward's second wife, Rafaelle Davidson-Kennedy, described Mallaby-Deeley as 'a professional buyer-upper of estates on the rocks', but this does scant justice to a more deserved reputation as an intrepid speculator. He was no carpetbagger; the evidence, as we shall see in the next chapter, points to the fact that he behaved decently in all of his dealings with the FitzGerald family. Edward's granddaughter, Rosemary FitzGerald, would claim many years later that Mallaby-Deeley and his son, Meyrick, behaved 'most honourably throughout the entire history';[43] Edward's son, Gerald, simply admitted that his father had made a bad deal and Mallaby-Deeley a good one.

Edward continued (and would do so for most of his life) to live a nomadic lifestyle. He was completely restless – his second wife recalled that 'he had the nervous energy of a racehorse'[44] – and was literally happiest on the road, often driving aimlessly for up to 400 miles per day, sometimes at speeds well in excess of 100 miles per hour. One of his passengers, Sir Gavin Lyle, later recalled: 'he always thought he was in a grand prix ... everything was done on the wrong side of the road'.[45] He moved between modest flats in London (Curzon Street, Hertford Street and Portland Place), holiday cottages of friends in places such as Huntingdonshire, more impressive continental holiday homes of the D'Abernons in France, and exclusive hotels. He was not welcome at Carton.

In March 1919, he was declared bankrupt for a second time. When the first meeting of his creditors was held in April, the receiver, Daniel Williams, told the Bankruptcy Court, that gross liabilities were estimated at £76,000 of which £25,000 was unsecured. The aforementioned Frederick Salaman was appointed to ensure the payment of as many of the debts as possible and his own were his priority. The fact that he was now heir apparent to the dukedom of Leinster generated international media attention. It also meant that Maurice's condition came under closer scrutiny. Thus, in September 1919, one American newspaper reported during the bankruptcy proceedings that Maurice had 'been under restraint for the last two years as a confirmed and incurable imbecile'.[46] It may have been the first newspaper to have disclosed this information.

                                    X

During the early months of 1920, Maurice's condition deteriorated rapidly. In May it was reported that he 'continues to take fits fairly frequently' and his moods were becoming increasingly erratic; he was 'at times excitable and communicative' and at other times 'morose and taciturn'.[47] By November 1921 he was taking up to fifteen seizures per month, mainly at night.[48] On the evening of 28 January 1922, Maurice developed a high temperature. All that day his mood had been distinctly melancholic. Following a chest examination, crepitations were found at the base of his right lung and it was noted that these sharp cracking rattles were usually the signs of pneumonia. By the following day his temperature had risen to 103°F; his lung congestion had increased greatly and his blood pressure had dropped. He reacted violently to a pneumococcal vaccination. For the next two days his breathing difficulties worsened and his blood pressure continued to fall. Finally, his kidneys failed and he died at 12.10 a.m. on the morning of 2 February from what was officially recorded as 'lobar pneumonia (4 ½ days); epilepsy (25 years)'.[49] He was just thirty-four years old.

Maurice was buried, according to his wishes, in the private cemetery at Carton.[50] His obituary in the *Irish Independent* could not decide whether he was vivacious and talented or destined to live the life of an invalid suffering from a 'nervous malady'.[51] In a sense it summed up his life: vivacious and talented is what his family would have desired the heir to Ireland's leading aristocratic family to have been; a mentally unstable young man who suffered from epilepsy was the reality of what he became. Edward, who was holidaying in Italy at the time of Maurice's death, did not come home for the funeral: 'There was no point', he later said.[52] And that largely summed up his character.

Shortly after Maurice died, Lord Frederick's solicitors, Johnson Raymond-Barker & Co., began to make enquiries as to where his physicians at Craighouse – Walshe, Cramie and Power – had moved. It was an indication of how little contact they had with the asylum, particularly during the war years, that they only then realized his doctors had all left. They wanted to ascertain Maurice's state of mind when he changed his will on 5 July 1911, 21 February 1912 and 1 January 1913. The three doctors had been witnesses to the various versions. Presumably, the trustees were hoping to find a way to safeguard the family heirlooms bequeathed to Edward. Maurice's medical reports showed that at each time he had changed his will, he had been delusional and upset over various things: in July 1911, he felt the birds singing outside were deliberately trying to provoke him on Donald Pollock's instructions; in February 1912 he wrote a letter claiming plots were being made to disinherit him and in May 1912, a few months before his final will, he had become violently upset by the news of Edward's engagement. Ironically, it was because Pollock had been the other witness to all wills and codicils that in January 1923 Mr Justice Hill pronounced for the final will (of January 1913), decreeing that 'the late duke was of testamentary capacity'.[53] It was a twist that Maurice might very well have enjoyed, given his disdain for Pollock.

It may be reasonably assumed that with Maurice's death, Lord Frederick's worst fears were realized. Edward had been reared as the 5th duke's son, and was now recognized as such. Frederick and, indeed, all of aristocratic society, knew Edward to be a disreputable rake who would jeopardize the family fortune. The loss of Carton to the family must have represented a huge disappointment and a severe blow to Frederick's prestige. He had weathered economic, social and political storms until the early 1920s with aristocratic confidence; now, it was family misfortune, over which he had no control, which ultimately proved the undoing of all he had worked for and believed in.

CHAPTER NINE

Henry Mallaby-Deeley: 'the fairy godfather of the estate'

In Carton grounds in old Maynooth
There stands a mansion grand …
Its stately halls and lovely rooms
Look out on gardens fair
But never more its noble heirs
Are seen to wander there.[1]

Anon.

The thirteen years that Maurice had spent in Craighouse had seen great changes for the aristocracy, not only in Ireland but in Britain and wider Europe; as David Cannadine has put it, they became: 'aristocrats in an era of democracy, patricians in an age of landed decline'.[2] For the likes of Mary Elcho, the Great War had changed aristocratic living forever: 'shaking all things to their foundations, wasting the treasures of the past, and casting its sinister influence far into the future'.[3] Such moods were compounded by the huge sense of loss. In Ireland, one of Hermione's best friends, Elizabeth Fingall, later recalled:

I used to think and say, during the war, that if ever that list of dead and wounded would cease, I would never mind anything or grumble at anything again. But when the Armistice came at last, we seemed drained of all feeling. And one felt nothing. We took up our lives again, or tried to take them up. The world we had known had vanished. We hunted again but ghosts rode with us. We sat at table, and there were absent faces.[4]

The transformation of the social and political order that resulted in the almost total marginalization of the aristocracy in Ireland was completed when a war of independence (1919–21) and civil war (1922–3) followed. Around 300 country houses were burned by Irish Republican Army or agrarian agitators (often one and the same) for a variety of reasons that can be loosely categorized as military (to prevent their occupation as temporary barracks by the crown forces); agrarian (to force the redistribution of lands in landlords' possession); and ancestral (because country house owners had become stigmatized since the Land War as colonial oppressors). The number destroyed was a small percentage of the total in existence – less than 10 per cent – but it was the symbolism that was striking. Many more times that number were subsequently abandoned and demolished as their owners could no longer afford their upkeep without their great estates and because their investment portfolios were decimated in the economically depressed decades that followed.[5] By the end of the twentieth century only a handful of great houses remained in the ownership of their original families and they struggled in a political and cultural climate largely unsympathetic to their plight.

For a time, the FitzGeralds and Carton remained the exception. In June 1922, just after the civil war had ended, the local nationalist newspaper once again extolled the role of the FitzGeralds as Irish patriots and rebels, in much the same way that the address to Gerald FitzGerald as earl of Offaly had done exactly fifty years before:

> They were not many generations in the country until having made common cause with the people they became more Irish than the Irish themselves. For centuries the Geraldines held a foremost place in the Irish national struggle. The names of Garret Oge, Silken Thomas and Lord Edward are as imperishable as Irish history itself.[6]

During the so-called Troubles, Carton had remained untouched. Local lore has it that a flying column of IRA men arrived at the front door during the War of Independence and demanded entrance so that they could set it alight but the butler showed them a portrait of Lord Edward by Hugh Douglas Hamilton (1739–1808), which to this day hangs in Carton, and asked them if they could justify destroying the home of one of the founding fathers of Irish republicanism. The men left peacefully, said to have been humbled by their experience. It probably never happened. In fact, the story is more likely to have grown out of a myth perpetuated locally to justify the reasons for *not* burning Carton and not ridding the area of a ducal family: it was better to save it as the home of Lord Edward than proclaim the loyal attachment of the people of Maynooth to it, mainly for economic reasons (see plate 8).[7]

But in 1922, the FitzGeralds and Carton faced a much graver threat than a handful of Republicans. Hermione's indiscretion, the tragic loss of Desmond during the Great War, the premature death of Maurice after a lifetime of personal tragedy and the profligacy of the illegitimate Edward meant that the fall of one of Ireland's most famous families was seemingly inevitable.

II

When Edward became 7th duke of Leinster his binding agreement with Sir Henry Mallaby-Deeley – he had been knighted in 1922 during the Lloyd George administration – came into play. No documentary evidence of the actual agreement has been found but what follows is based on the most reliable information available that has been gathered from receiver's reports presented at bankruptcy proceedings against Edward and information in newspapers (but this has been treated with some caution given the nature of the lore which has grown around the agreement).

Under the 1919 resettlement of the estate, the duke was entitled to the income from the estate entailed with the dukedom but he had no authority to meddle with the investment portfolio without the sanction of the trustees; in that way the capital investment was protected. Subsequently, Mallaby-Deeley became entitled to the income that he was obliged to use 'to do all such works and repairs as may from time to time be reasonably required for keeping up and preserving from injury or destruction any mansions remaining subject to the limitations of this settlement'. He was not bound to use any of his own personal wealth. Edward had the option to buy the reversionary rights from Mallaby-Deeley for a sum variously estimated at between about £180,000 and £400,000, but he was bankrupt a second time (see below) when he inherited and, therefore, not in a position to do so. Moreover, the trustees remained opposed to the repurchase. Their argument was simple: the repurchase could only be financed through the decimation of the share portfolio and this would leave very little to maintain a residence such as Carton into the long-term future.[8]

A 1922 investment portfolio has survived and shows that changes had taken place since the first was constructed in 1904. In particular, it was more diversified. The most significant shift was the reduction in the level of personal mortgages to £314,300 but still accounting for 46 per cent of the total portfolio. The Hastings mortgage was still extant while the others had been dramatically reduced or paid off. There were eight new mortgagees but, as with the previous portfolio, their choice is somewhat baffling. The largest loan was to R.A. Gough (£100,000) but nothing has been found to positively identify him. Waldorf Astor, 1st Viscount Astor (1848–1919), the American property owner and newspaper tycoon, had received £35,000.[9] In 1890, he had inherited $100 million from the family newspaper and property businesses, moved to England, invested in English estates and country houses at Cliveden in Buckinghamshire and later Hever Castle in Kent, and through his philanthropic

30 Henry Mallaby-Deeley (1863–1937).

works and contributions to the Conservative Party was created Baron Astor in 1916 and viscount the following year.[10] Why would Astor, one of the wealthiest men in the world, borrow from the trustees? Might it have had anything to do with his search for social position in Britain?[11] Were family links a consideration: his grandson, John Jacob (1886–1971), was an Etonian contemporary of the FitzGerald boys and he served with Desmond in the Irish Guards.[12]

Lady Eleanor Georgiana Shelley-Rolls (1872–1961) was granted a mortgage of £27,000. She was daughter of John Allan Rolls (1837–1912), 1st Baron Llangattock, of the motor manufacturing family, and provincial grand master of the freemasons in Monmouthshire. She was married to Sir John Shelley (1871–1951), 6th baronet of Castle Goring in Sussex, who in 1917 had assumed the additional name of Rolls by royal licence. Their family fortune had grown significantly in the nineteenth century from investments in London property.[13] Again, what was her need of a mortgage? Captain R.A. Vansittart (1851–1928), who had received £14,248, was a lifetime army officer who came from a patrician family in Kent, served in the Boer War with the 7th Dragoon Guards and later became recruiting officer for the Ministry of National Service.

Major Margesson (possibly Major Edward Cuninghame Margesson killed in the Dardanelles in 1915) had received £11,000; and finally the renowned sportsman, Reginald 'Tip' Foster (1878–1914), had been loaned £9,000. Foster is the only man to have captained both the English soccer and cricket teams. His sporting prowess would have brought him well into Lord Kinnaird's orbit. The fact that he died young from severe diabetes may suggest that at some stage he had a need for money to take care of medical expenses.[14]

Notably, the interest rates charged on these later mortgages had risen considerably, on average to almost 5.5 per cent in comparison to the previous portfolio average of 3.6 per cent. There was also a significant shift to fixed income bonds, while the equity component consisted mainly of quasi-corporate bonds such as debentures, guaranteed stock and preference shares. In total the bond element of the portfolio stood at £357,700 or 53 per cent of the total. Diversity was much greater than in the mortgage portfolio: over fifty different securities were held with no single security accounting for more that 5 per cent of the total value. The overall income yield had increased from 3.57 per cent per annum in 1904 to 5.33 per cent in 1922, providing a total of just over £36,000 (about £1.3 million in today's values) compared to £23,700 in 1904. However, actual purchasing power would have diminished greatly in the interim and the introduction of a whole range of taxes by Lloyd George after 1909 would have undoubtedly impacted on net income. For example: while the absolute value of the portfolio increased marginally by 1.6 per cent in the eighteen years from £664,707 in 1904 to £675,446 in 1922, inflation in the period exceeded 40 per cent, which meant that the value of the portfolio in terms of 'purchasing power' or 'real value' declined by 39 per cent. This highlighted the absence of any capital appreciation potential in the 1904 portfolio.[15]

The rate of death duty on the bulk of the 6th duke's estate was payable at 28 per cent and succession duty at 5 per cent. The value of the property was estimated at just under £658,000 (personalty – personal property and chattels) and just under £82,000 (realty – property consisting of houses and lands). It was estimated that the upkeep of the estates would be £4,500 per annum. When deductions were made (including the capitalization of annuities payable to the children of the 5th duke at £9,600 and the upkeep of Kilkea at £7,500), the figure for death duty was finalized at £152,000. The net annual income of the estate was estimated at £32,430 (slightly lower than the figure given above). According to succession duty tables, the value of an annuity on a life aged twenty-nine years – Edward's age at succession – was £537,057. At 5 per cent this came to £26,853 which was payable in eight half-yearly instalments.[16]

Taken together, the duties were a significant, though not entirely debilitating financial burden. Thus, the estate finances were reasonably stable and Frederick must have cursed his family's luck that they were now in such a deplorable situation because of what was effectively a philandering bankrupt's gamble.

It must also have been difficult, even from a purely social perspective, for Lord Frederick to have to deal with Mallaby-Deeley, but this was imperative if only to ensure he had a home for the remainder of his life. At first, Mallaby-Deeley decided that a line of least resistance was the best approach to adopt. He, therefore, allowed Frederick to stay on and manage Carton (while his spinster sisters were allowed to remain at Kilkea) with a modest indoor staff for his personal use.[17] In June 1922, four months after Maurice was buried, Mallaby-Deeley told the *Daily Mail* that 'as far as I know the estate is being run as usual. I am bearing the whole expenses of the estate, and my agreement with the duke is that everything should be carried on exactly as it has been in the past'.[18]

This message was important. The situation may have changed dramatically upon the sale of the estate but around Maynooth (where the duke retained ground rents on many properties) the perceived importance of ducal patronage had not diminished. Local apprehensions were underpinned by the immediate fear of economic loss to the area, fuelled by rumours that the staff numbers were to be reduced. Thus, in June 1922, the *Leinster Leader*, picking up on the *Daily Mail* interview with Mallaby-Deeley, pointed out:

> Any severance of the FitzGerald family with the management of the Leinster property will be greatly regretted in Kildare, where despite the fact that the land has been largely sold to tenants they still retain large interests in the ground rents and many buildings and homes in practically all the towns being held from them. Very extensive employment is given on the demesnes, tillage being intensive and a splendid class of livestock bred. Being a resident family a very deep interest was taken in the welfare of the employees, who are comfortably housed and well treated. In addition the Leinster estate trustees always subscribed generously to any object that tended to benefit Kildare and its people.[19]

Mallaby-Deeley was later reminded by Charles Hamilton that 'Carton has been run in the past with the view of giving as much employment as possible to the people in Maynooth. If you wish to continue it on those lines there need be no reductions.' But Hamilton also hedged his bets; after all he wanted to retain his position, and so he added: 'If on the other hand you consider the expenditure too high I have no doubt the reductions can be made on the lines I have suggested'.[20]

III

In the first year or so, Mallaby-Deeley made no great fuss and interfered minimally. However, it soon became clear to him that Lord Frederick was continuing to draw down hefty funds from the estate income (through what legal mechanisms are not clear). At the beginning of 1923, Mallaby-Deeley's representatives began to investigate the level of expenditure at Carton. The first two account books sent by the trustees to Sir Henry showed that prior to the agreement the estate had been (allegedly) running at a loss of over £8,000 per annum. It was 'admitted that the rate of expenditure in the [6th] duke's lifetime had been lavish'.[21] This was a disingenuous attempt to lay the blame at Maurice's door. Some years later, Charles Hamilton would recall that Frederick drew around £6,000 per annum to run the house and maintain the lifestyle to which he had become accustomed.[22]

Sir Henry was not prepared to support this level of expenditure.[23] He wrote to Frederick inviting him to prepare a statement 'for certain economies in administration', which he did, but 'it showed an estimated expenditure not much less than that which was made during the duke's lifetime'.[24] The exchanges unwittingly reveal much about Lord Frederick's personality, sculpted as it was in the twilight years of the Irish aristocracy. There was a peevish resentment towards *arrivistes* such as Mallaby-Deeley. Frederick's strong sense of entitlement made him test Sir Henry's resolve. And, it seems, he was partially successful. In 1923, around £9,000 was diverted with the permission of Mallaby-Deeley from the Trust investments to cover estate expenses. That November a further £6,000 was diverted to pay estate duty; this was raised by selling around £4,600 in 3.5 per cent Hong Kong Inscribed Stock and the remainder in 4 per cent National War Bonds that were not due to mature until 1928.[25] In this way the invested capital was dwindling slowly but surely with inevitable consequences. In May 1923, one of Frederick's legal advisors, Henry Nix, calculated that income from the Leinster investments had diminished to around £23,500 per annum. This was a very significant drop from the estimated £36,000 only a year or so previously (and, according to Nix, less than half of what it had been a decade before).[26]

At this stage, in May 1923, as the worldwide economic depression began to impact, Mallaby-Deeley stated his desire to sell the reversionary right to some member of the family or to the trustees – 'but to no other person' – at a greatly reduced £180,000, with £5,000 to be paid on deposit.[27] The reduced price was a good indicator of the impact of the economic downturn but no individual member of the family was in a position to purchase so the onus fell on the trustees. Lord Frederick sought advice from his solicitors. He was informed that the only fund the trustees had for purchasing was the capital money that was subject to the 1919 settlement. This was complicated by the fact that what Mallaby-Deeley was selling was actually Edward's life interest in the capital money.[28] The estate solicitor, Charles Ashworth James, advised that such a transaction would be 'quite inconsistent with any principle of trust investment. It would in substance be paying the capital of the trust fund to the tenant for life.'[29] However, James prophetically warned that 'if something is not done, there is a danger and even a probability that Carton, the ancestral home of the FitzGerald family for centuries, will be lost to the family forever'.[30]

While Mallaby-Deeley was not financially desperate he certainly would have been aware of the effects of the economic downturn on the investment portfolio in the post-war period. To give some examples: 5 per cent war bonds with a nominal value of £36,662 had fallen to £34,210 by 1922; £15,150 Victory bonds had depreciated to £12,707; 4 per cent funding loans with nominal value of £51,00 had depreciated to £40,481 and an investment of £25,500 in India 2.5 per cent stock had depreciated to £10,582. Thus, his annual income was likely to diminish, so a once-off capital sum was preferable. His offer refused, Mallaby-Deeley now demanded quarterly estimates of expenditure from Lord Frederick and Charles Hamilton, the least he could expect, he contended, given 'the position he [was] entitled to occupy'.[31] When the first quarterly report arrived on 1 December 1923, Mallaby-Deeley was annoyed that proposed expenditure had not been reduced and so he insisted again that costs 'be further materially decreased, consistently with the due preservation of the property in proper repair'.[32] Of note here, is the fact that he consistently insisted that Carton was to be maintained to high standards.

In March 1924, Frederick died. He was sixty-seven years old.[33] As with Maurice's death, there was no great media attention in the local or national press, perhaps a further indication of the declining social position of the aristocracy in an independent Irish Free State. It is to be presumed that the last two years of his life were stressful as he oversaw the beginning of the end of the 750 years FitzGerald connection with Maynooth and with Carton of almost 200 years.

IV

Lord Henry FitzGerald (1863–1955) replaced his brother as trustee. He was determined to try to keep Carton in FitzGerald hands. In May 1924, he wrote to Hamilton: 'It [Carton] must be saved at all costs and not allowed to turn into a wilderness'.[34] He presumed to take over from Frederick and issued Hamilton with instructions to close down the original kitchen area of Carton because too much coal was being wasted and to let go some of the boys in the gardens. He wanted to show Mallaby-Deeley that Carton could be carried at 30–50 per cent less.[35] However, when Henry and Hamilton considered the possibility of dispensing with the cook, asking the housekeeper to double up and letting one of the housemaids go, Mallaby-Deeley was informed directly by the cook, Mrs Nelligan, that notices had been served.[36] Mallaby-Deeley let Hamilton know of his annoyance at people interfering in his business: 'May I point out to you that Lord Henry's approval is not in any way necessary as the decision in any matters of this kind rest entirely with myself, as also the appointing of the agent and his salary'.[37] In future, he instructed, no dismissals were to be carried out without his prior agreement. While Mallaby-Deeley was concerned about 'the very heavy and unnecessary cost of Carton', he was careful to balance any such diminishment in employment against 'causing friction and hardship' or 'any ill feeling' around Maynooth. Thus, he urged that redundancies should only be carried out 'in a gradual way' and to ease local tensions he was prepared to compensate those made redundant by paying them a gratuity of £1–2 per annum.[38]

Hamilton had taken it for granted that after Lord Frederick's death he would continue as agent but as Mallaby-Deeley's letter above suggested he did not see it that way and so he made Hamilton formally apply for the position. Hamilton wrote: 'I am sure you will understand that up to this I have been in a most difficult position not being in direct communication with you. All I want to do is to carry out your wishes with regard to Carton without causing ill feeling among the men.'[39] His position was ratified on 12 April 1924. After reasserting his authority, Mallaby-Deeley instructed Hamilton to sell Pebble Mill farm on the outskirts of the Carton demesne.[40] Outlying woods were also sold to Kildare County Council for £3,400.[41] And the gas plant that was wasting money on coal and manpower for very little return was closed.[42]

It was imperative that the demesne continued to be farmed. Following the establishment of the Free State, a new and far-reaching land act was passed in 1923, which gave the state the power to compulsorily acquire untenanted and demesne lands required for the relief of congestion and the creation of viable farms.[43] Carton had hundreds of acres of the finest agricultural land in Ireland and so could have been a prime target for the Irish Land Commission, which was charged with the redistribution of lands. Charles Hamilton thus told Mallaby-Deeley: 'we are more or less bound to do a certain amount of tillage to prevent the government from interfering with the demesne'. In April 1924, Mallaby-Deeley had also ordered that the Kerry herd of cattle should be sold. What he had not realized was that the Kerries – about twenty-four cows, six bulls and a few heifers and calves – were probably one of the reasons why the demesne did not come under the compulsory acquisition terms of the 1923 Land Act; any demesne that could prove to be rearing thoroughbred animals was allowed exemption and Kerries were a rare breed of dairy cattle (in 1983 it is said there were only 200 pedigree Kerries in the whole world and the Irish Department of Agriculture took steps to protect them as a species).[44]

In the Spring of 1924, Mallaby-Deeley was happy to go along with most of Hamilton's proposals to reduce expenditure – 'especially as you tell me this can be done without causing friction and hardship' – but he was not prepared to act on Hamilton's advice to reduce the wages of the men at Carton to 30s. per week, as it was only a short time before that he had raised them to 34s.[45] However, as the agricultural depression continued during the summer months, Mallaby-Deeley was forced to make redundant sixteen labourers at Carton, while also reducing farm wages and abolishing the traditional harvest bonus paid to labourers.[46] Hamilton assured Sir Henry: 'I expect to keep Carton up just as well if not better with the reduced number of men'.[47] But again Mallaby-Deeley warned that it had to be done 'without any friction or disagreeable results'.[48]

For the first time, the loss of ducal patronage began to be felt in the Maynooth area. Families who had been dependent upon the estate for employment, in some cases for generations, were threatened with hardship. Six of those made redundant were 'old hands'. Two, by the names of Hanlon and Doran, had been employed at Carton for a very long time, Hanlon as an odd man around the house and Doran on the farm where he particularly looked after the Kerries. Hamilton feared that neither would get work if they were left off, so he suggested they should be awarded pensions of 15s. per week instead of a once off gratuity of £25–30.[49]

In May 1924, Hamilton received a letter from Thomas Kennedy of the Irish Transport and General Workers Union: 'Considering that the cost of living is practically higher at present than it was a year ago, and that other employers in the district have not sought to reduce wages or abolish the harvest bonus, we cannot see any justifiable grounds for such disadvantages being imposed on our members at Carton'.[50] The bonus was of particular concern because this was deemed a special allowance to agricultural workers to compensate them for the lowness of their standard wages in comparison to the average industrial wage. Hamilton replied that cutbacks were necessary in light of heavy estate and succession duties, and an increase in rates and taxes. Kennedy asked permission to write to Mallaby-Deeley and Hamilton undertook to forward the ITGWU correspondence on their behalf but he told his employer: 'You need not take their letter too seriously; they are bound as union officials to make an effort to get the men kept on. I think you should just tell them that you cannot see your way to keep on so many hands for the reasons I have already given them.'[51] The redundancies led to a brief stand off with the ITGWU but the union was not yet well enough organized in the area to be effective.[52]

Carton was now empty except for a handful of servants. Meanwhile, Mallaby-Deeley continued to move between his homes at Mitcham Court in Surrey, the exclusive Chateau des Fayeres in Cannes and Ceylon with no intention of either living or even visiting Carton. In April 1924, he enquired if shutting Carton up would 'save any great expense'.[53] His private assistant wrote to Hamilton: 'Please let Sir Henry know what can be done, as he cannot go on bearing this enormous expense for the benefit apparently of nobody at all'.[54] Hamilton claimed to have tried unsuccessfully to find a tenant.[55] In fairness, it would have been difficult in the economic climate of the time, although Count John McCormack, the renowned tenor, was prepared to lease the much less impressive Moore Abbey in the same county. It is more likely that Hamilton did not try very hard, preferring instead to suggest that the duke's spinster aunts, the Ladies Alice and Nesta, be allowed to live there rent free. 'They are most anxious', he wrote to Mallaby-Deeley, 'for Carton to be preserved as the home of the Leinster family and are most grateful to you for what you have done… I have always heard all the members of the family I have met say how well you have acted about Carton in the last two years and how much they hoped that the place would be kept up and come back to the family eventually'.[56]

Mallaby-Deeley relented and allowed Lady Nesta to move in with a skeleton staff for which he bore full financial liability. In September 1926, when approached by Charles Hamilton for money for a new boiler at Carton, Sir Henry replied: 'I think one ought to be installed, it is not fit for Lady Nesta to be there in the winter without one'.[57] It was a measure of the decency with which he treated the FitzGerald family, but with the exception of Edward. All this time, Mallaby-Deeley had prevented Edward visiting Carton: his solicitors had warned him that 'no reliance can be placed on what the duke may or may not do' and there were suspicions that covert visits by him had resulted in the loss of a number of valuable heirlooms.[58]

V

Throughout this period, Edward's second bankruptcy case was playing itself out on the side. He had learned nothing from the first experience and, in fact, used his new-found status as duke even more recklessly than he had used his status as heir apparent. He continued to get into trouble with the law. In June 1923, he was arrested for borrowing money while a bankrupt and for giving false information that he 'was a very wealthy man being worth £5,000,000'.[59] On that occasion he was released on bail of £2,000.[60] A few weeks later he was found guilty at the Central Criminal Court in London on another charge of illegally obtaining credit. The jury added a recommendation to mercy.[61] In October, he was summonsed again at Marlborough Street, this time for causing unnecessary obstruction with a motor car.[62] And so the litany of misdemeanours went on but the fact that he was the duke of Leinster kept him out of jail.

In June 1922, he had issued a press statement to the *Irish Independent* denying that he had parted with his birthright and that he had a reversionary option at £350,000 (as noted above the figure seems to have been fairly arbitrary); that the estate was worth more than £2.5 million, the heirlooms a further £2 million and he had a guaranteed annual income of £45,000.[63] It was almost like a snare to capture other unsuspecting benefactors. But pronouncements to the press of his imaginary wealth actually became a signal light to his moneylenders to get their investments back. On 19 December 1922, just short of the first anniversary of Maurice's death, a petition of bankruptcy was lodged against Edward by Frederick Salaman and others. It is difficult to unravel exactly what happened as there is conflicting evidence in a mix of sources but it seems that Salaman had become frustrated by his inability to recoup his losses on unsecured loans (given at extortionate rates) from Edward. Now reading Edward's widely reported claims he began legal proceedings.[64]

The first meeting of creditors was held on 8 January 1923 where Salaman was appointed trustee in the bankruptcy. Edward's indebtedness was estimated at almost £56,600. Salaman proposed that in order to recoup these unsecured debts the furniture and heirlooms at Carton bequeathed by Maurice to his successor should be sold.[65] Salaman seems, however, to have been completely unaware of the legal binds of the 1919 resettlement that left Edward with no income from the estate and no power to sell the settled heirlooms without the joint permission of the trustees and Mallaby-Deeley. And the trustees were extremely reluctant to bail Edward out; when Salaman approached them the following month to enquire if they would be prepared to purchase the furniture and heirlooms, he was flatly refused.[66] On 13 April 1923, Lord Frederick was advised by his solicitors that Salaman's schemes were 'hopelessly wrong' and should not be contemplated.[67]

The protracted bankruptcy proceedings continued through 1924 and most of the following year, until in September 1925 the trustees, in agreement with Mallaby-Deeley, finally agreed to sell the settled heirlooms and furniture. By then, some of the more valuable heirlooms had probably been removed from Carton. In 1924, Lord Henry FitzGerald, who had replaced Frederick as trustee, fretted when he heard rumours that Mallaby-Deeley was contemplating the sale of three Cuyps and some of the family plate in order to raise £15,000 (for what reason is unknown).[68] He connived with Hamilton to remove some of the family engravings from Carton to add to his own personal collection at Knowle. He also had suspicions about the disappearance of some heirlooms from the house, believed to have been sold illegally by Edward.[69] And nobody was quite sure where the family plate had been deposited. It was thought it had been packed up and stored by Lord Frederick after the probate valuation by Bennett & Sons sometime in February 1922.[70] While the presentation trowels, spades, maces and silver batons were kept *in situ* at Carton, the plate went to a bank in Dublin but in 1924 nobody was sure which one.[71]

Salaman tried to get Mallaby-Deeley to have the sale in Carton itself, the general belief being that contents sold *in situ* would realize around 10 per cent more for provenance. Initially, Mallaby-Deeley was totally opposed to the idea – he said he did not want dealers prowling around the house – but in the end he consented.[72] A number of auctions followed. In early November, 'a valuable collection of old Irish and English silver, gold and jewelled boxes, miniatures and various other bijouterie' reportedly 'attracted widespread interest and brought remarkable prices'.[73] Collectors were there from all over Britain and 'between them they succeeded in acquiring the more valuable of the 300 lots'. Later that month came the sale of the fine arts, including Old French and Irish furniture, tapestries, European porcelain and rare Irish coins as well as 'a gallery of oil paintings of considerable merit by the Old Masters'.[74]

Mallaby-Deeley bought some of the contents though his offer of £1,500 for the soup plates and dinner plates and a silver gilt toilet set was adjudged too low.[75] In the end the bulk of the contents were purchased by the American newspaper tycoon, William Randolph Hearst (1863–1951), then in the process of acquiring many of the finest collections in Europe. Hearst was in the top 100 wealthiest men in America at the time with an income conservatively estimated at $15 million per annum.[76] According to John Harris he was 'prolific … as a magpie accumulator of salvages'.[77] Catholic in his tastes, he simply removed everything from Carton with little thought as to where it was going to end up. Elizabeth Fingall later recalled:

> Everything else was taken out to be sold that tragic day when fourteen pantenichons took away most of the treasures of Carton that were not entailed. Her [Hermione's] grand piano … was one of the things taken. And the music-room now is as bare as her own boudoir, with all the lovely furniture gone from it. The house is stripped of its greatest treasures. Even many of the precious books had to go. But it is still beautiful.[78]

In November 1925, the great library – including 'books printed in the 15th and 16th centuries, works on sport and topography, books relating to America, freemasonry and occultism' – was sold out of Bennett and Sons auction rooms on Ormond Quay.[79] The auction attracted national and international buyers including Quaritch, Maggs, Thorpe and Josephs from London, Hodges & Figgis and Fred Hanna from Dublin.[80]

There are no records of exactly how much was realized from the auction but Salaman secured £21,000.[81] As trustee for the bankruptcy he then disbursed the proceeds, the bulk of creditors receiving a dividend of around 4s. in the pound.[82] Subsequently, Edward's second bankruptcy was released in May 1928 but the sale of the FitzGerald family heirlooms had resulted in the dismantling of one of the country's most valuable private collections and its dispersal both sides of the Atlantic. It was a development which became all too familiar in Irish country houses from the 1920s onwards. It was a quick and ignominious end to centuries of collecting and a symbolic reminder of how quickly the Irish aristocracy had fallen. Edward showed no remorse then or at any stage in the future.

VI

Under the terms of the original agreement, Mallaby-Deeley was under no obligation to spend any of his personal income on boilers or any other form of maintenance at Carton, but he did, and this was not just out of consideration to the elderly FitzGerald ladies: the point has earlier been made that he was at all times adamant that Carton should not fall into dilapidation. He was equally considerate of the repercussions that the decline of the estate as an important place of employment might have on the local community, at least as much as he could be in the economic circumstances of the time. Moreover, he clearly took a certain pride in preserving Carton. In 1930, Mallaby-Deeley wrote to Hamilton: 'Lord Frederick wrote me not long before he died that I had been the fairy godfather as regards the estate, which, without me, would long ago have been in the hands of the d[uke]'s Jew moneylenders', the reference here being to Salaman, indicating not only his personal disdain for the man but, indeed, the anti-Semitism that was rife in contemporary Britain as it was in wider Europe.[83]

Mallaby-Deeley never considered a move to Carton, but, if he had, how might he have been received? Lore has it 'that he would have been shot if he set foot there'.[84] While that was hardly likely, there certainly was an outpouring of popular support and sympathy for the FitzGeralds when news of the deal broke and Mallaby-Deeley was unflatteringly introduced through the media to the Kildare and wider Irish public as a usurping speculator. The sobriquet of the 'fifty-shilling tailor' was also used in this introduction, not because he had sold suits at a price that broke the profiteering trade in London, but in a more derogatory manner to suggest he was not socially equipped to take over Carton and all it had stood for.[85] As it turned out Mallaby-Deeley was better for Carton than an impoverished and feckless heir would have been.[86]

CHAPTER TEN

To America in search of an heiress

My road to ruin was the gay road – the road of mad parties, reckless friends and lovely women.

Edward, 7th duke of Leinster, 1957[1]

By the late 1920s even astute and canny businessmen such as Sir Henry Mallaby-Deeley found it difficult to manoeuvre in a severely depressed international economic climate. During the First World War, super tax had been introduced in Britain on incomes in excess of £10,000 per annum, levied on gross rather than net income. The standard rate of income tax had increased from 5.8 per cent in 1914–15 to 30 per cent in 1920–1 and did not fall below 20 per cent in the late 1920s. In 1913–14 income and super tax combined provided revenue of £47.2 million but in 1939 this had multiplied almost tenfold to £400 million.[2] Thus, in 1923 the 17th earl of Derby complained: 'taxation at the present moment is so high that I may call myself a tax collector for the government. At present I am not living on my income. I am living on my capital.'[3] It was a familiar story for many, including Mallaby-Deeley. On 23 October 1929, just a week before the New York Stock Exchange crashed on Black Tuesday, he sent a cheque for £1,000 to Charles Hamilton, accompanied with a note regretting that it could not be the £2,000 requested towards the maintenance of Carton. He could not afford it, he said, until his dividend in the London and North Eastern Railway Co. was paid.[4]

Over the next few years, Mallaby-Deeley's financial difficulties worsened; Charles Hamilton acknowledged this in 1932: 'I fully realize the difficulties Sir Henry has owing to increase of taxation both income tax and super tax in England and also the war loan conversion I know have hit him very hard'.[5] Sir Henry had been one of the largest single contributors to the war loan but in 1932 when the British government took the decision to convert 5% War Loan Bonds (the largest single block of the national debt) to new 3.5% bonds, it greatly diminished his investment.[6] Without substantive evidence one can only presume that the Carton investment portfolio was also greatly diminished during these years of great uncertainty.

Meanwhile, in Ireland, Charles Hamilton was dismayed by the fact that the new Fianna Fáil government under Eamon de Valera, which came to power in 1932, increased income tax from 3.6s. in the pound to 5s., and while rates on agricultural lands were slightly reduced there was no relief on buildings.[7] The great country houses were now, more than ever, white elephants. Rather than pay the hefty rates imposed by the new Fianna Fáil government, hundreds of owners simply abandoned them and had their roofs removed. Within a short radius of Maynooth once-great houses such as Donadea, Hortland and Rathcoffey were abandoned to decay.

In 1932, de Valera's government also abolished the oath of allegiance to the British crown, and then refused to pay the land annuities to the British government that were outstanding on the loans provided for the purchase of farms in Ireland under the British land acts of 1881 to 1909. The British government retaliated by imposing special duties on Irish imports, especially cattle and dairy produce. A six-year economic war followed (compounded by other defence, constitutional and financial issues), which damaged Anglo-Irish relations and trade. Although its repercussions on the farming industry remain the subject of debate,[8] Charles Hamilton's correspondence articulated his early fears that the economic war would have a negative impact on the letting (conacre) value of Carton lands and that demesne livestock farming would show a heavy loss as the duty payable on cattle exported to England would rise to around £5 a head which he regarded as prohibitive.

Hamilton advised that retrenchment at Carton was now a priority and Mallaby-Deeley was in no financial position to disagree. First of all, labourers' wages were lowered to 25s. a week from a high a decade before of 36s., a dramatic decrease of 30 per cent. Hamilton then focused on the running of the mansion: as long as Lady Nesta resided there, a staff on board wages had to be maintained and a considerable amount of coal and coke and a large quantity of cleaning materials were being used annually. If Lady Nesta lived at Kilkea it would save the wages of the butler (£100), the cook (£52), the coachman (£90 without board wages) and several others. Hamilton contended that the housekeeper and a couple of maids 'to do the rough scrubbing' and a boy to light the furnace twice a week during the winter would be enough to keep the house aired and clean.[9] While Sir Henry was not anxious to disturb Lady Nesta and the old butler who had been there for forty-four years (he was seventy-five), his own financial exigencies made him reflect long and hard on what Hamilton advised.[10] He wondered if a paying tenant (without disturbing Lady Nesta) could be got but in December 1932 Hamilton informed him that it would be difficult to let Carton without electric light. The Shannon Electrical Lighting Scheme had reached Maynooth but the £1,500 required to install it at Carton seemed prohibitive: 'Wiring costs a good deal', he told Sir Henry, 'and nobody but a rich American would take it'.[11] All they could hope, he continued, was that the Fianna Fáil government would be put out of office the following spring.[12] Instead it lasted until 1948.

While the upkeep of Carton had been affordable in the good years, it was now a luxury that Sir Henry could no longer afford. He looked once again to the possibility of selling the reversionary rights to the duke. For Edward to be able to purchase, he would have to find the money from somewhere other than the unwilling trustees. So in 1932, during the worst year of the economic depression, Edward set off for America to seek an heiress whose family might be interested in investing a large dowry for the ennoblement of their daughter.

II

The plan was not as frivolous as it might at first appear. From the late nineteenth century, American society, particularly along the eastern seaboard, had been a good deal obsessed by the life and manners and pastimes of the British and wider European aristocracy.[13] Indeed, in December 1903, when the sale of the Leinster estate was reaching its conclusion, the *New York Times'* 'Gossip between games' column noted that 'the young duke of Leinster [Maurice] will be the next matrimonial catch in the market'. It was projected that the sale of the estate would realize $1.5 million; Maurice would become extremely wealthy and inherit a ducal title and palatial residence; he was already well travelled and 'a representative of the great house of FitzGerald', and was reported to have a number of American cousins. One of these alleged cousins was the daughter of General Louis FitzGerald of New York (1838–1908, recently retired president of the Mercantile Trust Company), who had recently married her cousin, another FitzGerald from Boston. Her husband was, therefore, also reported to have been related to the young duke: he 'greatly resembled his distant Irish cousin'.[14] General Louis FitzGerald was very real but his relationship to the duke of Leinster, or that of his new son-in-law, seems fictitious. The report said more about New York and Boston Society and the social aspirations of its upper echelons.

The wealth and power elite of America comprised just as close knit a community as the aristocracy in Britain. When C. Wright Mills published his influential study of the power elite in America in 1956, he made the point that 'no matter what else they may be, the people of these higher circles are involved in a set of overlapping "crowds" and intricately connected "cliques".'[15] Similarly, when Ferdinand Lundberg had earlier published his *America's 60 families* in

1937 he estimated that 'the United States is owned and dominated today by a hierarchy of its sixty richest families, buttressed by no more than ninety families of lesser wealth'. He contended that 'the continuation of intermarriage among millionaire families will, other factors remaining unchanged, in a generation or two give rise to a situation wherein all the big American proprietors will be blood relatives – first, second, or third cousins'.[16] The same forecast could have been made with regard to the British and Irish aristocracy at the beginning of the eighteenth century.

While the likes of Lundberg might have lamented that 'one of the many ironies of the situation [was] that the United States should be pumping forth dividends and rents to support persons in stations so alien to the American concept of social status',[17] there were those within the American elite, who, knowing that it was impossible to create a titled aristocracy, considered the next best thing to be a marriage arrangement between a daughter and the son of a British/European aristocrat. In 1909, Gustavus Myers, the American historian and journalist, had estimated that 500 such marriages had taken place with the subsequent transfer of $220 million to Europe.[18] Myers was scathing of the wasteful extravagance of the Vanderbilts, for example, in their quest to attract titles for their children. He estimated that 'their excursions into the realm of high-caste European nobility' had cost them about $20 million dollars:

> When impecunious counts, lords, dukes and princes, having wasted the inheritance originally obtained by robbery, are on the anxious look out for marriages with great fortunes, and the American money magnates, satiated with vulgar wealth, aspire to titled connections, the arrangement becomes easy. Romance can be dispensed with, and the lawyers depended upon to settle the preliminaries.[19]

Lundberg put it rather bluntly: 'The chief assets of the Europeans have been hereditary titles, leisure-class manners, perhaps a shabby estate or two, and passports into the world of snobbery'. Thus, he seems to have resented that 'American dollars have served very concretely … to re-establish, via marriage, hundreds of decadent European estates, an ironic contribution of American democracy to the peoples of Europe'.[20] In Britain, the number of American-born peeresses multiplied from 4 in 1880 to 50 in 1914. In all, it has been estimated that between 1880 and 1914 there were more than 100 marriages by peers' eldest sons and younger sons to Americans.[21] While the dilution of society might have been frowned upon when Lord Edward FitzGerald, as he then was, or some of his fellow peers married outside the aristocracy, exceptions could always be made where vast wealth was concerned; as Angela Lambert contends 'the xenophobic, anti-Semitic British upper classes were prepared to make an exception' where the likes of the de Rothschild family was concerned.[22] Thus, the illegitimate daughter of Alfred de Rothschild was married off to the 5th earl of Carnarvon; Lord Curzon married the daughter of a wealthy Chicago businessman; the 4th earl of Strafford married the widow of the founder of Colgate's soap. The Irish aristocracy could only have looked enviously at the Marquis Boni de Castellan who married American heiress, Anna Gould, who brought with her a massive three million pounds.[23] William Waldorf Astor 'voluntarily expatriated himself … and was transmuted by the sorcery of money into an English lord'.[24] In 1929, his granddaughter married David Bowes-Lyon, uncle of the future Queen Elizabeth II.

There was a deeper, veiled and much more controversial aspect of this world revealed when a scandal involving the British government selling titles for money was exposed in the 1920s and David Lloyd George was heavily implicated in this 'murky business'; between January 1921 and June 1922, as an election loomed, 26 peerages, 74 baronetcies and 295 knighthoods were created.[25] It has been estimated that the purchases ranged from around £10,000 for a knighthood to £40,000 for a baronetcy. (It was during this period that Henry Mallaby-Deeley became baronet of Micham Court.) The exposure of this scandal led to the passing of the Honours (Prevention of Abuses) Act in 1925, but for the old aristocracy it came too late; the dilution of aristocratic society was deplored by one critic who proclaimed: 'gentlemen received titles whom no decent man would allow into his home. Several of them would have been blackballed by any respectable London club.'[26]

One of those most heavily implicated in the scandal was the notorious Maundy Gregory (1877–1941), the son of a clergyman, who had a history of involvement in various illegal scams. Edward later claimed that it was Gregory who proposed that he should find himself an American bride prepared to pay £100,000 to become a duchess.[27] He recalled: 'Gregory tried so hard to get me to marry the woman … that I think he had already received payment from her'.[28] It is unclear who 'the woman' was but it may have been Huguette Clark Gower, daughter of the late Senator W.A. Clark (1839–1925) of Montana, who the *Irish Independent* at the beginning of 1931 had linked to Edward and even reported that he was to marry her.[29]

W.A. Clark had been known as the 'copper king' as a result of the fortune he had amassed from copper mining (later diversifying into banks, railroads, timber, newspapers, sugar, coffee, oil, gold and silver) and was believed to have been the second-richest man in America behind Rockefeller by the time of his death in the 1920s. (He still ranks to this day as one of the fifty wealthiest Americans of all time.)[30] He was once famously described by Mark Twain as being 'as rotten a human being as can be found anywhere under the flag; he is a shame to the American nation, and no one has helped to send him to the Senate who did not know that his proper place was the penitentiary, with a chain and ball on his legs'.[31] For Twain he had epitomized the excesses of the so-called 'Gilded Age' in America that gave rise to the 'robber barons'. After leaving the Senate in 1907, Clark had moved his second (and young) wife and two daughters, including Huguette, into the Beaux-Arts house he built at Fifth Avenue and 77th Street in New York. It had 121 rooms, 4 art galleries, Turkish baths, a vaulted rotunda thirty-six feet high, and even its own railroad line to bring in coal. Known as 'Clark's Folly', it cost over $7 million dollars to build, which, to put it in some perspective, was three times more than it would cost to build Yankee Stadium a decade later. He decorated it with paintings by Degas, Rubens, Rembrandt, Titian, van Dyck, Gainsborough, Cazin and many others. After it was sold in 1927, for less than half it cost to build, it was demolished to make way for apartments.[32]

After he died in 1925 at the age of eighty-six, Clark's children's share of his inheritance came to $300 million (or approximately $3.6 billion today). Huguette was eighteen years old. Three years later, in 1928, she married William Gower, a law student working within her father's corporation. They divorced two years later. And shortly afterwards, newspapers began to link her to the duke of Leinster. The rumours may have been nothing more than a figment of some social diarist's imagination but one recent source has claimed that after the rumours spread of Huguette's engagement to Leinster 'the pundits had a field day in newspaper cartoons – publicity which Huguette no doubt abhorred. She gave up her opera seat and was never mentioned in society news again'.[33] In the summer of 2010, when Huguette's estate came under the scrutiny of Inland Revenue – she was still alive at the age of 103 in a Manhattan hospital – stories of her liaison with 'an Irish nobleman' came to prominence once again.[34]

III

Edward certainly had relationships with other heiresses. Mildred Logan was the widow of a wealthy stockbroker. She was known as the 'Rolls-Royce specialist' because of her penchant for collecting that make of car.[35] Described as an 'attractive woman, dark, though greying a little and very vivacious', she and

31 Rafaelle Van Neck (1920–91), 7th duchess of Leinster, taken from Rafaelle, duchess of Leinster, *So brief a dream* (London and New York, 1973).

Edward actually got engaged. However, after a few months Edward absconded; he later claimed that he detested her obsession with horses: 'I could stand most things but not being married to a horse show'.[36]

Not long afterwards he met 'a honey', the married Rafaelle Van Neck (née Kennedy), who became as besotted with Edward's rank as with the man himself. Some years later, she recalled how she was enchanted by the aristocracy: 'They spoke so beautifully, and had such good manners, and a type of quality and breeding the like of which I had never known before'.[37] Rafaelle had been born in Brooklyn of Irish parentage on her father's side but and was brought up in Connecticut following her parents' separation.[38] She made her first visit to England in 1924, as Mrs Clare Van Neck, arriving on the *Olympic*: 'over-dressed, over-anxious and over-whelmed'.[39] In London, she met Edward at a large luncheon given for him by some wealthy Americans. She later remembered that 'not much came of our meeting, except that I liked his fey quality and he never took his eyes off me'.[40] It was by accident that Rafaelle bumped into him again at Child's restaurant on Fifth Avenue and 58th Street. Edward was once again being fêted by New York society. The following day he invited Rafaelle to a luncheon being given by Emily Lardenburg who lived alone with her parrot at the Ambassador Hotel on Park Avenue. Society columns soon began to report their affair but Rafaelle denied it: 'the duke of Leinster is a friend', she told reporters in November 1932, 'I wish to deny most emphatically that a marriage has been arranged between us or has ever been suggested'.[41]

Rafaelle thought him 'the kindest, most generous man in all the world, with absolutely no sense of money'.[42] He was 'the dreamer always thinking that tomorrow would solve all problems'.[43] However, she was not the wealthy heiress that he had been sent to the States to find; indeed, Rafaelle later claimed that when the New York gossip columns began to write about her and Edward, Mallaby-Deeley was greatly disappointed.[44]

Rafaelle recorded in her memoirs several significant details that came out of her early conversations with Edward: his son, Gerald, was a ward of chancery who 'had been brought up to deplore his father by the FitzGeralds at Johnstown Castle in Ireland'; their relationship never improved so that when they met, 'They seemed complete strangers and rather stiff with each other'; Mallaby-Deeley had a 'hold over him'; Edward worshipped his dead mother who he barely remembered; and he was very close to his aunt Helen, Viscountess D'Abernon, 'the nearest thing he had to family', as the FitzGeralds had 'written him off' because of the disgrace he had brought to the family name.[45] She also claimed that the FitzGerald family bitterness was the reason they refused to provide Edward with a home. It was a poignant observation, as it was probably the loss of his home from childhood and more particularly the loss of both parents when still a child that conditioned Edward's personality. Two years before he met Rafaelle, during his unsavoury divorce case against May Etheridge in 1930, Lord Mackay had raised the question of Edward's domiciliation and concluded that he 'never had an Irish home in any sense except for the first two or three months of his life'.[46] If his mother was 'an unquiet soul', he was a lost soul and Rafaelle recognized this:

> To this day [c.1970] I earnestly believe that had the FitzGeralds been able to give us a small property on or near the Leinster estates, where Edward would have felt welcome and that he really belonged, it would have made all the difference to our marriage and our life together … Couldn't the family have given us a second place and a second chance? But alas, they couldn't: Edward had sold his life interest, so there was nothing to give.[47]

Rafaelle could do little to prevent his continued profligacy. In January 1933, while on honeymoon with her, he was sued by a creditor, Emily Grigsby, for repayment of a £2,000 loan.[48] In June he was back in Chancery Division in London having paid only £200 off the £2,000; his solicitor pleaded that 'he was entirely without means' and that it had only been with 'the kind assistance of friends' that he had managed to pay that much.[49] (That more of his fellow peers were going the same way was evidenced in the fact that on the same day in the same court, a judgment summons was taken by another creditor against the duke of Manchester and a commital order made against Lord Kinnoull for debts of around £10 to Harrods Ltd.)[50] Three months later, in September, Edward was fined £15 at Fort William sheriff's court in Scotland 'for driving a motor car recklessly' (estimated by a witness to be at 60 m.p.h.) and knocking down and injuring Alexander Morrison, a labourer, who subsequently spent five months in hospital.[51] And, in October, another five judgment summonses were made against him in the Chancery Division. As always Edward promised through his solicitor 'to pay a certain sum within the next week or so'.[52]

In 1936, three years after their marriage, Edward attempted to bring Rafaelle to see Carton for the first time. It is not clear when he had last been there himself, but, as noted in the previous chapter, he had neither been welcomed by the family nor encouraged to visit by Mallaby-Deeley. On 7 July, Edward wrote from Craughwell in Co. Galway informing Sir Henry that he was intending to visit the following day but knowing that Sir Henry would completely disapprove, Edward warned: 'I am taking with me a reporter on the *Irish Times* and another on the *Daily Express*; these will not publish anything at all unless we encounter any form of unpleasantness from you'.[53] Sir Henry's legal representatives informed Charles Hamilton that his visit was to be regarded as trespass and would not be tolerated. Lady Nesta was reportedly 'greatly disturbed and annoyed by the duke's imminent arrival'.[54] Mallaby-Deeley wrote to advise her to return temporarily to Kilkea, while his solicitors wrote to Charles Hamilton:

> You are authorized on Sir Henry's behalf, as soon as Lady Nesta has left Carton, to take all steps which you may think useful or convenient to make the duke's residence there impossible and, if necessary, you are to proceed to close the entire house … It is considered at present that it will be preferable to proceed in this way, rather than to commence an action in the courts which might prove long and costly.[55]

Hamilton was encouraged to 'avoid any publicity as far as possible, and not to have anything done that would furnish sensational copy to the newspapers'.

The attitude to the duke was easily discernible in the correspondence: 'it is probable that it is the duke's hope that publicity of this kind will follow – in fact he expressly threatens that – and if it does not, he will probably consider that it is not worth his while to stay'.[56] The instructions continued:

> We would suggest that if it is possible for you to do so, you should remove and exclude from the house and estate any servant or other person whom he has brought with him. We also suggest that you might be able to deny him access to the gardens and to prevent his obtaining any supplies from them or otherwise enjoying any of the amenities of the estate. Every step which you can take to interfere with his enjoyment of the premises in any way will be in order. It will equally be in order for you, if you think fit, to make public to shopkeepers in the neighbourhood the fact that the duke is not authorized to reside at Carton and that his residence there will not continue. This might have some influence with the local shopkeepers and make it awkward for him to obtain supplies.[57]

Rafaelle's description of events is more imaginative and inventive. The authenticity of her memoirs is somewhat dubious, but her reflections are still illuminating. She recalled that a small crowd of local people had gathered at the main entrance of Carton to welcome Edward and her. She remembered their deference, how they 'touched their caps or forelocks' as they smiled and waved (then again she also 'remembered' how it was the Jesuits who had established a seminary in the town of Maynooth!). As they came into view of the house, Edward ordered the chauffeur to stop so that they could walk the last mile or so, past the shell cottage, the lake covered with blue pond lilies and the American garden. When they crossed the bridge and walked up the slight incline towards the house they saw a great pennant being carried by the staff which read 'Welcome Home'. The agent, Charles Hamilton, local dignitaries and some of the town tenants had gathered as well as a band (probably the St Mary's Brass and Reed Band) which played 'America, my America' in honour of the new duchess. But Edward had disappeared, scuttling behind one of the pillars at the front of the house, leaving his new bride to make her own introductions. She sensed that all present hoped she was 'Lady Bountiful, or at least a Barbara Hutton!' (the so-called 'poor little rich girl', granddaughter of F.W. Woolworth and daughter of F.L. Hutton who on coming of age inherited perhaps up to €150 million in 1933, making her one of the wealthiest women in the world).[58]

While Mallaby-Deeley's correspondence advised Lady Nesta to leave, Rafaelle distinctly remembered her being there, armed 'with her disapproving manner and spinster chill'. Nesta was too old worldly to appreciate an American duchess of dubious lineage, not to mention a duke who was the illegitimate son of another duchess she had neither trusted nor liked. Rafaelle's memories of the house at this time are interesting (but again should be treated with some caution). She was impressed by the fine rooms 'each with traces of past beauty and elegance'; she knew not to pull the beautiful silk damask curtains or they would 'fall to the floor as dust'; and she greatly admired the pictures including the portrait of Lord Edward (the United Irishman) in the dining-room and the full-length portrait of Hermione which hung at the top of the stairs. Her favourite rooms were the magnificent Gold Saloon with its organ that she longed to play, and the Chinoiserie that had been converted into a bedroom. But her abiding impression was that 'Carton was a glorious un-lived-in, un-loved-house [that] held no warmth or welcome for me'.[59]

Yet, it was at Carton that Rafaelle began to appreciate the devastating psychological effect that the death of Hermione had on Edward. At night the two of them would secretly rummage through the cupboards of the house looking for photographs or other memorabilia of Hermione:

> There were boxes of family snapshots; he would go through them with care and stuff his pockets with all he could find of her and tell me as much as he could remember about this aunt or that uncle, but his whole search was for his mother.[60]

They found a miniature of Hermione with supposedly a lock of Edward's hair at the back of the frame. Nesta found out they were rummaging and became extremely angry.[61] According to Rafaelle, Edward, in the eyes of Nesta and her other spinster sisters at Kilkea, simply did not live up to his eighteenth-century namesake:

> Their hero was Lord Edward FitzGerald, who had led the rebellion for the Irish. His portrait hung in the dining-room – Nesta nearly genu-flected in front of it – and had kept Carton a shrine during the Troubles [1920–3]. My own Lord Edward had led his own rebellion against the Geraldines himself, and stripped the shrine of all its glory. So his portrait will never hang in the dining-room or any other room … Naturally the Geraldines resented what he had done and felt it deeply. So did his young son Gerald, who would succeed him.[62]

IV

After his marriage to Rafaelle, Mallaby-Deeley gave up on Edward finding a wealthy wife or, indeed, any of the FitzGeralds repurchasing the reversionary rights. In 1936, Edward was declared bankrupt for the third time, he owed almost £140,000. He had continued to borrow at extortionate rates: one creditor who had lent £50 claimed £3,075 while another who lent £2,000 demanded £10,000. Rafaelle remembered his small dressing-room in their house at Portland Place as 'an untidy mess of racing books, unpaid bills, threatening letters – and trouble'.[63] She was regularly called to his hotels when it was discovered he did not have the money to pay his bills. Often he was detained by the police until she could get someone to cover his expenses. Rafaelle recalled 'con men and con women, moneylenders, down and outs and riff raff' chasing him once more.[64] It is perhaps remarkable that he survived the sordid world in which he moved.

Edward and Rafaelle continued to live on the annual allowance of £1,000 from Mallaby-Deeley and roughly the same allowance from Rafaelle's mother. They could afford a butler, a cook, a housemaid, a between-maid, a lady's maid, a chauffeur and part-time secretary. As the premier peer of Ireland they still got invited to the grand occasions but as an un-discharged bankrupt Edward was not allowed to attend the coronation in 1937 of King George VI. Rafaelle went alone and later recalled:

> What a sight! What a sight! Never had I or mother dreamed of anything like this! How could we? It only happened in books! I was transfixed by the beauty of it all, and sat there holding my breath, for it was real! How I wished that 'My Imp' [Edward] was there to take his place and see what he too had never seen, yet given me the right to enjoy.[65]

How would she have reacted had she known that Edward had an affair with Wallis Simpson during the abdication crisis of the previous year?[66] King Edward VIII had regarded the duke of Leinster as one of his closest friends and, of course, he had regarded his brother, Desmond, as his 'greatest friend' before the latter was killed in the Great War. It was another measure of how unscrupulous and unprincipled Edward could be.

After he divorced Rafaelle, Edward married Denise 'Jo' Wessel (1884–1960) in 1946, another former gaiety girl whose stage name had been Denise Orme (but who had been born Jessie Smither, reputedly the daughter of a Sussex bicycle shop owner). Rafaelle described her as: 'small, very pretty, with a lovely shaped face and great grey eyes under thick false eyelashes, which she used with skill to get what she wanted'.[67] She was the former wife of John Yarde-Buller, Lord Churston, whom she had divorced in 1928 (their grandson was Aly Khan IV). It was another marriage doomed to disaster as Edward continued his wayward lifestyle. Within a few years he had also deserted Denise.[68] For a time he lived in France, started a relationship with a thirty-four year old named Yvonne Probyn, had a son, Adrian, by her in 1952, divorced Denise, and ended up, true to form, abandoning Yvonne Probyn and his son.

In the 1950s Edward also abandoned his title and preferred to call himself 'Mr FitzGerald'. He sold his life story, 'My forty years of folly', to the *Sunday Dispatch* for £5,000. In sensationalized style, true to the genre that the newspaper represented, he told how his 'road to ruin was the gay road – the road of mad parties, reckless friends and lovely women'; how he had thrown away a fortune worth £1,000 a week; how he had dined with an Eastern sultan while usurpers stormed his palace, 'supped with a girl who caused a revolution and cost a king his crown and his life', and 'courted some of the world's most-moneyed women'.[69] Less than ten years later, in 1965, he married his fourth and final wife, Vivien Connor, the housekeeper at the block of flats where he then lived. She subsequently sold her story to the *News of the World* which was published weekly under such headlines as 'My crazy life with the penniless duke' and 'Living on baked beans we dodged the creditors'.[70] Although hardly the most reliable source, Vivien's descriptions of his 'terrific way with women'; 'dashing life of debt'; 'eggs and bacon one day, champagne another'; pawning 'a diamond tie-pin for half a crown to buy a meal' mirrored the reality of Edward's degenerate lifestyle. This series of articles possibly represented his lowest point and brought further disgrace upon him in British aristocratic circles.

V

Edward lived his life driven by what one commentator has called 'an incendiary wilfulness'.[71] At the same time he was also an aristocratic heir in a very changing world. He was not a patrician landowner, a politician or a statesman. He had only two of the eleven 'abiding aristocratic preoccupations' identified by David Cannadine, namely rank and title; the others – fame and fortune, power and prestige, place and office, ancestor worship and family pride – all eluded him.[72] As we have seen throughout this book, the FitzGeralds' use of history became a key component in their ability to survive for as long as they

32 From left to right: Gerald, 8th duke of Leinster; seated on his lap is Thomas, earl of Offaly (killed in a car accident in 1997); Edward, 7th duke of Leinster; Maurice, 9th duke of Leinster. This photograph was taken *c.*1975.

did and to create a legacy that ensured they escaped the venomous nationalist rhetoric directed against so many of their peers from the late nineteenth century onwards. Even Maurice, in his madness, had desired to live in Ireland as his ancestors had done. But Edward had none of Maurice's attachment to family or place or what Cannadine calls 'the sense of interconnection between the generations dead, living and yet unborn' that Edmund Burke (1729–97), the Irish philosopher (among other things), identified as being 'the very essence of aristocracy'.[73]

Moreover, Edward had inherited by accident rather than design, and he was ill-prepared to do so. Many years after Sir Henry Mallaby-Deeley had passed away Edward recalled their first meeting and remembered him as a 'well-dressed, shrewd and charming' man.[74] The latter two adjectives suggest that Edward may have wanted others to sympathize with him for having been somehow duped into his ill-fated arrangement. However, it was probably that very arrangement that saved the FitzGerald Palladian mansion at Carton.

Given Edward's profligate lifestyle, and the fact that he was declared bankrupt twice more after Sir Henry's death, it would be difficult to imagine that the house would have survived; more likely it would have been abandoned by the 1940s just to save the rates, left roofless and decaying, to disappear from the Irish landscape.[75]

In 1943, Edward's position as a duke was put into perspective in a *Life* special by Lord Kinross.[76] Kinross traced the changing fortunes of Britain's dukes back to Lloyd George's 1909 budget and 'the radical policy of taxing the lands of the rich to give the money to the poor'. Lloyd George, he contended, had raised 'howls of joy from the slumhouses of Limehouse' and 'howls of rage from the squares of Belgravia'. Of the twenty-six dukes (who on average had 8.5 titles, 1.1 wives, 2.2 children, 3.6 homes, and 46,000 acres), half of them were millionaires, and only four had incomes of less than £10,000 per annum. The duke of Leinster was categorized as the poorest of all; in fact, Kinross contended, 'too poor' to be a duke.[77]

Kinross contrasted the exalted position of the duke of Devonshire in the eighteenth and nineteenth centuries when he lived at Chatsworth and retained six other houses (including Lismore Castle in Ireland), with how his descendants lived at Bolton Abbey in 1943, unable to afford Chatsworth, and having sold Devonshire House in Picadilly to make way for a block of apartments. He went on to speculate that 'one of these days this duke, or some other duke, will dream ... that he is living not at Chatsworth etc. etc. or any such mansion, but in a labour-saving flat or a four-room cottage. He will wake up and find that it is true.'[78] It did not happen to the Devonshires – their fortunes have been dramatically revived in recent years – but in 1976 the eighty-four-year-old Edward FitzGerald, 7th duke of Leinster, was found dead by his fourth wife, Vivien Connor, in a one-room bedsit flat in St George's Drive, Westminster, London. He had taken his own life through an overdose of alcohol and barbiturates.[79] He had acquired the sobriquet 'The bed-sit duke'.[80] He left 'little more than the watch on his wrist and the clothes that flapped from his body'.[81] Marcus Scriven contends that his exit 'might have been suffered by any of London's genteel poor'; there was certainly nothing ducal about his funeral ceremony except that the arrangements were carried out by J.H. Kenyon, London, undertakers to the Royal family for generations.[82]

Five years after Kinross' article, in 1948, Sir Henry Mallaby-Deeley's family came to a decision with the agreement of the trustees and Edward's son, Gerald, marquess of Kildare, to sell Carton but to allow the FitzGeralds to retain Kilkea Castle and seventy-three acres of land as a family residence. It was the 150th anniversary of the death of Lord Edward FitzGerald and a year before Ireland was officially declared a republic of a type very different to what he had aspired to, and where aristocratic title had no meaning. A family representative informed Charles Hamilton: 'Sad though this is I feel that there would not be the remotest chance of Kildare or his successors being able to afford to live at Carton what with taxation and the crippling death duties'.[83] Hamilton was informed that his tenure as agent would be terminated and that 'proper compensation' would be made by way of a 3 per cent commission on the sale monies.[84] The almost 800-year-old FitzGerald connection with Maynooth had come to an inglorious end.

Epilogue

> Hence learn, whenever, in some unhappy day, you light on the ruins of
> so great a mansion, of what worth he was who built it, and how frail all
> things are, when such memorials of such men cannot outlive misfortune.

Foundation stone of Leinster House

The above lines are said to have been inscribed *c.*1745 on the foundation stone
of the great FitzGerald town house on Kildare Street in Dublin. Its
architectural grandeur certainly reflected the 'worth' of the family who built it
and while it may not have become a ruin the radical change in its function, to
become the seat of power of the government of the Irish Republic, nevertheless
symbolizes the fall of the dukes of Leinster who did not 'outlive misfortune'.

The same is true of the Leinster country house at Carton. In 1949, it was
sold by the representatives of Henry Mallaby-Deeley to the wealthy brewer,
Ronald Nall-Cain, 2nd Baron Brocket, for £80,000.[1] For almost thirty years he
farmed the demesne, using the produce to supply his Irish hotels. For a time he
leased it to the Hon. Desmond Guinness and his wife, Mariga, and it was
there, in 1957, that they founded the Irish Georgian Society. Twenty years later,
Carton was sold again, this time to an engineering firm, Powerscreen Ltd. A
member of Brocket's family later regretted that 'we had to leave Carton because
we could not find those thousands [to maintain the buildings and the
demesne], while paying the new taxes …'[2]

In the late 1970s, one of the founders of Powerscreen Ltd, Lee Mallaghan,
purchased the house and over a period of time transformed it and the demesne
into a country house hotel with two championship golf courses and a leisure
complex.[3] Like the town house, Carton's role and function dramatically
changed over time. However, it remains an impressive reminder of the
FitzGerald legacy in Maynooth, as do the ruins of the great medieval castle,
Leinster Street (Main Street), Leinster Cottages, the Duke's Harbour, Bere
Street, Nelson Street, Stoyte House (and St Patrick's College), Carton Avenue
and so on. Further afield the FitzGerald legacy is to be found in Dublin in

Leinster House and Kildare Street and in London where one finds Leinster Gardens in Bayswater (where there is also the Duke of Leinster Hotel) and Leinster Square near Notting Hill.

In 1872, when this book opens, the Leinsters were wealthy, at least in terms of being asset rich, though not nearly as rich as most ducal families in Britain; Augustus, 3rd duke, and his family lived in private, if not entirely affordable, splendour; they controlled local society and politics through inherited power, patronage and paternalism that begot deference; their sons served the country and empire (and undoubtedly made material gains from the same); they were leisured and attended by an army of staff; and they believed in preserving the family lineage, most notably symbolized in the vast collection of family portraits that hung at Carton and Kilkea and, indeed, in the preservation of Maynooth Castle, the most prominent physical legacy of their ancestors who had settled in Ireland over 700 years previously.

In popular memory, the FitzGeralds became, to use the old cliché, more Irish than the Irish themselves and this arguably raised them above most of the settler classes who arrived under later plantation and confiscation schemes. Their defiance of central authority, beginning with the Tudor regime, ensured a legacy that was to serve them well in the future. This was especially true around their core estate in Maynooth. In October 1936, in an ironic historical twist, Gerald FitzGerald, marquess of Kildare, and later 8th duke of Leinster, married Joane McMurrough Kavanagh, a direct descendant of Diarmait Mac Murchada, who, of course, had invited the Anglo-Normans to Ireland in 1169 in an attempt to safeguard his position as high king of Leinster. Prior to the wedding, the people of Maynooth presented Gerald with a silver salver in the Leinster Arms Hotel. The celebration had echoes of his namesake's coming-of-age in 1872. A procession through the town was led by the St Mary's Brass and Reed band, while 'a large gathering assembled outside the hotel and fireworks were exploded'.[4] The Catholic parish priest of Maynooth, Fr Killeen, told those gathered:

> In particular they remembered the thoughtfulness and generosity that provided the sites for the church of St Mary, their schools and their parochial house, and they recalled with pride and gratitude that it was a head of the Leinster house who gave them the site for the great College of St Patrick's which had added such fame to their town.[5]

In response, the marquess told the audience that he hoped it would not be long before he and his wife would come back to reside in Carton, but, of course,

33 Wedding photograph of Gerald FitzGerald (1914–2004), marquess of Kildare and later
8th duke of Leinster, and Joane McMurrough Kavanagh (courtesy of David Cusker).

that was never to happen. When the Irish Land Commission stripped Kilkea
Castle of its farmland, he had no option but to vacate the same and he took the
path of most Irish nobles in the post-independence period and settled outside
Ireland, in his case Oxfordshire, where he pursued a successful career in
business as chairman of CSE Aviation.[6] If the family had been in a position to
come back to Maynooth in the 1930s, it seems that the locals would not have
objected.

The controversy and intrigue that had followed the family for centuries did
not suddenly end after they departed Ireland. When Edward, 7th duke, died in
1976, his successor, Gerald FitzGerald, had to contest a claim from a San
Francisco school teacher, Leonard FitzGerald, that he was the rightful heir to
the dukedom of Leinster, alleging that Maurice had not died in Craighouse but
had made his way to America. Gerald's legal team countered that in fact this
'pretender' – an ironic throwback to the late fifteenth century when Garret

More FitzGerald almost lost his power for supporting 'the pretender', Lambert Simnel, against King Henry VII – was the son of man named Charlie Tyler who it seems, Mitty-like, had got caught up in his own fantasies that he was a duke. This remarkable affair has been well documented;[7] suffice to say here that while Leonard gave up his eighteen-year campaign in 1994 due to ill health, his son, Paul, a property developer, resurrected the claim after Gerald died in 2004. This time it was based on the premise that his grandfather (aka Charlie Tyler) was actually Desmond, who had not died during the First World War but had faked his death, emigrated to America and had a family there.[8] Again, given the evidence of Desmond's death presented here, it seems extraordinary that it was even countenanced but still it dragged on until, in 2006, Paul FitzGerald's claim was allowed to be submitted simultaneously with Maurice FitzGerald's to the lord chancellor and secretary of state for constitutional affairs.[9] It was not until 2010 that Baron Falconer of Thoroton, the lord chancellor, dismissed Paul FitzGerald's claim.

The present and 9th duke of Leinster, Maurice FitzGerald, a landscape gardener based in Oxfordshire, and his family, have reconnected with Carton and are regular guests there of the Mallaghan family. Maurice's only son, Thomas, earl of Offaly, was tragically killed in a car accident in 1997. The title will now pass to Maurice's brother, John, and then to his son, Edward, an iconic FitzGerald name. Rather ironically his sister, Hermione, is a professional golfer whose career regularly brings her back to Carton in a much different guise to that of her namesake and great-great-grandmother.

Notes

Preface and acknowledgments

1 David Cannadine, *Aspects of aristocracy* (London, 1995 ed.), p. 9.
2 See, for example, Douglas Smith, *Former people: the last days of the Russian aristocracy* (London, 2012).
3 For the wider picture, see Terence Dooley, *The decline of the big house in Ireland* (2001); Olwen Purdue, *The big house in the north of Ireland: land, power and social elites, 1878–1960* (Dublin, 2009); and for Britain, David Cannadine, *The decline and fall of the British aristocracy* (London, 1994); Peter Mandler, *The fall and rise of the stately home* (London, 1997).
4 Marcus Scriven, *Splendour and squalour: the disgrace and disintegration of three aristocratic dynasties* (London, 2009), p. 16.
5 Quoted in Michael Estorick, *Heirs and graces: the claim to the dukedom of Leinster* (London, 1981), p. 90.

CHAPTER ONE
Gerald FitzGerald's coming-of-age, 1872

1 Anon., *Journal of the County Kildare Archaeological Society* (hereafter *JCKAS*), 6, 1909–11 (1911), p. 101.
2 David Cannadine, *The decline and fall of the British aristocracy* (London, 1990), p. 10.
3 *Morning Post*, 19 Aug. 1872.
4 On this subject see Kevin McKenna, 'Power, resistance and ritual: paternalism on the Clonbrock estates, 1826–1906' (PhD, NUI Maynooth, 2011); Howard

Newby, *Property, paternalism and power: class and control in rural England* (London, 1979); idem, 'The deferential dialectic', *Comparative Studies in Society and History*, 17 (1975), pp 139–64; David Roberts, *Paternalism in early Victorian England* (New Brunswick, NJ, 1979).
5 See below for rebellion of Silken Thomas, 10th earl of Kildare.
6 *Leinster Express*, 24 Aug. 1872.
7 Address to the earl of Offaly on the occasion of his attaining his majority, 16 August 1872 (Carton House).
8 On such issues see, D. Cannadine, *Aspects of aristocracy.*
9 How this socio-economic elite came into being in the post-Famine period will be discussed below.
10 See chapter 2.
11 Quoted in Art Cosgrove (ed.), *A new history of Ireland: ii, medieval Ireland 1169–1534* (Oxford, 1993), p. 45.
12 Thomas Wright (ed.), *The historical works of Giraldus Cambrensis* (London and New York, 1892), p. 246; Seán Duffy, *Ireland in the Middle Ages* (Dublin, 1997), p. 63.
13 Colm Lennon, 'The making of the Geraldines: the Kildare FitzGeralds and their early historians' in Patrick Cosgrove, Terence Dooley and Karol Mullaney-Dignam (eds), *Aspects of Irish aristocratic life: essays on the FitzGeralds of Kildare and Carton House* (Dublin, 2014), pp 71–8.
14 Quoted in Duffy, *Ireland in the Middle Ages*, p. 101.
15 S.G. Ellis, *Ireland in the age of the Tudors 1447–1603: English expression and the end*

of *Gaelic rule* (London, 1998), p. 106;
Colm Lennon, 'The FitzGeralds of
Kildare and the building of a dynastic
image' in William Nolan and Thomas
McGrath (eds), *Kildare: history and society*
(Dublin, 2006), p. 197.

16 See, for example, Steven Ellis, 'Tudor
policy and the Kildare ascendancy in the
lordship of Ireland, 1496–1534', *Irish
Historical Studies*, 20:79 (1977), pp 235–
71; Mary Ann Lyons, 'Sidelights on the
Kildare ascendancy: a survey of Geraldine
involvement in the church, *c*.1470–
c.1520', *Archivium Hibernicum*, 48
(1994), pp 73–87.

17 V.P. Carey, 'Collaborator and survivor:
Gerald the eleventh earl of Kildare and
Tudor Ireland', *History Ireland*, 2:2
(Summer 1994), p. 14.

18 S.G. Ellis, 'Bastard feudalism and the
Kildare rebellion, 1534–35: the character
of rebel support' in Nolan and McGrath
(eds), *Kildare*, p. 221.

19 See chapters eight and nine.

20 Mary Ann Lyons, 'FitzGerald, Gerald
(Gearoid Mor), 8th earl of Kildare'
in James McGuire and James Quinn
(eds), *Dictionary of Irish biography*
(Cambridge, 2009) [http://dib.
cambridge.org/viewReadPage.do?articleId
=a3148, accessed 9 July 2011].

21 For more details see
www.louvre.fr/llv/oeuvres/detail_notice;
see also Michael Potterton, 'Introduction:
the FitzGeralds, Florence, St Fiachra and
a few fragments' in Michael Potterton and
Thomas Herron (eds), *Dublin and the
Pale in the Renaissance c.1540–1660*
(Dublin, 2011), p. 28. Potterton suggests
Garret Oge may have met Lisa when
visiting the court of Cosimo I de'Medici.

22 Lodovico Ariosto, *Orlando Furioso* (canto
x, st. 87–8); www.gutenberg.org/cache/
epub/3747/pg3747.html [accessed 20 July
2012]; www.gutenberg.org/cache/epub/
615/pg615.html [accessed 20 July 2012].

23 *Important and scarce books selected for sale
with the consent of the trustees of His Grace,
the Duke of Leinster, from the library at
Carton County Kildare to be sold by
Bennett & Sons, 11 Nov. 1925 and
following two days* (National Library of
Ireland).

24 For more on Gerald's life see Vincent
Carey, *Surviving the Tudors: the 'Wizard
Earl' of Kildare and English rule in Ireland,
1537–1586* (Dublin, 2002).

25 There is an extensive literature on this
period of the family's life; see, for
example, Colm Lennon, 'The FitzGeralds
of Kildare and the building of a dynastic
image, 1500–1630' in Nolan and
McGrath (eds), *Kildare*, pp 195–212;
Mary Ann Lyons, 'Revolt and reaction:
the Geraldine rebellion and monastic
confiscation in Co. Kildare 1535–1540',
*Journal of the Kildare Archaeological
Society*, 18 (1992–93), pp 39–60; for the
place of the FitzGeralds within the wider
context of Irish political and social
developments, see V.P. Carey, *Surviving
the Tudors*; S.G. Ellis, *Tudor Ireland:
crown, community and the conflict of
cultures, 1470–1603* (London and New
York, 1985); Laurence McCorristine, *The
revolt of Silken Thomas: a challenger to
Henry VIII* (Dublin, 1987).

26 Raymond Gillespie, *Sixteenth-century
Ireland* (Dublin, 2006), p. 14.

27 Lennon, 'The building of a dynastic
image', p. 207.

28 Ibid.

29 A.B. Grosart (ed.), *The Lismore papers*
(London, 1886), 1st series, iv, p. 45;
quoted in Horner, *Maynooth*, p. 3.

30 Horner, *Maynooth*, p. 2.

31 Cullen, *Maynooth*, p. 28.

32 Quoted in ibid.; see also 'Text of talk
given by 5th duke of Leinster to Kildare
Archaeological Society, 1893', *JCKAS*
(1893–94), p. 233.

33 FitzGerald, 'Carton', p. 12.

34 Ibid.; Arnold Horner, 'Land transactions and the making of Carton demesne', *JCKAS*, 15 (1971–6), p. 391.

35 http://www.dia.ie/architects/view/347/CASTLE-RICHARD [accessed 7 January 2012].

36 See Patrick Walsh, 'Biography and the meaning of an Irish country house: William Conolly and Castletown' in Terence Dooley and Christopher Ridgway (eds), *The Irish country house: its past, present and future* (Dublin, 2011), pp 21–39.

37 Toby Barnard, *Making the grand figure: lives and possessions in Ireland, 1641–1770* (New Haven and London, 2004), p. 69.

38 Anne Crookshank, 'The visual arts, 1603–1740' in T.W. Moody and W.E. Vaughan (eds), *A new history of Ireland; iv, eighteenth-century Ireland 1691–1800* (Oxford, 1986), pp 487–8.

39 J.T. Gilbert, *A history of the city of Dublin* (Shannon, 1972 ed., [1st ed., 1854–9]), p. 316. An interesting piece of family lore attributes Castle's coming to Ireland to the 19th earl. The story goes that during his grand tour he had gone specifically to Italy to see first hand some of the best examples of Palladian architecture and while there stayed with Monsignor Rinaldo Pisani, a member of one of the most powerful and influential Venetian families, who was patron to a young emerging architect named Richard Castle. Both Pisani and Castle accompanied the earl for two months visiting Palladian villas in Venice and before he left, the earl invited Castle to Ireland. While more authentic evidence shows that it was at the invitation of Gustavus Hume that Castle came to Ireland, but the anecdote is illuminating in terms of the family's notions that they were responsible for introducing Castle to Ireland, and by extension in bringing Palladianism to prominence in the country; 'Notice of FitzGeralds, 1876' (National Library of Ireland, FitzGerald papers, MS 48,188); Kay O'Higgins, 'Carton: seat of the former duke of Leinster', *Irish Tatler and Sketch* (Dec. 1955), pp 21–7; also idem, 'Carton Co. Kildare, residence of Lord and Lady Brocket', *Irish Tatler and Sketch* (Jan. 1956), pp 33–40.

40 Quoted in Peter Somerville-Large, *The Irish country house* (London, 1995), p. 167; see also Alison FitzGerald, '"Desiring to look sprucish": objects in context at Carton' and William Laffan and Brendan Rooney, 'Painting Carton: the 2nd duke of Leinster, Thomas Roberts and William Ashford', both in Cosgrove et al. (eds), *Aspects of Irish aristocratic life*, pp 118–27, 128–37.

41 'Introduction', *The Irish Georgian Society Records of eighteenth-century domestic architecture and decoration in Ireland*, 5 (1913), p. 23; Edward McParland, 'Building in the grand manner: Sir Richard Morrison's country houses – II', *Country Life*, 31 May 1973, p. 1540; John Cornforth, 'The Francini in England', *Country Life*, 148, 12 Mar. 1970, pp 634–6; McDonnell, *Irish eighteenth-century stuccowork*, pp 1–2; Brian de Breffny, 'The Lafranchini brothers' in *The GPA Irish Arts Review Yearbook* (1988), pp 212–21.

42 McDonnell, *Irish eighteenth-century stuccowork*, p. 4.

43 For a wider discussion on this theme, see Malcolm Bull, *The mirror of the gods: Classical mythology in Renaissance art* (London, 2005), p. 342; also Jean Seznac, *The survival of the pagan gods: the mythological tradition and its place in Renaissance humanism and art* (Princeton, 1981), p. 5.

44 See Arnold Horner, 'Land transactions and the making of Carton demesne', *JCKAS*, 15 (1971–6), pp 387–96; idem, 'Carton, Co. Kildare: a case study of the

making of an Irish demesne', *Quarterly Bulletin of the Irish Georgian Society*, 18 (nos. 2 & 3), Apr.–Sept. 1975, pp 45–104; Finola O'Kane, *Landscape design in eighteenth-century Ireland; mixing foreign trees with the natives* (Cork, 2004), pp 89–130.

45 Quoted in Padraig Ó Snodaigh, 'Notes on the politics of Kildare at the end of the eighteenth century', *JCKAS*, 17:3 (1981–2), p. 264.

46 Ibid., p. 292.

47 Jacqueline Hill, *From Patriots to unionists: Dublin civic politics and Irish protestant patriotism, 1660–1840* (Oxford, 1997), p. 132.

48 Quoted in 'Introduction', *The Irish Georgian Society Records of eighteenth-century domestic architecture and decoration in Ireland*, 4 (Shannon, 1969 ed.), p. 48.

49 Hill, *From Patriots to unionists*, p. 118.

50 Eoin Magennis, 'Fitzgerald, James, first duke of Leinster (1722–1773)', *Oxford dictionary of national biography*, Oxford University Press, 2004; online edn., May 2010 [http://www.oxforddnb.com/view/article/9565, accessed 11 Sept. 2011]; Edith Mary Johnston considered him as being 'amongst the politicians who had dominated the reign of George II'; Edith Mary Johnston, *Ireland in the nineteenth century* (Dublin, 1974), p. 129; for more on his popularity see 'Introduction', *The Irish Georgian Society Records of eighteenth-century domestic architecture and decoration in Ireland*, 4 (Shannon, 1969 ed.), p. 48.

51 Untitled newspaper account, July 1813 (PRONI, Leinster papers, D3078/6/1).

52 Ibid.; it would be a mistake, however, to presume that everybody who visited Carton was impressed. On 3 June 1799, Alexander Hamilton of Knock recorded in his diary: 'We got to Carton in good time. We met there the duke of Leinster and his four unmarried daughters …

Dinner was soon announced. Though served on plate it was the shabbiest dinner I ever saw at a great man's table. To be sure there were nine dishes at the first course, but two of them were marrow bones, and two were potatoes at opposite corners.' He was more impressed by 'a very good supper' in the inn at Maynooth; Diary of Alexander Hamilton, 3 June 1799 (Calendar of Hamwood papers, PRONI).

53 See A.P.W. Malcomson, *The pursuit of the heiress: aristocratic marriage in Ireland, 1740–1840* (Belfast, 2006), pp 41–3.

54 FitzGerald, *Lord Kildare's grand tour*, p. 145.

55 William FitzGerald to Emily, duchess of Leinster, 25 Feb. 1776 (NLI, Walter FitzGerald papers, MS 13,022).

56 William FitzGerald to Emily, duchess of Leinster, 5 Oct. 1777 (NLI, Walter FitzGerald papers, MS 13,022).

57 Patrick M. Geoghegan, 'Fitzgerald, William Robert, 2nd duke of Leinster' in James McGuire and James Quinn (eds), *Dictionary of Irish biography* (Cambridge, 2009), [http://dib.cambridge.org/viewReadPage.do?articleId=a3195, accessed 10 June 2012].

58 Quoted in FitzGerald, *Lord Kildare's grand tour*, p. 153; Geoghegan, 'Fitzgerald, William Robert 2nd duke of Leinster'.

59 Cormac Begadon, 'The 2nd duke of Leinster and the establishment of St Patrick's College, Maynooth' in Cosgrove et al. (eds), *Aspects of Irish aristocratic life*, pp 138–47.

60 Hill, *From Patriots to unionists*, p. 292.

61 McParland, 'Sir Richard Morrison's country houses', p. 1538.

62 *The Times*, 20 Aug. 1817.

63 McParland, 'Sir Richard Morrison's country houses', p. 1539.

64 Typescript from 'Notices of the FitzGeralds: an account of the earl of Donoughmore's visit to Maynooth and

Carton, 5–6 Jan. 1822 (PRONI, Leinster papers, D3078/1/2/8).

65 Ibid.; McParland, 'Sir Richard Morrison's country houses', p. 1540.

66 Typescript from 'Notices of the FitzGeralds: an account of the earl of Donoughmore's visit to Maynooth and Carton, 5–6 Jan. 1822 (PRONI, Leinster papers, D3078/1/2/8).

67 D.A. Fleming and A.P.W. Malcomson, 'A volley of execrations': the letters and papers of John Fitzgibbon, earl of Clare, 1772–1802 (Dublin, 2005), pp 343, 344; for a scholarly insight to the reasons for the fall of the 2nd duke see, Liam Chambers, Rebellion in Kildare, 1790–1803 (Dublin, 1998).

68 Daniel O'Connell to Lord Cloncurry, 14 May 1820, quoted in Maurice O'Connell (ed.), The correspondence of Daniel O'Connell, 1815–1823 (Shannon, 1972), vol. ii, p. 261; for his role in educational reform see, D.H. Akenson, The Irish educational experiment: the national system of education in the 19th century (London, 1970), p. 89.

69 Quoted in Oliver MacDonagh, O'Connell: the life of Daniel O'Connell, 1775–1847 (London, 1991), p. 532. In 1832 O'Connell later wrote of Leinster: 'he is the first of his race who was un-Irish and he is un-Irish to the backbone'. However, by 1840, O'Connell made his peace, realizing the need for the support of Leinster; Daniel O'Connell to duke of Leinster, 28 Mar. 1840 in W.J. Fitzpatrick (ed.), Correspondence of Daniel O'Connell, the Liberator (London, 1888), pp 230–1; J.H. Murphy, Abject loyalty: nationalism and monarchy in Ireland during the reign of Queen Victoria (Cork, 2001), p. 449.

70 See below.

71 Freeman's Journal, 18 Dec. 1839.

72 Fr Theobald Mathew to duke of Leinster, 24 Oct. 1856; copy letter duke of Leinster to Fr Theobald Mathew, 25 Oct. 1856 (both PRONI, Leinster papers,

D3078/4/6); Fr Mathew to duke of Leinster, 29 Feb. 1853 (NLI, FitzGerald papers, MS 41,552 (67)).

73 See below.

74 For an interesting letter on the dismantling of Lord Edward's house, see that from 'Horatio' in Freeman's Journal, 1 Sept. 1880.

75 Eugene Curry to (3rd) duke of Leinster, 18 Aug. 1846 (NLI, FitzGerald papers, MS 18849 (1)).

76 Tom Nelson, 'Lord Frederick FitzGerald (1857–1924) and local politics in county Kildare' in Cosgrove et al. (eds), Aspects of Irish aristocratic life, pp 197–209.

77 Quoted in Chambers, Rebellion in Kildare, p. 15.

78 W.E. Vaughan, Landlords and tenants in mid-Victorian Ireland (Oxford, 1994), p. 226; Joseph Lee, The modernization of Irish society, 1848–1918 (Dublin, 1973), pp 89–90.

79 Toby Barnard has estimated there were around fifty servants at Carton at this time; Toby Barnard, Lives and possessions in Ireland, 1641–1770 (New Haven and London, 2004), p. 84.

80 'Copy of the marquis of Kildare's household account book, 1758' (in private possession); see also Terence Dooley, '"Till my further orders": rules governing servants at Carton in the mid-eighteenth century' in Cosgrove et al. (eds), Aspects of Irish aristocratic life, pp 106–17; Patricia McCarthy, 'Vails and travails: how Lord Kildare kept his household in order' in Irish Architectural and Decorative Studies: the Journal of the Irish Georgian Society, 6 (2003), pp 120–39; see also Jeremy Musson, Up and down stairs: the history of the country house servant (London, 2009), esp. pp 90–140.

81 Quoted in Ganly, A tribute to a noble life, p. 30.

82 Horner, Maynooth, p. 5.

83 Quoted in ibid., p. 4.

84 Caesar Otway, *A tour in Connaught, comprising sketches of Clonmacnoise, Joyce country and Achill* (1839), p. 13. My thanks to Dr Ciarán Reilly for this reference.

85 For more on this, see chapter two; see also Ciarán Reilly, 'A middleman in the 1840s: Charles Carey and the Leinster estate', Cosgrove et al. (eds), *Aspects of aristocratic life*, pp 178–86.

86 My thanks to Ciaran Reilly for bringing these references to my attention; *Leinster Express*, 14 Apr., 12, 19 May 1849; Karel Kiely, 'Poverty and famine in county Kildare 1820 to 1850' in Nolan and McGrath (eds), *Kildare*, pp 503, 523.

87 Frank Taafe, 'Athy and the Great Famine' in Kildare County Council, *Lest we forget: Kildare and the Great Famine* (Kildare, 1995), p. 65.

88 www.athyheritagecentre-museum.ie/religious_diversity [accessed 9 Feb. 2011].

89 *Report of her majesty's commissioners of enquiry into the working of the Landlord and Tenant (Ireland) Act, 1870 and the acts amending the same*, [C 2779], HC 1881, xviii (Earl of Bessborough, chairman); similarly Finlay Dun, *The Times* correspondent who did a tour of Irish estates in 1880–1, found that of the 400 or so tenants on the estate most occupied from 75 to 400 acres and that Augustus' successor was reluctant to let holdings of less than forty acres; Dun, *Landlords and tenants in Ireland*, p. 21.

90 N.W. Senior, *Journals, conversations and essays relating to Ireland* (London, 1868), p. 85.

91 See Dun, *Landlords and tenants in Ireland*, p. 21.

92 Whether Augustus deserved this reputation remains a matter of conjecture. First of all his reputation is very much based on his early work during the Famine. He was originally a member of the Mansion House committee to enquire into its causes, a position he would have been expected to take as the premier peer in Ireland. He became president of the General Central Relief Committee which was established in Dublin in 1846 which raised approximately £63,000. But he then fell back to the comfort zone of supporting the prevailing philosophy of *laissez-faire*. He publicly criticized the efforts of the Royal Agricultural Society in establishing relief employment schemes for the labouring classes and shortly after resigned his position as president. He denied the need for local public relief committees in Kildare; he may have believed that if he accepted the need for them it would have reflected negatively on his own estate management; Christine Kinealy, *This great calamity: the Irish Famine, 1845–52* (Dublin, 1994), p. 162; for Charles Trevelyan's criticisms of Leinster, see Robert Haines, *Charles Trevelyan and the Great Irish Famine* (Dublin, 2004), p. 266.

93 'F. S.' quoted in *The Times*, 9 Dec. 1872.

94 *Morning Post*, 19 Aug. 1872.

95 Untitled newspaper (PRONI, Leinster papers, D3078/6/1).

96 Akenson, *The Irish educational experiment*, p. 128.

97 William Nolan, 'Poverty and Famine in County Kildare, 1820–1850' in Nolan and McGrath (eds), *Kildare*, p. 495.

98 Cecil Woodham-Smith, *The Great Hunger* (London, 1962), pp 18, 295.

99 Quoted in Cannadine, *Aspects of aristocracy*, p. 18.

1 *Freeman's Journal*, 1, 2 Nov. 1847.

2 Ibid., 2 Nov. 1847.

3 R.V. Comerford, 'County Kildare and the Famine' in Kildare County Council, *Lest we forget: Kildare and the Great Famine* (Kildare, 1995), p. 13.

4 Taafe, 'Athy and the Great Famine', p. 70.

5 Quoted in J.H. Murphy, *Abject loyalty: nationalism and monarchy in Ireland during the reign of Queen Victoria* (Cork,

2001), p. 95; 'Notices of the FitzGeralds: the queen's description of her visit to Carton, 10 Aug. 1849' (PRONI, Leinster papers, D3078/1/2/8).

6 'Notices of the FitzGeralds: the queen's description of her visit to Carton, 10 Aug. 1849 (PRONI, Leinster papers, D3078/1/2/8).

7 See, for example, [?] Michael Hackett to duke of Leinster, n.d. (PRONI, Leinster papers, D3078/3/6/7).

8 P.J. Corish, *Maynooth College, 1795–1995* (Dublin, 1995), pp 101–5; Padraic O'Farrell, *A history of county Kildare* (Dublin, 2003), pp 80–1.

9 Quoted in Cullen, *Maynooth*, p. 16.

10 *Leinster Express*, 24 Aug. 1872; untitled newspaper (PRONI, Leinster papers, D3078/6/1).

11 Untitled newspaper (PRONI, Leinster papers, D3078/6/1); http://allpoetry.com/Thomas_Osborne_Davis [accessed 2 July 2012]; see also *The Athenaeum*, 5 June 1858, p. 71.

12 John O'Rourke, *The history of the Great Irish Famine of 1847* (Dublin, 1874); see also R.V. Comerford, 'Canon John O'Rourke: historian of the Great Famine' in Thomas Kabdebo (ed.), *Beyond the library walls: John Paul II annual lectures* (Maynooth, 1995), pp 58–68.

13 John Molony, 'Davis, Thomas Osborne' in James McGuire and James Quinn (eds), *Dictionary of Irish biography* (Cambridge, 2009). (http://dib.cambridge.org.jproxy.nuim.ie/quicksearch.do;jsessionid=9FAD6CBBC20B2B76D50B9E50F50502A3#) [accessed 31 Aug. 2011].

14 Untitled newspaper (PRONI, Leinster papers, D3078/6/1).

15 Ibid.

16 *Saunders' Newsletter*, 15 Oct. 1874; for other reports on his death see *Freeman's Journal*, 12 Oct. 1874.

17 For a fuller discussion on this agrarian agitation see following chapters.

18 *Leinster Express*, 24 Aug. 1872.

19 My thanks to Dr Kevin McKenna for this particular insight.

20 See chapter 3; Eric Hobsbawn, *The age of empire, 1875–1914* (London, 2002 ed.), p. 54.

CHAPTER TWO
Land war and politics in a changing society, 1872–85

1 Untitled newspaper (PRONI, Leinster papers, D3078/6/1).

2 See R.V. Comerford, 'Isaac Butt and the Home Rule Party, 1870–77' in W.E. Vaughan (ed.), *A new history of Ireland;* vi, *Ireland under the Union, pt 2, 1870–1921* (Oxford, 1996), pp 1–25; idem, *The Fenians in context: Irish politics and society, 1848–82* (Dublin, 1998); R.F. Foster, *Modern Ireland, 1600–1972* (London, 1988), pp 395–9.

3 J.C.W. Wylie, *Irish land law* (3rd ed., Dublin, 1997), p. 32.

4 Foster, *Modern Ireland*, p. 397.

5 *The Times*, 6 Dec. 1872; untitled and undated newspaper (PRONI, Leinster papers, D3078/2/15/3); for other details on the lease see Samuel Clark, *Social origins of the Irish Land War* (Princeton, NJ, 1979), pp 177–8.

6 *Report of her majesty's commissioners of enquiry into the working of the Landlord and Tenant (Ireland) Act, 1870 and the acts amending the same*, [C 2779], HC 1881, xviii (Earl of Bessborough, chairman).

7 Ibid.

8 Ibid.

9 'F. S.' quoted in *The Times*, 9 Dec. 1872.

10 *The Times*, 6 Dec. 1872.

11 C.W. Hamilton to *The Times*, 10 Dec. 1872.

12 http://hansard.millbanksystems.com/commons/1873/feb/24/irish-land-act-1870-the-12th-clause [accessed 21 Jan. 2010].

13 'F. S.' quoted in *The Times*, 9 Dec. 1872.

14 Thomas Robertson quoted in *The Times*, 16 Dec. 1872.

15 Leinster to Charles Hamilton, 22 Dec. 1872 (private possession).

16 *Saunders' Newsletter*, 15 Oct. 1874.

17 Ibid., 13 Oct. 1874.

18 Ibid., 13 Oct. 1874.

19 Ibid., 13, 15 Oct. 1874.

20 Ibid., 15 Oct. 1874.

21 *Freeman's Journal*, 18 May 1877.

22 James S. Donnelly, Jn, *The land and people of nineteenth-century Cork: the rural economy and the land question* (London, 1975), p. 6; also Vaughan, *Landlords and tenants in mid-Victorian Ireland*, pp 208–16.

23 See Tom Nelson, 'The career of John T. Heffernan', *JCKAS*, 19:4 (2006–7), pp 618–33; also Virginia Crossman, *Politics, pauperism and power in late nineteenth-century Ireland* (Manchester, 2006), pp 46–7.

24 Quoted in Nelson, 'John T. Heffernan', p. 618; another cousin offered him the conflicting view that it was 'the worst oppressed and afflicted country in the world'; ibid.

25 F.S.L. Lyons, *John Dillon: a biography* (London, 1968), pp 37–8.

26 Nelson, 'John T. Heffernan', p. 622.

27 *Kildare Observer*, 25 Dec. 1880, 15 Jan. 1881.

28 Dun, *Landlords and tenants in Ireland*, p. 23.

29 J.L. Hammond, *Gladstone and the Irish nation* (London, 1938), p. 189.

30 Lord Cloncurry to his Newport tenantry, 15 Apr. 1881; quoted in *Irish Times*, 2 May 1881.

31 *An act to further amend the law relating to the occupation and ownership of land in Ireland and for other relating purposes thereto* (33 and 34 Vict., c. xlvi (22 Aug. 1881)).

32 Quoted in Nelson, 'John T. Heffernan', p. 623.

33 Quoted in English and Saville, *Strict settlement*, p. 106

34 Dun, *Landlords and tenants in Ireland*, p. 23.

35 Quoted in T.W. Moody and Richard Hawkins (eds), *Florence Arnold-Forster's Irish journal* (Oxford, 1988), p. 35.

36 Ibid., p. 36.

37 Charles Hamilton to Leinster, 31 May 1882 (private possession).

38 Charles Hamilton to Leinster, 4 June 1882 (private possession).

39 Charles Hamilton to Leinster, 16 June 1882 (private possession).

40 Charles Hamilton to Leinster, 11 July 1882 (private possession).

41 Charles Hamilton to Leinster, 11 July 1882 (private possession).

42 Charles Hamilton to Leinster, 11 June 1882 (private possession).

43 Moody and Hawkins (eds), *Florence Arnold-Forster's Irish journal*, p. 440.

44 Nolan, 'The land of Kildare', p. 575.

45 Quoted in Nolan, 'The land of Kildare', p. 576; there is an extensive literature on the Catholic church and the land question: see, for example, Emmet Larkin, *The Roman Catholic Church in Ireland and the fall of Parnell, 1888–91* (Liverpool, 1979); idem, *The Roman Catholic Church and the Plan of Campaign, 1886–88* (Cork, 1978); on Russell and Walsh, see T.J. Morrisey, *William J. Walsh, archbishop of Dublin, 1841–1921* (Dublin, 2000); Ambrose Macaulay, *Dr Russell of Maynooth* (London, 1983); on the college, see P.J. Corish, *Maynooth College, 1795–1995* (Dublin, 1995).

46 See his William J. Walsh, *A plain exposition of the Irish Land Act of 1881* (Dublin, 1881).

47 My thanks to R.V. Comerford for bringing this to my attention.

48 *Report of her majesty's commissioners of enquiry into the working of the Landlord*

and Tenant (Ireland) Act, 1870 and the acts amending the same, [C 2779], HC 1881, xviii (Earl of Bessborough, chairman).

49 Ibid.

50 Quoted in ibid.

51 Ibid.

52 Ibid.

53 Ibid.

54 Ibid.

55 Kildare Observer, 28 June 1901.

56 Ibid., 6 Aug. 1904.

57 For some insights, see William FitzGerald to Emily, duchess of Leinster, 21 Oct., 21 Nov., 17 Dec. 1775 (NLI, Walter FitzGerald papers, MS 13,022); William Nolan, 'The land of Kildare: valuation, ownership and occupation 1850–1906' in Nolan and McGrath (eds), Kildare, p. 555.

58 Charles FitzGerald to Lady Emily (?), 5 Nov. 1802 (PRONI, Leinster papers, D3078/3/6/31).

59 Quoted in Donnelly, The land and people of nineteenth-century Cork, p. 305.

60 The Times, 9 Dec. 1882; for a fuller discussion, see Terence Dooley, The decline of the big house in Ireland, pp 79–111.

61 Quoted in Cannadine, Decline of the British aristocracy, p. 62.

CHAPTER THREE
The marriage of Gerald and Lady Hermione Duncombe, 1884

1 Quoted in Christopher Hussey, 'Duncombe Park, Yorkshire – II', Country Life, 12 Dec. 1957, p. 1328.

2 Hermione Duncombe, 'December 1883' (Somerset Record Office, de Vesci papers, DD/DRU/90).

3 See Giles Worsley, 'Duncombe Park, Yorkshire – I', Country Life, 24 May 1990, pp 116–21; idem, 'Duncombe Park, Yorkshire – II', Country Life, 31 May 1990, pp 138–43; Duncombe Park guide book (privately published, undated), p. 2.

4 Duncombe Park, p. 2.

5 http://www.touruk.co.uk/houses/house yorkshire_duncombe.htm [accessed 22 Apr. 2010].

6 Hermione to Evelyn de Vesci, n.d., DD/DRU/90; for a description of the splendour of the gardens and parkland, see Hussey, 'Duncombe Park', pp 1328–31.

7 Shane Leslie memoirs (NLI, Leslie papers, MS 22,885).

8 Penny Illustrated, 9 Mar. 1881.

9 See, for example, Penny Illustrated, 1 July 1881; Belfast Newsletter, 20 Sept. 1881.

10 Quoted in Michael Estorick, Heirs and graces: the claim to the dukedom of Leinster (London, 1981), p. 90.

11 Elizabeth Fingall, Seventy years young (London, 1937), p. 71.

12 Fingall, Seventy years young, pp 176, 177; for other descriptions of her beauty see Marchioness of Londonderry [Edith Vane-Tempest-Stewart], Retrospect (London, 1938), p. 16; Anita Leslie, Edwardians in love (London, 1972), p. 99; The Lady of the House, 15 Dec. 1891.

13 Scriven, Splendour and squalour, p. 16.

14 Leslie, Edwardians in love, p. 99.

15 The Lady of the House described Hermione as 'the eldest of a quartet of sisters almost equally renowned for their grace and beauty'; The Lady of the House, 15 Dec. 1891.

16 M.C. Rintoul, Dictionary of real places and people in fiction (London, 1993), p. 919.

17 Quoted in Clayre Percy and Jane Ridley (eds), The letters of Edwin Lutyens to his wife Lady Emily (London, 1985), p. 117.

18 Thomas and Florence Hardy, Thomas Hardy (Hertfordshire, 2007), p. 269.

19 Liverpool Mercury, 23 Oct. 1883; see also Freeman's Journal, 24 Dec. 1883.

20 Quoted in Kildare Observer, 17 Nov. 1883.

21 Belfast Newsletter, 18 Jan. 1884.

22 'Obituary of Gerald FitzGerald, 5th duke of Leinster', *JCKAS* (1894–5), p. 155.

23 *Belfast Newsletter*, 18 Jan. 1884.

24 Epitome of deeds to be executed on the marriage of the marquess of Kildare and Lady Hermione Duncombe, n.d. (PRONI, Leinster papers, D3078/1/3/5/59).

25 *Belfast Newsletter*, 18 Jan. 1884.

26 *The World*, 14 Nov. 1883.

27 *The Times*, 19 Jan. 1884.

28 *Belfast Newsletter*, 18 Jan. 1884.

29 Mark Stocker, 'Louise, Princess, duchess of Argyll (1848–1939)', *Oxford dictionary of national biography*, Oxford University Press, 2004; online ed., Jan. 2008 [http://www.oxforddnb.com/view/article/34601, accessed 18 July 2011].

30 *The Court Journal*, 19 Jan. 1884.

31 Ibid.; see also *Freeman's Journal*, 18 Jan. 1884.

32 A clock with a case of tortoise shell inlaid with metal or ivory perfected by André-Charles Boulle (1642–1732).

33 *The Court Journal*, 19 Jan. 1884; also *Lady's Pictorial*, 26 Jan. 1882.

34 *The Court Journal*, 19 Jan. 1884.

35 Amongst the dignitaries was Count Karolyi, the Austro-Hungarian ambassador, who, with his wife, was known to entertain lavishly at his home on the same square. http://www.blakeneymanor.com/books/links/link6.html [accessed 18 July 2011].

36 K.D. Reynolds, 'Gower, Harriet Elizabeth Georgiana Leveson-, duchess of Sutherland (1806–1868)', *Oxford dictionary of national biography*, Oxford University Press, 2004 [http://www.oxforddnb.com/view/article/16544, accessed 18 July 2011].

37 F.M.L. Thompson, 'Grosvenor, Hugh Lupus, first duke of Westminster (1825–1899)', *Oxford dictionary of national biography*, Oxford University Press, 2004; online ed., May 2006 [http://www.oxforddnb.com/view/article/11667, accessed 18 July 2011].

38 See following chapters.

39 *Kildare Observer*, 19 Jan. 1884.

40 Lord Walter FitzGerald, 'Kilkea Castle', *JCKAS*, 11 (1896–9), p. 25.

41 'Obituary of Gerald FitzGerald, 5th duke of Leinster', *JCKAS* (1894–5), p. 155.

42 *Kildare Observer*, 23 Mar. 1895.

43 'Introduction', *The Irish Georgian Society Records of eighteenth-century domestic architecture and decoration in Ireland*, 5 (1913), p. 23; Edward McParland, 'Building in the grand manner: Sir Richard Morrison's country houses – II', *Country Life*, 31 May 1973, p. 1540.

44 Robert P. Stewart to Lily Hutton, 28 Mar. 1891, cited in Olinthus J. Vignoles, *Memoir of Sir Robert P. Stewart* (London, 1898), p.162; my thanks to Dr Karol Mullaney-Dignam for this reference.

45 Fingall, *Seventy years young*, p. 179.

46 Household bill, Jan. 1884 (PRONI, Leinster papers, D3078/2/13).

47 The total is the estimated number who attended the 4th duke's funeral in 1887; *Kildare Observer*, 19 Feb. 1887; List of servants at Carton, January 1884 (PRONI, Leinster papers, D3078/2/13).

48 C.W. Ganly, *A tribute to a noble life: in memoriam of Gerald, duke of Leinster* (Dublin, n.d.), p. 3.

49 Arnold Horner, 'Carton, Co. Kildare: a case study of the making of an Irish demesne', *Quarterly Bulletin of the Irish Georgian Society*, 18 (nos. 2 & 3), Apr.-Sept. 1975, pp 45–104; idem, 'Land transactions and the making of Carton demesne', *JCKAS*, 14:4 (1974–5), pp 387–96; Finola O'Kane, *Landscape design in eighteenth-century Ireland; mixing foreign trees with the natives* (Cork, 2004), pp 89–130.

50 Hermione to Evelyn, n.d., DD/DRU/90.

51 Ibid.

52 http://www.unitetheunion.org/pdf/Esher%20History.pdf [accessed 2 Feb. 2012].

53 Hermione to Evelyn, n.d., DD/DRU/90.

54 Ibid.

55 Fingall, *Seventy years young*, p. 181.
56 Ibid.
57 Maurice FitzGerald to Evelyn, 6 Aug. 1905, DD/DRU/90.
58 For details of births and so on, see below.
59 Hermione to Evelyn, n.d., DD/DRU/90.
60 The standard work on this remains Laurence Geary, *The Plan of Campaign, 1886–1891* (Cork, 1986).
61 Charles Hamilton to Leinster, 1 May 1886 (private possession).
62 George Patterson to Charles Hamilton, 23 Apr. 1886 (private possession).
63 Charles Hamilton to Leinster, undated (private possession).
64 Charles Hamilton to Leinster, 14 Mar. 1885 (private possession).
65 Charles Hamilton to Leinster, 15 Mar. 1885 (private possession).
66 Ibid.
67 Valuation of diamonds and jewellery for his Grace, the duke of Leinster, 1883 (PRONI, Leinster papers, D3078/2/10/2); *Catalogue of pictures, plate and antiquities at Carton, Kilkea Castle and 13 Dominick St Dublin and 6 Carlton Terrace, London* (Dublin, n.d. [1885]).
68 *Catalogue of old Irish silver plate sold by order of trustees of late Lord Fitzgerald at Christie's, 4 Dec. 1902* and *Catalogue of ancient and modern pictures sold at Christie's, 6 Dec. 1902* (PRONI, Leinster papers, D3078/2/10//6/2–3).
69 Charles Hamilton to Leinster, 24 Apr. 1886 (private possession).
70 http://hansard.millbanlssystems.com/commons/1890/aug/14/ireland-the-duke-of-leinster [accessed 21 Jan. 2009].
71 Comparative statement of net rents, 1893–8 (PRONI, Leinster papers, D3078/2/15/17).
72 *St Stephen's Review*, 31 July 1886.
73 *Freeman's Journal*, 2 Dec. 1893.
74 Servants wages account, 31 Dec. 1887, 30 June 1888 (PRONI, Leinster papers, D3078/2/1/13).
75 Cannadine, *Decline and fall of the British aristocracy*, p. 26.
76 B.B. Gilbert, 'David Lloyd George: land, the budget and social reform', *American Historical Review*, 81 (1976), p. 1066.
77 *The Graphic*, 9 Dec. 1893.
78 Charles W. Ganly, *A tribute to a noble life: in memoriam Gerald, Duke of Leinster* (Dublin, n.d.), pp 5–6.
79 For a fuller understanding of this see R.V. Comerford, *Ireland* (London and New York, 2003) [in series 'Inventing the nation'].
80 *Daily Express*, 2 Dec. 1893.H

CHAPTER FOUR
'In this black dog haunted place': Hermione's melancholia

Much of this chapter is based on the letters of Hermione to Lady Evelyn de Vesci, now on deposit in Somerset Record Office. They are cited below as simply Hermione to Evelyn. The vast majority of these letters are undated and contained in one file, DD/DRU/90.

1 Hermione to Evelyn, n.d., DD/DRU/90.
2 Leslie, *Edwardians in love*, p. 22; on this see also Nicola Beauman, *Cynthia Asquith* (London, 1987), p. 5.
3 Hermione to Evelyn, n.d., DD/DRU/90.
4 Hermione to Ms Morton (PRONI, Leinster papers, D 3078/3/55/5).
5 Hermione to Evelyn, n.d., DD/DRU/90.
6 Ibid.
7 Ibid.
8 Ibid.
9 Fingall, *Seventy years young*, p. 180.
10 Hermione continued to refer to Gerald as 'Kildare' even after he became duke.
11 Quoted in Estorick, *Heirs and graces*, p. 94.
12 Hermione to Evelyn, n.d., DD/DRU/90.
13 Ibid.
14 Ibid.
15 Quoted in Estorick, *Heirs and graces*, p. 94.
16 Quoted in ibid., pp 94–5.

17 John Stuart Mill, *The subjection of women* (London, 1869), p. 272; quoted on http://plato.stanford.edu/entries/mill/#St aWom [accessed 27 May 2012].

18 John Stuart Mill, *The subjection of women* (London, 1869); quoted in Lisa Appignanesi, *Mad, bad and sad: a history of women and the mind doctors from 1800 to the present* (London, 2008), p. 122.

19 Lambert, *Unquiet Souls*, p. 56.

20 Hermione to Evelyn, n.d., DD/DRU/90.

21 *Kildare Observer*, 20 May 1899.

22 *Irish Times*, 2 Dec. 1893.

23 Hermione to Evelyn, n.d., DD/DRU/90.

24 *The Lady of the House*, 15 Dec. 1891, p. 38.

25 Hermione to Lord Houghton, 29 Jan. 1891 (in private possession); Lady Sybil, a widow, was eight years older than Wyndham when they married in 1887. I would like to thank Colette Jordan for bringing this reference to my attention.

26 Jane Ridley and Clayre Percy (eds), *The letters of Arthur Balfour and Lady Elcho* (London, 1992), p. 77.

27 Ridley and Percy (eds), *Arthur Balfour and Lady Elcho*, p. 10.

28 Fingall, *Seventy years young*, pp 73–4.

29 Hermione to Evelyn, n.d., DD/DRU/90.

30 Quoted in Estorick, *Heirs and graces*, pp 95–6.

31 Hermione to Evelyn, n.d., DD/DRU/90.

32 Ibid.

33 Ibid.

34 Ibid.

35 Leslie, *Edwardians in love*, p. 259; Jane Ridley and Clare Percy, 'Charteris, Mary Constance, countess of Wemyss (1862–1937)', *ODNB* [www.oxforddnb.com/view/article/40735, accessed 4 Dec. 2009]; Alvin Jackson, 'Wyndham, George (1863–1913)', *ODNB* [www.oxforddnb.com/view/article/37052, accessed 14 Feb. 2010].

36 Violet Bonham-Carter, 'The Souls', *The Listener*, 30 Oct. 1947.

37 Wilfred S. Blunt, *My diaries: being a personal narrative of events, 1888–1914* (1919), p. 53.

38 N.W. Ellenberger, 'The Souls and London society at the end of the nineteenth century', *Victorian Studies*, 34:2 (Winter, 1982), pp 133–60, at pp 138–40, 144.

39 Ibid.; see also Frances Balfour, *Ne obliviscaris* (London, 1930), pp 55–7.

40 Ellenberger, 'The Souls and London society', p. 159; Asquith, *Autobiography*, vol. I, p. 391.

41 George Wyndham to Countess Grosvenor, 12–13 Jan. 1888 (PRONI, Wyndham papers, T3221/1/2A).

42 Quoted in Lambert, *Unquiet Souls*, p. 57.

43 Quoted in ibid., p. 32.

44 Viscount D'Abernon, *Portraits and appreciations* (London, n.d.), pp 91–6.

45 Cynthia Asquith, *Remember and be glad*, p. 108.

46 Leslie, *Edwardians in love*, p. 13.

47 Ellenberger, 'The Souls and London society', p. 151; see also below.

48 Hermione to Evelyn, n.d., DD/DRU/90.

49 Quoted in Lambert, *Unquiet Souls*, p. 17.

50 Ibid., p. 58.

51 Ridley and Percy, 'Charteris, Mary Constance'.

52 Ridley and Percy (eds), *Arthur Balfour and Lady Elcho*, p. 10; see also Cynthia Asquith, *Haply I may remember* (London, 1950), pp 76–8, 128–30.

53 Quoted in Leslie, *Edwardians in love*, p. 259.

54 Quoted in Ellenberger, 'The Souls and London society', p. 149.

55 Ridley and Percy, 'Charteris, Mary Constance'; Beauman wrote that Hugo had always been 'charming and easily bored [and] always had a mistress'; Beauman, *Cynthia Asquith*, p. 13.

56 Hermione to Evelyn, n.d., DD/DRU/90.

57 Hermione to 'Darling', n.d., DD/DRU/90.

58 Hermione to Evelyn, n.d., DD/DRU/90.

59 Ibid.
60 Leslie, *Edwardians in love*, p. 263.
61 Beauman, *Cynthia Asquith*, p. 15.
62 Hermione to Evelyn, n.d., DD/DRU/90.
63 Ibid.
64 See Elizabeth Longford, *Pilgrimage of passion: the life of Wilfrid Scawen Blunt* (London, 1979); for more details see following chapters.
65 Beauman, *Cynthia Asquith*, p. 308.
66 Hermione to Evelyn, n.d., DD/DRU/90.
67 Ibid.
68 Leslie, *Edwardians in love*, p. 15.
69 Lambert, *Unquiet Souls*, pp 37–8.
70 Hermione to Evelyn, n.d., DD/DRU/90.
71 H. Steinberg, 'The sin in the aetiological concept of Johann Christian August Heinroth (1773–1843). part 1: between theology and psychiatry. Heinroth's concepts of "whose being", "freedom", "reason" and "disturbance of the soul", *History of Psychiatry*, 15 (59, part 3), (Sept. 2004), pp 329–44; part 2, *History of Psychiatry*, 15 (59, part 3), 16 (60, part 4), (Dec. 2004), pp 437–54.
72 Quoted in Estorick, *Heirs and graces*, p. 96.
73 Quoted in ibid., p. 97.
74 Leslie, *Edwardians in love*, p. 265.
75 Davidson-Kennedy, *So brief a dream*, p. 70.
76 Hermione to Evelyn, n.d., DD/DRU/90.
77 Hermione [from Cadogan Square] to Evelyn, n.d., DD/DRU/90.
78 Cannadine, *Decline and fall of the British aristocracy*, p. 62.
79 Hermione to Evelyn, n.d., DD/DRU/90.
80 *Freeman's Journal*, 2 Dec. 1893; *Irish Times*, 2 Dec. 1893.
81 *Freeman's Journal*, 2 Dec. 1893.
82 *Irish Times*, 2 Dec. 1893.
83 Ganly, *A tribute to a noble life*, p. 26.
84 Maurice to Evelyn, n.d., DD/DRU/90.
85 Quoted in *Kildare Observer*, 19 Feb. 1887.
86 Ganly, *A tribute to a noble life*.
87 *Kildare Observer*, 9 Oct. 1893.
88 Ibid.
89 *Freeman's Journal*, 2 Dec. 1893.
90 Untitled and undated newspaper clipping (PRONI, D 3078/2/15/3).
91 K.T. Hoppen, *Elections, politics and society in Ireland, 1832–1885* (Oxford, 1984), p. 136.
92 Quoted in Ganly, *A tribute to a noble life*, p. 8.
93 Hermione to Evelyn, n.d., DD/DRU/90.
94 Cindy Chung and James Pennebaker, 'The psychological function of function words' in K. Fiedler (ed.), *Social communication* (New York, 2007), p. 352.
95 Hermione to Evelyn, n.d., DD/DRU/90.
96 Ibid.
97 Ibid.
98 Ibid.
99 Quoted in Estorick, *Heirs and graces*, p. 97.
1 Fingall, *Seventy years young*, p. 178.
2 Ibid., p. 179.

CHAPTER FIVE
Hermione's death

1 Mabel, countess of Feversham to Evelyn de Vesci, 24 May [189?], DD/DRU/89.
2 Hermione to Evelyn, n.d., DD/DRU/90.
3 Hermione, untitled poem, DD/DRU/90.
4 See E.L. Hart and M.N. Smith (eds), *Open me carefully: Emily Dickinson's intimate letters to Susan Huntington Dickinson* (Paris, 1998).
5 Arthur Balfour to Mary Elcho, 16 July 1891; quoted in Ridley and Percy (eds), *Arthur Balfour and Lady Elcho*, p. 74.
6 Fingall, *Seventy years young*, p. 184; Frances Clarke and Patrick Maume, 'Lawless, Emily' in James McGuire and James Quinn (eds), *Dictionary of Irish biography* (Cambridge, 2009) http://dib.cambridge.org.jproxy. nuim.ie/quicksearch.do;jsessionid=69311 B097223541521AC8E0A7C834BE3 [accessed 8 Aug. 2007].
7 Clarke and Maume, 'Lawless, Emily'.
8 Balfour to Mary Elcho, 8 Aug. 1894; in Ridley and Percy (eds), *Arthur Balfour and Lady Elcho*, p. 109.

9 George Wyndham to Countess
   Grosvenor, 10 Jan. 1902 (PRONI,
   Wyndham papers, T3221/2B/281).
10 Fingall, *Seventy years young*, p. 184.
11 Hermione to Evelyn, n.d., DD/DRU/90.
12 Ibid.
13 Ibid., DD/DRU/90.
14 Ibid., DD/DRU/90.
15 Ibid., DD/DRU/90.
16 Ibid., DD/DRU/90.
17 Mabel to Evelyn, DD/DRU/89.
18 Hermione to Evelyn, n.d., DD/DRU/90.
19 J.H. Bennet, *Winter and spring on the
   shores of the Mediterranean* (1870) on
   www.jahtours.com/menton/Bennet
   _1_2.html [accessed 5 Feb. 2010].
20 Ibid.
21 Ibid.
22 W.C. Devereaux, *Fair Italy: the Riviera
   and Monte Carlo* (London, 1884) on
   www.gutenberg.org.files/23959-8
   [accessed 5 Feb. 2010].
23 Ibid.
24 Hugo Charteris to Evelyn, n.d.,
   DD/DRU/102.
25 Mabel to Evelyn, n.d., DD/DRU/89.
26 Mabel to Evelyn 18 Feb. [189?],
   DD/DRU/89.
27 Ibid.
28 Hugo Charteris to Evelyn, n.d.,
   DD/DRU/102.
29 Hugo Charteris to Evelyn, 20 Mar. 1895,
   DD/DRU/102.
30 Hugo Charteris to Evelyn, n.d.,
   DD/DRU/102.
31 Lambert, *Unquiet Souls*, p. 61.
32 Ibid., p. 63.
33 Hugo Charteris to Evelyn, n.d.,
   DD/DRU/102.
34 Lambert, *Unquiet Souls*, p. 65.
35 Hugo Charteris to Evelyn, n.d.,
   DD/DRU/102.
36 Quoted in Lambert, *Unquiet Souls*, p. 67.
37 Mabel to Evelyn 18 Feb. [189?],
   DD/DRU/89.
38 Mabel to Evelyn, 26 Oct. [189?] (from
   Monte Carlo), DD/DRU/89.
39 Hugo Charteris to Evelyn, 20 Mar. 1895,
   DD/DRU/102.
40 *Belfast Newsletter*, 26 Mar. 1895; *Pall Mall
   Gazette*, 26 Mar. 1895.
41 *The Graphic*, 30 Mar. 1895.
42 *Freeman's Journal*, 28 Mar. 1895.
43 Ibid.
44 *Freeman's Journal*, 28 Mar. 1895.
45 *Kildare Observer*, 30 Mar. 1895; Fingall,
   Seventy years young, p. 185.
46 *Freeman's Journal*, 28 Mar. 1895.
47 Copied in *Kildare Observer*, 30 Mar. 1895.
48 *Kildare Observer*, 23 Mar. 1895.
49 Receipt from Alexandra College for bust
   of Hermione, duchess of Leinster, 21 Oct.
   1908 (PRONI, FitzGerald papers, D
   3078/8/3/55/7).
50 Katharine Carmarthen, 'In memoriam
   the duchess of Leinster' (PRONI,
   FitzGerald papers, D3078/3/55/9).
51 Ganly, *A tribute to a noble life*, p. 2.
52 Quoted in Beauman, *Cynthia Asquith*, pp
   28–29; see also Lambert, *Unquiet Souls*,
   p. 65.
53 Quoted in Longford, *A pilgrimage of
   passion*, p. 283.
54 Quoted in Lambert, *Unquiet Souls*, p. 67.
55 Lord Frederick FitzGerald to Evelyn, n.d.,
   DD/DRU/94.
56 There is a huge literature on this topic;
   see, for example, N.M. Melhem, G.
   Porta, W. Shamseddeen, M. Walker
   Payne, D.A. Brent, 'Grief in children and
   adolescents bereaved by sudden parental
   death', *Archives of General Psychiatry*,
   2011:68 [http://www.sciencedaily.com
   /releases/2008/05/080505162849.htm,
   accessed 27 May, 2012].
57 Edward, Prince of Wales, to Lady Cynthia
   Graham, 3 Mar. 1916 (in private possession); also Queen Mary to Lady Cynthia,
   5 Mar. 1916 (in private possession).
58 See, for example, *Irish Independent*, 17
   Sept. 1906, 1 Oct. 1907.
59 Hermione to Evelyn, n.d., DD/DRU/90.

CHAPTER SIX
The sale of the Leinster estate, 1903

1   Quoted in C.B. Shannon, *Arthur J. Balfour and Ireland, 1874–1922* (Washington, 1988), p. 124.

2   See Bryan Robson, *The road to Kabul* (London, 2007), p. 3; E. Hutton, *A brief history of the King's Royal Rifle Corps, 1755–1915* (London, 1917 [2nd ed.]), pp 23–5.

3   *Daily Telegraph*, 13 Mar. 1924.

4   *Freeman's Journal*, 18 Jan. 1882; *Kildare Observer*, 21 Jan. 1882.

5   *Kildare Observer*, 6 May 1882.

6   Nicholas Fishwick, 'Kinnaird, Arthur Fitzgerald, eleventh Lord Kinnaird of Inchture and third Lord Kinnaird of Rossie (1847–1923)', *Oxford dictionary of national biography*, Oxford University Press, 2004 [http://www.oxforddnb.com/view/article/50297, accessed 28 Aug. 2011]; see also 'Arthur Fitzgerald, eleventh Lord Kinnaird', *Spread Eagle*, 37 (1962), pp 4–6. A. Gibson and W. Pickford, *Association football and the men who made it*, 4 vols [London, 1905–6], vol. 3, pp 129–31; *The Times,* 31 Jan. 1923, 3 Feb. 1923.

7   Thomas Nelson, 'Lord Frederick FitzGerald' in Cosgrove et al. (eds), *Aspects of Irish aristocratic life*, pp 197–209.

8   Ibid.

9   *Leeds Mercury*, 22 Jan. 1895.

10 *Kildare Observer*, 22 Apr. 1899, 13 May 1899, 8 July 1899.

11 Quoted in Cannadine, *Decline of the British aristocracy*, p. 36.

12 Hoppen, *Elections, politics and society*, p. 339.

13 Buckland, *Irish Unionism I*, p. xiv.

14 Speech of James F. Egan, March 1899; quoted in *Freeman's Journal*, 20 Mar. 1899.

15 *Leinster Leader*, 28 Feb. 1899.

16 Pauric Travers, 'A bloodless revolution: the democratization of Irish local government 1898–9' in Mary Daly (ed.), *County and town: one hundred years of local government in Ireland* (Dublin, 2001), p. 12.

17 *The Times*, 2 May 1907.

18 *Freeman's Journal*, 20 Mar. 1899.

19 See Thomas Nelson, 'Kildare county council, 1899–1926' (PhD, NUI Maynooth, 2007), pp 71–80.

20 *Freeman's Journal*, 20 Mar. 1899.

21 Ibid., 9 Feb. 1899.

22 Ibid., 13 Mar. 1899.

23 See also Thomas Moore, *The memoirs of Lord Edward FitzGerald* (ed. M. Mac Dermott, 1897); Stella Tillyard, *Citizen lord: Edward FitzGerald, 1763–1798* (London, 1997); Liam Chambers, 'FitzGerald, Lord Edward (1763–1798)' [www.oxforddnb.com/view/article/9546].

24 *Kildare Observer*, 24 Dec. 1898.

25 *Glasgow Herald*, 21 Aug. 1897.

26 *Kildare Observer*, 19 Aug. 1899.

27 Nelson, 'Kildare county council', p. 69.

28 *The Times*, 25 Apr. 1899.

29 For Frederick's obituary, see *Kildare Observer*, 22 Mar. 1924.

30 Nelson, 'Lord Frederick FitzGerald' in Cosgrove et al. (eds), *Aspects of Irish aristocratic life*, pp 197–209.

31 Minutes of Kildare County Council, 22 Apr. 1899; quoted in ibid.

32 *Return of the resolution and statement adopted by the Irish Landowners' Convention on 10 Oct. 1902…HC 1903, lvii, 321.*

33 *An act to amend the law relating to the occupation and ownership of land in Ireland and for other purposes relating thereto, and to amend the Labourers (Ireland) Act*, [3 Edw. 7], Ch 37, 14 Aug. 1903.

34 See, for example, Dunraven, *Crisis in Ireland*, p. 21;

35 Much of what follows echoes Patrick J. Cosgrove's 'The sale of the Leinster estate under the Wyndham Land Act, 1903', *Journal of the County Kildare*

Archaeological Society, 20 (2008–9), pp 9–25, which can largely be explained by the fact that we worked simultaneously off shared newspaper sources available in Leinster papers.

36 Hansard 4, xxx, 521 (22 Feb. 1904); quoted in Patrick J. Cosgrove, 'The Wyndham Land Act, 1903: the final solution to the Irish land question?' (PhD, NUI Maynooth, 2008), p. 169.

37 F.S.L. Lyons, John Dillon: a biography (London, 1968), p. 219.

38 Fingall, Seventy years young, p. 270.

39 Quoted as hearsay in ibid., p. 270; on Wyndham and his land act, see, for example, Alvin Jackson, 'Wyndham, George (1863–1913)', Oxford dictionary of national biography (Oxford, 200); online ed., Jan. 2008. [http://www.oxforddnb.com/view/article/37052, accessed 9 Mar. 2012]; also Paul Bew, Conflict and conciliation in Ireland, 1890–1910 (Oxford, 1987); Philip Bull, Land, politics and nationalism: a study of the Irish land question (New York, 1996); Fergus Campbell, 'Irish popular politics and the making of the Wyndham Land Act, 1901–3', Historical Journal, 45:4 (2002), pp 755–73; Andrew Gailey, Ireland and the death of kindness: the experience of constructive unionism, 1890–1905 (Cork, 1987); Alvin Jackson, The Ulster Party: Irish unionists in the House of Commons, 1884–1911 (Oxford, 1989); Eunan O'Halpin, The decline of the union: British government in Ireland, 1892–1920 (Dublin, 1987), esp. chap. 2.

40 Shannon, Arthur J. Balfour, p. 126.

41 Irish Times, 25 Sept. 1903.

42 http://www.kildare-nationalist.ie/tabId/215/itemId/10748/Historic-links-between-Athy-and-France.aspx [accessed 9 Mar. 2012].

43 Leinster Leader, 19 Sept. 1903.

44 Nationalist and Leinster Times, 17 Oct. 1903.

45 Cosgrove, 'The Wyndham Land Act', p. 158.

46 Ibid., p. 164.

47 Nationalist and Leinster Times, 19 Sept. 1903.

48 Ibid., 26 Sept. 1903.

49 Ibid., 3 Oct. 1903.

50 Ibid.

51 The Nationalist, 17 Oct. 1903.

52 'A Leinster Tenant' in Irish Times, 5 Oct. 1903.

53 Land Purchase (Ireland) Act, 1903 (3 Ed., c.xxxvii (1 Nov. 1903)).

54 Quoted in Freeman's Journal, 6 Oct. 1903.

55 This was a figure widely reported in the media; see, for example, Irish Times, 25 Sept. 1903; Daily Mail, 31 Oct. 1903.

56 Statement of application of funds received on the sale of the Leinster estates in Ireland (PRONI, Leinster papers, D3078/2/15/10); Statement of moneys realized … and the distribution thereof (PRONI, Leinster papers, D3078/2/15/5).

57 http://gpih.ucdavis.edu/files/England_1209–1914_(Clark).xls [accessed 25 Aug. 2011].

58 Irish Times, 25 Sept. 1903.

59 Charles P. Johnson to Lord Frederick FitzGerald, 31 Jan. 1905 (PRONI, Leinster papers, D3078/2/15/9).

60 The Nationalist, 3 Oct. 1903.

61 Statement of application of funds received on the sale of the Leinster estates in Ireland (PRONI, Leinster papers, D3078/2/15/10).

62 Ibid.; Statement of moneys realized … and the distribution thereof (PRONI, Leinster papers, D3078/2/15/5).

63 Cosgrove, 'The Wyndham Land Act', 1903, p. 173.

64 The Nationalist, 3 Oct. 1903.

65 Quoted in Freeman's Journal, 10 Oct. 1903.

66 Quoted in Ibid.

67 William O'Brien, *An olive branch in Ireland* (London, 1910), p. 301.

68 For contemporary opinion to this effect, see *Irish Times*, 25 Sept. 1903.

69 *Irish Times*, 30 Sept. 1903; see also earlier editorial of ibid., 25 Sept. 1903.

70 *Hansard* 5, 111, 194–5 (30 Mar. 1909); quoted in Cosgrove, 'The Wyndham Land Act', 1903, p. 174.

71 Statement of moneys realized … and the distribution thereof (PRONI, Leinster papers, D3078/2/15/5).

72 T.H.S. Escott, *England: its people, polity and pursuits* (1885), pp 314–15; quoted in P.J. Cain and A.G. Hopkins, *British imperialism, 1688–2000* (Essex, 2001), p. 124.

73 I am indebted to Tony McCarthy for all of his insights on this discussion regarding investment behaviour.

74 Cannadine, *Decline of the British aristocracy*, p. 94.

75 Ibid., p. 134.

76 Quoted in ibid., pp 134–5.

77 Tony McCarthy to author, 13 Dec. 2011.

78 *Return of the resolution and statement adopted by the Irish Landowners' Convention on 10 Oct. 1902 …* HC 1903, lvii, 321.

79 *Irish Times*, 30 Sept. 1903.

80 Quoted in Niall Ferguson, *The ascent of money: a financial history of the world* (London, 2008), p. 237.

81 Statement of application of funds received on the sale of the Leinster estates in Ireland (PRONI, Leinster papers, D3078/2/15/10); Statement of moneys realized … and the distribution thereof (PRONI, Leinster papers, D3078/2/15/5).

82 Cannadine, *Decline of the British aristocracy*, pp 134–5; Dooley, *Decline of the big house in Ireland*, pp 120–1; Alvin Jackson, *Col. Edward Saunderson: land and loyalty in Victorian Ireland* (Oxford, 1995), p. 208.

83 Quoted in O'Brien, *An olive branch in Ireland*, p. 478.

84 Dunraven, *Crisis in Ireland*, p. 35

85 Cosgrove, 'Irish landlords and the Wyndham Land Act, 1903', p. 101.

86 Quoted in ibid., p. 101.

87 Quoted in ibid.

88 Quoted in ibid.

89 Warner Turner to [?] Bailey, 14 May 1916 (University of Nottingham archives, PL F10/7/6/56); on 1922 portfolio, see chapter 8.

90 See Catherine Bailey, *Black diamonds: the rise and fall of an English dynasty* (London, 2008).

91 See chapter seven.

92 C. Wright Mills, *The power elite* (new ed., Oxford, 2000), first ed. 1956, p. 4.

CHAPTER SEVEN
Maurice: epilepsy and madness

1 Hermione to Evelyn, n.d., DD/DRU/90.

2 Maurice FitzGerald [Kildare] to Evelyn de Vesci, 5 Apr. 1906, DD/DRU/90.

3 Maurice FitzGerald [Kildare] to Evelyn de Vesci, n.d., DD/DRU/90.

4 Mario Corrigan, 'Carton House through the pages of the *Kildare Observer*, 1880–1935', http://www.kildare.ie/library/ehistory/2012/02/carton_house_through_the_pages.asp [15 Mar. 2012].

5 Ibid.

6 See chapter eight.

7 Nicola Gordon Bowe, 'Preserving the relics of heroic time: visualizing the Celtic Revival in early twentieth-century Ireland' in Brian Cliffe and Nicholas Grene (eds), *Synge and Edwardian Ireland* (Oxford, 2012), pp 58–9.

8 *Kildare Observer*, 7 Mar. 1908.

9 Ibid.

10 *Carlow Sentinel*, 7 Mar. 1908.

11 *Kildare Observer*, 7 Mar. 1908.

12 I am grateful to Dr Kevin McKenna for sharing with me his, 'Elites, ritual and the

legitimation of power on an Irish landed estate, 1855–90' in Ciaran O'Neill (ed.), *Irish elites in the nineteenth century* (Dublin, 2013).

13 *Carlow Sentinel*, 7 Mar. 1908.

14 *Kildare Observer*, 7 Mar. 1908; *Carlow Sentinel*, 7 Mar. 1908.

15 R.W. Crone, 'Pollock, Sir (John) Donald, baronet (1868–1962)', rev. *Oxford dictionary of national biography*, OUP, 2004 [http://www.oxforddnb.com/view/article/35565, accessed 4 Dec. 2009].

16 Medical certificate signed by T.S. Clouston, 16 June 1909 (Lothian Health Service Archive, LHB7, 52.915); Pollock's entry in the 1937 edition of *Who's Who* stated that he was 'General adviser and personal physician to the late duke of Leinster 1907–12' and the 1956 edition said from 1907 to 1926; neither were correct, it was from 1907 to 1922.

17 Hermione to Evelyn, n.d., DD/DRU/90.

18 Ibid.

19 *San Francisco Examiner*, 22 Feb. 1922.

20 Hermione to Evelyn, n.d., DD/DRU/90.

21 Ibid.

22 Ibid.

23 Ibid.

24 Ibid.

25 *The Times*, 8 Feb. 1894.

26 Hermione to Evelyn, n.d., DD/DRU/90.

27 Case book 73, 2 Feb. 1922, LH B7/51/73.

28 Quoted in Bailey, *Black diamonds*, p. 25.

29 Quoted in ibid., p. 31.

30 Ibid., p. 31.

31 Ibid., p. 26.

32 W.M. Thackeray, *Catherine: a story* (London, 1869), pp 163–4; there are interesting parallels between Hermione and Thackeray's wife, Isabella. She also had three children and suffered what would now be recognized as severe post-natal depression after each. When an infant daughter, Jane, died, Isabella

'descended into madness' and was institutionalized in a Paris asylum; see Melisaa Fegan, '"Isn't it your own country?": the stranger in nineteenth-century Irish literature', *Yearbook of English Studies*, vol. 34 (2004), p. 32. I am grateful to Lisa Butterly for this reference.

33 Emily to James, 1st duke of Leinster, 12 May 1955; quoted in Brian FitzGerald (ed.), *Correspondence of Emily, duchess of Leinster (1731–1814)* (Dublin, 1949), vol. i, p. 13.

34 Maurice to Evelyn, 22 Aug. [?], DD/DRU/90.

35 Maurice to Evelyn, 6 Mar. 1907, DD/DRU/90.

36 Maurice to Evelyn, n.d., DD/DRU/90.

37 Maurice to Evelyn, 5 Apr. 1906, DD/DRU/90.

38 Maurice to Evelyn, n.d., DD/DRU/90.

39 Maurice to Evelyn, n.d., DD/DRU/90.

40 Mabel to Evelyn, 19 May 1906, DD/DRU/93.

41 Maurice to Evelyn, 6 Mar. 1907, DD/DRU/90.

42 Maurice to Evelyn, 25 Dec. 1912, DD/DRU/90.

43 Eton School register, part vii, 1899–1909, p. xxix (Eton School Archives).

44 Quoted in Donald Leinster-Mackay, *The rise of the English prep school* (Sussex, 1984), p. 40.

45 Ibid.

46 Ibid., pp 40–1.

47 Report by Walker D. Chambers, Mar. 1910, LHB7, 52.915.

48 Ibid.

49 See, for example, Louise A. Jackson, *Child sexual abuse in Victorian England* (London, 2000), pp 28, 46, 112; in 1992, W.D. Mosher found that there were only nineteen articles mentioning either sexual abuse or incest in English-language psychoanalytical journals from 1920 to 1986; Lisa Appignanesi, *Mad, bad and sad: a history of women and the mind*

doctors, 1800 to the present (London, 2008), p. 459.

50 Louise A. Jackson, *Child sexual abuse in Victorian Ireland* (London and New York, 2000), p. 4.

51 Sigmund Freud, *The aetiology of hysteria* (London, 1962 ed., 1st ed. 1896), p. 203; for introductions to this area of study, see John and Rita Sommers-Flanagan, *Counselling and psychotherapy: theories in context and practice* (Hoboken, NJ, 2004); on Freud and psychoanalysis, see, for example, Todd Dufresne, *Killing Freud: twentieth-century culture and the death of psychoanalysis* (New York, 2003); N.G. Hale Jr, *Freud and the Americans: the beginning of psychoanalysis in the United States, 1876–1917* (New York, 1971); J.M. Masson, *The assault on truth: Freud's suppression of the seduction theory* (New York, 1998).

52 Royal Edinburgh Hospital case files, Maurice FitzGerald, 7 Mar. 1912 (Lothian Archive, LH B7 folders 1–2); see also Royal Edinburgh Hospital, case book 73 (LH, B7/51/73).

53 Maurice FitzGerald case file, 7 Mar. 1912, LH B7 folders 1–2.

54 Ibid.

55 Maurice FitzGerald case file, 8 Jan. 1911, LH B7 folders 1–2.

56 Maurice FitzGerald case file, 6 Sept. 1912, LH B7 folders 1–2.

57 A. Bifulco, G.W. Brown, Z. Adler, 'Early sexual abuse and clinical depression in adult life', *The British Journal of Psychiatry*, 159 (1991), pp 115–22.

58 Revd Bowlby's House Debating Society journal, 1899–1906, p. 176 (Eton School Archives).

59 MS of Shane Leslie's autobiography (NLI, Shane Leslie papers, MS 22,884).

60 Shane Leslie, *The Oppidan* (London, 1922), pp ix, xi–xii.

61 Ibid., pp 11, 29, 44.

62 Maurice to Evelyn, 29 Oct. 1905, DD/DRU/90.

63 Cynthia to Evelyn, 31 Dec. 1909, DD/DRU/93.

64 Cynthia to Evelyn, 10 Jan. 1910, DD/DRU/93.

65 Cannadine, *Decline and fall of the British aristocracy*, p. 327.

66 Ibid., p. 328.

67 *Vanity Fair*, 31 Jan. 1902; *Irish Society and Social Review*, 7 Mar. 1908; *New York Daily Tribune*, 18 Dec. 1905; *Evening Sun* [New York], 11 Sept. 1919.

68 *New York Daily Tribune*, 18 Dec. 1905.

69 *Irish Independent*, 17 Dec. 1907.

70 *Irish Society and Social Review*, 7 Mar. 1908.

71 Ibid.

72 *Irish Independent*, 12 Dec. 1907.

73 Ibid., 29 Feb. 1908.

74 R.W. Crone, 'Pollock, Sir (John) Donald, baronet (1868–1962)', rev. *Oxford dictionary of national biography*, OUP, 2004 [http://www.oxforddnb.com/view/article/35565, accessed 4 Dec. 2009].

75 A noted philanthropist, Pollock died leaving an estate of almost £1 million; R.W. Crone, 'Pollock, Sir (John) Donald, baronet (1868–1962)', rev. *Oxford dictionary of national biography*, OUP, 2004 [http://www.oxforddnb.com/view/article/35565, accessed 4 Dec. 2009].

76 Quoted on www.sudep.org/sudep_story.asp [accessed 13 Oct. 2009].

77 Johnson Raymond-Barker & Co. to Lord Frederick, 27 June 1923 (PRONI, Leinster papers, D3078/1/3/69).

78 Ibid.

79 Will of Maurice, 6th duke of Leinster, 14 July 1908 (PRONI, Leinster papers, D3078/1/3/71).

80 Ibid.

81 *Irish Independent*, 1 Sept. 1908.

82 Ibid., 15 Sept. 1908.

83 Ibid., 21 Nov. 1908.

84 Maurice to Evelyn, 30 Jan. 1909, DD/DRU/90.

85 *Irish Independent*, 4 May 1909.

86 Medical Certificate no. II signed by

Angus Matheson, 16 June 1909, LHB7, 52.915.

87 For more on these delusions see below.

88 Allan Beveridge, 'Clouston, Sir Thomas Smith (1840–1915)', ODNB [www.oxforddnb.com/view/article/38634, accessed 26 Nov. 2009].

89 Clouston's pioneering *Manic depressive insanity and paranoia* (1921) is still widely referenced; my thanks to Lisa Butterly for recommending this source to me.

90 Quoted in Estorick, *Heirs and graces*, p. 148.

91 David Wright, 'Getting out of the asylum: understanding the confinement of the insane in the nineteenth century', *Society for the Social History of Medicine*, 10 (1997), p. 137; see also Mark Finnane, *Insanity and the insane in post-Famine Ireland* (London, 1981); for the asylum as an 'arbiter of social and familial conflict', see Mark Finnane, 'Asylums, families and the state', *History Workshop Journal*, 20 (1985), p. 135.

92 'In lunacy, in the matter of the most noble Maurice, Duke of Leinster, a person alleged to be of unsound mind', 13 July 1909 (PRO, C 211/71).

93 Chantal Stebbings, 'Conflicts and tensions in lunacy jurisdiction: the case of *Re Earl of Sefton* [1898]' in Charles Mitchell and Paul Mitchell (eds), *Landmark cases in equity* (Oxford, 2012), pp 453–77. I would like to thank Prof Stebbings for allowing me read pre-publication drafts of this article as well as her 'Protecting the property of the mentally ill: the judicial solution in nineteenth-century lunacy law', *Cambridge Law Journal* (July 2012).

94 Inquisition findings filed 26 July 1906 (PRO, C 211/71).

95 Petition to the sheriff of Lothian to admit a patient into the Royal Edinburgh Asylum, 17 June 1909, LHB7, 52.915.

96 Duke of Leinster's consent to purchase of plate and pictures from the

representatives of the late Lord William FitzGerald, 16 Dec. 1902 (PRONI, Leinster papers, D3078/2/10/11); Maurice, duke of Leinster to Lord Frederick, 1 Nov. 1906 (PRONI, Leinster papers, D3078/2/10/13); Pictures purchased during the minority of the duke of Leinster (Leinster papers, D3078/2/10/6–7).

97 See chapter eight.

98 Prof. Chantal Stebbings to author, 15 May 2012; See *An act to amend the law in Ireland relating to Commissions of Lunacy, and the proceedings under the same, and the management of the estates of lunatics; and to provide for the visiting and the protection of the property of lunatics in Ireland; and for other purposes*, [34 Vict], ch 22, 25 May 1871, sect. 63.

99 See below.

1 Craighouse was renamed the Thomas Clouston Clinic in 1972. It was closed in the 1990s.

2 *British Medical Journal*, 3 Nov. 1894, pp 994–5.

3 See Brendan D. Kelly, 'Mental health law in Ireland, 1821 to 1902: building the asylums', *Medico-legal Journal*, 76:1 (2008), part i, pp 19–25.

4 Quoted in Estorick, *Heirs and graces*, pp 150–1.

5 *British Medical Journal*, 3 Nov. 1894, p. 995.

6 Leslie Topp, 'The modern mental hospital in late nineteenth-century Germany and Austria: psychiatric space and images of freedom and control' in James Moran and Leslie Topp, 'Introduction: interpreting psychiatric spaces' in Leslie Topp, James E. Moran and Jonathan Andrews (eds), *Madness, architecture and the built environment: psychiatric spaces in historical context* (London & New York, 2007), p. 243.

7 See Barry Edington, 'A space for moral management: the York retreat's influence on asylum design' in Leslie Topp, James

E. Moran and Jonathan Andrews (eds), *Madness, architecture and the built environment: psychiatric spaces in historical context* (London & New York, 2007), pp 85–104, esp. p. 90; for how German asylum designers created this impression see Leslie Topp, 'The modern mental hospital in late nineteenth-century Germany and Austria: psychiatric space and images of freedom and control' in Topp, Moran and Andrews (eds), *Madness, architecture and the built environment*, pp 241–62; David Wright, 'Getting out of the asylum: understanding the confinement of the insane in the nineteenth century', *Society for the Social History of Medicine*, 10 (1997), p. 137; as Bailey points out, several 'aristocratic asylums' flourished throughout Britain; the likes, for example, of Shillingthorpe were 'modelled on grand country houses, [and] boasted aviaries and bowling greens, cricket pavilions and pagodas'; Bailey, *Black diamonds*, p. 28.

8 Maurice to Evelyn, 23 Dec. 1909, DD/DRU/90.

9 Ibid.

10 Maurice to Evelyn, 10 Jan. 1910, DD/DRU/90.

11 Letter of obligation for payment of board signed by Lord Frederick FitzGerald, 16 June 1909, LHB7, 52.915.

12 Estorick, *Heirs and graces*, p. 149.

13 Royal Edinburgh Hospital case files, Maurice FitzGerald, 6 Jan. 1912, LH B7 folders 1–2; see also Royal Edinburgh Hospital, case book 73, LH, B7/51/73.

14 Maurice FitzGerald case file, 29 July 1911, LH B7 folders 1–2.

15 Report by Walker D. Chambers, Mar. 1910, LH B7 folders 1–2.

16 Ibid.

17 Maurice FitzGerald case file, 17 June 1909.

18 Report by Walker D. Chamber, Mar. 1910, LH B7 folders 1–2.

19 Allan Beveridge, 'Voices of the mad: patients' letters from the Royal Edinburgh Asylum, 1873–1908', *Psychological Medicine*, 27 (1997), p. 902.

20 Ibid., p. 901.

21 Maurice FitzGerald case file, 18 June 1911, LH B7 folders 1–2.

22 Maurice FitzGerald case file, 20 May 1911, LH B7 folders 1–2.

23 Maurice FitzGerald case file, 1 July 1911, LH B7 folders 1–2.

24 Maurice FitzGerald case file, 20 May 1911, LH B7 folders 1–2.

25 Notes from case book, 1910, LH B7 folders 1–2.

26 Maurice FitzGerald case file, 20 June 1911, LH B7 folders 1–2.

27 Ibid.

28 Maurice FitzGerald case file, 22 June 1909, LH B7 folders 1–2.

29 Maurice FitzGerald case file, 27 Sept. 1912, LH B7 folders 1–2.

30 Maurice FitzGerald case file, 1 Dec. 1912, LH B7 folders 1–2.

31 Cynthia to Evelyn, 11 Jan. 1910, DD/DRU/93.

32 Maurice FitzGerald case file, 9 May 1913; for Edward's engagement see chapter eight.

33 Maurice FitzGerald case file, [?] Sept. 1913, LH B7 folders 1–2.

34 Maurice FitzGerald case file, 8 Nov. 1914, LH B7 folders 1–2.

35 Maurice FitzGerald case file, 20 Sept. 1914, LH B7 folders 1–2.

36 Maurice FitzGerald case file, 25 Oct. 1914, LH B7 folders 1–2.

37 Maurice FitzGerald case file, 8 Nov. 1914, LH B7 folders 1–2.

38 Maurice FitzGerald case file, 27 Mar. 1915, 24 Apr. 1915, 19 June 1915, LH B7 folders 1–2.

39 Maurice FitzGerald case file, 5 May 1911, LH B7 folders 1–2.

40 Maurice FitzGerald case file, 23 June 1911, LH B7 folders 1–2.

41 Maurice FitzGerald case file, 4 Dec. 1912, LH B7 folders 1–2.

42 Maurice FitzGerald case file, 2 Sept. 1912, LH B7 folders 1–2.

43 Maurice FitzGerald case file, 16 Oct. 1915, LH B7 folders 1–2.

44 Hermione to Evelyn, n.d., DD/DRU/90.

45 http://www.pbs.org/wnet/redgold/basics/ bloodlettinghistory.html [accessed 22 July 2012].

46 Julius Althus, *A treatise on medical electricity: theoretical and practical* (Philadelphia, 1870), 2nd ed., p. v; for other contemporary contributions on this subject, see G.M. Beard, 'The treatment of insanity by electricity', *British Journal of Psychiatry*, 19 (Oct. 1873), pp 355–60; A.H. Newth, 'The value of electricity in the treatment of insanity', *British Journal of Psychiatry*, 30 (Oct. 1884), pp 354–9.

47 http://www.goodreads.com/author/ quotes/1938.Friedrich_Nietzsche [accessed 1 June 2012].

48 *Irish Independent*, 11 Mar., 4 May 1910.

49 See, for example, *Carlow Sentinel*, 13 Aug. 1910.

50 *Kildare Observer*, 15 Oct. 1910.

51 Ibid., 22 Oct. 1910.

52 Ibid., 11 Mar. 1911.

53 Maurice FitzGerald case file, 29 July 1911, LH B7 folders 1–2.

54 Ibid.; a similar report appeared in *Daily Mirror*, 1 Aug. 1916.

55 Maurice FitzGerald case file, 25 Mar. 1916, LH B7 folders 1–2; for example of such reports see *Gentlewoman*, 5 Aug. 1916.

56 Maurice FitzGerald case file, 8 Feb. 1918, LH B7 folders 1–2.

57 *London Mail*, Sept. 1918.

58 Case book 73, 18 May 1919 (LH B7/51/73); Maurice FitzGerald case file, 18 Nov. 1919, LH B7 folders 1–2.

59 *Gentlewoman*, 26 July 1919.

CHAPTER EIGHT
War and debt, 1914–22

1 Hermione to Evelyn, n.d., DD/DRU/90.

2 Such descriptions are to be found in Hermione's letters to Evelyn.

3 FitzGerald notes (NLI, MS 48,177).

4 *Eton Calendar, 1907*, p. 127.

5 Revd H.T. Bowlby's House Debating Society, 1899–1906, p. 198 (Eton School Archives).

6 Desmond's obituary by H.T. Bowlby in *Eton College Chronicle*, 6 July 1916, p. 48.

7 Revd H.T. Bowlby's House Debating Society, 1899–1906, pp 198, 213–14, 230–1 (Eton School Archives).

8 Eton School register, part vii, 1899–1909 (Eton School Archives).

9 *Eton College Chronicle*, 30 Nov. 1907, p. 178.

10 'The Wall Game', [http://www.eton college.com/WallGame.aspx, accessed 24 Aug. 2012].

11 *Eton College Chronicle*, 6 July 1916, p. 48.

12 Maurice to Evelyn, 30 Jan. 1909, DD/DRU/90; *Eton College Chronicle*, 6 July 1916, p. 48.

13 *Irish Times*, 2 Dec. 1893.

14 Revd H.T. Bowlby's House Debating Society, 1899–1906, pp 198, 213–14, 230–1 (Eton School Archives).

15 *Sunday Dispatch*, 10 Feb. 1957.

16 Maurice to Evelyn, 30 Jan. 1909, DD/DRU/90.

17 Estorick, *Heirs and graces*, p. 11.

18 Public examination of the debtor [Edward Fitzgerald] in the High Court of Justice, 21 Nov. 1923 (PRO, B 9/953).

19 George Cornwallis-West, *Edwardian hey-days: a little about a lot of things* (1930), p. 132.

20 *Irish Independent*, 6 May 1913.

21 Un-named source quoted in *Irish Independent*, 6 Feb. 1922.

22 Mark Bence-Jones, *Twilight of the ascendancy* (London, 1987), p. 94; Estorick, *Heirs and graces*, p. 91.

23 Quoted in Bailey, *Black diamonds*, p. 164.

24 Quoted in ibid.

25 Fingall, *Seventy years young*, p. 119.

26 Quoted in Scriven, *Splendour & squalor*, pp 24–5.

27 Quoted in *Irish Independent*, 6 May 1913.
28 Ibid.
29 Ibid., 13 June 1913.
30 Ibid., 6 Feb. 1922.
31 Scriven, *Splendour & squalor*, p. 27.
32 Ibid.
33 Ibid., p. 26.
34 Estorick, *Heirs and graces*, p. 14.
35 Scriven, *Splendour & squalor*, p. 28.
36 *Telegraph*, 7 Dec. 2004.
37 Gerald Fitzgerald to May, duchess of Leinster, n.d. (in private possession).
38 *Irish Independent*, 7 Jan. 1926.
39 Quoted in Scriven, *Splendour & squalor*, p. 35.
40 http://www.1914–1918.net/dukes.htm [accessed 23 July 2011].
41 *Irish Independent*, 16 Aug. 1915.
42 Quoted in Scriven, *Splendour & squalor*, p. 33.
43 See Dooley, *Decline of the big house*, pp 122–7; also Peter Martin, '*Dulce et Decorum*: Irish nobles and the Great War, 1914–19' in Adrian Gregory and Senia Paseta (eds), *Ireland and the Great war: 'a war to unite us all'?* (Manchester, 2002), pp 28–48.
44 Buckland, *Irish unionism I*, p. 32; Dooley, *Decline of the big house*, pp 122–7.
45 See, for example, Molly Keane's *Mad Puppetstown* (1931) and *The rising tide* (1937); also Elizabeth Bowen, *The last September* (1929).
46 Quoted in Lennox Robinson, *Bryan Cooper* (London, 1931), p. 80.
47 *Burke's landed gentry of Ireland* (London, 1958 ed.), p. xviii.
48 Robinson, *Bryan Cooper*, p. 131.
49 Ibid., p. 74.
50 *Kildare Observer*, 1 Aug. 1914.
51 Ibid., 22 Aug. 1914.
52 Ibid., 26 Aug., 2 Sept. 1916.
53 Ibid., 16 Sept. 1916.
54 Lord D'Abernon, 'In memoriam of Major Lord Desmond FitzGerald, 21 September 1888 to 3 March 1916', *JCKAS*, 8 (1915–17), p. 424.
55 Quoted in Estorick, *Heirs and graces*, p. 151.
56 Desmond FitzGerald to Aunt Dolly, 16 Nov. 1916 (in private possession).
57 Note written by Desmond FitzGerald, 17 Nov. 1914 (in private possession).
58 www.victorianweb.org/authors/farningham/bio.html [26 Feb. 2010].
59 Quoted in Cannadine, *Decline and fall of the British aristocracy*, p. 75.
60 Copy W.H.L. McCarthy to Lord de Vesci, 2 Apr. 1916 (in private possession).
61 Lord D'Abernon, 'In memoriam of Major Lord Desmond FitzGerald, 21 September 1888 to 3 March 1916', *JCKAS*, 8, 1915–17, p. 424.
62 Copy W.H.L. McCarthy to Lord de Vesci, 2 Apr. 1916 (in private possession).
63 Ibid.
64 Quoted in Lennox Robinson, *Bryan Cooper*, p. 80.
65 Cynthia Asquith, *Diaries, 1915–18*, p. 92; Leslie, *Edwardians in love*, p. 265.
66 Cynthia Asquith, *Diaries, 1915–18*, p. 97.
67 Quoted in Leslie, *Edwardians in love*, p. 264.
68 Quoted in ibid., p. 271.
69 Rudyard Kipling, *The Irish Guards in the Great War: edited and compiled from their diaries and papers* (1923), vol. 1, at www.telelib.com/authors/k/kiplingrudyard/prose/irishguardsv1/index.html [accessed 6 June 2012].
70 Desmond's obituary by H.T. Bowlby in *Eton College Chronicle*, 6 July 1916, p. 48.
71 Kipling, *The Irish Guards*.
72 Simon Winchester, *Their noble lordships: class and power in modern Britain* (New York, 1981), p. 40.
73 Desmond's obituary by H.T. Bowlby in *Eton College Chronicle*, 6 July 1916, p. 48.
74 Edward, Prince of Wales, to Cynthia Graham, 3 Mar. 1916 (in private possession).
75 Queen Mary to Cynthia Graham, 5 Mar. 1916 (in private possession.)

76 Edward, Prince of Wales, to Cynthia Graham, 14 Apr. 1916 (in private possession).

77 Taaffe, 'Athy in the Great War', pp 615, 621.

78 D'Abernon, 'In memoriam of Major Lord Desmond FitzGerald', p. 423

79 Ibid., p. 423.

80 Ibid., p. 424.

81 *Kildare Observer*, 25 Mar. 1916.

82 Ibid., 18 Mar. 1916.

83 Minutes of Kildare County Council, 29 May 1916; quoted in Thomas Nelson, 'Lord Frederick FitzGerald, 1857–1924' in Cosgrove et al. (eds), *Aspects of Irish aristocratic life.*

84 Ibid.

85 Joseph Doran to Lord Frederick, n.d. (in private possession).

86 Cannadine, *Decline of the British aristocracy*, p. 84.

87 Marie Coleman, 'Buachalla (Ua Buachalla), Domhnall (Donal/Daniel Richard Buckley)' in James McGuire and James Quinn (eds), *Dictionary of Irish biography* (Cambridge, 2009). (http://dib.cambridge.org/viewReadPage. do?articleId=a6284 [accessed 22 Mar. 2012]).

88 Cannadine, *Decline of the British aristocracy*, p. 335; see also chapter 10 for the purchase of honours scandal.

89 Dunraven, *Past times and pastimes*, vol. i, p. 196.

90 Maurice FitzGerald case file, 11 Mar. 1916, LH B7 folders 1–2.

91 This is evident in his letters to Evelyn de Vesci quoted earlier.

92 Maurice FitzGerald case file, 29 July 1911, LH B7 folders 1–3.

93 Ibid., 3 Apr. 1915.

94 Ibid., 20 Dec. 1914.

95 Ibid., 23 July 1915.

96 Ibid., 16 Oct. 1915.

97 Edward FitzGerald, duke of Leinster, 'My forty years of folly', *Sunday Dispatch*, 10 Feb. 1957.

98 Quoted in Scriven, *Splendour & squalor*, p. 35.

99 Public examination of the debtor [Edward Fitzgerald] in the High Court of Justice, 21 Nov. 1923 (PRO, B 9/953).

1 *Irish Independent*, 22 Nov. 1923; Public examination of the debtor [Edward Fitzgerald] in the High Court of Justice, 21 Nov. 1923 (PRO, B 9/953).

2 Henry Mallaby-Deeley to Charles Hamilton, 1 Apr. 1930 (in private possession).

3 See below.

4 Public examination of the debtor [Edward Fitzgerald] in the High Court of Justice, 21 Nov. 1923 (PRO, B 9/953).

5 Ibid.; Official Receiver's report to the court heard on 25 June 1953 (PRO, B 9/953).

6 Public examination of the debtor [Edward Fitzgerald] in the High Court of Justice, 21 Nov. 1923 (PRO, B 9/953); Official Receiver's report to the court heard on 25 June 1953 (PRO, B 9/953).

7 Quoted in Mark Bence-Jones, *Twilight of the ascendancy* (London, 1987), p. 197.

8 Cannadine, *Decline of the British aristocracy*, pp 413, 416.

9 Public examination of the debtor [Edward Fitzgerald] in the High Court of Justice, 21 Nov. 1923 (PRO, B 9/953).

10 Rafaelle, duchess of Leinster, *So brief a dream*, p. 76.

11 Public examination of the debtor [Edward Fitzgerald] in the High Court of Justice, 21 Nov. 1923 (PRO, B 9/953).

12 Estorick, *Heirs and graces*, pp 10–11.

13 *The Times*, 19 July 1922.

14 Ibid., 26 Apr., 9, 15 May 1923; Official Receiver's report to the court heard on 25 June 1953 (PRO, B 9/953).

15 Public examination of the debtor [Edward Fitzgerald] in the High Court of Justice, 21 Nov. 1923 (PRO, B 9/953).

16 Ibid.

17 Official Receiver's report to the court heard on 25 June 1953 (PRO, B 9/953).

18 E.H. Short and Arthur Compton-Rickett, *Ring up the curtain: being a pageant of English entertainment* (1938), p. 171.

19 Harold Philip Clunn, *The face of London* (London, 1970), p. 152.

20 *Dundalk Democrat*, 13 Mar. 1920.

21 Obituary, *The Times*, 13 Feb. 1937.

22 George Hamilton Cunningham, *London, being a comprehensive survey of the history, tradition & historical associations of buildings and monuments, arranged under streets in alphabetical order* (London, 1927), p. 496.

23 Mark Frost, *The greatest game ever played: Vardon, Ouimet and the birth of modern golf* (London, 2002), p. 11.

24 Derek Birley, *Playing the game: sport and British society, 1910–45* (Manchester, 1995), p. 34; Geoffrey Cousins, *Golf in Britain: a social history from the beginnings to the present day* (London, 1975), p. 52.

25 George Wyndham to Countess Grosvenor, 12–13 Jan. 1888 (PRONI, Wyndham papers, T3221/1/2A).

26 Quoted on http://www.mitcham common.org/golfclub.html [accessed 17 Nov. 2009].

27 In 1907, Mallaby-Deeley also designed and developed the Prince's Golf Club at Sandwich opened by Balfour; Birley, *Playing the game*, p. 35; Cousins, *Golf in Britain*, pp 49, 50; http://www.mitcham golfclub.co.uk/mitcham-golf-club-history.php [accessed 23 July 2011].

28 http://www.number10.gov.uk/history-and-tour/prime-ministers-in-history/david-lloyd-george/1909-peoples-budget-transcript [accessed 8 Feb. 2010].

29 Cannadine, *Decline of the British aristocracy*, p. 48.

30 *New York Times*, 12 Oct. 1913.

31 Cannadine, *Decline of the British aristocracy*, p. 49.

32 R.E. Prothero, *Whippingham to Westminster: the reminiscences of Lord Ernle* (London, 1938), pp 213–14.

33 *The Times*, 7 Aug. 1911.

34 'Liberal newspaper' quoted in *New York Times*, 13 Dec. 1913.

35 Ibid.; see also 'The Bedford estate: the sale of the estate', *Survey of London: vo. 36: Covent Garden* (1970), pp 48–52, on history.ac.uk/report.aspx?compid=46089 [accessed 30 July 2009].

36 *New York Times*, 17 Dec. 1913.

37 *Daily Telegraph*, 7 July 1914; 'The Bedford estate: the sale of the estate' [www.british-history.ac.uk/report.aspx?compid=46089, accessed 23 July 2011].

38 'The Bedford estate: the sale of the estate'.

39 Quoted on http://www.mitcham common.org/golfclub.html [17 Nov. 2009].

40 Scriven, *Splendour & squalor*, p. 36.

41 Public examination of the debtor [Edward Fitzgerald] in the High Court of Justice, 21 Nov. 1923 (PRO, B 9/953).

42 Official Receiver's report to the court heard on 25 June 1953 (PRO, B 9/953); *Sunday Dispatch*, 10 Feb. 1957.

43 Quoted in Scriven, *Splendour & squalor*, p. 37.

44 Rafaelle, duchess of Leinster, *So brief a dream*, p. 60.

45 Quoted in Scriven, *Splendour & squalor*, p. 29.

46 *Evening Sun* [New York], 11 Sept. 1919.

47 Maurice FitzGerald case book 73, 25 May 1920, LH B7/51/73.

48 Ibid., and 11 Nov. 1921.

49 Ibid., 2 Feb. 1922.

50 Will of Maurice, duke of Leinster, 14 July 1908 (PRONI, Leinster papers, D3078/1/3/71).

51 *Irish Independent*, 6 Feb. 1922.

52 Estorick, *Heirs and graces*, p. 13.

53 *The Times*, 23 Jan. 1923.

CHAPTER NINE

Henry Mallaby-Deeley: 'the fairy godfather of the estate'

The MSS quoted in this and the following chapters are in private possession except where location is given. H M-D refers to Sir Henry Mallaby-Deeley.

1 Anon., quoted in Patricia Condron, Muireann Ní Bhrolcháin and Dominick Hyland (eds), *Cannonballs and crosiers: a history of Maynooth* (Maynooth, 1994), p. 58.

2 Cannadine, *Aspects of aristocracy*, p. 240.

3 Lambert, *Unquiet Souls*, p. 166.

4 Fingall, *Seventy years young*, p. 386.

5 See Dooley, *Decline of the big house in Ireland*, pp 170–207.

6 *Leinster Leader*, 17 June 1922.

7 See below. Elizabeth Fingall related another version of this story in which a group of Republicans allegedly raided Carton in 1922 and took away Lord Desmond's revolver, which had been sent back from France with his other personal effects but 'by the kind intervention of the last governor general of Ireland, then a rebel leader, it was given back'. This, of course, was the aforementioned Domhnall Ua Buachalla; Fingall, *Seventy years young*, p. 386.

8 Official Receiver's report to the court heard on 25 June 1953 (PRO, B 9/953).

9 R.J.Q. Adams, 'Astor, Waldorf, second Viscount Astor (1879–1952)', *Oxford dictionary of national biography*, Oxford University Press, 2004; online edn, Jan. 2008 [http://www.oxforddnb.com/view/article/30490, accessed 2 Aug. 2011]

10 John Turner, 'Astor, William Waldorf, first Viscount Astor (1848–1919)', rev. *Oxford dictionary of national biography*, Oxford University Press, 2004; online edn, Jan. 2008 [http://www.oxforddnb.com/view/article/37131, accessed 2 Aug. 2011].

11 R.J.Q. Adams, 'Astor, Waldorf', *Oxford dictionary of national biography*, online ed., Jan. 2008 [http://www.oxforddnb.com/view/article/30490, accessed 14 Mar. 2012].

12 Derek Wilson, 'Astor, John Jacob, first Baron Astor of Hever (1886–1971)',

Oxford dictionary of national biography, Oxford University Press, 2004; online edn, Jan. 2011 [http://www.oxforddnb.com/view/article/30773, accessed 2 Aug. 2011].

13 For Llangattock's obituary see, *The Times*, 25 Sept. 1912.

14 http://www.ouafc.com/varsity/players/150 [accessed 14 Mar. 2012].

15 Once again, I would like to express my deepest gratitude to Tony McCarthy for sharing his expertise with me on these financial matters.

16 Notes on Messrs Smith and Hudson's estimate of death duties and Mr Salaman's statement of income and charges thereon, n.d. [Apr. 1923]; Estimate of death duties [with modifications] (in private possession).

17 Ibid.

18 Quoted in *Leinster Leader*, 17 June 1922.

19 Ibid., 17 June 1922.

20 Charles Hamilton to H M-D, 8 Apr. 1924.

21 Freshfields Leese and Munns to Johnson Raymond-Barker & Co., 18 Jan. 1923.

22 Charles Hamilton to Mr Arnott, 14 Aug. 1932; Lord Henry FitzGerald to Henry Nix, 24 Mar. 1938.

23 Freshfields Leese and Munns to Johnson Raymond-Barker & Co., 18 Jan. 1923.

24 Ibid.

25 Cecil Raymond-Barker to Lord Frederick, 26 Nov. 1923.

26 Henry Nix to Lord Frederick, 30 May 1923.

27 Duke of Leinster's estate: opinion of C. Ashworth James, 29 May 1923; also *Leinster Leader*, 17 June 1922.

28 Duke of Leinster's estate: opinion of C. Ashworth James, 29 May 1923.

29 Johnson Raymond-Barker & Co. to Lord Frederick, 27 June 1923 (PRONI, Leinster papers, D3078/1/3/69).

30 Duke of Leinster's estate: opinion of C. Ashworth James, 29 May 1923.

31 Freshfields Leese and Munns to Johnson Raymond-Barker & Co., 18 Jan. 1923.

32 Freshfields, Leese, Munns to Charles Hamilton, 1 Dec. 1924.

33 *Kildare Observer*, 7 June 1924.

34 Henry FitzGerald to Charles Hamilton, 24 May 1924, 3 Apr. 1924.

35 (?)Henry FitzGerald to Charles Hamilton, 20 Mar. 1924.

36 Cecil Raymond-Barker to G.F.C. Hamilton, 14 Mar. 1924.

37 H M-D to Charles Hamilton, 5 Apr. 1924.

38 H M-D to Charles Hamilton, 12 Apr. 1924, 16 Aug. 1924.

39 Charles Hamilton to H M-D, 8 Apr. 1924.

40 H M-D to Charles Hamilton, 5 Apr. 1924.

41 H M-D to Charles Hamilton, 12 Apr. 1924.

42 Charles Hamilton to H M-D, 8 Apr. 1924.

43 For a fuller understanding of this act, see Terence Dooley, '*The land for the people*: the land question in independent Ireland' (Dublin, 2003), esp. pp 27–56.

44 http://www.ansi.okstate.edu/breeds/cattle/kerry/ [accessed 1 June 2012].

45 Charles Hamilton to H M-D, 8 Apr. 1924.

46 H M-D to Charles Hamilton, 10 May 1924; Charles Hamilton to H M-D, 24 May 1924; Charles Hamilton to H M-D, 5 Dec. 1932; Charles Hamilton to H M-D, 8 Apr. 1924, 24 July 1924.

47 Charles Hamilton to H M-D, 12 May 1924.

48 H M-D to Charles Hamilton, 24 Nov. 1925.

49 Charles Hamilton to H M-D, 20 May 1924.

50 Thomas Kennedy to Charles Hamilton, 29 May 1925.

51 Charles Hamilton to H M-D, 20 May 1924.

52 Thomas Kennedy to Charles Hamilton, 29 May 1925.

53 H M-D to Charles Hamilton, 12 Apr. 1924.

54 H M-D to Charles Hamilton, 21 July 1924.

55 Charles Hamilton to H M-D, 24 July 1924.

56 Charles Hamilton to H M-D, 21 July 1924, 24 July 1924.

57 H M-D to Charles Hamilton, 29 Sept. 1926.

58 Duke of Leinster's estate: opinion of C. Ashworth James, 29 May 1923; H M-D to Charles Hamilton, 21 July 1924.

59 Information and complaint of Straker Squire Ltd, 9 May 1923 (PRO, CRIM 1/237).

60 *The Times*, 19 June 1923.

61 Ibid., 10 July 1923.

62 Ibid., 20 Oct. 1923.

63 Quoted in *Irish Independent*, 13 June 1922.

64 See, for example, *Irish Independent*, 9, 19 Jan. 1923; *The Times*, 9 Jan. 1923.

65 *The Times*, 9 Jan. 1923.

66 F.S. Salaman to Johnson Raymond-Barker & Co., 26 Feb. 1923.

67 Henry Nix [of Johnson Raymond-Barker & Co.] to Lord Frederick, 13 Apr. 1923.

68 Lord Henry FitzGerald to Charles Hamilton, 18 Apr. 1924; Lord Henry FitzGerald to Charles Hamilton, 12 Nov. 1925.

69 Lord Henry FitzGerald to Charles Hamilton, 18 Apr. 1924; Lord Henry FitzGerald to Charles Hamilton, 12 Nov. 1925.

70 Cecil Raymond-Barker to G.F.C. Hamilton, 14 Mar. 1924; Cecil Raymond-Barker to G.F.C. Hamilton, 16 May 1924; Bennet & Son to Cecil Raymond-Barker, 25 Feb. 1922.

71 Cecil Raymond-Barker to G.F.C. Hamilton, 10 Dec. 1924.

72 H M-D's private secretary to Charles Hamilton, 14 Feb. 1925; Cecil Raymond-Barker to G.F.C. Hamilton, 19 Feb. 1925; Cecil Raymond-Barker to G.F.C. Hamilton, 27 July 1925.

73 *Irish Independent*, 4 Nov. 1925.

74 Ibid., 28 Nov. 1925.

75 Cecil Raymond-Barker to G.F.C. Hamilton, 24 Sept. 1925.

76 Ferdinand Lundberg *America's 60 families* (New York, 1937), p. 267; John Harris, *Moving rooms: the trade in architectural salvages* (New Haven and London, 2007), p. 219.

77 Harris, *Moving rooms*, p. 219.
78 Fingall, *Seventy years young*, p. 180.
79 *Irish Independent*, 24 Oct. 1925.
80 Ibid., 12, 13 Nov. 1925.
81 Official Receiver's report to the court heard on 25 June 1953 (PRO, B 9/953).
82 Statement showing position of estate, 8 Sept. 1927 (PRO, B 9/953).
83 H M-D to Charles Hamilton, 1 Apr. 1930; D'Abernon was married to Helen Duncombe, sister of Hermione and, therefore, Lord Edward's uncle-in-law.
84 Estorick, *Heirs and graces*, p. 13.
85 *Leinster Leader*, 17 June 1922.
86 See next chapter.

CHAPTER TEN
To America in search of an heiress

1 Quoted in *Sunday Dispatch*, 10 Feb. 1957.
2 Richard Whiting, *The Labour Party and taxation: party identity and political purpose in twentieth-century Britain* (Cambridge, 200), pp 17–19.
3 Quoted in Cannadine, *Decline of the British aristocracy*, p. 98.
4 H M-D to Charles Hamilton, 23 Oct. 1929.
5 Charles Hamilton to Mr Arnott, 14 Aug. 1932.
6 *The Times*, 15 Aug. 1932.
7 Charles Hamilton to Mr Arnott, 14 Aug. 1932.
8 See, for example, Deirdre McMahon, *Republicans and Imperialists: Anglo-Irish relations in the 1930s* (New Haven, CT, 1984); Kevin O'Rourke, 'Burn everything British but their coal: the Anglo-Irish economic war of the 1930s', *Journal of Economic History*, 51:2 (June 1991), pp 357–66.
9 Charles Hamilton to Mr Arnott, 14 Aug. 1932; Charles Hamilton to H M-D, 5 Dec. 1932.
10 Charles Hamilton to H M-D, 5 Dec. 1932.
11 Ibid.
12 Ibid.
13 For an interesting contemporary insight, see W.T. Stead, *The Americanization of the world* (London, 1902), especially chapter v, 'Marriage and society', pp 121–9; my thanks to Prof. Joe Cleary for bringing this to my attention.
14 *New York Times*, 20 Dec. 1903.
15 C. Wright Mills, *The power elite* (Oxford, 2000 ed., 1st ed. 1956), p. 11.
16 Ferdinand Lundberg, *America's 60 families* (New York, 1937), pp 3, 9.
17 Ibid., p. 15.
18 Gustavus Myers, *History of the great American fortunes* (Chicago, 1910), vol. ii, p. 274; Lundberg, *America's 60 families*, p. 9; see also, M.C. Howard, *Transnationalism and society: an introduction* (Jefferson, 2011), esp. chapter four.
19 Myers, *History of the great American fortunes*, pp 273–4.
20 Lundberg, *America's 60 families*, p. 9.
21 Cannadine, *Decline of the British aristocracy*, pp 347, 398.
22 Lambert, *Unquiet Souls*, p. 7.
23 Cannadine, *Decline and fall of the British aristocracy*, p. 25.
24 Lundberg, *America's 60 families*, p. 14.
25 *The Times*, 25 Mar. 2006; Cannadine, *Decline of the British aristocracy*, p. 316.
26 Quoted in Cannadine, *Decline of the British aristocracy*, p. 316.
27 Scriven, *Splendour & squalor*, p. 41; in Edward's account of his life in the *Sunday Dispatch*, 17 Feb. 1957, he claimed he went to America bankrolled by a conman named Gilbert Marsh.
28 Quoted in Scriven, *Splendour & squalor*, p. 41.
29 *Irish Independent*, 29 Jan. 1931.
30 Michael Klepper and Robert Gunther, *The wealthy 100: from Benjamin Franklin to Bill Gates, a ranking of the richest Americans, past and present* (New York, 1996).

31 See William Mangam, *The Clarks: an American phenomenon* (New York, 1941); http://www.msnbc.msn.com/id/3547001 1/ns/business-huguette_clark_mystery/ [accessed 25 Apr. 2011].

32 http://www.msnbc.msn.com/ id/35470011/ns/business-huguette_clark_ mystery/ [accessed 25 Apr. 2011].

33 www.beadinggem.com/2012/04/ reluctant-heiress-jewels.html [accessed 8 Nov. 2012].

34 *New York Daily News*, 7 Sept. 2010; http://www.msnbc.msn.com/id/3547001 1/ns/business-huguette_clark_mystery/ [accessed 25 Apr. 2011]; Huguette died in 2011, aged 104, leaving $300 million to charity and nothing to her family; www.beading gem.com/2012/04/reluctant-heiress-jewels.html [accessed 8 Nov. 2012].

35 *Sunday Dispatch*, 10 Feb. 1957.

36 Ibid.

37 Rafaelle, duchess of Leinster, *So brief a dream* (London & New York, 1973), p. 19.

38 Ibid., pp 12–13.

39 Ibid., *So brief a dream*, p. 20.

40 Ibid., p. 47.

41 *Irish Independent*, 15 Nov. 1932.

42 Rafaelle, duchess of Leinster, *So brief a dream*, pp 48, 50.

43 Ibid., pp 51–2.

44 Ibid., p. 50.

45 Ibid., pp 54, 58.

46 *The Times*, 30 June 1930; see also *Irish Independent*, 1 May 1930.

47 Rafaelle, duchess of Leinster, *So brief a dream*, p. 61.

48 *Irish Independent*, 24 Jan. 1933.

49 Ibid., 23 May 1933.

50 Ibid.

51 Ibid., 23 Sept. 1933.

52 Ibid., 31 Oct. 1933.

53 Leinster to H M-D, 7 July 1936.

54 Freshfields Lees and Munns to Charles Hamilton, 9 July 1936.

55 Freshfields, Lees and Munns to Charles Hamilton, 22 July 1936.

56 Freshfields Lees and Munns to Charles Hamilton, 9 July 1936.

57 Ibid.

58 Rafaelle, duchess of Leinster, *So brief a dream*, p. 68; on Barbara Hutton, see Dean Jennings, *Barbara Hutton: a candid biography* (London, 1968); C.D. Heymann, *Poor little rich girl: the life and legend of Barbara Hutton* (London, 1984).

59 Rafaelle, duchess of Leinster, *So brief a dream*, p. 69.

60 Ibid., p. 70.

61 Ibid.

62 Ibid., pp 71–2.

63 Ibid., p. 87.

64 Ibid., p. 73.

65 Ibid., p. 82.

66 'Gerald FitzGerald: the last duke of Leinster to call Carton his home', *Irish Times*, 18 Dec. 2004; John Tribe, 'Bankruptcy, insolvency and corporate rescue: peerage and MP ledger: Edward FitzGerald', http://bankruptcyand insolvency.blogspot.com/2010/05/peerage -and-mp-ledger-edward-fitzgerald.html [accessed 14 Apr. 2012]; http://www. windsorknot.org/thefacts.htm [accessed 14 Apr. 2012]; Turtle Bunbury and Art Kavanagh, *The landed gentry and aristocracy of Kildare* (Dublin, 2004), p. 101.

67 Rafaelle, duchess of Leinster, *So brief a dream*, p. 105.

68 Ibid., p. 145; Scriven, *Splendour & squalor*, p. 46.

69 *Sunday Dispatch*, 10 Feb. 1957.

70 *News of the World*, 18, 25 June 1967.

71 Scriven, *Splendour & squalor*, p. 13.

72 David Cannadine, *Aspects of aristocracy*, p. 1.

73 Ibid.

74 Estorick, *Heirs and graces*, p. 12.

75 On the third bankruptcy see *The Times*, 17 July 1953.

76 Lord Kinross, 'The dukes of England: splendid relics of the past', *Life*, 15 Nov. 1943.

77 Ibid.
78 Ibid.
79 *Irish Independent*, 20 Mar. 1976.
80 The Westminster coroner, Dr Thurston, wrote: 'I have no doubt that this is a deliberate self-poisoning. He died by poisoning which was self-administered while he was suffering from depression'; *Irish Independent*, 20 Mar. 1976.
81 Marcus Scriven, *Splendour & squalor*, p. 11.
82 Ibid.
83 Denis FitzGerald to Charles Hamilton, 28 Nov. 1948.
84 F.R. Allen to Charles Hamilton, 22 Nov. 1948; today the family continues to reside at Hamwood, an important Palladian house, on the outskirts of Maynooth, not far from the Carton demesne.

Epilogue

1 Estorick, *Heirs and graces*, p. 18.
2 David Nall-Cain to Patrick Duffy, 22 Apr. 1992.
3 On the debate about the sustainability of the country house in the twenty-first

century and Carton's centrality to it, see Christopher Ridgway, 'Triumph or travesty? Carton House, Co. Kildare', *Country Life*, 18 Feb. 2009, pp 70–5; idem, 'Making and meaning in the country house: new perspectives in England, Ireland and Scotland' in Terence Dooley and Christopher Ridgway (eds), *The Irish country house: its past, present and future* (Dublin, 2011), pp 203–43.
4 Untitled and undated newspaper (PRONI, Leinster papers, D3078/6/2).
5 Ibid.
6 F.R. Allen to Charles Hamilton, 22 Nov. 1948; obituary in *Telegraph*, 7 Dec. 2004.
7 This episode in the FitzGerald family history has been dealt with in Michael Estorick, *Heirs and graces: the claim to the dukedom of Leinster* (London, 1981) and Marcus Scriven, *Splendour & squalor: the disgrace and disintegration of three aristocratic dynasties* (London, 2009), chapter one.
8 *Telegraph*, 7 Dec. 2004; on this see Estorick, *Heirs and graces*.
9 *The Times*, 29 Jan. 2006; *The Telegraph*, 27 Feb. 2006.

Bibliography

PRIMARY SOURCES

I MANUSCRIPTS

Eton School Archives
Eton School register, part vii, 1899–1909
Revd Bowlby's House Debating Society journals, 1899–1906

Lothian Health Service Archive, Edinburgh
Medical file of Maurice, 6th duke of Leinster.
Royal Edinburgh Hospital case files, Maurice FitzGerald.
Royal Edinburgh Hospital, case book 73 (LH, B7/51/73).
Petition to the sheriff of Lothian to admit a patient into the Royal Edinburgh Asylum,
17 June 1909 (LHB7, 52.915).

National Library of Ireland

Cloncurry papers
Conolly papers
Conolly-Napier papers
De Vesci papers
FitzGerald [Walter] papers

Leinster papers
Lennox/FitzGerald/Campbell papers
Leslie Papers
Redmond [John] papers

Public Record Office
In lunacy, in the matter of the most noble Maurice, Duke of Leinster, a person alleged
      to be of unsound mind, 13 July 1909 (PRO, C 211/71).
Public examination of the debtor [Edward Fitzgerald] in the High Court of Justice, 21
      Nov. 1923 (PRO, B 9/953).
Inquisition findings filed 26 July 1906 (PRO, C 211/71).
Official Receiver's report to the court heard on 25 June 1953 (PRO, B 9/953).
Information and complaint of Straker Squire Ltd, 9 May 1923 (PRO, CRIM 1/237).

Public Record Office of Northern Ireland
Dufferin papers
De Vesci papers
George Wyndham papers
Hamilton of Hamwood papers (Register of Archives, no. 9)
Leinster papers (consulted on microfilm, NUIM)

Somerset Record Office
De Vesci papers

In private possession
'Copy of the marquis of Kildare's household account book, 1758'
Correspondence of Charles Hamilton
Correspondence of Edward, Prince of Wales, to Lady Cynthia Graham
Correspondence of Queen Mary to Lady Cynthia Graham
Correspondence of Lord Desmond FitzGerald

2 GOVERNMENT PUBLICATIONS

Report of her majesty's commissioners of enquiry into the working of the Landlord and Tenant (Ireland) Act, 1870 and the acts amending the same, [C 2779], HC 1881, xviii (Earl of Bessborough, chairman).
An act to amend the law in Ireland relating to Commissions of Lunacy, and the proceedings under the same, and the management of the estates of lunatics; and to provide for the visiting and the protection of the property of lunatics in Ireland; and for other purposes, [34 Vict.], ch 22, 25 May 1871, sect. 63.
An act to amend the law relating to the occupation and ownership of land in Ireland and for other purposes relating thereto, and to amend the Labourers (Ireland) Act, [3 Edw. 7], ch 37, 14 Aug. 1903.
Hansard 4, xxx
Dáil Debates
Seanad Debates

3 NEWSPAPERS, PERIODICALS AND JOURNALS

Belfast Newsletter
British Medical Journal
Carlow Sentinel
Country Life
Daily Express
Daily Mirror
Dundalk Democrat
Eton College Chronicle
Evening Sun [New York]
Freeman's Journal
Gentlewoman
Glasgow Herald
Irish Independent
Irish Press

Irish Society and Social Review
Irish Times
Kildare Observer
Leeds Mercury
Leinster Express
Leinster Leader
Life
Liverpool Mercury
London Mail
Morning Post
Nationalist and Leinster Times
News of the World
New York Daily News
New York Daily Tribune

Pall Mall Gazette
Penny Illustrated
San Francisco Examiner
Saunders' Newsletter
St Stephen's Review
Sunday Dispatch
The Court Journal

The Graphic
The Lady of the House
The Listener,
The Nationalist
The Times
The World
Vanity Fair

4 DIRECTORIES, GUIDES AND WORKS OF REFERENCE

Burke's landed gentry of Ireland (London, various edns).
Cunningham, George Hamilton, *London, being a comprehensive survey of the history, tradition & historical associations of buildings and monuments, arranged under streets in alphabetical order* (London, 1927).
Dooley, Terence, *The big houses and landed estates of Ireland: a research guide* (Dublin, 2007).
Lewis, Samuel, *A topographical dictionary of Ireland, vol. ii* (London, 1838).
Rintoul, M.C., *Dictionary of real places and people in fiction* (London, 1993).
Who's Who (various editions).

5 CONTEMPORARY PUBLICATIONS

Adams, R.J.Q., 'Astor, Waldorf, second Viscount Astor (1879–1952)', *ODNB* (Oxford, 2004); online ed., Jan. 2008 [http://www.oxforddnb.com/view/article/30490, accessed 2 Aug. 2011].
Althus, Julius, *A treatise on medical electricity: theoretical and practical* (Philadelphia, 1870), 2nd ed.
Balfour, Frances, *Ne obliviscaris* (London, 1930).
Beard, G.M., 'The treatment of insanity by electricity', *British Journal of Psychiatry*, 19 (Oct 1873), pp 355–60.
Beddington, Mrs Claude, *All that I have met* (London, 1929).
Bennett, J.H., *Winter and spring on the shores of the Mediterranean* (New York, 4th ed., 1870).
Blunt, Wilfred S., *My diaries: being a personal narrative of events, 1888–1914* (New York, 1922).
Bowen, Elizabeth, *The last September* (New York, 1929).
Catalogue of pictures, plate and antiquities at Carton, Kilkea Castle and 13 Dominick St Dublin and 6 Carlton Terrace, London (Dublin, n.d. [1885]).
Catalogue of old Irish silver plate sold by order of trustees of late Lord Fitzgerald at Christie's, 4 Dec. 1902).
Catalogue of ancient and modern pictures sold at Christie's, 6 Dec. 1902.
Cornwallis-West, George, *Edwardian hey-days: a little about a lot of things* (London, 1930).

D'Abernon, Viscount, *Portraits and appreciations* (London, n.d.).

Davidson, Rafaelle, [duchess of Leinster], *So brief a dream* (London & New York, 1973).

Devereaux, W.C., *Fair Italy: the Riviera and Monte Carlo* (London, 1884).

Dun, Finlay, *Landlords and tenants in Ireland* (London, 1889).

Escott, T.H.S., *England: its people, polity and pursuits* (London, 1885).

'Excursion meeting, 1893', *JCKAS* (1894–5), pp 213–15.

Fingall, Elizabeth, Countess of, *Seventy years young* (London, 1937).

FitzGerald (ed.), Brian, *Correspondence of Emily, duchess of Leinster (1731–1814)* (Dublin, 1949), vol. i.

FitzGerald, Elizabeth, *Lord Kildare's grand tour, 1766–1769* (Cork, n.d.).

FitzGerald, Gerald [5th duke of Leinster], 'Maynooth Castle' [text of paper delivered at Maynooth Castle, Sept. 1893], *JCKAS* (1893–4), pp 223–33.

FitzGerald, Walter, 'Kilkea Castle', *JCKAS*, 2 (1896–9), pp 3–32.

—, 'Portraits of Lord and Lady Edward FitzGerald', *JCKAS*, 2 (1896–9), pp 382–3.

—, 'Kilkea Castle', *JCKAS*, 2 (1896–9), p. 25.

—, 'Carton', *JCKAS*, 4 (1903–5), pp 1–34.

Fitzpatrick, W.J. (ed.), *Correspondence of Daniel O'Connell, the Liberator* (London, 1888).

Fleming, D.A., and A.P.W. Malcomson (eds), *'A valley of execrations': the letters and papers of John Fitzgibbon, earl of Clare, 1772–1802* (Dublin, 2005).

Freud, Sigmund, *The aetiology of hysteria* (London, 1962 ed., 1st ed., 1896).

Ganly, C.W., *A tribute to a noble life: in memoriam of Gerald, duke of Leinster* (Dublin, n.d.).

Gibson, A., and W. Pickford, *Association football and the men who made it*, 4 vols (London, 1905–6).

Gilbert, J.T., *A history of the city of Dublin* (Shannon, 1972 ed., [1st ed., 1854–59]).

Hart, E.L. and M.N. Smith (eds), *Open me carefully: Emily Dickinson's intimate letters to Susan Huntington Dickinson* (Paris, 1998).

Hutton, E., *A brief history of the King's Royal Rifle Corps, 1755–1915* (London, 1917 [2nd ed.]).

Important and scarce books selected for sale with the consent of the trustees of his grace, the duke of Leinster, from the library at Carton County Kildare to be sold by Bennett & Sons, 11 Nov. 1925 and following two days.

Keane, Molly, *Mad Puppetstown* (1931).

—, *The rising tide* (1937).

Kipling, Rudyard, *The Irish Guards in the Great War: edited and compiled from their diaries and papers* (1923), vol. 1.

Lecky, W.E.H., *A history of Ireland in the eighteenth century* (London, 1892), vol. ii.

Leslie, Anita, *Edwardians in love* (London, 1972).

Leslie, Shane, *The Oppidan* (London, 1922).

Londonderry, marchioness of [Edith Vane-Tempest-Stewart], *Retrospect* (London, 1938).

Lundberg, Ferdinand, *America's 60 families* (New York, 1937).

MacDonagh, Michael, *The viceroy's postbag* (London, 1904).

Mangam, William, *The Clarks: an American phenomenon* (New York, 1941).

Mills, C. Wright, *The power elite* (Oxford, 2000 ed., 1st ed. 1956).

Mill, John Stuart, *The subjection of women* (London, 1869).

Moody, T.W., and Richard Hawkins (eds), *Florence Arnold-Forster's Irish journal* (Oxford, 1988).

Moore, Thomas, *The memoirs of Lord Edward FitzGerald* (ed. M. Mac Dermott, 1897).

Myers, Gustavus, *History of the great American fortunes* (Chicago, 1910), vol. ii.

Newth, A.H., 'The value of electricity in the treatment of insanity', *British Journal of Psychiatry*, 30 (Oct. 1884), pp 354–9.

'Obituary of Gerald FitzGerald, 5th duke of Leinster', *JCKAS* (1894–5), pp 155–8.

O'Brien, William, *An olive branch in Ireland* (London, 1910).

O'Connell, Maurice (ed.), *The correspondence of Daniel O'Connell, 1815–1823* (Shannon, 1972).

O'Rourke, John, *The history of the Great Irish Famine of 1847* (Dublin, 1874).

Otway, Caesar, *A tour in Connaught, comprising sketches of Clonmacnoise, Joyce country and Achill* (1839).

Percy, Clayre, and Jane Ridley (eds), *The letters of Edwin Lutyens to his wife Lady Emily* (London, 1985).

Prothero, R.E., *Whippingham to Westminster: the reminiscences of Lord Ernle* (London, 1938).

Ridley, Jane, and Percy, Clayre (eds), *The letters of Arthur Balfour and Lady Elcho* (London, 1992).

Robinson, Lennox, *Bryan Cooper* (London, 1931).

Senior, N.W., *Journals, conversations and essays relating to Ireland* (London, 1868).

Short, E.H., and Arthur Compton-Rickett, *Ring up the curtain: being a pageant of English entertainment* (London, 1938).

Thackeray, W.M., *Catherine: a story* (London, 1869).

Vignoles, Olinthus J., *Memoir of Sir Robert P. Stewart* (London, 1898).

Walsh, William J., *A plain exposition of the Irish Land Act of 1881* (Dublin, 1881).

Wright, Thomas (ed.), *The historical works of Giraldus Cambrensis* (London and New York, 1892).

SECONDARY SOURCES

Akenson, D.H., *The Irish educational experiment: the national system of education in the 19th century* (London, 1970).

Appignanesi, Lisa, *Mad, bad and sad: a history of women and the mind doctors from 1800 to the present* (London, 2008).

Aylmer, R.J., 'The duke of Leinster withdraws from Ireland: October 1797', *JCKAS*, 19 (part I) (2000–1), pp 161–3.

Bailey, Catherine, *Black diamonds: the rise and fall of an English dynasty* (London, 2008).

Barnard, Toby, and Jane Fenlon, *The dukes of Ormonde, 1610–1745* (Woodbridge, 2000).

Barnard, Toby, *Making the grand figure: lives and possessions in Ireland, 1641–1770* (New Haven and London, 2004).

—, 'Mrs Conolly and Castletown 1720–1752' in Nolan and McGrath (eds), *Kildare*, pp 327–48.

Beard, Geoffrey, *Stucco and decorative plasterwork in Europe* (London, 1983).

Beauman, Nicola, *Cynthia Asquith* (London, 1987).

Begadon, Cormac, 'The 2nd duke of Leinster and the establishment of St Patrick's College, Maynooth' in Cosgrove et al. (eds), *Aspects of Irish aristocratic life*, pp 138–47.

Bence-Jones, Mark, *Twilight of the ascendancy* (London, 1987).

Beveridge, Allan, 'Voices of the mad: patients' letters from the Royal Edinburgh Asylum, 1873–1908', *Psychological Medicine*, 27 (1997), pp 899–908.

Beveridge, Allan, 'Clouston, Sir Thomas Smith (1840–1915)', *ODNB* [www.oxford dnb.com/view/article/38634, accessed 26 Nov. 2009].

Bew, Paul, *Conflict and conciliation in Ireland, 1890–1910* (Oxford, 1987).

Bifulco, A., G.W. Brown and Z. Adler, 'Early sexual abuse and clinical depression in adult life', *The British Journal of Psychiatry*, 159 (1991), pp 115–22.

Birley, Derek, *Playing the game: sport and British society, 1910–45* (Manchester, 1995).

Bolton, G.C., *The passing of the Irish Act of Union: a study in parliamentary politics* (London, 1966).

Bowe, Nicola Gordon, 'Preserving the relics of heroic time: visualizing the Celtic Revival in early twentieth-century Ireland' in Brian Cliffe and Nicholas Grene (eds), *Synge and Edwardian Ireland* (Oxford, 2012), pp 58–83.

Bull, Philip, *Land, politics and nationalism: a study of the Irish land question* (New York, 1996).

Bunbury, Turtle, and Art Kavanagh, *The landed gentry and aristocracy of Kildare* (Dublin, 2004).

Bull, Malcolm, *The mirror of the gods: Classical mythology in Renaissance art* (London, 2005).

Cain, P.J., and A.G. Hopkins, *British imperialism, 1688–2000* (Essex, 2001).

Campbell, Fergus, 'Irish popular politics and the making of the Wyndham Land Act, 1901–3', *Historical Journal*, 45:4 (2002), pp 755–73.

Cannadine, David, *The decline and fall of the British aristocracy* (New Haven and London, 1990).

—, *Aspects of aristocracy: grandeur and decline in modern Britain* (New Haven and London, 1994).

Carey, V.P., 'Collaborator and survivor: Gerald the eleventh earl of Kildare and Tudor Ireland', *History Ireland*, 2:2 (Summer 1994).

—, *Surviving the Tudors: the 'Wizard Earl' of Kildare and English rule in Ireland, 1537–1586* (Dublin, 2002).

Chambers, Liam, *Rebellion in Kildare, 1790–1803* (Dublin, 1998).

—, 'FitzGerald, Lord Edward (1763–1798)', *ODNB* [www.oxforddnb.com/view/article/9546].

Chung, Cindy, and James Pennebaker, 'The psychological function of function words' in K. Fiedler (ed.), *Social communication* (New York, 2007).

Clarke, Frances, and Patrick Maume, 'Lawless, Emily', James McGuire and James Quinn (eds), *Dictionary of Irish biography*, (Cambridge, 2009) [http://dib.cambridge.org.jproxy.nuim.ie/quicksearch.do;jsessionid=69311B097223541521A C8E0A7C834BE3].

Clark, Samuel, *Social origins of the Irish Land War* (Princeton, NJ, 1979).

Clements, C.M.L., '100 years of the county Kildare Archaeological Society', *JCKAS*, 17 (1987–91), pp 5–7.

Clunn, Harold P., *The face of London* (London, 1970).

Coleman, Marie, 'Buachalla (Ua Buachalla), Domhnall (Donal/Daniel Richard Buckley)' in James McGuire and James Quinn (eds), *Dictionary of Irish biography* (Cambridge, 2009) [http://dib.cambridge.org/viewReadPage.do?articleId=a6284, accessed 22 Mar. 2012].

Comerford, R.V., 'County Kildare and the Famine' in Kildare County Council, *Lest we forget: Kildare and the Great Famine* (Kildare, 1995), p. 13.

—, 'Canon John O'Rourke: historian of the Great Famine' in Thomas Kabdebo (ed.), *Beyond the library walls: John Paul II annual lectures* (Maynooth, 1995), pp 58–68.

—, 'Isaac Butt and the Home Rule Party, 1870–77' in W.E. Vaughan (ed.), *A new history of Ireland*; vi, *Ireland under the Union, part 2, 1870–1921* (Oxford, 1996), pp 1–25.

—, *The Fenians in context: Irish politics and society, 1848–82* (Dublin, 1998).

—, *Ireland* (London and New York, 2003) [in series 'Inventing the nation'].

Condron, Patricia, Muireann Ni Bhrolcháin and Dominick Hyland (eds), *Cannonballs and crosiers: a history of Maynooth* (Maynooth, 1994).

Corish, P.J., *Maynooth college, 1795–1995* (Dublin, 1995).

Cosgrove, Art (ed.), *A new history of Ireland*; ii, *medieval Ireland 1169–1534* (Oxford, 1993)

Cosgrove, Patrick J., 'The sale of the Leinster estate under the Wyndham Land Act, 1903', *JCKAS*, 20 (2008–9), pp 9–25.

Cosgrove, Patrick, Terence Dooley and Karol Mullaney-Dignam (eds), *Aspects of Irish aristocratic life: essays on the FitzGeralds of Kildare and Carton* (Dublin, 2014).

Costello, Con, *A class apart: the gentry families of county Kildare* (Dublin, 2005).

Cousins, Geoffrey, *Golf in Britain: a social history from the beginnings to the present day* (London, 1975).

Craig, Maurice, *The architecture of Ireland from the earliest times to 1880* (London, 1982).

Crone, R.W., 'Pollock, Sir (John) Donald, baronet (1868–1962)', rev. *ODNB* (Oxford, 2004)[http://www.oxforddnb.com/view/article/35565, accessed 4 Dec. 2009].

Crookshank, Anne, 'The visual arts, 1603–1740' in T.W. Moody, W.E. Vaughan (eds), *A new history of Ireland*; iv, *eighteenth-century Ireland 1691–1800* (Oxford, 1986), pp 487–8.

Crossman, Virginia, *Politics, pauperism and power in late nineteenth-century Ireland* (Manchester, 2006).

Curran, C.P., *Dublin decorative plasterwork of the 17th and 18th centuries* (London, 1967).

de Breffny, Brian, 'The Lafranchini brothers', *The GPA Irish Arts Review Yearbook* (1988), pp 212–21.

Donnelly, James S. Jr, *The land and people of nineteenth-century Cork: the rural economy and the land question* (London, 1975).

— *The Great Irish Potato Famine* (Stroud, 2002).

Dooley, Terence, *The decline of the big house in Ireland: a study of Irish landed families, 1860–1960* (Dublin, 2001).

—, *'The land for the people': the land question in independent Ireland* (Dublin, 2003).

—, 'National patrimony and political perceptions of the Irish country house in post-independence Ireland' in Terence Dooley (ed.), *Ireland's polemical past: views of Irish history in honour of R.V. Comerford* (Dublin, 2010), pp 192–212.

Duffy, Seán, *Ireland in the Middle Ages* (Dublin, 1997).

Dufresne, Todd, *Killing Freud: twentieth-century culture and the death of psychoanalysis* (New York, 2003).

Edington, Barry, 'A space for moral management: the York retreat's influence on asylum design' in Leslie Topp, James E. Moran and Jonathan Andrews (eds), *Madness, architecture and the built environment: psychiatric spaces in historical context* (London & New York, 2007), pp 85–104.

Ellenberger, N.W., 'The Souls and London society at the end of the nineteenth century' in *Victorian Studies*, xxv, no. 2 (Winter, 1982), pp 133–60.

Ellis, S.G., 'Tudor policy and the Kildare ascendancy in the lordship of Ireland, 1496–1534', *Irish Historical Studies*, 20:79 (1977), pp 235–71.

—, *Tudor Ireland: crown, community and the conflict of cultures, 1470–1603* (London and New York, 1985).

—, *Ireland in the age of the Tudors 1447–1603: English expression and the end of Gaelic rule* (London, 1998).

—, 'Bastard feudalism and the Kildare rebellion, 1534–35: the character of rebel support' in William Nolan and Thomas McGrath (eds), *Kildare: history and society* (Dublin, 2006), pp 213–32.

Estorick, Michael, *Heirs and graces: the claim to the dukedom of Leinster* (London, 1981).

Fegan, Melisa, '"Isn't it your own country?": the stranger in nineteenth-century Irish literature', *Yearbook of English Studies*, 34 (2004), pp 31–45.

Ferguson, Niall, *The ascent of money: a financial history of the world* (London, 2008).

Finnane, Mark, *Insanity and the insane in post-Famine Ireland* (London, 1981).

—, 'Asylums, families and the state', *History Workshop Journal*, 20 (1985).

Fishwick, Nicholas, 'Kinnaird, Arthur Fitzgerald, eleventh Lord Kinnaird of Inchture and third Baron Kinnaird of Rossie (1847–1923)', *ODNB* (Oxford, 2004) [http://www.oxforddnb.com/view/article/50297].

Foster, R.F., *Modern Ireland, 1600–1972* (London, 1988).

Frost, Mark, *The greatest game ever played: Vardon, Ouimet and the birth of modern golf* (London, 2002).

Gailey, Andrew, *Ireland and the death of kindness: the experience of constructive unionism, 1890–1905* (Cork, 1987).

Geary, Laurence, *The Plan of Campaign, 1886–1891* (Cork, 1986).

Gilbert, B.B., 'David Lloyd George: land, the budget and social reform', *American Historical Review*, 81 (1976), pp 1058–66.

Gillespie, Raymond, *Sixteenth century Ireland* (Dublin, 2006).

Geoghegan, Patrick M., 'Fitzgerald, William Robert 2nd duke of Leinster' in James McGuire and James Quinn (eds), *Dictionary of Irish biography* (Cambridge, 2009) [http://dib.cambridge.org/viewReadPage.do?articleId=a3195, accessed 10 June 2012].

Gray, Peter, *Famine, land and politics: British government and Irish society, 1843–1850* (Dublin, 1999).

Griffin, David, 'Carton and Isaac Ware', *JCKAS*, 18 (1992–3), pp 163–75.

Guinness, Desmond, and William Ryan, *Irish houses and castles* (London, 1971).

Haines, Robert, *Charles Trevelyan and the Great Irish Famine* (Dublin, 2004).

Hale, N.G., Jr, *Freud and the Americans: the beginning of psychoanalysis in the United States, 1876–1917* (New York, 1971).

Hammond, J.L., *Gladstone and the Irish nation* (London, 1938).

Harris, John, *Moving rooms: the trade in architectural salvages* (New Haven and London, 2007).

Heymann, C.D., *Poor little rich girl: the life and legend of Barbara Hutton* (London, 1984).

Hill, Jacqueline, *From Patriots to Unionists: Dublin civic politics and Irish protestant patriotism, 1660–1840* (Oxford, 1997).

Hobsbawn, Eric, *The age of Empire, 1875–1914* (London, 2002 ed.).

Hoppen, K.T., *Elections, politics and society in Ireland, 1832–1885* (Oxford, 1984).

Horner, Arnold, 'Carton, Co. Kildare: a case study of the making of an Irish demesne', *Quarterly Bulletin of the Irish Georgian Society*, 18 (nos. 2 & 3), Apr.–Sept. 1975, pp 45–104.

Horner, Arnold, 'Land transactions and the making of Carton demesne', *JCKAS*, 15:4 (1974–5), pp 387–96.

Howard, M.C., *Transnationalism and society: an introduction* (Jefferson, NC, 2011).

Hussey, Christopher, 'Duncombe Park, Yorkshire – II', *Country Life*, 12 Dec. 1957, pp 1328–31.

Jackson, Alvin, *The Ulster Party: Irish unionists in the House of Commons, 1884–1911* (Oxford, 1989).

—, *Col Edward Saunderson: land and loyalty in Victorian Ireland* (Oxford, 1995), p. 208.

—, 'Wyndham, George (1863–1913)', *ODNB* [www.oxforddnb.com/view/article/37052].

Jackson, Louise A., *Child sexual abuse in Victorian England* (London, 2000).

Jefferies, H.A., 'The Kildare revolt: accident or design', *JCKAS*, 19:3 (2004–5), pp 447–59.

Jennings, Dean, *Barbara Hutton: a candid biography* (London, 1968).

Johnston, Edith Mary, *Ireland in the nineteenth century* (Dublin, 1974).

Kelly, Brendan D., 'Mental health law in Ireland, 1821 to 1902: building the asylums', *Medico-legal Journal*, 76:1 (2008), pp 19–25.

Kiely, Karel, 'Poverty and famine in county Kildare, 1820–1850' in Nolan and McGrath (ed.), *Kildare*, pp 493–534.

Kinealy, Christine, *This great calamity: the Irish Famine, 1845–52* (Dublin, 1994).

Klepper, Michael, and Gunther, Robert, *The wealthy 100: From Benjamin Franklin to Bill Gates, a ranking of the richest Americans, past and present* (Brunswick, NJ, 1996).

Larkin, Emmet, *The Roman Catholic Church and the Plan of Campaign, 1886–8* (Cork, 1978).

—, *The Roman Catholic Church in Ireland and the fall of Parnell, 1888–91* (Liverpool, 1979).

Lee, Joseph, *The modernization of Irish society, 1848–1918* (Dublin, 1973).

Leinster-Mackay, Donald, *The rise of the English prep school* (Sussex, 1984).

Lennon, Colm, 'The FitzGeralds of Kildare and the building of a dynastic image, 1500–1630' in William Nolan and Thomas McGrath (eds), *Kildare: history and society* (Dublin, 2006), pp 195–212.

—, 'The making of the Geraldines: the Kildare FitzGeralds and their early historians' in Patrick Cosgrove, Terence Dooley and Karol Mullaney-Dignam (eds), *Aspects of Irish aristocratic life: essays on the FitzGeralds of Kildare and Carton* (Dublin, 2014), pp 71–8.

Longford, Elizabeth, *Pilgrimage of passion: the life of Wilfrid Scawen Blunt* (London, 1979).

Lyons, F.S.L., *John Dillon: a biography* (London, 1968).

Lyons, Mary Ann, 'Revolt and reaction: the Geraldine rebellion and monastic confiscation in Co. Kildare 1535–1540', *JCKAS*, 17 (1992–3), pp 39–60.

—, 'Sidelights on the Kildare ascendancy: a survey of Geraldine involvement in the church, *c.*1470–*c.*1520', *Archivium Hibernicum*, 48 (1994), pp 73–87.

—, 'FitzGerald, Gerald (Gearoid Mor) 8th earl of Kildare' in James McGuire and James Quinn (eds), *Dictionary of Irish biography* (Cambridge, 2009) [http://dib.cambridge.org/viewReadPage.do?articleId=a3148].

McCarthy, Patricia, 'Vails and travails: how Lord Kildare kept his household in order', *Irish Architectural and Decorative Studies: the Journal of the Irish Georgian Society*, 6 (2003), pp 120–39.

McCorristine, Laurence, *The revolt of Silken Thomas: a challenger to Henry VIII* (Dublin, 1987).

MacDonagh, Oliver, *O'Connell: the life of Daniel O'Connell, 1775–1847* (London, 1991).

McKenna, Kevin, 'Elites, ritual and the legitimation of power on an Irish landed estate, 1855–90' in Ciaran O'Neill (ed.), *Irish elites in the nineteenth century* (Dublin, 2013), pp 68–82.

McMahon, Deirdre, *Republicans and Imperialists: Anglo-Irish relations in the 1930s* (New Haven, CT, 1984).

McParland, Edward, 'Building in the grand manner: Sir Richard Morrison's country houses – II', *Country Life*, 31 May 1973, pp 1538–41.

Macaulay, Ambrose, *Dr Russell of Maynooth* (London, 1983).

Magennis, Eoin, 'Fitzgerald, James, first duke of Leinster (1722–1773)', *ODNB* (Oxford, 2004); online edn, May 2010 [http://www.oxforddnb.com/view/article/9565, accessed 11 Sept. 2011].

Malcomson, A.P.W., *Virtues of a wicked earl: the life and legend of William Sydney Clements, 3rd earl of Leitrim, 1806–78* (Dublin, 2008).

—, *The pursuit of the heiress: aristocratic marriage in Ireland, 1740–1840* (Belfast, 2006).

—, *Archbishop Charles Agar: churchmanship and politics in Ireland, 1760–1810* (Dublin, 2002).

Martin, Peter, '*Dulce et Decorum*: Irish nobles and the Great War, 1914–19' in Adrian Gregory and Senia Paseta (eds), *Ireland and the Great War: 'a war to unite us all'?* (Manchester, 2002), pp 28–48.

Masson, J.M., *The assault on truth: Freud's suppression of the seduction theory* (New York, 1998).

Melhem, N.M., G. Porta, W. Shamseddeen, M. Walker Payne, D.A. Brent, 'Grief in children and adolescents bereaved by sudden parental death', *Archives of General Psychiatry*, 2011:68 [http://www.sciencedaily.com /releases/2008/05/080505162849.htm].

Morrisey, T.J., *William J. Walsh, archbishop of Dublin, 1841–1921* (2000).

Murphy, J.H., *Abject loyalty: nationalism and monarchy in Ireland during the reign of Queen Victoria* (Cork, 2001).

Musson, Jeremy, *Up and down stairs: the history of the country house servant* (London, 2009).

Nelson, Thomas, 'The career of John T. Heffernan', *JCKAS*, 19:4 (2006–7), pp 618–33.

—, 'Lord Frederick FitzGerald (1857–1924) and local politics in county Kildare' in Cosgrove, Dooley and Mullaney-Dignam (eds), *Aspects of Irish aristocratic life*, pp 197–209.

Newby, Howard, 'The deferential dialectic', *Comparative Studies in Society and History*, 17 (1975), pp 139–64.

—, *Property, paternalism and power: class and control in rural England* (London, 1979).

Nolan, William, and Thomas McGrath (eds), *Kildare: history and society* (Dublin, 2006).

Nolan, William, 'The land of Kildare: valuation, ownership, and occupation 1850–1906' in Nolan and McGrath (eds), *Kildare*, pp 549–84.

—, 'Poverty and Famine in County Kildare, 1820–1850' in Nolan and McGrath (eds), *Kildare*, pp 459–84.

O'Farrell, Padraic, *A history of county Kildare* (Dublin, 2003).

O Halpin, Eunan, *The decline of the union: British government in Ireland, 1892–1920* (Dublin, 1987).

O'Higgins, Kay, 'Carton: seat of the former duke of Leinster', *Irish Tatler and Sketch* (Dec. 1955), pp 21–7.

—, 'Carton Co. Kildare, residence of Lord and Lady Brocket', *Irish Tatler and Sketch* (Jan. 1956), pp 33–40

O'Kane, Finola, *Landscape design in eighteenth-century Ireland; mixing foreign trees with the natives* (Cork, 2004).

O'Rourke, Kevin, 'Burn everything British but their coal: the Anglo-Irish Economic War of the 1930s', *Journal of Economic History*, 51:2 (June, 1991), pp 357–66.

Ó Snodaigh, Padráig, 'Notes on the politics of Kildare at the end of the eighteenth century', *JKAS*, 17:3 (1981–2), pp 264–71.

Palumbo-Fossati, *Carlo, Gli stuccadori Ticinese Lanfranchini in Inghiliterra e in Irlande nel secola XVIII* (Lugano, 1982).

Prendergast, Muiriosa, 'The Geraldine League: the attempted restoration of the House of Kildare or a study in political opportunism' *JCKAS*, 19:3 (2004–5), pp 460–73.

Purdue, Olwen, *The big house in the north of Ireland: land, power and social elites, 1878–1960* (Dublin, 2009).

Reilly, Ciarán, 'Clearing the estate to fill the workhouse: King's County land agents and the Irish Poor Law Act of 1838' in Virginia Crossman and Peter Gray (eds), *Poverty and welfare in Ireland, 1838–1948* (Dublin, 2011), pp 145–62.

—, *John Plunket Joly and the Great Famine in King's County* (Dublin, 2012).

—, 'A middleman in the 1840s: Charles Carey and the Leinster estate' in Patrick Cosgrove et al. (eds), *Aspects of Irish aristocratic life* (Dublin, 2014), pp 178–89.

Reynolds, K.D., 'Gower, Harriet Elizabeth Georgiana Leveson-, duchess of Sutherland (1806–1868)', *ODNB* (Oxford, 2004) [http://www.oxforddnb.com/view/article/16544].

Ridgway, Christopher, 'Triumph or travesty? Carton House, Co. Kildare', *Country Life*, 18 Feb. 2009, pp 70–5.

—, 'Making and meaning in the country house: new perspectives in England, Ireland and Scotland' in Terence Dooley and Christopher Ridgway (eds), *The Irish country house: its past, present and future* (Dublin, 2011), pp 203–43.

Ridley, Jane, and Clare Percy, 'Charteris, Mary Constance, countess of Wemyss (1862–1937)', *ODNB* [www.oxforddnb.com/view/article/40735, accessed 4 Dec. 2009].

Roberts, David, *Paternalism in early Victorian England* (New Jersey, 1979).

Robson, Bryan, *The road to Kabul* (London, 2007).

Scriven, Marcus, *Splendour & squalor: the disgrace and disintegration of three aristocratic dynasties* (London, 2009).

Seznac, Jean, *The survival of the pagan gods: the mythological tradition and its place in Renaissance humanism and art* (Princeton, 1981).

Shannon, C.B., *Arthur J. Balfour and Ireland, 1874–1922* (Washington, 1988).

Somerville-Large, Peter, *The Irish country house* (London, 1995).

Sommers-Flanagan, John and Rita, *Counselling and psychotherapy: theories in context and practice* (New Jersey, 2004).

Stead, W.T., *The Americanization of the world* (London, 1902).

Stebbings, Chantal, 'Protecting the property of the mentally ill: the judicial solution in nineteenth-century lunacy law', *Cambridge Law Journal* (2012), vol. 71, no. 2, pp 384–411.

Steinberg, H., 'The sin in the aetiological concept of Johann Christian August Heinroth (1773–1843); part 1: between theology and psychiatry. Heinroth's concepts of "whose being", "freedom", "reason" and "disturbance of the soul", *History of Psychiatry*, 15 (59, part 3), Sept. 2004, pp 329–44; part 2, *History of Psychiatry*, 15 (59, part 3), 16 (60, part 4), Dec. 2004, pp 437–54.

Stocker, Mark, 'Louise, Princess, duchess of Argyll (1848–1939)', *ODNB* (Oxford University Press, 2004); online ed., Jan. 2008 [http://www.oxforddnb.com/view/article/34601].

Taaffe, Frank, 'Athy and the Great Famine' in Kildare County Council, *Lest we forget: Kildare and the Great Famine* (Kildare, 1995).

Thompson, F.M.L., 'Grosvenor, Hugh Lupus, first duke of Westminster (1825–1899)', *ODNB* (Oxford, 2004); online edn., May 2006 [http://www.oxforddnb.com/view/article/11667].

Tillyard, Stella, *Citizen lord: Edward FitzGerald, 1763–1798* (London, 1997).

—, *Aristocrats* (London, 1995).

Topp, Leslie, 'The modern mental hospital in late nineteenth-century Germany and Austria: psychiatric space and images of freedom and control' in Topp, Moran and Andrews (eds), *Madness, architecture and the built environment* (London, 2007), pp 241–62.

Topp, Leslie, 'Introduction: interpreting psychiatric spaces' in Topp, Moran and Andrews (eds), *Madness, architecture and the built environment: psychiatric spaces in historical context* (London, 2007), pp 1–16.

Turner, John, 'Astor, William Waldorf, first Viscount Astor (1848–1919)', rev. *ODNB* (Oxford, 2004); online ed., Jan. 2008 [http://www.oxforddnb.com/view/article/37131, accessed 2 Aug. 2011].

Vaughan, W.E., *Landlords and tenants in mid-Victorian Ireland* (Oxford, 1994).

Walsh, Patrick, 'Biography and the meaning of an Irish country house: William Conolly and Castletown' in Terence Dooley and Christopher Ridgway (eds), *The Irish country house: its past, present and future* (Dublin, 2011), pp 21–39.

Whiting, Richard, *The Labour Party and taxation: party identity and political purpose in twentieth-century Britain* (Cambridge, 2006), pp 17–19.

Wilson, Derek, 'Astor, John Jacob, first Baron Astor of Hever (1886–1971)', *ODNB* (Oxford, 2004); online ed., Jan. 2011 [http://www.oxforddnb.com/view/article/30773, accessed 2 Aug. 2011].

Winchester, Simon, *Their noble lordships: class and power in modern Britain* (New York, 1981), p. 40.

Woodham-Smith, Cecil, *The Great Hunger* (London, 1962).

Worsley, Giles, 'Duncombe Park, Yorkshire – I', *Country Life*, 24 May 1990, pp 116–21.

—, 'Duncombe Park, Yorkshire – II', *Country Life*, 31 May 1990, pp 138–43.

Wylie, J.C.W., *Irish land law* (3rd ed., Dublin, 1997).

Unpublished theses

Cosgrove, Patrick J., 'The Wyndham Land Act, 1903: the final solution to the Irish land question?' (PhD, NUI Maynooth, 2008).

McKenna, Kevin, 'Power, resistance and ritual: paternalism on the Clonbrock estates, 1826–1906' (PhD, NUI Maynooth, 2011).

Nelson, Thomas, 'Kildare county council, 1899–1926' (PhD, NUI Maynooth, 2007).

Websites

www.athyheritagecentre-museum.ie/religious_diversity

http://allpoetry.com/Thomas_Osborne_Davis

www.beadinggem.com/2012/04/reluctant-heiress-jewels.html

http://www.blakeneymanor.com/books/links/link6.html

http://www.dia.ie/architects/view/347/CASTLE-RICHARD

http://hansard.millbanksystems.com/commons/1873/feb/24/irish-land-act-1870–the-12th-clause

http://www.kildare.ie/library/ehistory/2012/02/carton_house_through_the_pages.asp

http://www.mitchamcommon.org/golfclub.html

http://www.msnbc.msn.com/id/35470011/ns/business-huguette_clark_mystery/

http://www.touruk.co.uk/houses/houseyorkshire_duncombe.htm

List of Illustrations

FIGURES

PLATES

(between pages 160 and 161)

Index

By Catherine Murphy

Browne, Stephen, 126, 140
Buckingham Palace, 174
Burgh, William, 20
Burke, Edmund, 110, 224
Burton, John Hill, 159

Cadogan Square, London, 93
Cairo, 155
Calais, 177, 180–1
Cambrensis, Giraldus, 14
Campbell, George, 8th duke of Argyll, 94
Campbell, John, marquess of Lorne, 63
Cannadine, David, 72, 133, 152, 190–1,
    196, 223–4
Carlow Sentinel, 143
Carlton Club, 189
Carmarthen, Katharine, 110
Carton demesne, 35, 44, 55, 177, 204
Carton House, 9, 29, 32, 34, 37, 44–5,
    48, 54, 62, 66, 80–1, 89, 92–3,
    96–8, 109, 112, 116–17, 123, 128,
    139, 143, 155, 165, 173, 183, 194–
    5, 197, 202–4, 210–11, 224, 226
  7th duke's visit 1936, 219–21
  changing role, 227
  contents and sale of contents, 208–9
  estate employees, 67
  expenditure, 204
  fine art collection, 157
  Gold Saloon, 19, 67, 221
  landscape, 22, 68
  library, 16, 67, 100
  mortgages, 198–9
  paintings, 70
  portraits, 67, 228
  redundancies at, 205–6
  remodelling of, 23
  retrenchment at, 212,
  sale of estate, 123ff
Castle, Richard, 18
Castledermot, 12, 45, 50, 126, 129
Castletown, 18, 54
Castletown, Clare, 68

Catholic Emancipation, 23
Caulfield, Joseph, 31
Caulfield, Peter, 66
Cavendish Hotel, 174, 176
Cavendish, Lord Frederick, 50
Celbridge, 35
Celbridge Board of Guardians, 95
Celtic Revival, 141
Central Criminal Court, London, 187,
    207
Ceylon, 206
Chambers, Dr Walker, 149, 160–1
Chandeler, John, 30
Charteris, Cynthia, 180
Charteris, Ego, 180
Charteris, Francis Richard, 10th earl of
    Wemyss, 80
Charteris, Hugo, Lord Elcho, 84–7, 90,
    92, 106–8, 111, 147, 170, 180, 183
Charteris, Yvo, 180
Chateau des Fayeres, Cannes, 206
Chatsworth, 225
Cheam Preparatory School, 147, 151,
    167
China Clay Corporation, 192
Churchill, Winston, 59
Clark Deeley, William, 189
Clark Gower, Huguette, 215–16
Clark, Senator W.A., 215–16
Clery, Stephen, 46
Cliveden, 198
Cloncurry, Lord, 47, 59
Clouston, Dr (later Sir) Thomas, 156–8
Cobden, Richard, 48
Cogan, D.J., 127
Cogan, W.H.F., 12, 43
Connaught Hotel, 188
Connecticut, 217
Connemara, 155
Connor, Vivien, 223, 225
Conolly folly, 54
Conolly, Lady Louisa, 18
Conolly, William, 18